翻译讲堂

Essays:
Translation
and Analyses

英汉·汉英

〔澳〕林巍　译析

商务印书馆
The Commercial Press

图书在版编目（CIP）数据

短文译析：英汉汉英 /（澳）林巍译析 .—北京：商务印书馆，2023
ISBN 978-7-100-22446-8

Ⅰ.①短⋯　Ⅱ.①林⋯　Ⅲ.①英语—翻译—研究　Ⅳ.① H315.9

中国国家版本馆 CIP 数据核字（2023）第 076085 号

权利保留，侵权必究。

翻译讲堂
短文译析
（英汉·汉英）
〔澳〕林巍　译/析

商务印书馆出版
（北京王府井大街36号　邮政编码100710）
商务印书馆发行
北京冠中印刷厂印刷
ISBN 978 - 7 - 100 - 22446 - 8

2023 年 11 月第 1 版　　开本 880×1230　1/32
2023 年 11 月北京第 1 次印刷　印张 16 1/8
定价：80.00 元

简 介

在当今互联网、自媒体时代，何止是"信息爆炸"，甚至"信息泛滥"亦成为一种世界现象，于是如何选择阅读、阅读精品成为一个课题，本书正是这样背景下的一部作品。

本书作者长期在高校翻译专业主持日常翻译竞赛和《英语世界》"翻译擂台"栏目，与翻译专业师生和广大翻译爱好者有着广泛互动，因而为实地点评提供了鲜活的材料。原文多选自未曾翻译过的经典著作、媒体时文(包括佚名作品)及作者随笔，涉及政治、经济、文化、历史、科技等诸多方面，经编辑加工，短小精悍；译文则重对比，讲分析。整体分为"英译汉部分"与"汉译英部分"，每篇由原文、译析、参考译文组成。

从来精炼费功夫。希望这些"浓缩品"能集知识性、专业性、可读性于一体，真正雅俗共赏。

目录

I. 英译汉部分

1. Human History ······················· 3
   人类的历史 ························ 8
2. Human Uniqueness ················ 10
   人类的特性 ······················· 15
3. Social Space ························ 17
   社会空间 ·························· 22
4. True Self-Reliance ················· 23
   真正的自立 ······················· 27
5. Be Yourself ························· 29
   做你自己 ·························· 32
6. Self-Assertion ······················ 33
   坚定自信地表达自己 ············ 37
7. What You See Is the Real You ···· 39
   人所见到的是你所展现的 ······· 44

8. Adventures of Daily Life ·· 45
   日常生活中的"冒险" ·· 51
9. On Being Introduced ··· 53
   所谓"被人介绍" ··· 56
10. Acknowledgements ··· 58
    致谢 ··· 62
11. Getting Less Sleep ··· 64
    被减少的睡眠 ··· 68
12. The Value of Sleep Deprivation ··· 70
    不睡觉的代价 ··· 72
13. Exercises Put You in a Good Mood ······································ 74
    锻炼可怡人 ··· 77
14. How Does Exercise Work? ·· 79
    锻炼的益处 ··· 84
15. Fighting Diabetes Complications ·· 86
    如何应对糖尿病并发症 ··· 90
16. Seniors and the City ··· 91
    老人与城市 ··· 97
17. Entry ··· 98
    入对行当 ·· 102
18. Family Relationship in Ancient China ·································· 104
    中国古代家庭关系一瞥 ·· 108
19. The Mooncake ··· 109
    月饼 ·· 113

20. The Better Robots ·· 115
    更好的机器人 ·· 120
21. Thought and Computer ·· 121
    人脑与电脑 ·· 125
22. Discovery of Gravitational Waves ································ 126
    发现引力波 ·· 130
23. The Role of Time ·· 131
    时间的作用 ·· 137
24. Scientific Revolution ··· 139
    科学革命 ·· 143
25. What Is Wisdom? ··· 144
    什么是智慧？ ·· 148
26. What Is Culture? ·· 149
    文化是什么？ ·· 155
27. Interpreters and Translators: Good Prospects ············· 156
    口笔译者，前程乐观 ··· 161
28. Thanksgiving ·· 163
    感恩节 ··· 167
29. All Saints' Day ··· 169
    万圣节 ··· 175
30. Looking for an Honest Person ···································· 176
    寻觅诚实人 ·· 182
31. A Year ·· 184
    一年之中 ··· 189

32. What You Learn from the Games ·············· 191
    运动所得 ························· 196
33. The Sunrise ························· 198
    日出 ···························· 202
34. The Sunset ························· 203
    日落 ···························· 207
35. Understanding Travel ··················· 209
    懂得旅行 ························· 214
36. A Green Hill Far Away ·················· 215
    远方的青山 ······················· 219
37. The Philosopher ······················ 220
    哲学家 ·························· 226
38. An Invisible Hand ····················· 227
    看不见的手 ······················· 232
39. New World Order ····················· 233
    世界新秩序 ······················· 237
40. The Persuaders ······················· 239
    说客种种 ························· 244
41. Theatre ···························· 245
    戏剧 ···························· 248
42. Power and Discourse ··················· 250
    权力与话语 ······················· 253
43. Conflict Management ··················· 255
    冲突管控 ························· 259

44. Early Capitalist Society ········· 261
　　早期资本主义社会 ············· 265
45. Global Exchanges ············· 267
　　国际交流 ···················· 269
46. Individual Engagement ········ 270
　　各尽所能 ···················· 275
47. The Asking Animal ············ 277
　　不断探究的物种 ··············· 281
48. The Gifted Children ··········· 283
　　天才儿童 ···················· 288
49. Be Ordinary ················· 290
　　安于平凡 ···················· 293
50. Studying Abroad ············· 295
　　留学 ······················· 299

II. 汉译英部分

1. 汤显祖与莎士比亚 ················ 303
　　Tang Xianzu and Shakespeare ········ 308
2. 过年 ···························· 309
　　Celebrating the New Year ··········· 312
3. 岁月的流逝 ······················ 314
　　As Years Go By... ················· 319

4. 老家的端午节 ································ 320
   The Dragon Boat Festival in My Hometown ········ 325
5. 心与脑 ····································· 327
   Heart and Brain ································ 330
6. 知识结构 ··································· 332
   The Knowledge Structure ························ 338
7. 注意力的分配 ······························· 340
   The Distribution of Attention ·················· 345
8. 系统的功能（上）··························· 347
   The Function of System（Ⅰ）···················· 352
9. 系统的功能（下）··························· 354
   The Function of System（Ⅱ）···················· 359
10. 痛苦也是财富（上）······················· 361
    Suffering Is Also an Asset（Ⅰ）················ 366
11. 痛苦也是财富（下）······················· 368
    Suffering Is Also an Asset（Ⅱ）················ 370
12. 丝绸之路 ································· 372
    The Silk Road ································· 377
13. 孟子的"性善论" ·························· 379
    Mencius' Original Goodness of Human Nature ···· 382
14. 适应自然的能力 ··························· 384
    Abilities to Cope with the Environment ········ 385
15. 可爱的中国 ······························· 387
    My Beloved Motherland—China ··················· 393

16. 陈独秀在法庭上的抗辩 ······ 394
   Chen Duxiu's Objection in Court ······ 397
17. 一条公益广告 ······ 398
   A Public Service Advertising ······ 402
18. 开始写作 ······ 403
   How I Start to Write ······ 407
19. 我的小说写法 ······ 409
   My Way of Writing a Novel ······ 412
20. 其他侧面 ······ 414
   Other Aspects ······ 417
21. 我住处的景色 ······ 419
   The Scenery Surrounding My Place ······ 422
22. 白雪与青草 ······ 424
   Snow and Grass ······ 428
23. 旧梦重温 ······ 430
   Revisiting My Dream ······ 433
24. 老刀 ······ 434
   Old Dao ······ 437
25. 电商的挑战 ······ 439
   The Challenge Presented by E-Commerce ······ 442
26. 区块链 ······ 444
   Blockchain ······ 449
27. 学生比例 ······ 451
   Proportion of International and Domestic Students ······ 454

28. 不可厌倦 …………………………………………… 455
   Never Be Bored …………………………………… 459
29. 人生即劳作 ………………………………………… 461
   Life Is Labor ……………………………………… 466
30. 国之少年 …………………………………………… 468
   The Youth of Our Nation ………………………… 475
31. 潇洒的欧洲青年 …………………………………… 477
   Burdenless European Youth ……………………… 481
32. 女排精神 …………………………………………… 483
   The Spirit of Chinese Women Volleyball ………… 486
33. 杭州师范大学第二届全球青年学者论坛 ………… 487
   The Second Global Youth Scholars Forum of HZNU ……… 492
34. 珠海校区与珠海政府（上）……………………… 494
   Zhuhai Campus and Zhuhai Municipal Government（Ⅰ）…… 496
35. 珠海校区与珠海政府（下）……………………… 498
   Zhuhai Campus and Zhuhai Municipal Government（Ⅱ）…… 501

I. 英译汉部分

1

Human History

By J. M. Roberts

[1] When does history begin? It is tempting to reply "In the beginning", but like many obvious answers, this soon turns out to be unhelpful. As a great Swiss historian once pointed out in another connexion, history is the one subject where you cannot begin at the beginning. If we want to, we can trace the chain of human descent back to the appearance of vertebrate, or even to the photosynthetic cells which lie at the start of life itself. We can go back further still, to almost unimaginable upheavals which formed this planet and even to the origins of the universe.

[2] Yet this is not "history". Commonsense helps here: history is the story of mankind, of what it has done, suffered or enjoyed. We all know that dogs and cats do not have histories, while human beings do. Even when historians write about a natural process beyond human control, such as the ups and downs of climate, or the spread of disease, they do so only because it helps us to understand why men and women have lived (and died) in some ways rather than others.

[3] This suggests that all we have to do is to identify the moment at which the first human beings step out from the shadows of the remote past. It is not quite as simple as that, though. First we have to know what we are looking for but most attempts to define humanity on the basis of observable characteristics prove in the end arbitrary and cramping, as long arguments about "ape-men" and "missing links" have shown.

译 析

本文选自一历史教科书《新世界史》(*The New History of the World*)序言的片段，作者为约翰·莫里斯·罗伯特斯（J. M. Roberts, 1928—2003），英国著名历史学家，其写作风格言简意赅，颇具含义。

首先要提醒的是，有的参赛者没有翻译该文的题目，这是不完整的，自然也会影响其成绩。

[1] 中讲到 in the beginning，人们很容易想到《圣经》里的 In the beginning was the Word, and the Word was with God, and the Word was God（太初有话，话与神同在，话就是神）。对此，有参赛者译成："在它开始的时候""在一开始的开始""从它最开始的时候开始"等，似乎没有错，但要注意措辞的简练、讲究；这里不妨译为"太初之始""天地之始""混沌初开"等。

对于 this soon turns out to be unhelpful，参赛者们的表述差异很大，如："这样的回答无济于事""但不用多长时间，这个答案就会跟许多平白无力的答案一样，变得一文不值"等，其实不妨译为"很快便会显得缺乏说服力"。而对于 in another connexion，其中的 connexion 是 connection 的变体，意指 reference or relation to something else; context，例如，In this connection, the agreement can be seen as a step toward peace.（就此而言，该协议可视为迈向和平的一步。）。故 pointed out in another connexion，可译为"在相关著述中指出"。

关于 If we want to, we can trace the chain of human descent back to the appearance of vertebrate, or even to the photosynthetic cells which lie at the start of life itself. We can go back further still, to almost unimaginable upheavals which formed this planet and even to the origins of the universe，有参赛者译成"如果我们想的话，我们大可把人类的血脉追溯到脊椎动物出现时，甚至是象征生命发迹的能进行光合作用的细胞出现时。我们还能追溯得更久远些，到形成这座星球的那次超乎想象的剧变之时，甚至一直到宇宙的起源""如果需要的话，我们可以追溯人类血统的链条，从脊椎动物的出现或者甚至从本身就存在于原始生命体内的光合细胞开始。我们还可以再一步往回倒退，回到几乎无法想象的那个产生了地球乃至宇宙发端的大剧变时期。"总的讲，是可以接受的，但其中的下画线为本人所加，标明可进一步推敲。该句不妨译为"若非要如此，人类的沿袭纽带便要追溯到脊椎动物的出现，或孕育生命起源的光合细胞。我们仍可追寻得更远，上溯到形成地球的那难以想象的沧桑巨变，甚至宇宙的起源"。

Ⅰ. 英译汉部分

[2] 中对于 Commonsense helps there: history is the story of mankind, of what it has done, suffered or enjoyed，有同学译成"这里我们可以用常识来帮助理解：历史是人类的故事，它讲述人类曾经的事迹、苦难，或欢乐"，固然不错，但有些太拘泥于原文了，其实不妨译为"由常识便不难得知，……"。

就此段落而言，Even when historians write about a natural process beyond human control, such as the up and downs of climate, or the spread of disease, they do so only because it helps us to understand why men and women have lived (and died) in some ways rather than others. 有参赛者译为"他们之所以这样做只是为了帮助我们理解为什么男人跟女人会有与其他生物不一样的生死。"，显然有理解和表达的错误；另有参赛者译为"即使史官记录了人力所能控制范围之外的自然过程，诸如气候变化，疾病肆虐，也是为了使我们后来者明白为何人们以某种方式活着（或死亡）而非其他"，虽无大错，但其中画线之处值得商榷；主要是作为翻译学院的学生，应有更高的要求，以使译文经得住推敲。此句不妨译为"即便历史学家记述下来非人类所能控制的自然过程，如气候的变迁、疾病的传播等，也仅是为了有助于理解我们男女众生为什么以这样而不是以那样的方式生存或死去"。

[3] 中对于 This suggests that all we have to do is to identify the moment at which the first human beings step out from the shadows of the remote past，有参赛者译成"它表明我们所应该做的就是认识到人类是从何时第一次从古老过去的阴影里走出来"，其中 the shadows of the remote past, 不必一定要按字面意思译为"古老过

去的阴影",而整句不妨译为"这似乎提示,我们只需确定人类是在何时最早走出了远古的蒙昧状态"。

对于 We have to know what we are looking for first and most attempts to define humanity on the basis of observable characteristics prove in the end arbitrary and cramping, as long arguments about "ape-men" and "missing links" have shown,其中的 define humanity,有参赛者译成(大多数以显著特征来)"定义人类",似有更确切的词语,而 to define humanity on the basis of observable characteristics,有同学译为"用显性特征来定义人类""在浅显现象的基础上更深入地定义人类"等等,虽无大错,但欠确切。其实,不妨译为"基于可观察到的外部特征来界定人类"。

就 cramping 而言,其意为 a compressing or restraining force, influence, or thing(约束,束缚压缩或限制的力量、影响或事物),例如"他们被关在了一个小卧室中。"(They are cramped in a tiny cubicle.)由于 ape-men 和 missing links 是一种英文中的专业术语,故在引用时应将其附于中译文之后,故此句不妨译为"……而基于可观察到的外部特征来界定人类的多种尝试,最终都证明是武断和有限的,诚如'猿-人'(ape-men)、'衔接缺失'(missing links)等长期争论的问题所表明的那样"。其中,对于较为专业的词语,如"猿-人""衔接缺失",需给出其英文原文,以示明确。简言之,"猿-人"生存于距今三十万年以前,具有人和猿的双重生理构造,被认为是现代人类的直接祖先;而"衔接缺失"则是人类学及考古学研究中的重要课题,即科学家们根据达尔文的进化论,执意寻找介于猿与现代人类之间的生物化石，但至今未果。

值得指出的是，参考材料是可以用的，参赛者之间也可以互相探讨，但是不能抄袭；从此次翻译中，似可看到一些痕迹，须引起注意。

参考译文

人类的历史

J. M. 罗伯特斯

[1] 历史源于何时？人们自然会答道"天地之始"。然而，如同许多浅白的回答那样，这很快便会显得缺乏说服力。正如瑞士一位大历史学家在相关著述中所指出的，对历史这一课题，你简直就无法从头开始。若非要如此，人类的沿袭纽带便要追溯到脊椎动物的出现，或孕育生命起源的光合细胞。我们仍可追寻得更远，上溯到形成地球的那难以想象的沧桑巨变，甚至宇宙的起源。

[2] 但是，这些都不是"历史"。由常识便不难得知，历史就是人类的故事，它述说着以往的经历、磨难和喜悦。众所周知，人类是有历史的，而猫狗则没有。即便历史学家记述下来非人类所能控制的自然过程，如气候的变迁、疾病的传播等，也仅是为了有助于理解我们男女众生为什么以这样而不是以那样的方式生

存或死去。

[3] 这似乎提示，我们只需确定人类是在何时最早走出了远古的蒙昧状态。不过，事情并非如此简单。我们必须明白，自己首先要得到的是什么，而基于可观察到的外部特征来界定人类的多种尝试，最终都被证明是武断和有限的，诚如"猿-人"（ape-men）、"衔接缺失"（missing links）等长期争论的问题所表明的那样。

Human Uniqueness

By J. M. Roberts

[1] Some people have suggested that human uniqueness lies in language, yet other primates possess vocal equipment similar to our own; when noises are made with it which are signals, at what point do they become speech?

[2] Another famous definition is that man is a tool-maker, but observation has cast doubt on our uniqueness in this respect, too, long after Dr Johnson scoffed at Boswell for quoting it to him. What is surely and identifiably unique about the human species is not its possession of certain faculties or physical characteristics, but what it has done with them—its achievement, or history, in fact.

[3] Humanity's unique achievement is its remarkably intense level of activity and creativity, its cumulative capacity to create change. All animals have ways of living, some complex enough to be called cultures.

[4] Human culture alone is progressive: it has been increasingly built by conscious choice and selection within it as well as by accident

and natural pressure, by the accumulation of a capital of experience and knowledge which man has exploited.

[5] Human history began when the inheritance of genetics and behaviour which had until then provided the only way of dominating the environment was first broken through by conscious choice.

译 析

本文选自一历史教科书《新世界史》(*The New History of the World*)序言的片段，作者为约翰·莫里斯·罗伯特斯（J. M. Roberts, 1928—2003），英国著名历史学家，其文言简意赅，含义精辟。

就该标题的翻译，各式各样，但综合考虑，不妨译为"人类的特性"（有些同学竟然没有翻译题目）。

[1] 中对于... when noises are made with it which are signals, at what point do they become speech, 有同学将其中的noises译成"噪声"，其实该词亦可为"声音"，如The only noise was the wind in the pines（唯一的响声是松林中的风声）；而将speech译成"演讲""交流"等，是不够准确的，可译为"言语"，其英文解释为the faculty or act of expressing or describing thoughts, feelings, or perceptions by the articulation of words（表达能力，用连续的字词表达或描述思想、情感或知觉的能力），以区别于其他动物的发声。有的在句子理解上出现了错误，如"尽管其他灵长类动物也有与我们相似的发音特征；但是当它们发出的信号却是噪声时，

怎么能成为言语呢？"其实，此句不妨译为："有人认为人类的特性在于其语言；然而，其他灵长类动物也有类似于我们的发音机能。如果信号是通过发声而传送的，那么声音在哪一环节上转化成了言语？"

[2] 中 Another famous definition is that man is a tool-maker, but observation has cast doubt on our uniqueness in this respect, too, long after Dr Johnson scoffed at Boswell for quoting it to him. 此句为典型的英文表述，由于句子成分位置的不同，令同学的理解和表述出现了许多问题，比较典型的，如"另一个著名的解释是，人类是一个工具制造者。观察报告也把怀疑放在我们的独特性这个方面，在很久以后，Johnson博士还因为Boswell引用它而嘲讽他"，似乎与原文的顺序相当吻合，但内涵和表述却颇有差异。如果将该句的顺序变化一下，便不难理解：Another famous definition is that man is a tool-maker, long after Dr Johnson scoffed at Boswell for quoting it to him, the observation has cast doubt on our uniqueness in this respect. 当然这不是好的英文表述。因而，此句不妨译为"另一有名的定义是人能制造工具，然而约翰逊（Johnson）博士对于博斯韦尔（Boswell）引用这一观点不屑一顾；很久以来，经过观察，对于我们在这方面的独特性人们也开始怀疑起来"。

同样，对于 What is surely and identifiably unique about the human species is not its possession of certain faculties or physical characteristics, but what it has done with them—its achievement, or history, in fact, 有参赛者也过分依照原文的顺序，译成"无疑人类更显而易见的独特性并非是其拥有特定的能力或物理特性，而

是他们实际已经完成的事——其成就或历史"。其实，除了将其中的词义译得更准确外，亦可在词序上作相应的调整："可以确认的是，人类的独特性不在于其所具有的某种机能或生理特征，而在于人类利用其做了些什么，即取得了哪些成就，创造了哪些实际意义上的历史。"

[3] 中 Humanity's unique achievement is its remarkably intense level of activity and creativity, its cumulative capacity to create change. All animals have ways of living, some complex enough to be called cultures. 对此，大部分参赛者都能将主要意思翻译出来，但在具体词义的表述上，似可进一步推敲。比较典型的，如"人类的独特性在于其显著的活跃力和创造力，它积累的能力能够创造变化。所有动物都有自己的生活方式，而一些悠久曲折的被称作文明"。不妨对比如下"人类的独特成就在于其非凡的高水准的活力与创造力，以及不断积蓄起来的改变世界的能力。所有动物都有其生活方式，有些达到了某种复杂程度，可称之为'文化'"。

[4] 中 Human culture alone is progressive: it has been increasingly built by conscious choice and selection within it as well as by accident and natural pressure, by the accumulation of a capital of experience and knowledge which man has exploited. 对此，许多同学将其中的 alone 译成"单独来说"，将 capital 译成"资本"，显然是照搬字典的结果，而好的翻译来自对具体语境的准确把握，故不妨对比一下："然而只有人类的文化积淀了下来，这种文化靠着自身内部的有意识的选择以及偶发事件和自然势力、通过经验和知识实

力的积累，日益厚重起来。"

[5] 中 Human history began when the inheritance of genetics and behaviour which had until then provided the only way of dominating the environment was first broken through by conscious choice. 对此，大部分同学可能不太理解其含义，即在人类这种智能动物出现并主宰这个世界之前，支配自然界万物的是一种天然、本能的力量，而人类的历史改变了这一切。

以下是一些参赛者比较典型的译文："人类的历史开始了透过在遗传基因和行为上继承是支配环境的唯一方式，是第一个被有意识的选择打破""人类的历史始于基因遗传和行为的继承，直至有一种可主宰环境的力量由有意识的选择打破""当基因与行为的遗传首次因意识性选择发生突破时，人类历史的帷幕便拉开。这些遗传一直到后来都为我们提供控制自然的唯一方法""在人类开创历史之前，人类只能用行为支配自然环境，然而当基因有了继承以及从人类行为飞跃到人类意识时，人类的历史才真正的开始"，等等。可以说，都源于对原文没有透彻的理解。参赛者在翻译完之后，要读几遍，看看是否有道理（英文说 Does it make sense?），是否能够说服自己，否则"以己昏昏"焉可"使人昭昭"？故此，不妨译为："遗传和行为的继承，曾一直支配着万物的生存环境，而当这种唯一的方式被有意识地打破时，人类历史便开始了。"

此外，关于"格式"问题，许多同学还是没有遵守，很是遗憾，也影响了其成绩。包括学院、年级等的标明，标题的处理（要用黑体，但首先不要忘记翻译！），段落的开头（要空两格），标点符号的正确使用（如句号不能与英文的混同），等等，作为大学生，如果在这些基础方面还错误百出，实在说不过去。

同时，还须说明，获奖同学的译文并不意味着没有错误了，而只是相比较而言的，甚至不乏鼓励的成分。译海无涯，要不断严要求，再进步。

参考译文

人类的特性

J. M. 罗伯特斯

[1] 有人认为人类的特性在于其语言；然而，其他灵长类动物也有类似于我们的发音机能。如果信号是通过发声而传送的，那么声音在哪一环节上转化成了言语？

[2] 另一有名的定义是人能制造工具，然而约翰逊（Johnson）博士对于博斯韦尔（Boswell）引用这一观点不屑一顾；很久以来，经过观察，对于我们在这方面的独特性人们也开始怀疑起来。可以确认的是，人类的独特性不在于其所具有的某种机能或生理特征，而在于人类利用其做了些什么，即取得了哪些成就，创造了哪些实际意义上的历史。

[3] 人类的独特成就在于其非凡的高水准的活力与创造力，以及不断积蓄起来的改变世界的能力。所有动物都有其生活方

式，有些达到了某种复杂程度，可称之为"文化"。

[4] 然而只有人类的文化积淀了下来，这种文化靠着自身内部的有意识的选择以及偶发事件和自然势力、通过经验和知识实力的积累，日益厚重起来。

[5] 遗传和行为的继承，曾一直支配着万物的生存环境，而当这种唯一的方式被有意识地打破时，人类历史便开始了。

3

Social Space

[1] The social space is partly symbolic and invisible and hence dealt with through gestures, postures, language. But it is also partly physical, and hence can be observed in body distances. The range of acceptable body distance varies with the degree of intimacy and equality that is thought to exist in the relationship.

[2] In some societies there seems to be little appreciation of privacy, separateness, the need for a protected zone of intimacy into which no one intrudes. I remember vividly the shock of living in a village in Nepal where the door was open and people dropped in constantly and commented on everything I was doing. They followed us on our trips out of the village when we were trying to create a little personal space, and even going to the toilet out in the fields in private was a difficult exercise.

[3] It is therefore interesting that many of the English effect a compromise; more or less the same physical distance is maintained for everybody, whether they are intimate or distant from us. Everyone stands under one law, the law of compromise, not too far

apart, nor too close.

译 析

该文是一篇短小的论说文，言简意赅，有理有据；有事实，有理论，亦有东西文化间的对比，而这些都融汇于一篇200字的小文之中，难能可贵。对于其翻译，看似简单，但要做到准确、清晰、简洁，亦非易事。

就题目而言，可译为"社会空间"或"社交空间"。

[1]中对于partly，不必刻板地译为"部分地"，而"某种程度""一定程度上"或"多少"则更为自然。deal with在一般意义上是"处理""解决"，但在这里不妨根据特殊语境译为"体现""体会""感知"等。对于physical，许多参赛者译成了"物理的"等，固然不错，但显然受了词典的约束；其实这里应理解为"客观的""实体的"或"有形的"，如the physical environment（客观环境）、the physical world around us（我们身边的物质世界）、Don't be put off by his physical appearance（别因为他的外貌而讨厌他）等；observe也不一定要译为"观察"（甚至不一定要译出来）；body distances是指人们之间的身体距离，且开头两句之间是有内在对比关联的，故不妨译为："社会空间多少具有象征性，是无形的，因而需要通过手势、姿态和语言来体会；然而，它又多少带有实体性，由此体现于彼此身体间的距离。"

对于The range of acceptable body distance varies with the degree of intimacy and equality that is thought to exist in the relationship，有参赛者译得比较死板，如"人与人之间可接受的距离范围是随着亲密程度和平等程度而改变的，这一现象被认为是存在于人际关系当中的"，有些过度就范于原文了。同时，the degree of intimacy and equality 也不必完全按原文的顺序译出；因在中文里将重要的放在前面，故此句不妨译为"……与人际关系中的平等度与亲密度有关"。

[2] 中对于 In some societies there seems to be little appreciation of privacy, separateness, the need for a protected zone of intimacy into which no one intrudes，其中的 appreciation，不必刻板地译为"赞赏""理解"等，而其本义只是（不太）"在意"；对于 the need 和 protected，也不必一定要将"需要""受到保护"的字眼译出，而只要将其含义融合在译文当中即可，故不妨译为："有些社会似乎不大在意隐私和独处这回事，不理解为什么人们要有一块不受他人干扰的'私密领地'。"注意，原文中的 zone of intimacy 未加引号，但在中文里却是有必要的，可见标点符号也未必要"屈从"于原文。

对于 I remember vividly the shock of living in a village in Nepal where the door was open and people dropped in constantly and commented on everything I was doing，有参赛者译为"我很清晰地记得住在尼泊尔的一个村庄中给我带来的震撼，那里各家各户都不关门，人们可以不断来拜访，甚至可以对我正在做的一切事情评头论足""这次经历在我脑海里历历在目。让人奇怪的是，在尼泊尔的村庄，当地人的家都是大门敞开的，而且村民们络绎不绝地相互串门,并谈论我的所作所为""我深刻地记得居住在尼泊尔的一个村庄时让我惊讶的经历:房间的大门敞开着,人们不断地来拜访,而且评论任何我正在做的事"等,这些大错都没有,但有两种明显倾向:一方面有拘泥于原文的痕迹,如将shock译为"震撼";另一方面又有些渲染过度,如将people dropped in constantly译为"村民们络绎不绝地相互串门"等,这些"伤痕"都可进一步"抹平"。故此,不妨译为:"想起我在尼泊尔村庄生活时的情景,至今历历在目,惊讶不已。那里的大门总是敞开的,人们可随意进来,对你所做的任何事情评头品足。"

对于They followed us on our trips out of the village when we were trying to create a little personal space, and even going to the toilet out in the fields in private was a difficult exercise,有参赛者译为"我们在试图创造一个小的私人空间,而他们却跟着我们到村子外去游览,甚至在野外自己上厕所也是一件很难的事情""我们试图创造一点儿私人空间,于是走出村子去旅行,无奈村民们也跟着去了,结果就连单独在野外上个厕所也变得十分困难"等,其中将trip都译为了"游览""旅行",其实根据上下文,该词在这里只是"走出去"的意思,而going to the toilet亦可隐讳为"方便一下"等,故该句不妨译为:"我们想去村外找一点'私人空间',他们却一路跟来;就是到野地里去独自'方便'一下,也很困难。"

[3] 中对于It is therefore interesting that many of the English effect a compromise; more or less the same physical distance is

maintained for everybody, whether they are intimate or distant from us. Everyone stands under one law, the law of compromise, not too far apart, nor too close，需综合考虑、整体理解，否则会翻译得非常繁琐、复杂。例如："因此十分有趣的是，很多英国人对此达成妥协。无论他们对待我们是亲近还是疏远，我们对每个人都差不多保持同样的距离。每个人都遵循这样一个经过妥协的原则：彼此间既不要靠得太近，也不要离得太远。"再如，"有趣的是，很多英国人因此采取了折中的办法：无论是我们保持亲密还是保持疏远，每个人之间所保持的身体距离都大致是差不多的。人与人之间都是在处于一种这样的定律，是折中定律，让我们之间的关系既不太远，又不太近"。其实，作者在此笔锋一转，讲到了西方文化，特别是英国人的态度，由此形成了鲜明对照。因而，therefore可为"由此看来"，以示转折与衔接；interesting不一定译为"有趣的"，而可译为"有意味的"；之后的law，有同学翻译成"法律"，在此是不妥的，而应译为"规则""原则"或"定律"，如the laws of tennis（网球规则）、Newton's law（牛顿定律）、the laws of nature（自然规律）等。

总之，是英国人宁愿恪守这样一种"折中"的规则，故整句不妨译为："由此看来，英国人大都采取的那种折中的办法，颇有意味，那就是，不论亲疏，人人都保持一种大致相同的距离——人们实际遵守的是一种一视同仁、不近也不远的折中定律。"

参考译文

社会空间

[1] 社会空间多少具有象征性,是无形的,因而需要通过手势、姿态和语言来体会;然而,它又多少带有实体性,由此体现于彼此身体间的距离。可接受的身体距离,因人而异,与人际关系中的平等度与亲密度有关。

[2] 有些社会似乎不大在意隐私和独处这回事,不理解为什么人们要有一块不受他人干扰的"私密领地"。想起我在尼泊尔村庄生活时的情景,至今历历在目,惊讶不已。那里的大门总是敞开的,人们可随意进来,对你所做的任何事情评头品足。我们想去村外找一点"私人空间",他们却一路跟来;就是到野地里去独自"方便"一下,也很困难。

[3] 由此看来,英国人大都采取的那种折中的办法,颇有意味,那就是,不论亲疏,人人都保持一种大致相同的距离——人们实际遵守的是一种一视同仁、不近也不远的折中定律。

4

原 文

True Self-Reliance

[1] In a community everyone is dependent on the service of others, while he himself contributes to the needs of others. But, so long as we are doing our fair share, we are not dependents; for mutual help and cooperation is quite consistent with individual independence and self-reliance.

[2] The contemptible dependence on others, which is the opposite of self-reliance, is the depending on others for the goods and services which we could and should provide for ourselves. This kind of dependence may be due to laziness, or lack of confidence. Idlers, who shrink from honest work, attach themselves like parasites to rich and influential people, and by flattery and servile adulation get money and favors from them. Such hangers-on are to be despised. People who are afraid to rely on their own opinions and efforts are to be pitied, and, if possible, taught self-confidence and self-reliance.

[3] True self-reliance therefore means knowledge of one's own powers, a reasonable self-confidence, and a determination to be independent and to stand on one's own feet. As a poem goes: "His

brow is wet with honest sweat / He earns whatever he can / And looks the whole world in the face / For he owes not any man."

译 析

　　本文是一篇随笔式论文，从一个侧面论述了个人与社会、自己与他人、付出与索取的辩证关系，富有含义。其相应的翻译，应在充分理解的基础上，言简意赅。

　　就题目而言，有参赛者译成"真正的自力更生"；然而，"自力更生"的主体一般是指一个群体、民族或国家，而这里主要指的是个人，故以"自立"为宜；当然，有同学译成"真正的自食其力""自助的真谛"等，也未尝不可。

　　[1] 中对于 community，有的同学译成"社区""社团"等一般含义，但与个人相对而言，不妨将其译为"社会"。类似的，如 community problems（社会问题）、the international community（国际社会）、community facilities（公共设施）、the trend is towards reintegrating mentally ill people into the community（目前的趋势是将精神病人重新融入社会当中）等。

　　In a community everyone is dependent on the service of others, while he himself contributes to the needs of others. 该句叙述的是"人人为我，我为人人"的事实，即不必将其顺序颠倒，如有的同学所译："每个人在尽己之所能解他人之需的同时，亦依赖着他人提供的服务"，而不妨顺其自然，译为"在社会里，其实人人都有赖于他人的服务，而自己也为别人的需求做贡献"。

But, so long as we are doing our fair share, we are not dependents; for mutual help and cooperation is quite consistent with individual independence and self-reliance. 对于其中的 fair share，有的同学译为"进行公平分配""在公平的分享"等，显然有所偏颇，不如"承担着自己的分内之事""做自己所承担的部分"等更靠谱。实际上，该词组在英文里有"应当有的那一部分"之意，如 We should pay our fair share of tax（我们应交自己的那份税款），故此句不妨译为"只要我们尽了自己的努力……"。而 is quite consistent with，正如大部分同学所译，"相一致""相辅相成"等，都符合原意。

[2] 中 The contemptible dependence on others, which is the opposite of self-reliance, is the depending on others for the goods and services which we could and should provide for ourselves. 其中 contemptible dependence 是指"依赖"，而非"人"，而有参赛者将其译成"那些可鄙地依赖着别人、与自力更生截然不同的人""卑微地依赖于人，正与自立相反"等，需再作斟酌；而其中的插入语 which is the opposite of self-reliance 可用括号来处理，故该句不妨译为"那种令人鄙视的对他人的依赖（与'依靠自己'背道而驰）是从别人那里得到本来应该靠自己可以得到的物品和服务"。

This kind of dependence may be due to laziness, or lack of confidence. Idlers, who shrink from honest work, attach themselves like parasites to rich and influential people, and by flattery and servile adulation get money and favors from them. 其中的 shrink 与 from 连

用，意思为 to avoid doing something difficult or unpleasant，如 We should not shrink from making necessary changes in our schedule（我们不会回避对日程作必要的修改）、A shy man shrinks from meeting strangers（羞怯的人怕见生人）等。对于此句，大部分同学都能较为准确地翻译出来，其基本意思为："这种依赖性可能是出于懒惰或缺乏自信。懒汉们不愿辛勤劳动，如寄生虫那样依附于富豪与权贵，靠阿谀奉承得到钱财和实惠。"

Such hangers-on are to be despised. People who are afraid to rely on their own opinions and efforts are to be pitied, and, if possible, taught self-confidence and self-reliance. 对于其中的 to be pitied，需留意：首先是被动的，其次应拿捏住其准确意思——大部分同学译成了"可悲的""可怜的"等，只有一个参赛者译成了"同情的"，我以为更加适宜。同时，这当中还有一种微妙的语气，即对于 hangers-on 和 people who are afraid to rely on their own opinions and efforts 两种人应持不同的态度，并且，对于后者亦有"固然值得……，但还应……"的委婉，对此只有一些参赛者体会到了，故该句不妨译为"对这类寄食者自当嗤之以鼻，而对于不敢依靠自己想法和努力的人，固然值得同情，但亦应告诫他们需自信和自立"。

[3] 中 True self-reliance therefore means knowledge of one's own powers, a reasonable self-confidence, and a determination to be independent and to stand on one's own feet. 其中需注意，knowledge 这里应理解为动词，而 on one's own feet，有"恢复""独立意志"之意，如 We'll soon have you on your feet again（我们很快就

会使你恢复健康), I need to get back on my feet again and forget all this(我得重新站起来,忘掉这一切)等。几位同学对此翻译如下:"真正的自力更生意味着对自身权利的认识、拥有适当的自信以及争取独立和自食其力的决心""真正的自立意味着了解自己的能力,恰到好处的自信以及独立自主的决心""真正的自强包含着对自己的力量的了解,理智的自信,独立自主的果决和顶天立地",这些固然都有各自不同的理解,但亦有欠准确、可"细加工"之处,故此句不妨译为"真正的自立,是指对自己能力的把握、有实力的自信以及独立自主的意志"。

至于最后的诗句,正如有参赛者指出的,引自诗歌《乡村铁匠》第二小节,作者为美国著名诗人亨利·沃兹沃斯·朗费罗(Henry Wadsworth Longfellow, 1807—1882),是19世纪美国最伟大的浪漫主义诗人之一。对其翻译,参赛者都做了有益的尝试,注重了诗意与音韵,值得称赞;但在音韵美的和谐上,似可进一步完善。

参考译文

真正的自立

[1] 在社会里,其实人人都有赖于他人的服务,而自己也为别人的需求做贡献。然而,只要我们尽了自己的努力,我们便不

是"依赖者",因为互相帮助及合作,与个人独立和依靠自己是相辅相成的。

[2] 那种令人鄙视的对他人的依赖(与"依靠自己"背道而驰)是从别人那里得到本来应该靠自己可以得到的物品和服务。这种依赖性可能是出于懒惰或缺乏自信。懒汉们不愿辛勤劳动,如寄生虫那样依附于富豪与权贵,靠阿谀奉承得到钱财和实惠。对这类寄食者自当嗤之以鼻,而对于不敢依靠自己想法和努力的人,固然值得同情,但亦应告诫他们需自信和自立。

[3] 真正的自立,是指对自己能力的把握、有实力的自信以及独立自主的意志。如诗所云:"辛勤汗水溢满头,自挣自花不用愁;坦然无羞对世人,无欠无愧乐悠悠。"

5

> 原 文

Be Yourself

By Steve Jobs

[1] Your time is limited, so don't waste it living someone else's life.

[2] Don't be trapped by dogma—which is living with the results of other people's thinking.

[3] Don't let the noise of other's opinions drown out your own inner voice.

[4] And most important, have the courage to follow your heart and intuition. They somehow already know what you truly want to become. Everything else is secondary.

> 译 析

本期原文节选自史蒂夫·乔布斯（Steve Jobs）在美国斯坦福大学（Stanford University）毕业典礼上的一次演讲。了解这个背景很有必要，在应用语言学、翻译学上属"语外衔接"。

众所周知，翻译的基本原则是"信、达、雅"，这看似老生常谈，但具体应用中，问题仍层出不穷。"信"，是对原文的忠实，也是对译者的一种限制，而"达""雅"则多少给了译者发挥的空间，但亦囿于范围，不能如同创作般任意发挥。句[1]，有的译文，如"一寸光阴一寸金。因此，不要在别人的故事中流着自己的眼泪"，显然离原文过远。[1]中的your，是第二人称代词，看似简单，很多都译成了"你"，也可泛指成"人"，即people in general；或省去指称，比如You have to be 21 or over to buy alcohol in Florida，可译为"在佛罗里达，必须年满21岁才能买酒"。许多译文若脱离语境看还算不错，但要身临其境，有面对大学毕业生讲话的感觉，便应为"你们"。然而，又可变通，既泛指大家，又特指个体，所以[3][4]中的you / your，不妨译成"你""你的"或"自己的"等，以增加亲近感。

[2]中，固然可以紧贴字面译成"不要陷入教条之中，那是根据别人的思考结果来生活"，但显臃赘。所谓"达"，是指文思的通达和文气的顺达，故不妨译为"不要被条条框框所束缚；那些是别人思考的结果"。

[4]中的heart and intuition，许多人都分别译成了"内心和直觉"，其实两词意思相近、互补，不妨简化为"内心的感悟"，正如：completely and perfectly不必译成"完全和完整"，而可为"完美"；proper and right不必是"恰当和正确"，"得体"即可。

对于[4]，许多译文是按原文的句式、标点符号翻译的，如"最为关键的是，要勇敢地追随你的内心和直觉。它们其实早已知晓你真正的归宿。而其他的一切，无非是过眼云烟"，形式稍显死板。这里完全可在理解其含义的基础上，将三句打通处理，如"最重要的，是有勇气听从你内心的感悟——那些知道你想要的是什么，而其他都是次要的"等。

以"雅"而言，还包括文体、选词、精练等内涵。此次亦有以文言文翻译的。应当说，中国的语言文字，自五四运动以来，有两大划时代的事件，一是白话文写作，一是汉语拼音方案。当代人以当代文表述，是历史的趋势，不应逆转，更何况此文是讲演稿。不可想象，一个当代英语演讲者，满口用的竟然是16世纪莎士比亚式的古典英文！乔布斯语言风格的特点是朴实无华，即用简单、通俗的词汇和句式说出真实的感受和耐人寻味的道理，这无疑使他的演讲广受欢迎。同样，正确、标准、地道、朴实、简练、生动地以现代汉语写作，即老老实实地讲好现代人的"人话"（通俗易懂、打动人心的语言），并不比蹩脚甚至不伦不类地使用生僻文言文更容易；相反，更难，也更有价值。所以，就我们现在的日常实践而言，除特殊情况外，以文言文翻译英文，不值得提倡。

就选词来说，应注意准确和变化。如：将living someone else's life译成"为他人而活"，容易产生歧义，因中文这一表述是褒义的，英文实为living for others、man is here for the sake of others、a man for others等，故不妨译为"生活在他人世界"。再如：将Don't let the noise of other's opinions drown out your own inner voice译成"不要让其他人的意见掩埋了你内心的想法"，就忽略了noise与voice的对比呼应，故不妨改译为"不要让他人的噪音淹没了自己的心声"。同时，应注意行文的变化，避免重复。如：有的译文将someone else、other people一概译成"别人"，其实还可译成"他人""旁人""外人"等；将you一律译成"你"，其实还可译成"自己""自我"等。"文似看山不喜平",中、英文皆然;而以中文之丰富,足以应对。

不够精练,是大部分译文存在的问题。鲁迅说,写完之后至少看两遍,将可有可无的字、句、段删去。以下段译文为例:

每个人的一生都是十分短暂的,所以请不要浪费自己的生命去按照别人的意志生活,不要被那些灌注了他人思想的教条主义所束缚,……最重要的是,我们要敢于听从自己内心的声音和相信自己的直觉。因为我们的内心和直觉早已它们知晓我们真正想要的是什么。这样一来,而任何其他的声音都已经不重要了。

其中,画线部分为可删去部分,而涂灰部分为可增加部分。

精练也是"雅"的一种境界,需要的是化繁为简的功力。

参考译文

做你自己

史蒂夫·乔布斯

[1] 时间宝贵,切莫生活在他人世界,浪费光阴!

[2] 不要被条条框框所束缚;那些是别人思考的结果。

[3] 不要让他人的噪音淹没了自己的心声。

[4] 最重要的,是有勇气听从你内心的感悟——那些知道你想要的是什么,而其他都是次要的。

6

原　文

Self-Assertion

[1] Assertiveness is the ability to clearly represent your thoughts and feelings in a mutually respectful way. It does not infringe on the rights of others or rely on guilt for results. Assertiveness starts with the premise that each human being is given rights that do not depend on status or performance. You have the right to express your perspective. You have the right to assume personal responsibility and to decline responsibility for others. How you govern yourself in relation to these rights is important for "valued" communication.

[2] Communication is valued when both parties, the sender and the receiver, are respected. There are three primary styles of communication: passive, assertive, and aggressive. The difference between passive, assertive, and aggressive communication rests with the exchange between parties and quality of the message. Passiveness diminishes your capacity to be heard and validated. Aggressiveness exerts differential power to promote a certain end result that is not based on mutual respect. Only assertiveness respectfully engages both parties for valued communication.

[3] In order to achieve assertive communication, one needs a level of self-confidence, self-worth, and self-awareness. Self-confidence is projected, not performed. It has to radiate from within and does not rely on others. Self-worth comes from believing that you are a worthwhile individual who deserves the best that life has to offer. Self-awareness develops from personal monitoring. One learns of strengths and weaknesses by making internal assessments. Self-assertion is a natural process for individuals who are confident and aware. In essence, you must have confidence within before you can demonstrate it in the midst of others.

译 析

本文节选自短文"坚定自信地表达自己",收录于常青藤语言教学中心编译的《如果坠落时也有星光》,作者佚名。

标题"Self-Assertion"的英文解释是the act or an instance of putting forward one's own opinions, etc., esp. in a bold, aggressive or conceited manner,即表达自己观点的行为或者事实,尤其强调以一种大胆的、自负的,或咄咄逼人的方式来表达自己的观点。从感情色彩来看,它是一个中性词,可褒亦可贬。通读全文之后,我们发现作者是以肯定的语气来论述一个人应该大胆地和自信地表达自己的观点。由此可见,将标题译为"坚持己见""自我肯定""自我主张",不符合原文的感情色彩,因为这些表达在汉语中或多或少包含着贬义。将标题处理为"自信",没能将原文的全部意义表达出来。译为"坚定自信地表达自己""大胆地说出你的想法""自信地表达自己"更为合适。那么，assertiveness是指坚定自信地表达自己的能力或者状态。

[1] 中对于rely on guilt for results，不少同学理解不够准确，译成"存有对他人的内疚""会为了结果而内疚""因为不理想的结果而内疚"等，而这部分的真正含义是：坚定自信的表达不会为达到目的而不择手段，因而心存愧疚。对于performance，有同学译为"性能"，显然忽略了语境对它的语义制约，在此应该理解为"成就""业绩"。

对于You have the right to assume personal responsibility and to decline responsibility for others，不少同学的理解有误。这句话紧跟着上一句，举例说明坚定自信地表达以天赋人权为前提，这些权利不取决于后天的社会地位和成就，包括有权为自己的行为承担责任，同时谢绝为他人的行为承担责任。有同学将后半部分译为"拒绝对他人负责"显然是错误的。此外，还有不少同学将decline译为"减少"，不符合原文的语境，而且逻辑上也行不通。

对于How you govern yourself in relation to these rights is important for "valued" communication，一些同学译为"如何处理自身与这些权利之间的关系对于'有价值'的沟通极为重要"，读来非常拗口。译者应该灵活变通，通过结构调整，使译文符合汉语的表达习惯。此句可处理为"能否实现'有价值'的沟通，关键在于你如何支配自己的这些权利"。另外，有个别同学将communication译为"传播"，在语域上与原文不一致，因为这不是一篇传播学专业方面的文章，而是泛指人与人之间的交流和沟通。

[2] 中对于 aggressiveness，不少同学译为"进攻型""侵略型"，用来描述人与人之间的沟通方式，显得语气过重。对该词的理解和翻译应该对比前面提到的两种沟通方式，一是消极被动地接受，二是大胆自信地表达自己。第三种沟通方式译为"迫使对方接受"比较合适。对于 Passiveness diminishes your capacity to be heard and validated，不少同学直译为"消极被动的接受会使你被聆听和被认可的能力下降"，读来十分别扭，通过调整和变通，可以处理为"一味消极被动地接受，很难使自己的观点被对方接受和认可"。

对于 Aggressiveness exerts differential power to promote a certain end result that is not based on mutual respect，其中 exerts differential power，有同学译为"利用有差别的权力""利用微分影响力""特意释放能量"，我想这样的译文没有经过仔细的推敲，连译者自己都不明白是什么意思，更不用说准确地向读者传达原文的意思了。根据上下文，通过推理我们可以发现作者试图表达的意思是：迫使对方接受，是指一方为了达到目的不惜利用自己手中的权力优势。这显然不是建立在双方相互尊重的基础上，而是依靠自己手中掌握的比对方更大的权力。

[3] 中对于 Self-assertion is a natural process for individuals who are confident and aware，不少同学译为"对于一个自信和自知的人，自信是一个很自然的过程"，这里译文不符合逻辑，因为自信不应该是一个过程，获得自信才是一个过程，可以译为"一个人有了自信和自知之明，自然就会坚定自信地表达自己"。

此外，有些同学望文生义，不顾上下文而随便摘取词典中的词义来译，造成译文表达错误或晦涩难懂，如将parties、primary、projected译为"党派""初级的""被投射的"等等。这既是语言的基本功，也体现了译者的态度，希望大家尽量克服这一点。

另外，有个别同学从网络上直接下载译文，或者稍作改动后交来参赛，这违背了"'每月一题'翻译之星"的宗旨，不利于提高译者的翻译水平，当然也不可能获奖，希望大家牢记这一点！

参考译文

坚定自信地表达自己

[1] 坚定自信的表达就是在双方互相尊重的基础上，能够清晰地说出你的看法和感受。它不会侵犯别人的权利，也不会为达到目的而不择手段，因而心存愧疚。坚定自信的表达以天赋人权为前提，这些权利不取决于后天的社会地位和成就。比如，你有权利为自己的行为承担责任，并谢绝为他人的行为承担责任。能否进行"有价值"的交流，关键在于你如何支配自己的这些权利。

[2] 当沟通的双方——讲述者和倾听者相互尊重时，交流才

有价值。主要的沟通方式有三种：消极被动地接受，坚定自信地交流和迫使他人接受。三者的差异性在于交流方式和信息质量的不同。一味消极被动地接受，很难使自己的观点被对方接受和认可；迫使对方接受，是为了达到目的而利用自己的权力优势。这显然不是建立在双方相互尊重的基础上，而是依靠自己手中掌握的比对方更大的权力。只有坚定自信地交流才能使双方都受到尊重，才能进行有价值的交流。

[3] 一个人需要有一定程度的自信、自我肯定和自知之明，才能进行坚定自信的交流。自信，是要从内心凸显，而不是伪装出来的。它源自内心，不依赖于任何人。自我肯定，即相信自己的价值，相信自己是生活中美好事物的承载者。自知之明，源于自我控制，它能通过对自身评价获知自己的优缺点。一个人有了自信和自知之明，自然就会坚定自信地表达自己。唯有内心充满自信，才能自信地与他人交流，这是最根本的。

7

原 文

What You See Is the Real You

(Excerpts)

By Willard Gaylin

[1] The inside of the man represents another view, not a true one.

[2] A man may not always be what he appears to be, but what he appears to be is always a significant part of what he is.

[3] A man is the sum total of all his behavior.

[4] To probe for unconscious determinants of behavior and then define him in their terms exclusively, ignoring his overt behavior altogether, is a greater distortion than ignoring the unconscious completely.

[5] The inner man is a fantasy. If it helps you to identify with one, by all means, do so; preserve it, cherish it, embrace it, but do not present it to others for evaluation or consideration, for excuse or exculpation, or, for that matter, for punishment or disapproval.

[6] Like any fantasy, it serves your purposes alone. It has no standing in the real world which we share with each other.

[7] Those character traits, those attitudes, that behavior—that

strange and alien stuff sticking out all over you — that's the real you!

译 析

该文节选自 What You See Is the Real You，作者威拉德·盖林（Willard Gaylin, 1925—2022），美国著名社会学与伦理学家，纽约黑斯廷斯社会伦理暨生命科学学院院长，著有《报效国家》（*In the Service of Their Country*）等多种著作。

关于题目，有人按字面意思译成"你所见到的即是那真正的你"，显然有误；自己怎么能够见到自己？原因是没有恰当理解 you，该词在这里泛指"人们"，如 You don't have to be a mathematician to solve this problem（不是非得数学家才能做出这道题），即指任何一般人（都可这样做）等，故这里不妨译为"人所见到的是你所展现的"。

在[1]中，The inside of the man represents another view, not a true one，被译成"一个人的内在部分往往呈现的是另一副面貌，但却未必是那更真实的面貌"，有些欠妥。其中 represent 固然有"代表""呈现"之意，但不必刻意译出；inside of... another view 是"另一副面貌"吗？显然"状况"更为合适；not a true one，是"那更真实的面貌"？"那更"和"的面貌"都是多余而冗赘的，应删去。故此，不妨译为"人的内在是另一种状况，未必真实"。

在[2]中，A man may not always be what he appears to be, but what he appears to be is always a significant part of what he is 被译

成"一个人不一定时时都是他表现在外面的,但那表现在外面的却无疑是他真正情况的一个重要部分",似乎不错,但经推敲,发现其用词啰嗦。"表现在外面的",难道还有"表现在里面的"吗?"却无疑是他真正情况的一个重要部分"其中画线部分可以省略,而斜体部分亦可改进。故此,不妨译为"一个人不一定总是如他外在所现,但其外在所现一定是其真实自己的重要部分"。

在[3]中,A man is the sum total of all his behavior,译成"一个人即是他全部行为的总和",其中的画线部分可以删除;同时,为了强调"人",可将其顿开处理。故此,不妨译为"人,是其全部行为的总和"。

在[4]中,To probe for unconscious determinants of behavior and then define him in their terms exclusively, ignoring his overt behavior altogether, is a greater distortion than ignoring the unconscious completely,被译成"只去探索人的行为的无意识决定因素,然后再全部使用这类的词语来勾画出他这个人,丝毫也不考虑他的外部行为,这一做法的谬误程度实在要比完全忽略了那无意识的部分要严重得多",其中有许多可商榷之处。probe固然可以译成"探索"(其基本意思为"多方寻求答案,解决疑问"),但鉴于作者是社会学家和伦理学家,此处讨论的又是学术问题,故不妨用"探究"。将then define him in their terms exclusively译成"然后再全部使用这类的词语来勾画出他这个人"显得十分笨拙,原因是太拘泥于字面意思。具体而言,define的实质是to determine the essential quality or nature of someone or something，故不是在表面上的"来勾画出他这个人"，而是判断、断定某个人；exclusively 意为 without any others being included or involved，即"排除其他"，而 in their terms 不一定是"用他们的词语"，而是据他们的理解、以他们的方式等，如 He allows them to view the situation in their terms and offers a solution that they can understand（他允许他们以自己的观点来考虑这个情况，并提供他们能够理解的办法）；而将 ... is a greater distortion than ignoring the unconscious completely 译成"这一做法的谬误程度实在要比完全忽略了那无意识的部分要严重得多"，就更显冗赘；实则为"不亚于……行为"。故此，不妨译为"只探究人的行为的无意识因素，完全不考虑其外在表现，并据此来断定一个人，其荒谬程度，不亚于完全忽视人的无意识行为"。

在[5]中，将 The inner man 译成"那内在的人"不如"内在之人"专业；而将 If it helps you to identify with one, by all means, do so 译成"如果这种认识能帮助你辨出谁谁，那当然完全请便"就更加离谱：什么是"谁谁"？而"那当然完全请便"不但不是专业用语，甚至不是规范的书面语言；preserve it, cherish it, embrace it 译成了"你尽可以对其保存之，珍视之，爱护之"，相对前面的"口语化"，这里又半文半白，极不协调；but do not present it to others for evaluation or consideration, for excuse or exculpation, or, for that matter, for punishment or disapproval 译成"只是不应<u>提到</u>他人面前作为评价或考虑的根据，作为原谅或开脱的根据，或者仅<u>为这点</u>而决定其惩处"，其中画线部分显然欠妥，可加改进。故此，不妨译为"'内在之人'是种幻觉；如果这有助于识别人，则尽可为之。对此不妨保留、珍视、利用，但不可提供给他人作为考量、评判的依据，亦不可据此当借口，加以开脱，进行诋毁或处罚"。

在[6]中，Like any fantasy, it serves your purposes alone. It has no standing in the real world which we share with each other 译成"正像一切其他幻觉那样，它的功用往往不出你个人范围"，其中的"它"在规范或学术译文中应尽量避免，在此处则更没有必要；"不出"是源于 no standing，显然太拘泥于字面，其实可通融处理。故此，不妨译为"正如许多其他幻觉，其功能专属个人，不可与他人分享"。

在[7]中，Those character traits, those attitudes, that behavior—that strange and alien stuff sticking out all over you—that's the real you!，译成"那些性格特点，那些举止态度，那种行为——那种从你周身冒出的奇特和异样的东西——那才是那真正的你！"其中的 attitude 的实质是 the opinions and feelings that usually have about something (*Longman Dictionary of Contemporary English*) 即主要是一种思想和感觉，而"举止"与后面的"行为"（behavior）重叠；"冒出的"又是欠规范的书面语；后面的两个"那"可以删去。故此，不妨译为"那些特性、态度、行为——那些你身上焕发出的奇光异彩——才是真正的你！"

固然，译文要忠实于原文，但这种忠实不可僵化，亦不可出格。

参考译文

人所见到的是你所展现的

（节选）

威拉德·盖林

[1] 人的内在是另一种状况，未必真实。

[2] 一个人不一定总是如他外在所现，但其外在所现一定是其真实自己的重要部分。

[3] 人，是其全部行为的总和。

[4] 只探究人的行为的无意识因素，完全不考虑其外在表现，并据此来断定一个人，其荒谬程度，不亚于完全忽视人的无意识行为。

[5] "内在之人"是种幻觉；如果这有助于识别人，则尽可为之。对此不妨保留、珍视、利用，但不可提供给他人作为考量、评判的依据，亦不可据此当借口，加以开脱，进行诋毁或处罚。

[6] 正如许多其他幻觉，其功能专属个人，不可与他人分享。

[7] 那些特性、态度、行为——那些你身上焕发出的奇光异彩——才是真正的你！

8

原 文

Adventures of Daily Life

By Jack Handey

[1] Most people think that the exciting events are those for which you take huge steps, long strides. Traveling to foreign countries, passionate romantic affairs, daring schemes, or perilous adventures. But it became clear to me, that by simply walking downstairs from the city station to the restaurant center, I had come across an adventure. And it took the form of a bowl of black pasta.

[2] I took the fork and spoon and scooped a healthy-sized serving onto my plate. The first sensation I experienced as the spaghetti noodle touched my tongue was not disgust, but interest. It was indeed bizarre, strange, but interesting. My friends smiled at me from across the table. With their teeth and lips as black as night they looked like exhumed corpses... Adventures, after all, like people, come in all shapes, sizes, and colors. It is said, "The true voyage of discovery lies not in seeking new landscapes, but in having new eyes".

[3] Our days are filled with mini-adventures that are passed over so quickly without a thought. I would have missed out on this

adventure completely if I had actually known what I was ordering when I ordered it, but I was thankful for the mistake. Could I have gotten this dish in the States? Maybe, maybe not. I wasn't looking for it. Thanks to a bowl of squid ink pasta, I have been reminded of how many mini-adventures I'd been missing out on.

[4] You don't need to cross an ocean to find excitement. You can take a walk, talk to the person next to you in the train, or order a different dish in your favorite restaurant. Life's lessons are everywhere and adventures abound!

译 析

杰克·汉迪（Jack Handey）所写的 Adventures of Daily Life 是就日常生活有感而发的一篇随笔，平易而有启发性。

参加本期翻译练习的，有近百位同学，不仅有翻译学院的，也有其他学院的。由于该文不是很难，在整体意思上，大都把握得不错，但推敲起来，仍有许多问题。

就该文的标题而言，有的同学译成"生活中的历险""……冒险""……奇遇""平中见奇"等都可以，但"精彩的人生无处不在"，便有些"过"了。

在[1]中 Most people think that the exciting events are those for which you take huge steps, long strides. Traveling to foreign countries, passionate romantic affairs, daring schemes, or perilous adventures. 其中的 Most people think，一般译成了"大多数的人

都认为",其实可更加简练为"人们大都认为";take huge steps,有人译成"迈出一大步""重大步骤"等,有些生硬,实则不妨为"大规划、大动作的"等。而对于整段,有同学译成"大多数人都认为,只有那些需要采取重大措施的事才够撩动心弦,像长距离徒步,出国旅行,激动人心的风流韵事,充满勇气的宏图大计亦或是九死一生的冒险远征,但它对我清楚地表明,仅仅从城市车站下楼到餐饮中心,我就经历了一次冒险""我们的生活充满着无数奇遇,它们转瞬即逝,让人措手不及"。

这些意思都不错,但有些"夸张"了,即多少有些"过度翻译"。好的翻译是"适度翻译",而"过度翻译"如同"过度包装",是一种累赘、浪费和不真实。

But it became clear to me, that by simply walking downstairs from the city station to the restaurant center, I had come across an adventure. 其中的 simply 不是"简单地",而是"只是""只不过""仅仅"等;同时,此句不妨与下一句结合起来翻译,即"仅从市车站的台阶下来步入餐饮中心,便会经历一场'冒险',而冒险的形式不过是一碗黑乎乎的意大利面条"。

在[2]中 I took the fork and spoon and scooped a healthy-sized serving onto my plate. The first sensation I experienced as the spaghetti noodle touched my tongue was not disgust, but interest. It was indeed bizarre, strange, but interesting. My friends smiled at me from across the table. With their teeth and lips as black as night they looked like exhumed corpses... 其中, a healthy-sized serving, 有同学译成"健康规模的服务",这显然讲不通,实为"合适的一部

分""一大块";而有同学误将 disgust 以为是 digest,因而将此句译成"它给我的第一感觉就是很难消化,但是口感很奇特",这说明在翻译中要仔细再仔细,要勤于查字典。对于整段,有同学译成"我用叉子和勺子舀取了健康适量的面,将它放到盘子上。意大利面触及我舌尖的第一感觉就是:不是很难吃,反而让我有兴趣继续吃下去。这确实是一种很奇怪,陌生的,但是很有趣的味道。我的朋友们坐在桌子的另一边冲着我笑,他们就像刚挖出来的尸体,有着像黑夜一样黑的嘴唇和牙齿"。显然,其主要囿于字面意思的翻译,使得译文过于生硬、不自然;试比较:"我拿起勺叉,挖了一大块放在盘里。当舌头碰到通心粉那一刹那,我并不感到恶心,而是有趣。那的确是一种陌生、怪异而又得意的感觉。桌对面的朋友们冲着我笑,他们的牙齿和嘴唇都被染得漆黑一片,像是从墓地里挖出的死尸……"

对于 Adventures, after all, like people, come in all shapes, sizes, and colors 一句,也很容易译得生硬,如:"说到底,奇遇就像人一样,以各种各样的形状、大小和颜色来到世上";"冒险,终究就像人们走进所有的颜色、形状和尺寸"等,其实,可根据此处的语境,具体调整为:"冒险,说到底,恰如众人各异,有着形态、体型、肤色的不同。"

The true voyage of discovery lies not in seeking new landscapes, but in having new eyes. 对此,有同学译成"发现之旅并不是寻找新的风景,而是扩展眼界""真正的航海发现不在于寻到新大陆,而在于有了一双新的眼睛""真正的发现之旅不是为了寻找全新的景色,而是为了拥有全新的眼光""……而在于有一双不同的眼睛"等，显然，虽都抓住了主要意思，但又都不够准确。实际应用"不在于／乎……，而有了……"的句式，为"真正的发现之旅不在乎寻求新景观，而是有了新的眼光"。

在[3]中 Our days are filled with mini-adventures that are passed over so quickly without a thought，其中的 mini-adventures 可以译成"小的风险"或"迷你风险"；passed over 大部分同学都译成"稍纵即逝的"，固然不错，但还可加重语气，即全句为"我们的生活中充满了稍纵即逝的'迷你风险'"。

Could I have gotten this dish in the States? Maybe, maybe not. I wasn't looking for it. Thanks to a bowl of squid ink pasta, I have been reminded of how many mini-adventures I'd been missing out on. 其中的 States，有同学翻译成"州"是不对的，那是 state，不大写，没有复数；熟悉美国文化的都知道，美国人称自己的国家为 States，即 United States 的简称。对于 Maybe, maybe not. I wasn't looking for it. 有同学译成"我也许会点它，也许不会点它。我不会去寻找它"，显然是过于呆板地依附原文了，可变通为"既可能又不可能，但我想不会特意去要的"。

在[4]中，You don't need to cross an ocean to find excitement. You can take a walk, talk to the person next to you in the train, or order a different dish in your favorite restaurant，其后是有省略意思的，应当"填补"出来，如有的同学所译："这就足够了""你就可以感受到刺激""你就已经经历了一次冒险了"等，但大部分同学没有采用"增译"技巧（这是翻译课程中的一项内容）。整句不妨译为："你其实不必去跨洋过海寻找刺激，而只需闲来散步、在火车上与旁边的人搭讪聊天，或是到你喜欢的餐馆点上一道别致的菜肴，便能找到感觉。"

最后一句Life's lessons are everywhere and adventures abound!，同学们的典型译文有："生活的课程到处都有，奇遇也就大量存在！""生活的启示无处不在，奇遇也无所不在！""生活的课程无处不在，各种奇特冒险经历更是蕴含其中！""生活的哲理处处皆是，奇遇如是也！""生活的教训到处都是，人生的乐趣无处不在！"等，可见有的是"直译"，有的为"意译"；我们应当追求的，是在二者之间找到一种相对平衡，如："所以，生活处处可学习，'冒险'充斥你身旁！"

另外，值得提出的是，作为大学生的翻译、写作，其语言修辞应当更讲究一些，即不仅要"信"，还要力争"达""雅"。如下段译文："大多数人认为，激动人心的事情是那些你为之采取重要手段，大步向前的事：国外旅行，激情浪漫的情事，大胆的计划或是惊险的冒险。但我很清楚地知道，仅仅是从火车站走下楼到达餐饮中心，我就已经经历了一次冒险。吃一碗黑椒意面便是一次冒险"；"生活处处是课堂，处处充满奇遇"等等，其中画线之处，重复太多，应当更加斟酌，有所选择。有的同学很认真，甚至做了相关的注释，值得表扬。同时，有些错误又实在不该，如：将"林林总总"写成"林林种种"，甚至将省略号"……"写成"○○○○○○"，就显得很不严肃、不专业，希望在我们大学生的翻译、写作中再也不要出现这种（或类似的）不正规的符号或写法。

参考译文

日常生活中的"冒险"

杰克·汉迪

[1] 人们大都以为，让人兴奋的事情，一定是那些大规划、大动作的，如国外旅游、火热浪漫、大胆设想、惊奇探险等等，但我却日益感到，仅从市车站的台阶下来步入餐饮中心，便会经历一场"冒险"，而冒险的形式不过是一碗黑乎乎的意大利面条。

[2] 我拿起勺叉，挖了一大块放在盘里。当舌头碰到通心粉那一刹那，我并不感到恶心，而是有趣。那的确是一种陌生、怪异而又得意的感觉。桌对面的朋友们冲着我笑，他们的牙齿和嘴唇都被染得漆黑一片，像是从墓地里挖出的死尸……冒险，说到底，恰如众人各异，有着形态、体型、肤色的不同。俗话说，"真正的发现之旅不在乎寻求新景观，而是有了新的眼光"。

[3] 我们的生活中充满了稍纵即逝的"迷你风险"。我点菜时，若知道点的是什么，就可能完全错过了这次"冒险"，不过我要感谢这个错误。要是在美国，我会点这道菜吗？既可能又不可能，但我想不会特意去要的。由于那碗墨鱼汁黑酱意大利面，使我想起了以往错过的许多这样的"冒险"。

[4] 你其实不必去跨洋过海寻找刺激,而只需闲来散步、在火车上与旁边的人搭讪聊天,或是到你喜欢的餐馆点上一道别致的菜肴,便能找到感觉。所以,生活处处可学习,"冒险"充斥你身旁!

原 文

On Being Introduced

[1] Once the person introducing me bit his tongue so badly that blood poured over his necktie onto the index card on which he had inscribed my entire life. Another time one of the more combative younger poets introduced a colleague in terms so stark and acidulous the speaker seemed struck dumb: "If I were you," our host opined, "I'd go do something else, not listen to this genius's gibberish; he screws better than he writes."

[2] One day at the University of Tulsa, my introducer actually read aloud my entire curriculum vitae, taking up some thirty minutes, smitten at the outset by parroty echolalia and devastating nerves. Even as he spoke, on and on, I ran a 2B pencil through paragraphs of comparable length in my speech.

[3] Indeed, given time enough, we could have exchanged roles completely; the introduction would have supplanted the speech. I cannot think why someone has not attempted this—suddenly the audience twigs it that the introducer is the real draw after all and the ostensible speaker is a figment, a ghost who will slink away when no

one is looking.

译 析

[1] 中，Once the person introducing me bit his tongue so badly that... 其中，bit his tongue so badly，很多参赛者译成"狠狠地咬了一下舌头""狠狠咬了自己的舌头""他用力咬破舌头"等；其实，so badly固然可以表示程度很重，但此处更多的是就结果而言，而不是过程，"狠狠地"似乎更强调过程，且有意咬舌的嫌疑，不太合乎情理。而on which he had inscribed my entire life，不少人译成"那次经历我会一直记住""他那时的样子深深刻在了我的生命里"等。其实，index card是指的卡片，因而不可能有"印在我的心上"之类的含义，译成"记住"反映出对语言结构的错误理解；同时，inscribed 译成"记住"或者"刻在"，明显是机械照搬字典，未能从具体语境中理解词义。而our host opined看似简单，却有各式各样的歧义，如"主持人对他的同僚说""主持人对观众说""主持人对演讲者说""而且就连当晚的主持人都说""我的同事说道""我们的主持人向后者发表意见说""那次活动的东道主向我表示说""听得主持人都好像愣住了""主持人不满地说"等等。具体而言，此句指称人物的有younger poets, a colleague, the speaker, our host, this genius等。它们之间的关系，一是可以通过语法结构来确定，二是可以通过经验来确定。首先，one of the more combative younger poets introduced a colleague，指明了younger poet是介绍人，a colleague

是被介绍者。同时，host是指谁呢？请注意in terms so stark and acidulous the speaker seemed struck dumb后面使用的是冒号，说明冒号后面所引用的内容，正是younger poet介绍同行时所说的那些难听的话，由此，我们可以确定，host也是younger poet，而他所说的genius无疑是讽刺自己这位同行了。那么，the speaker则是那位被介绍的同行了。根据日常经验，我们也完全可以还原当时的情景：一位诗人要发表演讲（作为speaker），另一位诗人作为主持人，首先向听众介绍他，但他没有说恭维的话，而是讽刺和挖苦。这样理解便符合原文语境，因为该段都是讲在被介绍时发生的尴尬事件。

[2] 中，smitten at the outset by parroty echolalia and devastating nerves，是整段文字中错误最多的。有人译成"使我在最开始的时候就由于他的鹦鹉学舌和神经质而备受打击""其鹦鹉式的模仿语言和带有毁灭性的神经在开首对我进行了打击""可怜我的神经被百般蹂躏"等，根本的原因，是没有真正理解原文的语法形式。这里有两个关键点：一是smitten，二是devastating nerves。首先，smitten是smite的过去分词，也可作形容词，与with或by搭配，Oxford Dictionary上有两层含义：1. suddenly feeling that you in love with; 2. severely affected by a feeling, disease, etc. 而Merriam-Webster Dictionary上的一种解释是marked by foolish or unreasoning fondness。其次，具体到本句话，smitten引导的是状语，其主语显然就是主句的主语，而主句的主语即是my introducer，因而一切"使我受到打击""使我受到折磨"之类的翻译，均不正确；而smitten描写的是my introducer的状态，至于

其含义，可根据上下文来推断。

对于 devastating nerves，有同学提出质疑，认为搭配有误。其实，devastating 在字典里有 causing a lot of damage、extremely shocking 和 impressive and powerful 几种含义。而 nerves 作复数时，指 feelings of worry or anxiety，即"紧张"，因而 devastating nerves 的意思自然是"高度紧张"。此外，需要注意的是，parroty echolalia 和 devastating nerves 是并列的，都没有所有格修饰，因而都应该视作主语 my introducer 的行为表现，若译成"可怜我的神经被百般蹂躏"，显然是误译了主语。

[3] 中的 real draw，词面意思是"真画"，此处指"真正的主角"；ostensible 为表面的，如 He did not accept the ostensible explanation, but suspected that there was a nigger in the woodpile（他不同意那种表面解释，怀疑其中有不可告人之处）；此处结合后面的 speaker，可译为"所谓的演讲者"；slink away，为"偷偷溜走""溜之大吉"等，类似的，如 Don't slink away without apologizing（不要不道歉就偷偷溜走）等。

参考译文

所谓"被人介绍"

[1] 一次，介绍我的人咬到了舌头，鲜血从领带一直滴到写

有我简历的提示卡上，十分惨烈。另一次，有个争强好胜的年轻诗人，在介绍一个同行的时候，说了番非常直白而刻薄的话，惊得这位演讲者哑口无言："我要是你们"，这位主持人宣称，"我宁愿去干点别的，也不会在这听这位天才胡说八道；他随便瞎整点什么都比写诗强"。一天，在塔尔莎大学，介绍我的人只是把我的简历从头到尾大声地朗读了一遍，花了差不多半个小时。

[2] 从一开始，他便完全陷入了照本宣科、高度紧张的状态。在他滔滔不绝介绍我时，我用2B铅笔在演讲稿上划着，预习着整篇发言，结果我们用了差不多同样的时间。

[3] 其实，如果时间允许，我们完全可以互换角色；就让介绍代替演讲算了。不知为什么还没有人这么试过——听众刹那间明白了，原来那个介绍者才是真正的主角，而所谓的演讲者不过形同虚设，像个幽灵，要是没人看见便可溜之大吉。

10

Acknowledgements

By Yukiko Koshiro

[1] The suburbs of Yokohoma in the 1960s betrayed hardly any trace of Japan's Eurasian-Pacific War. Just two decades after surrender, the war was already a distant event of the past, and we children had little desire to feel any connection. Japanese society did not encourage us to do so either, other than imparting the rather powerful moral lesson that war, a very general and abstract concept lacking historical specificity, meant only killing and destruction and as such was inherently wrong. None of the adults around me who lived through the war—my immediate family, relatives, neighbors, and even teachers—talked about Japan's war at all, much less recounted their opinions and memories of it.

[2] The rare exceptions proved the rule. Every year at our New Year's family reunion, my grandmother would reminisce about the massive Yokohama air raid of May 29, 1945, that claimed ten thousand lives. As her house began burning, she fled with her small children and barely cheated death. She grabbed only an ohitsu (a

wooden container for cooked rice) and a pair of hair clippers. Feeding the children was her top priority during the war and so the ohitsu was a precious item. And the clippers? When the air raid began, she happened to be trimming the hair of one of her sons. At this point in the story, she giggled wryly. Her adult children, my aunts and uncles, laughed at her blunder, too.

[3] How many times I heard this episode I can't recall: it was one of the rare occasions my grandmother or anyone else in the family talked about their experiences in Japan's war. Only much later, when my uncles and aunts were in their sixties and seventies, did they begin sharing small episodes of the war, still selectively. Along the way I learned that some maternal and paternal relatives had lived and worked in Korea and Manchuria. No one has ever been forthcoming with details.

译 析

本文节选自《帝国的消融：二战前日本针对亚洲大陆的战略思想》(*Imperial Eclipse: Japan's Strategic Thinking about Continental Asia before August 1945*) 一书的致谢部分。作者小代有希子（Yukiko Koshiro）现任教于日本大学国际关系学院。翻译前，译者应该对原文的来源、作者的背景及原文涉及的历史题材做一定的调查。不然的话，动笔就会出错。例如，有些同学将Acknowledgements译为"承认""面对""承认战争""认错"，等等。此处应译为"致谢",译为"鸣谢""谢启""后记",不符合著作致谢部分的表达习惯。

[1]中对于The suburbs of Yokohoma in the 1960s betrayed hardly any trace of Japan's Eurasian-Pacific War,主语是the suburbs of Yokohoma in the 1960s,译成汉语时可以根据话题的需要进行调整,同时betrayed也不一定要翻译成"暴露"。整句可以处理为"20世纪60年代,横滨郊区几乎看不到日本亚欧-太平洋战争留下的丝毫踪迹了",或者"20世纪60年代,你在日本横滨郊区已几乎找不到当年亚欧-太平洋战争的痕迹"。对于Japanese society did not encourage us to do so either, other than imparting the rather powerful moral lesson that war, a very general and abstract concept lacking historical specificity, meant only killing and destruction and as such was inherently wrong,绝大多数同学理解有误。这句话的结构比较复杂,句子的主干是Japanese society did not encourage us to do so either, other than引出一个介宾结构,其中lesson后面带了一个同位语从句,用来说明lesson的内容,而同位语从句的主语war后面带了一个名词短语与之同位,用来描述主语war的性质和特征。理解和翻译这句话时,译者应该激活自己对战争的已有认识和了解,同时调动自己的逻辑思维能力。这句话表达了以下几层意思:一,日本社会也希望我们不要提及那次战争;二,除此之外,日本社会只是教育我们应该吸取战争的教训;三,教训的具体内容以及日本社会的教育方式是:战争带来的是死亡和破坏,因此战争本身是错误的,然而日本社会提到的战争不是指具体的哪次战争,更不是日本发动的战争,而是一

个抽象、笼统的概念。不少同学在理解和表达lacking historical specificity时没有经过逻辑推理,因而译文不合乎逻辑,更不用说符合译入语的表达习惯了。

[2]中对于The rare exceptions proved the rule,不少同学拘泥于英文的形式,停留在句子的表层结构,没有进入句子的深层结构,即没有把握该句的深层意义。这句话是一个承上启下的句子,因此译者应该结合语境,把握上文和下文之间的意义和逻辑关系。上文说到,我身边经历过那场战争的成年人,包括我的家人,亲戚,邻居甚至我的老师,都没有谈论过那场战争,更不会讲述他们对于那场战争的记忆和看法。下文却提到,每次新年的家庭聚会上,祖母总会回想起1945年5月29日规模浩大的横滨空袭,那场空袭夺去了上万人的生命。因此,此句表达的意思是"例外的情况总是有的",表达的逻辑关系是"转折",因而可以加上"然而"。有些同学将之译为"一些罕见的例外也证实了这条规律""极少的几次讲到这场战争还是证明了它的存在""少有的例外证明了这一点""少之又少的例外似乎都在证明这种潜规则",等等。试想,这样翻译的话,估计译者自己都不知所云,更不用说将原文的意思有效传递给译文读者。也有不少同学在理解原文遇到阻碍时,勇于突破原文形式的束缚,探寻原文的深层结构。不过,这种探寻应该在上下文提供的语境中合理进行。

对于Feeding the children was her top priority during the war and so the ohitsu was a precious item中priority一词,同学们处理得非常好,大多数同学将这一抽象名词具体化,译为"头等大事""最重要的事""首先考虑的事",等等。对于Her adult children, my aunts and uncles, laughed at her blunder, too 中 Her adult children, my aunts and uncles，有多种处理方法，可以将 adult 及 my aunts and uncles 表达的意思抽出来，单独表达，如"她的孩子们，如今已长大成人，也就是我的叔伯和姑妈们"。

最后需要强调的是，英译汉时译者应积极调动自己的常识、经验和知识，结合翻译语境，并通过逻辑推理，努力挖掘原文的深层结构，以确保译文本身的连贯性。因为译文内的连贯是实现原文与译文之间连贯的前提条件。

参考译文

致谢

小代有希子

[1] 20世纪60年代，横滨郊区几乎看不到日本亚欧-太平洋战争留下的丝毫踪迹了。日本宣布投降仅仅二十年后，那场战争就似乎已经离我们很遥远了，当时我还是个孩子，大家不太愿意提及与战争有任何联系的事。日本社会也希望我们不要提及那次战争，只是教育我们应该吸取战争的教训：战争带来的是杀戮和破坏，因此战争本身是错误的——不过这里提到的战争不是指具体的哪次战争，而是一个抽象、笼统的概念。我身边经历过那场战争的成年人，包括我的家人，亲戚，邻居甚

至我的老师，都没有谈论过那场战争，更不会讲述他们对于那场战争的记忆和看法。

[2] 然而，例外的情况总是有的。每次新年的家庭聚会上，祖母总会回想起1945年5月29日规模浩大的横滨空袭，那场空袭夺去了上万人的生命。房子被烧着后，祖母带着年幼的孩子逃生，险些遇难。当时她只抢带了一个盛饭的木质饭盒和一把理发的剪刀。当时最重要的是孩子能吃饱饭，因此，盛饭的木质饭盒对祖母来说显得弥足珍贵。为何要带上理发的剪刀呢？原来，空袭发生时，祖母正在给儿子修剪头发。说到这里，祖母一脸苦笑，而她的孩子们，如今已长大成人，也就是我的叔伯和姑妈们，也都忍不住笑了起来。

[3] 我已记不清楚曾经多少次听到过这段故事，虽然祖母和家里其他人平时很少谈论他们在日本战争中的经历。过了很长时间以后，直到叔伯和姑妈们渐入花甲和古稀之年，才开始谈论那场战争的一些细节，而且依然小心翼翼。从他们的谈论中，我得知一些亲戚当时在朝鲜和满洲里（现在的东北地区）生活和工作，不过他们当中没有任何人曾经提及过关于那场战争的具体细节。

11

原 文

Getting Less Sleep

(Excerpts)

By Walter Kirn

[1] The difference between night and day is not what it used to be for Tony Warren. After a couple of years of steady shift work, the 27-year-old Atlanta resident—a part-time waiter and full-time graduate student in computer engineering—has embraced an existence of almost non-stop wakefulness that would turn most normal human beings into drooling, hallucinating zombies.

[2] "My shifts are from 5 p.m. until 3 or 4 in the morning", he says. "When you get home late like that over and over again, then you just can't fall asleep as easy. So you stay up an hour. Then an hour becomes two hours. Then the next thing you know, the sun's coming up as you're going to bed". Eventually, Warren says, "you start to realize it's daytime and you could be doing something with your time, like schoolwork or whatever. Now it's easy to stay up. I can go a day and a half without sleep as long as I keep my mind active. Sleep becomes annoying once you realize how much you can accomplish".

[3] In this age of flexible work schedules, all-night dining, round-the-clock cable news and home espresso makers, the unwillingness to sleep may be far more common than people suspect. For certain restless, over-scheduled Americans intent on squeezing more labor, more fun, more family time and more sheer activity from their lives, the traditional 24-hour day has become an anachronistic inconvenience, much like the sit-down lunch meal.

译 析

本文节选自美国《时代周刊》的"Sleep Is for Sissies",作者沃尔特·科恩(Walter Kirn)为美国当代小说家、文学评论家、散文家,曾任《时代周刊》的特约编辑,其代表作为小说作品 *Up in the Air* 等。

总的来讲,参加翻译的同学们都能大致理解原文,译文相对完整,没有明显漏译,可以看出同学们是下了功夫的,都有不同程度的进步。

主要问题:1. 不细心或未查字典。例如,一些译文中,Tony 的原话引用部分,只有前引号,没有后引号;graduate student 直接译为"毕业生"(实则为"研究生");2. 长句处理欠妥,主要是最后一段第一句;3. 未能透彻理解原文、缺乏英文语感,主要问题存在于最后一段,问题比较普遍;4. 标点的误用,比较明显的是对逗号和顿号的使用方法不甚明了,属中文功底问题;5. 不应有的明显误译,如将 Tony 译为"汤姆",将 the 27-year-old

Atlanta resident—a part-time waiter 译为"这位27岁的兼职作家"，即把 waiter 当成 writer，而完全不顾上下文的逻辑关系，等等。

具体而言，关于题目 Getting Less Sleep 的翻译，有同学译成"越睡越少""压榨睡眠""越来越少的睡眠""不愿多睡""睡眠时间越缩越短""睡眠渐少""睡少点"等等，这些都还只是表面意思，在通读全篇后，便会知道这是一种被形势所迫、不得已的行为，故不妨用这个当下流行语"被"字，如："被出名了"即本来不想出名，"被放假了"本来不想放假等，故此处不妨译为"被减少的睡眠"。当然，"自经轮班少睡眠"，也是别有特色的。

[1] 中对于 The difference between night and day is not what it used to be for Tony Warren，有同学译成"白天和黑夜对于托尼沃伦来说没有什么不同了"，其中 is not what it used to be 实则为"不像以往那样明显了"。

在这一段，After a couple of years of steady shift work, the 27-year-old Atlanta resident—a part-time waiter and full-time graduate student in computer engineering—has embraced an existence of almost non-stop wakefulness that would turn most normal human beings into drooling, hallucinating zombies，其中 shift work 为"轮班工作"，non-stop wakefulness 为"全天候"的一种状态，而 drooling, hallucinating zombies 也不能完全按字典的定义"死译"，如"神志不清，口水直流的行尸走肉的几近不停的不眠生活""很可能早就胡说八道、神志不清、行动迟缓了""使很多正常人变得像嘴流口水、满是幻觉的僵尸"等等，而要根据原文的意思加以变通，使其具有可读性，故该段不妨译为"他今年27

岁，家住亚特兰大，计算机工程专业的全日制研究生，兼职服务生。在持续做了若干年轮班工作后，他已进入了一种似乎是'全天候'睡醒的生存状态。多数正常人，若像他那样，可能早已成了痴痴呆呆、幻想丛生的木讷者了"。

[2] 中对于 Eventually, Warren says, "you start to realize it's daytime and you could be doing something with your time, like schoolwork or whatever. Now it's easy to stay up. I can go a day and a half without sleep as long as I keep my mind active. Sleep becomes annoying once you realize how much you can accomplish", 有的同学翻译得过于口语化了，如"最后呢，沃伦说：'你意识到，哦，是白天了。在白天，你总得做点什么事儿，像学习啊什么的。现在，熬夜也就成了顺理成章的事。只要我的思维能保持活跃，我可以一天半不睡觉。一旦你意识到利用睡觉的时间你可以完成许多事，你就会觉得睡觉真是件惹人厌的麻烦事'"等，参考译文为："他最后说，'……现在熬夜倒是挺容易的；只要头脑清醒，我可以一天半不睡觉。一旦你意识到睡觉的时间可以用来做多少事情，睡觉便成了一件令人心烦的事'。"

[3] 中，主要问题出在以下下画线部分：In <u>this age</u> of <u>flexible work schedules</u>, all-night dining, round-the-clock cable news and home espresso makers, the unwillingness to sleep may be far <u>more common than people suspect</u>. For certain <u>restless</u>, over-scheduled Americans intent on squeezing more labor, more fun, more family time and more sheer activity from their lives, the traditional 24-hour day has become an anachronistic <u>inconvenience</u>, much like the sit-

down lunch meal. 请将这位同学的比较典型的译文与参考译文的相关部分加以比较："这个工作时间<u>允许调节</u>，饭店开始永不打烊，电视新闻全天播放，家用浓缩咖啡机大行其道的时代，让人们在夜晚<u>比他们所猜想的要更不想寐</u>。正因当代<u>坐立不安</u>，琐事缠身的美国人希望把从睡眠时间中挤出来的时间拿去工作、享乐、陪同家人，做一些有意义的事情，所以传统意义上一日24小时的概念同旧时代人们<u>正襟危坐</u>，服务生热情服务的正式午餐一样，变得过时而<u>不方便</u>。"

参考译文

被减少的睡眠

（节选）

沃尔特·科恩

[1] 对托尼·华伦（Tony Warren）而言，白天与黑夜间的区别，不像以往那样明显了。他今年27岁，家住亚特兰大，计算机工程专业的全日制研究生，兼职服务生。在持续做了若干年轮班工作后，他已进入了一种似乎是"全天候"睡醒的生存状态。多数正常人，若像他那样，可能早已成了痴痴呆呆、幻想丛生的木讷者了。"我的轮值时间是从下午五点至第二天凌晨三四点"，华伦说，"如果你一次次那样晚回家的话，便很难入睡了，于是

就熬上一小时,后来变成了两小时。等你要去睡的时候,你知道,太阳也出来了。"

[2] 他最后说,"这时你又会想,现在是大白天,应当利用这段时间干点什么,如做作业之类的。现在熬夜倒是挺容易的;只要头脑清醒,我可以一天半不睡觉。一旦你意识到睡觉的时间可以用来做多少事情,睡觉便成了一件令人心烦的事"。

[3] 当今时代,人们的工作时间灵活多变,餐馆通宵营业,有线新闻日夜播报,家用咖啡器具已普及;不愿睡觉的普遍状况可能超出了人们的想象。有些美国人总是闲不住,每天安排得满满的;一心想干更多的事,得更多的乐趣,挤出更多和家人在一起的时间,或纯粹就是想从事更多的活动。对他们来说,传统一天24小时的生活,犹如坐下来吃顿午餐那样,显得落伍、不合时宜了。

12

原文

The Value of Sleep Deprivation

(Excerpts)

By Walter Kirn

[1] Is the waking life actually worth living—or does it feel like a miserable, gray limbo of red eyes, dragging limbs and foggy thoughts? My own experience with Provigil, which I took for several weeks a few years ago during a season of heavy deadlines, convinced me that simple wakefulness is no replacement for genuine restedness. After two or three 18-hour days of writing, the quality of my work collapsed even as my fingers kept on typing.

[2] Though some switch deep inside my brain was stuck on "on", my soul and spirit had gone numb, incapable of emotion or creativity. I felt as if I were encased in a full-body cast that allowed me to neither lie down all the way nor sit up straight: a mummy man. Though researchers agree almost unanimously that far from granting superpowers, sleep derivation dulls the mind and nervous system—rapidly, profoundly and invariably—many people still insist that they are the exception.

[3] For them, the perceived satisfaction of heightened

productivity, extra hours spent with friends and family, and uninterrupted late-night sessions in front of the computer or television outweigh the supposed benefits of unconsciousness. Are they right— or does the altered state brought on by caffeine, fatigue and lack of slow-wave sleep merely make them believe they are right? It's a question they might do well to ponder—if only they had the time.

译 析

就题目而言，其中的value，许多人译成了"价值"，即"不睡觉的价值"，不大确切，实为"代价"。类似的，如If we lose the shipment, the extra value we have to pay will be too high（如果这批货搞砸了，我们的代价就太高了）。

[1]中，the waking life，字面是"醒着的生活"，实际为"不睡觉的生活"；将miserable译成"悲惨的"似有些过火，不妨以日常生活用语淡化，如"惨兮兮"等。simple wakefulness is no replacement for genuine restedness，其中的simple wakefulness不宜译成"简单地醒来"，而为"只是醒着"，相对而言，genuine restedness，则为"真正休息"。对于最后一句，有的译成"我的工作质量崩溃了而我的手指却一直还在打字"，显然是过于拘泥于原文了，甚至像是电脑软件的译文；实则不妨将其变通，调整为"尽管手指还在打字，但写出东西的质量急剧下降了"。

[2]中，多人将allowed me to neither lie down all the way nor sit up straight: a mummy man译成"不允许我躺下，也不允许我坐

下：一个木乃伊的男人",显然过于死板;不妨变通为"既不能直躺,亦无法直坐,简直成了一尊木乃伊"。sleep derivation dulls the mind and nervous system—rapidly, profoundly and invariably,其中的dull不是形容词而是动词,而rapidly, profoundly and invariably三个副词,在译文里可加以分解,如将invariably和rapidly译为"不可避免地迅速",而将profoundly译为"相当(迟钝)"。

[3]中第一句的主语似难确定,有的人从the perceived satisfaction开始,译成"感知到的好处……",于是接下来的文字就很冗长;其实,前面的在原文里是定语,可以提前译出,如"不睡觉可提高工作效率,可有更多的时间和朋友及家人在一起,可于深夜持续地坐在电脑或电视机面前",而"这些可感知的满足感"为主语同位语;outweigh the supposed有一种虚拟语气,不妨译为"似乎超过了……的好处",类似的if only they had the time,许多人译成"如果他们有时间的话",不如变换语气为"但愿他们有这个时间"。

参考译文

不睡觉的代价

(节选)

沃尔特·科恩

[1] 不睡觉的生活值得吗?抑或这样的生活只会惨兮兮的:

眼睛充血，四肢乏力，迷迷瞪瞪？几年前，有段时间，因为要赶着做事，我也服用过几个星期的"不夜神"。那段经历使我认识到，"只是醒着"的状态并不能代替"真正休息"过后的状态。我曾每日写作18个小时，两三天后，尽管手指还在打字，但写出东西的质量急剧下降。

[2] 尽管大脑深处的某个机关还在"开着"，但我的神情已经麻木，没了情感与创意；只觉得自己像被关在了一个与我同大的模具里，既不能直躺，亦无法直坐：简直成了一尊木乃伊。尽管研究者们几乎一致认同，不睡觉不但不会给人以"超强能力"，反而会让大脑和神经系统不可避免地迅速变得相当迟钝，但许多人仍坚持认为自己是个例外。

[3] 对他们来说，不睡觉可提高工作效率，可有更多的时间和朋友及家人在一起，可于深夜持续地坐在电脑或电视机面前，这些可感知的满足感，远比睡眠带来的种种所谓的感知不到的好处更重要。他们的观点正确吗？还是因为咖啡因、疲惫及缺乏深度睡眠而导致的身心变态使得他们相信了自己是正确的？这个问题值得他们深思——但愿他们有这个时间。

Exercises Put You in a Good Mood

[1] It's now clear that emotions can affect our physical health, but what about the reverse? Can physical activity affect the health of our minds? In fact, getting off the couch may help some people as much as psychotherapy. Exercise can improve anyone's mood and mental performance. It's free, it's fun and it doesn't take a whole lot of time.

[2] Whether they survey children or adults, researchers find that active people are happier than sofa jockeys, and less prone to depression and suicide. That doesn't prove that exercise make people happy (it could be that happiness makes people exercise), but studies are now confirming the therapeutic effects. The research on mental performance tells a similar story.

[3] Researchers have long noticed that active seniors suffer less cognitive decline than sedentary ones, and recent studies suggest that aerobic exercise may make us sharper at any age. The benefits accrue quickly, but they require constant reinforcement.

[4] When we are young and strong, we cannot imagine what it is to be weak and ailing. We are so used to vigorous health that we

take it for granted. The organs of our body work so smoothly that we scarcely know we have lungs and liver, heart and stomach. But when any of these get upset and give us pain and sickness, we learn by bitter experience what an unspeakable blessing it is to be well.

译 析

本文大部分节选自"运动之益"（The Serenity Workout），原文刊载于美国《新闻周刊》（*Newsweek*）。标题Exercises Put You in a Good Mood表意明确，大家提供了许多不错的译文，如"运动带来好心情""常运动，常开心""好心情，在运动""常运动，好心情"等等。

通读全文，我们发现整篇文章探讨运动对心理、情绪和智力表现的作用，因此选择词义时应该考虑这一整体语境。故[1]中的emotions应译为"情绪"而不是"情感"，physical activity应译为"体力活动"或"体育锻炼"，不能理解为"物理活动"。对于In fact, getting off the couch may help some people as much as psychotherapy，部分参赛者理解有误。这句话包含比较结构，比较对象是锻炼身体和心理治疗，比较点是帮助一些人摆脱心理疾病，因此整句话可以处理为"事实上，和心理治疗一样，少躺、少坐也能帮助一些人摆脱心理疾病"。其中，getting off the couch如果直译为"离开沙发"，没有表达出作者的真实意图；而mental performance中mental一词是个多义词，一般词典提供的词义有"内心的，精神的，思想的，心理的，智慧的，智（脑）力的",根据上下文提供的语境,我们可以推理出该词在这里主要指"智(脑)力的"。同样,performance也是个多义词,常见的词义有"履行,性能,表现,演出,业绩",通过词语搭配以及短文提供的整体语境,我们可以判断该词在这里是"表现"的意思。所以mental performance应该理解为"智力表现"或"思维能力",有的将其译为"性情心理""心理状况"或"心理表现",显然是不合适的。关于free一词,我们可以根据常识来判断,该词在这里指"免费的",而不是"自由自在的",因为"自由自在"不是体育锻炼的显著特征。需要补充的是,体育锻炼并非一定是免费的,因此It's free可以处理为"锻炼可以是免费的"。

[2]中,对于active people are happier than sofa jockeys, and less prone to depression and suicide,有些同学将active people译为"活跃的人"不太合适,因为活跃包含的意思太广,且包含思想上活跃,而此处更加具体,强调喜欢运动,所以处理为"喜欢运动的人"更好。另外,sofa jockeys指久坐沙发,很少运动的人,有同学将其译为"沙发骑师"或"沙发客",采用了"异化"的翻译方法,一方面保留了原文的形象性,另一方面给译文读者带来了一些理解上的困难。异化与归化之争,是翻译界经久不衰的话题,有兴趣的同学可以进一步了解异化与归化翻译的得与失。对于tell a similar story,有些同学没有把握该短语的深层意义,即"揭示出一个类似的情况",将其直译为"有一个类似的故事"或"展示了一个相似的故事"等,造成译文生硬,不符合汉语习惯。

[3]中,对于active seniors suffer less cognitive decline than sedentary ones,有些同学理解不够准确,将之译为"喜欢运动的

老年人比久坐不动的老年人，更不容易产生认知能力衰退"。这部分包含比较结构，比较点是老年人认知能力衰退的程度大小或高低，而不是认知能力是否衰退，而且常识告诉我们：老年人的认知力衰退是不可避免的，只是衰退的程度不一样而已。

[4] 中，翻译时应与原文保持适度的距离，距离太近时，容易受原文语言形式的束缚而造成译文生硬；距离太远时，容易歪曲原文的意思，或者随意增加原文没有的意思，从而混淆翻译与自由创作的界限。如：有人将 When we are young and strong, we cannot imagine what it is to be weak and ailing 处理为"当我们年轻有为、孔武有力时，我们很难想象恶病缠身、年老体衰时的情境"，其中"有为"是译者自己随意添加的意思，"恶病缠身"相比原文程度过强，这是我们在翻译时应该尽可能避免的。著名语言哲学家维特根斯坦曾经说过，语言的意义在于它的使用。

总之，对词义的选择一定要考虑其使用的环境。如 sharper、smoothly、learn 都是多义词，根据本文提供的上下文，应该分别理解为"反应更加灵敏""（运转）正常""领悟到"。

参考译文

锻炼可怡人

[1] 情绪可影响人们的身体健康，这已不言自明；那么，相

反的情况呢？体力活动会影响我们的心智健康吗？事实上，少躺、少坐对有些人可能像心理治疗那样有效。锻炼可改善人的情绪和智力表现。锻炼可以是免费、愉悦的，且可不用很多时间。

[2] 无论是对儿童或成人的调查，研究人员都发现，爱运动的人总是比卧在沙发上的人更愉快，更少患抑郁症或自杀。这并不证明锻炼使人愉快（也许是快活驱使人去锻炼），但研究正是要证实锻炼的治疗效果。对精神状态的研究也揭示出类似的情况。

[3] 长期以来，研究人员还注意到，爱活动的老人比久坐不动的老人，其认知力衰退的程度会更小，而最近研究表明，增氧健身运动可使任何年龄段的人反应更加灵敏。锻炼收效甚佳，但亦需持之以恒方可事半功倍。

[4] 年轻力壮时，我们想象不到体弱多病是怎样的滋味；我们如此习惯于生机勃勃的健康，认为是理所当然的。我们身体的各个器官如此正常运作，使我们很少意识到肺、肝、心、胃等功能。可是，一旦感觉哪个器官不适了，出现了疼痛或病症，我们便会从痛苦的经历中领悟到：身体健康是怎样一种难以言表的幸福啊！

How Does Exercise Work?

By H. Martin

[1] It is wise and necessary to learn in time, before we have lost our health, that it can be kept only by knowing and observing the laws of health. Nature's laws cannot be ignored with impunity. In the long run they will avenge themselves on us if we forget them, even if they do not do so at once. At first we may not feel the result of excesses and unhealthy habits; but we certainly shall some day.

[2] Besides improving circulation, exercise causes an array of chemical changes within the brain. It boosts the activity of mood-enhancing neurotransmitters such as dopamine and serotonin. It increases the production of brain-derived neurotrophic factor, a chemical that helps neurons multiply and form new connections. And it triggers the release of endorphins—morphinelike chemicals that blunt pain and foster relaxation. Studies show that even 10 minutes of vigorous exercise (producing a pulse rate of 100 to 120 beats per minute, depending on your age) can raise endorphin levels for an hour.

[3] As it is said that "you feel tired, but you feel good" and you have "comfortable pain". Exercise may be a tonic for the psyche, but that doesn't mean more is always better. Competitive swimmers and other endurance athletes, for example, can become gloomy and irritable during periods of intense training. Nevertheless, pick an activity you enjoy, and stick with it. You have nothing to lose but your sorrows, your fogginess and a few extra pounds.

译 析

本文摘选自"健康"（Health），载于美国《新闻周刊》（*Newsweek*），作者H. 马丁（H. Martin）现执教于美国西北大学梅迪尔新闻学院，为多份出版物供稿。

本期收到翻译学院及其他学院的学生来稿百余篇，质量参差不齐。现作一综合评析。

关于该文的题目How Does Exercise Work? 其中的work不是"工作"之意。同学们有许多不同的译法，如"运动是如何有益于身心健康的？""体质锻炼对人体产生怎样的影响？""运动如何发挥功效？"等，是比较"紧贴"原文的，而有些则加以改变，如"运动如何发挥作用""运动怎样使你健康"等，至于"流水不腐"等则有些偏离太远了。其实题目的翻译是很灵活的，如最近由美国索尼公司拍摄的影片*The Interview*，中文译为《刺杀金正恩》；类似的如最近《英语学习》上题为Rising to the Top 的一篇文章，被翻译成"亚裔美国学生：高分≠成功"，显然都有较大的发挥。故此处不妨译为"锻炼的益处"。

在[1]中对于 It is wise and necessary to learn in time... 的句式（其中的 learn 亦非"学习"之意），有两种译法，既可"置前"也可"置后"，如"必要和明智的做法是……"或"……是必要和明智的"，都是可以接受的。但有的同学在选词上不够准确，如"在还没失去健康前就开始适时锻炼是非常<u>聪明</u>也非常必要的""有一条我们需要及时学习的重要信息：想要保持身体健康，就要<u>知晓掌握</u>健康法则""在失去健康前，及时了解相关信息才是明智的和必要的，一旦失去，就只能<u>靠条条框框</u>保持健康了"，等等。对于 before we have lost our health, that it can be kept only by knowing and observing the laws of health. Nature's laws cannot be ignored with impunity，其中的 laws of health 为"健康法则"或"健康规律"，而 before lost health，为"失去健康之前"，有同学译成"在我们的身体亮红灯前"亦是可取的。Nature's laws cannot be ignored with impunity 是一种"否定之否定"的肯定。其中，impunity 为 without penalty，如 One cannot commit crimes with impunity（人不能犯了罪不受惩罚）；In a society where people can get away with it with impunity, they are encouraged to feel there is nothing wrong with it（在社会里，若人们可以逃脱罪责、免受惩罚，就等于鼓励他们的此种行为）；The certainty of a God giving a meaning to life far surpasses in attractiveness the ability to behave badly with impunity（神赋予了生活以意义，这种信仰的吸引力远超出了行恶而不受惩罚的权力）。其实此句的英文还可表述为 ...cannot be ignored without penalty 等。故此句不妨译为："必要和

明智的做法，是在没有失去健康时，我们应及时意识到，只有通过了解和遵循健康规律来保持健康；而无视健康规律，则不能不受到惩罚。"

关于 In the long run they will avenge themselves on us if we forget them, even if they do not do so at once. At first we may not feel the result of excesses and unhealthy habits; but we certainly shall some day，其中的 avenge 一般意思是"复仇"，其英文一般释为 If you avenge a wrong or harmful act, you hurt or punish the person who is responsible for it 等，但此处更多为受到自然规律的"报复"。对此句中的含义，有同学译为"或许逃得过初一，但是逃不过十五"是颇有创意的，有中文特色，也传达出原意；而有的，如"自然的没有附加条件的新陈代谢不可忽视，这种规律的威力即使不会立竿见影，但从长远来看，它们不容小觑"则有些用词不当。此句不妨译为"长远来看，如果我们忽视了自然规律，便会受到报复，即使不是即刻的。起初，我们可能感觉不到过火行为和不良习惯的后果，但总有一天会的"。

在[2]中，Besides improving circulation, exercise causes an array of chemical changes within the brain. It boosts the activity of mood-enhancing neurotransmitters such as dopamine and serotonin. It increases the production of brain-derived neurotrophic factor, a chemical that helps neurons multiply and form new connections. And it triggers the release of endorphins—morphinelike chemicals that blunt pain and foster relaxation. 其中涉及的一些科技词汇，同学们通过查找字典等工具大都可以准确译出，但在表述上可再自然、

通顺一些，如第一句Besides improving circulation, exercise causes an array of chemical changes within the brain，英文虽为句号，但在中文里与后面是紧密相关的，故不妨加上冒号，处理为"除了改善身体循环，体育锻炼可在大脑中引起一系列的化学变化："，下面则是对其进一步说明，即"可增强提高情绪的多巴胺、血清素之类的神经传质的活力，增加大脑衍生神经因子（帮助神经元繁衍和形成新连接物的一种化学物质），并能激发释放内啡肽（能减轻疼痛、促进放松的类吗啡的化学物质）"，其中的a chemical that helps neurons multiply and form new connections可理解为是对brain-derived neurotrophic factor的说明；而morphinelike chemicals that blunt pain and foster relaxation是对endorphins的诠释，故可放入括号中处理；当然，有的同学用了破折号也是可以的。

在下一句，Studies show that even 10 minutes of vigorous exercise (producing a pulse rate of 100 to 120 beats per minute, depending on your age) can raise endorphin levels for an hour，同学们一般都能按原文的标点符号作出恰当处理，如"研究表明，即便十分钟的剧烈运动（心跳在每分钟100—120的频率，视年龄不同而定），也可提高内啡肽水平达一小时之久"等。

在[3]中对于you feel tired, but you feel good可以译作"累并快乐着""虽然很累，但感觉很爽"等，更详细一点可译为"你会疲惫，但感觉良好"，而you have "comfortable pain"则是一种所谓的比喻的说法，译成"痛并快乐着"或"既舒适又疼痛"就不太恰当，而不妨顺其意为"舒服的疼痛"。就最后一段而言，Nevertheless, pick an activity you enjoy, and stick with it. You have nothing to lose but your sorrows, your fogginess and a few extra pounds，一些同学对此有着理解错误或用词不妥的地方，如"那么你所失去的只是悲伤、错觉和额外的零钱""所以，选一个你喜欢的活动，并且坚持下去。你会失去的无非是悲伤、迷惑和那么一点赘肉""除了你的悲伤、彷徨和多余的磅数之外，不会有任何损失""然后坚持下去，除了你的失意、迷茫和几磅多余的肥肉之外，你又不会损失其他任何东西"等等，而不妨译为"不管怎样，选择一项你所喜爱的运动并持之以恒，那么在运动中你所失去的便只有忧愁、迷茫和多余的重量"。

总之，需以有关健康知识为基础，结合具体内容选择最佳词语和句式。

参考译文

锻炼的益处

H. 马丁

[1] 必要和明智的做法，是在没有失去健康时，我们应及时意识到，只有通过了解和遵循健康规律来保持健康；而无视健康规律，则不能不受到惩罚。长远来看，如果我们忽视了自然规律，便会受到报复，即使不是即刻的。起初，我们可能感觉不到

过火行为和不良习惯的后果，但总有一天会的。

[2] 除了改善身体循环，体育锻炼可在大脑中引起一系列的化学变化：可增强提高情绪的多巴胺、血清素之类的神经传质的活力，增加大脑衍生神经因子（帮助神经元繁衍和形成新连接物的一种化学物质），并能激发释放内啡肽（能减轻疼痛、促进放松的类吗啡的化学物质）。研究表明，即便十分钟的剧烈运动（心跳在每分钟100—120的频率，视年龄不同而定），也可提高内啡肽水平达一小时之久。

[3] 人们常说，在运动中"你会疲惫，但感觉良好"，并会有一种"舒服的疼痛"。体育锻炼固然可以使人精神振奋，但并不总是意味越多越好。例如，游泳选手及其他耐力运动员，在集训期间会变得情绪低落、急躁易怒。不管怎样，选择一项你所喜爱的运动并持之以恒，那么在运动中你所失去的便只有忧愁、迷茫和多余的重量。

Fighting Diabetes Complications

By Dave Rockwell

[1] For people with diabetes, heart disease and stroke pose two serious and very real threats to their long-term health. Cardiovascular disease is the leading cause of death for people with diabetes, who are two to four times more likely to develop it than people who don't have diabetes. People who have diabetes are also more likely to die from a heart attack or stroke than others. Because of this, health care experts recommend that people with diabetes lower their risk factors for heart disease and stroke as much as possible.

[2] That means managing your ABCs of diabetes: A is for A1C (pronounced a-one-see), a test that measures your average blood sugar over the past two to three months; B is for blood pressure; and C is for cholesterol. Smoking and being overweight or physically inactive can also increase your risk for heart attack and other problems. Medications can also help ward off heart disease and stroke, in people with or without diabetes.

[3] Recent studies have found that certain classes of drugs can substantially reduced the threat of coronary artery disease, especially for people with type two diabetes. However, medications should never be seen as the total solution to preventing heart disease and stroke. Any good treatment plan should also include regular physical exercise, healthy meal planning and, if necessary, a weight-loss plan. Together, these steps can help reduce the risk of death from cardiovascular disease and other complications from diabetes and increase the chance of leading an active, healthy life.

译 析

本文是一篇如何对待糖尿病并发症的科普文章。对于题目中的fight，不是一般意义上的"战斗""斗争"等，而是一种"努力""对策"等，如He made a prompt decision, raised his head and began to carefully think about the future steps to fight（当机立断，他开始抬起头谨慎思考未来奋斗的步骤）; The chairman gave this long drawn out speech about how the company is going to fight the recession（董事长发表了长时间的演讲，大谈公司将怎样对付经济衰退期）等。但若翻译成"防治"，似也有不妥，因该词有prevent"防止"的意思，指未发生之前，故不妨译为"如何应对"。

在[1]中，这里的(people) with 是介词作动词用，如He is

walking in the park with an umbrella（他手拿雨伞在公园里散步）；Starting out with nothing but love（携手起步，一无所有，唯有爱心）等，此处为"患有（糖尿病）"。leading cause 可以是"头号杀手"，但更接近原文的为"首要死因"。Cardiovascular disease is the leading cause of death for people with diabetes, who are two to four times more likely to develop it than people who don't have diabetes，此句典型地体现出英文里介词在句子组合中的作用，有同学译成"冠心病是糖尿病患者的头号杀手，其并发率是正常人的两到四倍之多"，其中两点不妥：首先，cardiovascular disease 是泛指心血管病，类似的 cardiovascular system (circulatory system) 指心血管系统（the heart together with two networks of blood vessels—the systemic circulation and the pulmonary circulation）；而冠心病是 coronary heart disease，其中 corona，名词，一种冠或冠状结构，coronary 为其形容词。其次，people who don't have diabetes 并不等于"正常人"，因为他可能还有其他症状。故该句不妨译为"糖尿病患者出现心血管病的可能性是非糖尿病患者的2至4倍"。

在[2]中，That means managing your ABCs of diabetes，许多同学译得很直而生硬，如"这就意味着要管理好你的糖尿病中的ABCs"等，其实不妨译为"如此便要做好关于糖尿病ABC因素的管控"；A1C (pronounced a-one-see)，是一种拟音处理，不妨译为"A1C（英语中的发音是a-one-see）"；being overweight 不是"过重"，而是"肥胖"；physically inactive 不是"体力不活跃"，而是缺乏锻炼；medication 不是冥想（meditation），有人将二者混淆了,而是"药物",这里可译为"药物疗效";ward off 原义为"挡开""架开",可引申为"防治""预防""防范"等,如 One of the best products ever to ward off colds, allergies, and clear congestion(这是防治感冒、过敏和清除充血的从未有过的最好产品)等。

在[3]中,对于 type two diabetes 许多同学译成了"II类"等,实则为"2型";total solution 一般译为"整体解决方案",如 The business does not take ownership of the software, but instead subscribes to a total solution that is delivered remotely(这种业务并不获得软件的所有权,而是订阅远程交付的整体解决方案)等,但此处不宜僵化,如"最终解决方案""根本途径""唯一方法",而不妨变通为"预防心脏病或脑中风不能完全依赖药物治疗";if necessary, a weight-loss plan 固然可译成"若有必要,还可有减肥计划",但有时为了语境的顺达,亦可放入括号中处理,如"……以及相应的减肥步骤(若有必要的话)"等。对于 Together, ...and...,有同学将其译成两句,如"这些计划都有助于降低心血管疾病以及其他一些糖尿病并发症导致的死亡风险。与此同时,这些计划还很有可能促使患者去积极、健康地生活",显得很臃赘;其实,应将其尽量简化,如"总之,这些措施有助于……的死亡危险、增加……"等。

当然,还需注意各段句式之间的有机衔接。

参考译文

如何应对糖尿病并发症

戴夫·洛克威尔

[1] 对于糖尿病患者而言，心脏病和脑中风是他们长期健康中的两大实际的严重威胁。心血管病是糖尿病患者的首要死因；糖尿病患者出现心血管病的可能性是非糖尿病患者的2至4倍。同时，糖尿病患者较其他人更易死于心脏病或脑中风。正因如此，健康专家建议，患有糖尿病者，应尽可能地减低得心脏病和脑中风的因素。

[2] 如此便要做好关于糖尿病ABC因素的管控：A代表A1C（糖化血红蛋白，英语的发音是a-one-see），是一项检验过去2—3个月平均血糖水平的测试；B是指血压；C是指胆固醇。吸烟、肥胖或缺乏体力活动，也会增加糖尿病患者发生心脏病及其他疾病的风险。药物疗效，对于糖尿病或非糖尿病患者也会有助于防范其心脏病和脑中风的发生。

[3] 最近一些研究发现，通过服用某种药物，可显著降低冠心病的危险，特别是对于2型糖尿病患者。然而，预防心脏病或脑中风不能完全依赖药物治疗。任何合理的治疗方案还应包括有规律的体育锻炼、健康的饮食计划以及相应的减肥步骤（若有必要的话）。总之，这些措施有助于降低由糖尿病导致的心血管病及其他并发症的死亡危险、增加过上充满活力的健康生活的机会。

16

原 文

Seniors and the City

By Peg Tyre & Catharine Skipp

[1] The trickle of older folks returning to the city, which began in the mid-90s, has grown into a steady stream. While some cities, especially those with few cultural offerings, have seen an exodus of seniors, urban planners say others have become retiree magnets.

[2] In the next few years, as the 76 million baby boomers begin to enter retirement downtowns are expected to grow even grayer. Nobody's calling it the fountain of youth, but there may be hidden health benefits to city living, too. Some senior citizens moved from the suburbs to the city to ward off another, even more debilitating, byproduct of aging — social isolation.

[3] Recently they've discovered that disconnecting from their car may turn out to be a survival skill of sorts. When their suburban friends stop driving, they're trapped. Although they didn't plan it that way, learning to live without a car means they can keep enjoying paradise for a good long time. Maybe that's what they mean by the golden years.

译 析

本文节选自佩格·泰尔（Peg Tyre）和凯瑟琳·斯基普（Catharine Skipp）所写的一篇时事报道，刊于美国《新闻周刊》（*Newsweek*）（2004年10月11日），笔调清新、简练。

就题目而言，有的同学译成"城市老龄化""城市与老龄化""老龄化城市"等，都不准确；其实很简单，不妨就字面意思译为"老人与城市"。其中，seniors是对老年人的一种尊称，如senior citizens、the senior states men，等。

[1] 中The trickle of older folks returning to the city, which began in the mid-90s, has grown into a steady stream，是一种隐喻（亦称暗喻），即不用"如""像""似""好像"等比喻词，而用"是""成""就是""成为""变为"等词，把某事物直接比拟成和它有相似关系的另一事物，如"少年儿童是祖国的花朵""荷叶成了一把把撑开的小伞"。英文释义为metaphor: a figure of speech in which a word or phrase that ordinarily designates one thing is used to designate another, thus making an implicit comparison, as in "a sea of troubles" or "All the world is a stage"（Shakespeare）[隐喻是一种语言表达手法，通常用指某物的词或词组来指代他物，从而暗示它们之间的相似之处，如"忧愁之海"或"整个世界一台戏"（莎士比亚）]。

对于此处的隐喻翻译，有的同学作了释译处理，如"老年人慢慢地回流到城市已经成为平稳的趋势""老年人开始回归城市，到现在已经发展成为稳定的潮流"等，未尝不可，但是最好能够在尊重原文的基础上，以相对应的暗喻译出，如"自上世纪九十年代中期开始，老人们返回城市的涓涓细流，如今已形成滔滔江河"。

对于While some cities, especially those with few cultural offerings, have seen an exodus of seniors, urban planners say others have become retiree magnets的理解，翻译错误的同学较多。主要是没有弄懂especially those with few cultural offerings与整个句子的关系，同时没有弄清exodus的含义。根据上下文，总的意思是，老年人又开始重返了城市，但是especially...是一个转折，而并不包含在"重返"之列，如有的同学所译"包括这些没有什么文化的城市"，显然是不合理的；而对于others有同学译为"他人"，又显然讲不通。对于have become retiree magnets，也是一种暗喻，但若如有的同学所直接译成的"变成了退休者的磁石"，显然也不妥当。所以，要根据上下文，灵活处理。同时，exodus原指the departure of the Israelites from Egypt（以色列人逃离埃及），《圣经》里就有*Exodus*（《出埃及记》）一章，又如capital exodus（资本逃避），rural exodus（农村迁离）等。因而，该句不妨译为"虽然大批老人离开了一些城市，特别是那些没有什么文化活动的城市，城市设计者们仍认为，其他城市对退休者有着吸引力"。

[2]中对于In the next few years, as the 76 million baby boomers begin to enter retirement downtowns are expected to grow even grayer，其中的76 million，被译成了各种形式，如"76,000,000

人""七千六百万的人们",还有错译为"七百六十万"等,其实不妨译为"7600万人"简单、明了。短语"baby boomers"是指"婴儿潮时期",即美国第二次世界大战后的"4664"现象——从1946年至1964年,这18年间所出生的人口超过7000万人。该句的后半部应断为enter retirement 和 downtowns are expected to...两节,而不是retirement downtowns,如有的同学译成"退休城市中心"。对于grayer,许多同学译错了,如"灰色的""不景气""颓败的""更加冷清""面临更严重的衰落危机"等等;当然,也有相当一部分的同学译对了,即是指"老人"。英文释义为gray or white with or as if with age(灰白的;因年老而头发灰白的);having gray hair; hoary(有灰色头发的;头发灰白的);hair just turning gray(可怜白发生)。英文表述里常有这样的指称,如blue-blood,是指"出生贵族的""出身名门的""贵族的血统""贵族、王室的后代"等,因为上流社会的人皮肤白皙,可以清楚看到血管;血管看起来稍带蓝色,故用blue加以形容,如If you go there you will see a lot of blue-blood(到了那里你会看到许多贵族皇亲)。这里又不禁让人联想到塞缪尔·乌尔曼(Samuel Ullman)所写的《青春》(Youth)里的名句Youth is not a matter of rosy cheek, red lips(青春不是粉面丹唇),故亦可以"粉面丹唇"(rosy cheek and red lips)代指"青春"(youth)。

故此,该句不妨译为"今后几年,随着婴儿潮时期出生的7600万人进入退休年龄,市中心会见到更多的白发苍苍者"。

对于Nobody's calling it the fountain of youth, but there may be hidden health benefits to city living, too. Some senior citizens moved from the suburbs to the city to ward off another, even more debilitating, byproduct of aging — social isolation，其中，hidden health benefits to city living, too，有同学译成"隐匿在城市生活中的那些健康长寿的秘诀""在城市生活会获得隐性的医疗福利"等，意思上大致符合，但不够准确，不妨译为"城市生活对人们的健康可能有潜在的益处"。短语 ward off 意为 to prevent，即防止之意，而 debilitating，意为 to sap the strength or energy of; enervate（使衰弱；削弱……的力量或精力；使衰弱），有的同学译出了其中意思，但语言组织得欠佳，如"是为了避免另一个人口老龄化问题带来的副作用，那就是与社会隔绝，那会使人变得更加脆弱""为了避开其他垂暮之人，从郊外搬到城区，却被晚年的副产品——社会隔绝，折磨得更加老弱"等。其实，不妨译为"以防止与年迈随之而来的、甚至是更令人衰老的另一副产品——与世隔绝"。

[3] 中对于 Recently they've discovered that disconnecting from their car may turn out to be a survival skill of sorts. When their suburban friends stop driving, they're trapped，其中，"disconnecting"不宜直接译成"断开联系"，如有同学所译："由于他们的车而断开的联系可能促成一种多样的生存技能的诞生"；turn out，最早是指到场、出现，如 I was disappointed by the turn-out for our home match（我对我们主场比赛的观众到场人数感到失望），这里则意为"是""成为"等。再有，stop driving 不是"停止开车"，而是"不再开车"；trap，原意是"陷阱"，这里是动词，意为 to place in a confining or embarrassing position（使陷于困境；将……放到一个受限制或令人尴尬的境地中），有同学对此理解错误，

译成"当他们住在郊区的朋友都没有开车,他们也受到了诱惑"。实则,该句的意思为"最近,他们发现摆脱汽车生活,也是一种生存技巧。当他们的郊区朋友们不再开车时,便被'困住'"。

对于Although they didn't plan it that way, learning to live without a car means they can keep enjoying paradise for a good long time. Maybe that's what they mean by the golden years,其中didn't plan it that way,到底是指什么?同学们对此所译不一,如"虽然他们没有计划这样做""尽管不是有意为之"等,似乎都不大明确,实则为"他们搬到市区并非是打算从此不再开车了";enjoying paradise,有的译为"天堂般的生活",似太直白,不如"美化人生"。golden years或gold ager,为"流金岁月",在美国是指退休时期(一般65岁以上)的口语化、形象化表述。该词组与golden time或gold age不同,那是指"黄金时期""幸运时刻""黄金时代""幸福时光"等,二者毕竟有所不同。故该句不妨译为"他们搬到市区并非是打算从此不再开车了,但学会没有汽车的生活,意味着他们可享受很长时间的美好人生;也许,这就是他们所指的'黄金岁月'吧"。

本文中涉及的老年人问题,是西方世界普遍关注的,而英文的有关表述也是颇为丰富的。例如,超过70岁的老年称为borrowed time,因为根据《圣经》的启示,人生为70年一辈子(three-score years and ten),而对70岁以上的人,一般也不称old,而是young,如"75岁",称为"seventy years young"。对于女士,超过50岁以上的亦可称为girl,男长者亦为boy;老太太也不愿被称为grandma,而是aunt等。同时,在人们的交谈中,尽管对方年龄很大，一般也会称赞对方年轻，如 You still look young; you look younger than your age; no one thinks you look as old as you are，等等。

参考译文

老人与城市

佩格·泰尔和凯瑟琳·斯基普

[1] 自上世纪九十年代中期开始，老人们返回城市的涓涓细流，如今已形成滔滔江河。虽然大批老人离开了一些城市，特别是那些没有什么文化活动的城市，城市设计者们仍认为，其他城市对退休者有着吸引力。

[2] 今后几年，随着婴儿潮时期出生的7600万人进入退休年龄，市中心会见到更多的白发苍苍者。没人说城市生活是青春的源泉，但城市生活对人们的健康可能有潜在的益处。一些长者从郊区搬到了城市，以防止与年迈随之而来的、甚至是更令人衰老的另一副产品——与世隔绝。

[3] 最近，他们发现摆脱汽车生活，也是一种生存技巧。当他们的郊区朋友们不再开车时，便被"困住"。虽然，他们搬到市区并非是打算从此不再开车了，但学会没有汽车的生活，意味着他们可享受很长时间的美好人生；也许，这就是他们所指的"黄金岁月"吧。

17

原文

Entry

By Ashley Mears

[1] You've got a great look. That was what he told me as I sat in a Starbucks in downtown Manhattan. I had come in search of a quiet table at which to crack open a social theory book, one of a number of texts I was assigned as a new graduate student in sociology at New York University. Instead I found myself seated across from a model scout who was handing me his card and telling me that I could be making a fortune as a fashion model.

[2] While waiting in line for my coffee I overheard a man, flanked by two pretty young women at a nearby table, talking loudly about what it's like to work in the fashion modeling industry. He was in his forties, tan and balding; his two companions, who were listening to him intently, looked about twenty years younger.

[3] I took him to be a modeling agent out with two of his models, and I listened with feigned disinterest, having packed away my own modeling portfolio into my mom's attic just six months ago, content to start a new career in academia after what had been five years in

the business, at first part time in college, mostly small stuff for local department stores in my hometown of Atlanta.

[4] Later, school vacations would be spent modeling in Milan, New York, Tokyo, and Hong Kong. It seemed a lifetime ago; I had just celebrated my twenty-third birthday, well past retirement age for a model, and the books weighing down my shoulders were a reminder of a new career ahead.

译 析

本文节选自艾希莉·米尔斯（Ashley Mears）的 *Pricing Beauty: The Making of a Fashion Model* 一书第一章。作者系纽约大学社会学系博士，现为波士顿大学助理教授。因此书独特的研究对象，她成为了美国最受关注的年轻社会学家之一。Ashley Mears 在大学期间就开始做兼职模特。后来，她产生了研究模特业的想法。*Pricing Beauty* 一书，作为她在纽约大学社会学系的博士论文，便是实践这一想法的最终成果。

就标题而言，entry 一词的意义似乎不好确定，一是因为其本身的多义性，二是因为在没有全文的情况下，难以拿捏。该书作者曾经有过做模特的经历，后来中断了。在咖啡馆遇到了模特星探，他试图劝她入行。后来发生的故事就是，作者为了写她的博士论文，就答应了。尽管大多数同学不知道后面的事，但从星探的劝诱中，我们完全可以推测出该词的含义，即"进入模特行当"，因而翻译成"入行"，更准确地说，是"入对行当"；言外之意,她最终的目的是要进入学术界,做自己真正想从事的"行当"。

[1] 中,You've got a great look,有人译成"你是个尤物",虽然也表达出了"你很漂亮""你很好看"的意思,但这样的语言明显与对话发生的情景不相符。"尤物"虽然指容貌十分美好的女子,但在现代语言习惯中,却带有一定程度的对女性不够尊重、轻佻之意。即便是取正面意义,对一个陌生的女子,初次见面,使用该语,也不大得体,不符合一个商务人士的言行。而将 telling me that I could be making a fortune as a fashion model,有的译成"告诉我可以作为一个时尚模特谋生",其中的 making a fortune,不仅是"谋生",而更有"发大财""赚大钱"之意;然而,有的译成"扬言我若当模特,必能赚大钱",其中的"扬言"也显得有些"过"了。对于 one of a number of texts I was assigned as a new graduate student in sociology at New York University,有人将其中的 assigned 译成了"指派""指定""必须得"等,稍显死板,而有人译成"作为纽约大学社会学系的研究生新生,我得读一大堆书,而这是其中之一",其中的"得"颇有新意。此外,有人将 New York University 译成了"纽约州立大学",其实这是两所完全不同的学校。以后凡是遇到专有名词,应特别小心,可查找参考材料,不宜随意处理。

[2] 中,对于 looked about twenty years younger,不少人译成了"看起来20多岁""看起来不到20岁",可能是粗心所致,但将非常明确的信息弄错,尤其是涉及数字方面的,可视为大忌。对于 flanked by two pretty young women at a nearby table,有人将 flanked 译成"簇拥""环绕""包围"等,显然不准确;同时,将 flanked by two pretty young women 译成"身侧有两位佳人相伴",

虽然意思不差，但不够得体；其实，"佳人相伴"常常暗示男女之间有特殊关系。He was in his forties, tan and balding; his two companions, who were listening to him intently, looked about twenty years younger，虽然是在描述一个场景，但从中可以揣摩作者的立场和态度：一个四十多岁的谢顶大叔，滔滔不绝地向两个比自己小二十多岁的女孩讲述在模特界工作的情景，而两个女孩听得津津有味。其中的欺骗意味还不明显么？她们哪里知道作者将要揭示的模特业内部的黑暗和残酷！揣摩出了作者的态度，才能准确地理解某些词的具体含义，并从整体上把握译文的风格，而若将后文的 I listened with feigned disinterest 理解为作者非常向往这个行业，那就太离谱了。

[3] 中，对于 after what had been five years in the business, at first part time in college, mostly small stuff for local department stores in my hometown of Atlanta，问题较多，主要原因是没有弄清楚 business 和 small stuff 的含义，如将 business 译成"商界"，small stuff 译成"小东西""小商品""小职员"等，而将有关句子译成"在生意场上打拼了五年""混迹商界五年之后"以及"在家乡亚特兰大州本地百货商场做过卑微小职员之后""在家乡亚特兰大州本地百货商场卖些小东西""更多时候是在亚特兰大的家乡当地的百货商店当店员""作为小职员为当地的百货公司工作"等，显然是机械对照词典的结果，而未从具体语境出发。例如，in the business，具体而言，指的是"模特"行当，而不是"商界""商场"等；small stuff 显然是指模特所从事的工作，应该不只是"拍拍照片"，可能还有走秀等，只不过这些活动太小太不

起眼罢了,译成"拍拍照片"显然将原意缩小了。相反,也不可对原意有过度发挥,如对于as I sat in a Starbucks in downtown Manhattan,有人译成"我正在曼哈顿市中心的一家星巴克悠闲地坐着",这其中,"悠闲地"便超出了原意。

另外,at first part time in college, mostly small stuff for local department stores,有人理解为一开始是在大学里做兼职,但更多的时候是在百货商店工作,当成两项并列的工作了。这是没有注意in和for的区别,也没注意到part time和small staff是同位语。这句的意思是,大学期间做了兼职模特,而兼职的内容,大多数时候只能做点小活,不是那么盛大的走秀活动。

[4] I had just celebrated my twenty-third birthday, well past retirement age for a model,此句并不难理解,但有人将后半句well past retirement age for a model译成"模特退休的好时候",显然是误解了well的意思;该词实际指的是程度很深,即"早就过了……(23岁就算高龄了)",由此可见模特业的残酷。

参考译文

入对行当

艾希莉·米尔斯

[1] "你外形很不错",我在曼哈顿市区的一家星巴克里坐下

时,他对我这样说。本来,我想进去找张安静的桌子,坐下来读一本社会理论方面的书;作为纽约大学社会学系新入学的研究生,我有一大堆指定书目要读。结果,我发现自己对面坐着一位模特星探。他递上名片,说我要是做时装模特的话,可能早已赚了大钱。

[2] 在排队等咖啡时,无意间,我听到邻桌有个男人正高谈阔论在模特行当工作的情形。他坐在两个年轻漂亮的女孩中间,看起来有四十多岁,皮肤晒得黝黑,有点秃顶。那两个听得入神的,看起来比他小20来岁。

[3] 我想他应该是个模特经纪人,和自己的两个模特一起来的。而我,听着,装作毫无兴趣。就在半年前,我刚把做模特时的那些材料全部收拾好,封存在母亲的阁楼上了。在这一行摸爬滚打五年后,我很知足地转入了学术生涯。才做模特时,我只是在读大学期间边读书边当过兼职模特,主要是在我的家乡亚特兰大的百货公司接一些不起眼的小活。

[4] 后来在假期中,又去了米兰、纽约、东京和香港等地走秀——那好像是上辈子的事了。我刚过完23岁生日,这个年龄早该是退出模特行当的时候了,而肩上沉甸甸的书,正提醒着我前面还有一番新的事业。

18

原文

Family Relationship in Ancient China

[1] In still another story, we meet a mother behind the scenes of male feasting and become aware of her full authority. This mother was none other than Jing Jiang (敬姜), the widow known for her moral guidance of her son Wenbo (文伯). The setting was her son's house, where Wenbo was entertaining Nangong Jingshu (南宫敬叔), a cousin from another prominent aristocratic Lu family. Lu Dufu (露睹父), a minister, was present as the honored guest.

[2] When tortoises were served, Lu Dufu received a small one and became upset. As the guests invited each other to dine on the tortoises, Lu Dufu declined and left the banquet after saying that he would eat after the tortoise had grown up. Jing Jiang, who learned about the incident—how we do not know, but it must have been either through her own observation or through a report by the family's servants—reacted with rage and summoned Wenbo.

[3] She chided him, "I heard from my deceased father-in-law that at sacrifices the Impersonator for the ancestor should receive special provision and at banquets the honored guests should receive

special provision. For what reason do you have to offend a guest by being stingy with tortoises?" After this scolding, she drove Wenbo out of the house. It was five days before she allowed her son to return, following the intervention of a minister.

译 析

该文内容取材于《国语》中一个故事，由美籍华人学者 Yiqun Zhou 加以改写并翻译成了英文，作为 *Festivals, Feasts, and Gender Relations in Ancient China and Greece* 的一部分出版（Cambridge University Press, 2010）。

关于题目 Family Relationship in Ancient China，同学们有着各种译法，如"古代中国的家庭关系""古代中国家庭的长幼尊卑""先秦家宅关系"等，都有词序、语义不够准确的问题。"中国古代家庭关系"是可以的，但仍有欠缺。试想，此一篇短文何以能论述这样大的一个题目？故不妨译为"中国古代家庭关系一瞥"。

就译文的分段问题，可不必完全拘于原文，而可按其内容发展，分出段落，并以段落符号（[ ]）标出。有的同学对此做得不错。具体分段，可参见"参考译文"。

在[1]中，In still another story, we meet a mother behind the scenes of male feasting and become aware of her full authority，有同学译成"她在男人的宴席之后，开始意识到她对儿子的权威的重要性"，显然没有弄清叙述者、被叙述者及所要表述内容间的

关系。该文是以作者的角度来叙述的,故可译为"我们会看到一位男人宴请幕后的母亲,并感受到她的绝对威严"。This mother was none other than Jing Jiang(敬姜),the widow known for her moral guidance of her son Wenbo(文伯),这句许多同学翻译得不够通顺、自然。其中的none other than,不一定译成"不是别人,正是……",而"正是……"即可。如 It was none other than Professor Wu(那人正是吴教授); Because owners started keeping detailed records on them in 1860, due in part to the urging of none other than Charles Darwin(因为当地人从1860年就开始详细记录它们的情况,这部分真要归功于达尔文的劝说)等。故可译为"这位母亲正是敬姜,一个为儿子文伯作出道德示范而为人所知的遗孀"。同时,不用"寡妇""单亲妈妈"等这类不敬或现代词语。

The setting was her son's house,这里的setting是指环境、地点,如You already have the natural inclination for this type of thinking, if not in an academic setting(即使不是在学术环境中,你自然而然地早已经有了相同的、思考问题的方式),有同学译成"此背景是在她儿子的屋里",很死板。而...where Wenbo was entertaining Nangong Jingshu(南宫敬叔), a cousin from another prominent aristocratic Lu family,对这句的翻译有许多错误或不妥,如"他正在款待南宫敬叔——一个来自露家名媛贵族的亲戚",其中显然没有理解"名媛"、Lu family、cousin等意思,需查有关字典、资料弄清楚。故此句不妨译为"事情发生在文伯的住处,他招待其堂兄——出生于鲁国显赫贵族的南宫敬叔"。同时,a minister不是现代的"部长"而是"大臣"。

在[2]中，...tortoises were served，这个served不是一般意义上的"服务"，而是"提供""呈上""端上"，考虑后面的意思，这里应该更具体一点，即"端给了每人"。对于Lu Dufu declined and left the banquet after saying that he would eat after the tortoise had grown up，有同学翻译成"露睹父拒绝赴宴，离开了宴会，并说，等乌龟长大以后再来吃它"，显然"翻译腔"十足，原因是"跟随"原文太紧，没有能够将重点转到译出语（TL）的表述上，故不妨考虑："客人们相邀品尝，露公推辞，放下一句'等它长大了再吃吧'，便拂袖而去"。对于后面的—how we do not know...可以跟随其破折号的形式，亦可用括号，或二者都不用。而将reacted with rage译成"愤怒的反应"，显然有些生硬、过火。

在[3]中，敬姜的father-in-law，词面意思是"公公"，但试想，母亲是否会这样对儿子说："我公公曾说过，……"，显然不妥，所以，应改换角度为"你的已故祖父……"，这样才符合当事人口吻。而the Impersonator for the ancestor为当时的"祭养尸"；两个special provision突出的是一个"特"字。最后一句，是有时间顺序的，即following the... it was five days...，故为"经大臣说情，五天后才允许他回家"。

有同学用了文言文进行翻译，这固然值得赞赏，但不宜提倡。我们知道，自1919年新文化运动以后，白话文成为中国文化承载和表述的主体；文言文对于传承国学很有价值，但现代人还应使用现代文体，特别是在翻译中，尽管其内容是古代的。当然，不妨吸收一些文言文精练、凝重的成分。

在《国语·鲁语》中，有关该故事的记载如下："公父文伯饮南宫敬叔酒,以露睹父为客,羞鳖焉小,睹父怒,相延食鳖,辞曰:'将使鳖长而后食之。'遂出。文伯之母闻之,怒曰:'吾闻之先子曰:"祭养尸,飨养上宾。"鳖于何有?而使夫人怒也!'遂逐之。五日,鲁大夫辞而复之。"当然,在英文的描述中,做了一些演绎的加工,而译者也只能根据原文进行翻译。

参考译文

中国古代家庭关系一瞥

[1] 在另一故事中,我们会看到一位男人宴请幕后的母亲,并感受到她的绝对威严。这位母亲正是敬姜,一个为儿子文伯作出道德示范而为人所知的遗孀。事情发生在文伯的住处,他招待其堂兄——出生于鲁国显赫贵族的南宫敬叔。大臣露睹父也作为贵宾出席了。

[2] 甲鱼菜端给了每位,露公得到一个小的,故而不快。客人们相邀品尝,露公推辞,放下一句"等它长大了再吃吧",便拂袖而去。敬姜得知此事(是自己看到还是听家人禀告,不得而知),大怒,招来文伯。

[3] 她训斥道:"你的已故祖父曾告诫,'祭养尸优礼遇,待上宾有殊荣'。小子如今何以因吝惜一鳖而得罪贵客?"骂毕,将儿子赶出家门。经大臣说情,五天后才允许他回家。

原 文

The Mooncake

[1] Delicately designed, overwhelmingly dense and often an acquired taste for many in the West, mooncakes are one of the most famous foods found in Chinese communities around the world this time of year.

[2] Every year on the 15th day of the eighth month of the lunar calendar, Chinese and other Asian cultures celebrate the Mid-Autumn Festival. Mooncakes are as important to festivities as turkey is to Thanksgiving and latkes are to Hanukah.

[3] The Mid-Autumn Festival—when the moon is at its fullest and brightest—became an official celebration in China during the Tang dynasty (618–907 AD). The term "mooncake" was first found in 1274 AD in author Wu Zimu's *Book of Dreams*, and the first cookbook on how to prepare mooncakes was published in 1792.

[4] While there are many variations of mooncakes, the most famous is the classic Cantonese version: a soft pastry filled with sweet lotus seed paste and savory salted duck egg yolk.

译 析

2020年的国庆节与中秋节为同一天，属不多见，值得特殊庆祝。

然而，就题目而言，许多参赛者漏译了：月饼。有的译成"巧谈月饼"似无必要。

[1] 中，Delicately designed, overwhelmingly dense 看似简单，但并不好译；参赛者一般译成了"设计精巧、密度极高""制作精巧、口感馥郁""做工精致、味道浓郁"等，似乎并不十分贴切。考虑到中餐讲究色香味以及月饼是带馅儿的食品，不妨译为"形色讲究，馅料醇厚"。

...often an acquired taste for many in the West 中的 an acquired taste 为并非天生，而是后来养成的口味、嗜好等，《牛津高阶英汉双解词典》中对这一俗语的解释为：a thing that you do not like much at first but gradually learn to like 养成的爱好。该词典给的例句是：Abstract art is an acquired taste. 要慢慢培养才会欣赏抽象艺术。再如：Pumpkin pie for him is an acquired taste.（南瓜馅饼是他后来才喜欢吃的。）。有的参赛者将此句译成"在许多西方人看来是一种引进的食物"，显然对词义理解不够，而有的译成"广为西方人所喜爱""往往令许多西方人尝后回味无穷""每年都受到西方人士的追捧"等，则又有些过度了；相对而言，"慢慢喜欢上了吃月饼""逐渐习惯了这种口味"等译文比较适中，因为从中既体现了"后来形成"又有"颇为喜欢"的意思。著名翻译家傅雷说过，好的翻译就是要在"不够"与"过度"之间找"适中"。

同时，in Chinese communities，有的参赛者译成"华人社区"，其实这是一种泛指，即华人之中；而around the world是地点状语，this time of year为时间状语。固然，在词序上可对此作些调整，但亦不宜过于偏离原文。

综合而言，此句不妨译为："每年此时，在全球华人中，月饼是最负盛名的一种美食；它形色讲究，馅料醇厚，许多西方人常常品尝数次后便渐渐喜欢上这一口。"

[2] 中，Chinese and other Asian cultures celebrate the Mid-Autumn Festival参赛者一般译成"中国和其他亚洲国家都会庆祝中秋节""中国人和其他亚洲文化都会庆祝这个节日——中秋节"，似乎都不够准确，因为此处的Chinese，不只是"中国人"（这是一个政治概念），还包括遍布世界各地的华侨、外籍华人等，而此处的cultures亦应理解为具有某种文化认同感的民族，即为"华人及其他亚洲民族都会庆祝中秋节"。

are as important to... as大都译成了"如同……那样同等重要"，如"月饼之于中秋节，恰如火鸡之于感恩节、马铃薯饼之于光明节那般重要性""月饼对中秋节来说，就像火鸡对于感恩节，土豆烙饼对于光明节一样意义非凡""月饼对中秋节的重要性好比一只火鸡之于感恩节、土豆烙饼之于光明节"等，不免有些生硬；其实，该短语可根据具体语境作些变通，如Generally speaking, cell phones nowadays are as important as computers to an average family.（对普通家庭来说，现在手机和电脑一样，通常是必不可少的。)。

故此，该部分不妨译为："每年农历八月十五，华人及其他亚洲民族都会庆祝中秋节。而中秋节的月饼，犹如感恩节的火鸡、光明节的土豆饼，都是过节必不可少的。"

[3] 中的两个破折号可不必在译文中保留，如"中秋节——一年之中月亮最圆最明亮的时候，而在唐朝年间（公元618—907年）——正式成为法定节日"，而可根据中文表达习惯作相应顺达处理。

同样，对于"The term... in 1792."一句，亦不必拘泥其语序，而可相应作些调整，但如上所述，需注意相对的尺度与准确性。另外需要指出的是，不少参赛者没有仔细查考选文中提及的古籍，实属不应当。而做了一定查考的参赛者中，却又有很多将书名《梦粱录》错写成了《梦梁录》。进一步查考就会知道，该书得名自典故"黄粱梦"，如此恐怕就不会写错了吧。

此部分不妨译为："中秋节，是满月之时，在唐朝（618—907）便成为中国官方的庆祝活动。'月饼'一词最早出现在1274年吴自牧所著的《梦粱录》中，而第一本制作月饼的食谱于1792年出版。"

[4] 中，问题主要是过度发挥，如"几百年来，虽然月饼逐渐发展出了许多'版本'，但最为有名的还属经典广式月饼，香松软糯的薄面裹上香甜可口的莲籽糊，再加上风味十足的鸭蛋黄，这'莲蓉蛋黄'月饼真真是勾人心弦，让人回味无穷"。该句不妨译为："月饼种类众多，但最有名的还是经典的广式月饼，即一种包有可口莲蓉和咸鸭蛋黄的酥软糕点。"

的确，中秋，这个延绵千年的中华传统节日，曾引多少文人骚客望月感怀、饮酒赋诗、丹青流韵、翰墨生辉。来稿中亦有如下篇章：

小饼如嚼月

巧出饼师心，貌得婵娟月。揉搓细面尘，料稠馅绵嫩。有月秀可餐，西人日渐迷。南宫十五夜，月明中秋节。羡饼香四溢，名扬四海唐人街；慕文化同流，月下团圆东方国。秋夕共尝月，饼中寄相思。感恩乐万家，火鸡答天赐。九灯耀光明，薯饼忆旧时。尔问月满月明是何时，吾叹寒宫最寂无人知，尔幸佳节同庆盛唐始。似问月饼词归处，自牧《梦粱录》中述。月团秘谱第一出，品类纷呈不胜数。要数名月落谁家，月满广府甲天下。黄金月轮咸香溢，幽幽白莲清香里。

应当说，若无需对原文作较为忠实的比照，亦可欣赏一二。

参考译文

月饼

[1] 每年此时，在全球华人中，月饼是最负盛名的一种美食；

它形色讲究，馅料醇厚，许多西方人常常品尝数次后便渐渐喜欢上这一口。

[2] 每年农历八月十五，华人及其他亚洲民族都会庆祝中秋节。而中秋节的月饼，犹如感恩节的火鸡、光明节的土豆饼，都是过节必不可少的。

[3] 中秋节，是满月之时，在唐朝（618—907）便成为中国官方的庆祝活动。"月饼"一词最早出现在1274年吴自牧所著的《梦粱录》中，而第一本制作月饼的食谱于1792年出版。

[4] 月饼种类众多，但最有名的还是经典的广式月饼，即一种包有可口莲蓉和咸鸭蛋黄的酥软糕点。

> 原　文

The Better Robots

By Henry Charles

[1] Scientists are building robots that can walk on two legs like a toddler. The researchers say the breakthrough will lead to robots with increasingly human characteristics that could one day become the everyday servants depicted for decades in science fiction. Because walking has to be subtly altered according to the type of surface, the robots have to take the ground on which they stand into account.

[2] Calculations of the energy used by the robots as they walk suggest they are quite energy-efficient, consuming about the same amount of calories that a human walker would to cover the same distance. All the robots in the study move using a principle called passive-dynamic walking, which has been used for a century or more in a variety of walking toys that are, in effect, passive mechanical devices with moveable joints enabling them to walk down a slope under the force of gravity.

[3] Applying a source of motorized movement to the principle of passive-dynamic walking produced a robot with a remarkable

ability to walk like a human toddler. The researchers believe that the development of robots capable of walking on two legs like humans would help scientists to understand human movement better as well as aiding the development of a new generation of robotic artificial legs for accident victims.

译 析

本文改写自 Robotic "Toddlers" Can Walk Like Us，刊于 *The New Zealand Herald*（《新西兰先驱者报》）(21st Feb. 2005)，是一篇科普小文，具有科技英文的某些特点，即行文严谨，多用被动语态、从句、介词等，翻译时需作整体的考量及相应的变通。

总的讲，参赛者踊跃参加（收到约百余份译文），从多方面做了有益的尝试。

就标题而言，同学们的译文中有各种译法，如"更棒的机器人""前进中的机器人""更优秀的机器人""优化版机器人""会行走的机器人""更理想的机器人""改良版机器人""优化机器人""智能机器人"等等，固然都不错，但是还不应离原文太远，故不妨译为"更好的机器人"或"更先进的机器人"为宜。

[1] 中 Scientists are building robots that can walk on two legs like a toddler，其中的 build 可作些灵活处理，如 His argument is built on facts（他的论点是以事实为根据的），故此处不妨译为"研制"；The researchers say the breakthrough will lead to robots

with increasingly human characteristics that could one day become the everyday servants depicted for decades in science fiction. 其中的介词 with 在此处应译为动词，类似的如：He is walking in the park with an umbrella（他手里拿着把伞在公园里散步）；Strange enough, that he is having breakfast with wine（说来也怪，他竟然喝着酒吃早餐）等。对于 human characteristics，有同学译成"人性化""人类化"等，其实更准确的应为"人类特性"；everyday servants，有的译成"全职服务""起居仆人"等，其实可以很简单："日常佣人"。故整段不妨译为："科学家们正在研制如儿童学步那样用双脚走路的机器人。研究人员说，这项突破将使机器人更日益富有人类特性，并终有一日成为几十年来科幻小说中所描写的那种日常佣人。"

Because walking has to be subtly altered according to the type of surface, the robots have to take the ground on which they stand into account. 其中的 subtly 不必译成"精确地""精细地"，而结合 alter，可译为"敏捷调整"；而 take... into account 为"考虑""重视"，中间的 the ground on which they stand 为宾语，而其中的 on which... 又为定语从句。故此，整句不妨译为"因为走路须根据地面表层作出敏捷调整，机器人还要考虑所处地面的情况"。

[2] 中 Calculations of the energy used by the robots as they walk suggest they are quite energy-efficient, consuming about the same amount of calories that a human walker would to cover the same distance. 其中，对于 Calculations of the energy used by the robots

as they walk suggest 有同学译成"机器人行走时会进行耗能计算,具备节能的特性",显然表述不够准确。其实,这是一个倒装句,主语是 the robots; efficient,为"效能""效率""性能"等,如 This new copy machine is more efficient than the old one.(这台新复印机比那台旧的性能好。); a human walker 为"步行者"。故整句不妨译为"机器人行走耗能的计算表明,其能效相当之高,与步行者走过同等距离时所消耗的热卡量大致相同"。

All the robots in the study move using a principle called passive-dynamic walking, which has been used for a century or more in a variety of walking toys that are, in effect, passive mechanical devices with moveable joints enabling them to walk down a slope under the force of gravity. 其中的 All the robots in the study move using a principle called passive-dynamic walking,此句看似难以理解,主要是中间插入了 in the study,若将其放在句前,便一目了然:In the study, all the robots move using a principle…; passive-dynamic walking 可译为"被动动力行走",而 principle 此处不是"原则""标准"等,而应为"原理",该原理来自于20世纪80年代,加拿大学者迈克基尔(McGeer)提出的"被动动力学理论",并由此形成了"机器人被动行走"的概念;… that are, in effect, … 也是一种插入语方式,其中的 that 是指 principle,也是该句的主语; in effect,此处可理解为 in fact。故此,整句不妨译为"研制中所有机器人在运动中所应用的是一种称为'被动动力行走'原理,该原理已在各种行走玩具中应用了一个多世纪。实际上,这些具有可动关节的被动机械装置使得它们在重力作用下可沿斜坡

行走"。

[3] 中 Applying a source of motorized movement to the principle of passive-dynamic walking produced a robot with a remarkable ability to walk like a human toddler. 这里的 source 不是一般的资源,而是结合 motorized movement,故为"动力源";produce 原意为"产生",这里可为"制造";此处的 with,如上文所述,应译为动词"具有",故该句可译为:"将机械化运动的动力源运用于被动动力行走的原理,便能制造出具有非凡能力、像学步儿童那样行走的机器人。"

The researchers believe that the development of robots capable of walking on two legs like humans would help scientists to understand human movement better as well as aiding the development of a new generation of robotic artificial legs for accident victims. 值得指出的是,在 as well as 的句式中,强调的是"除了后者,还有前者",如:She as well as I waited for you for a long time.(我和她都等你好久了。);Hiking is fun as well as good exercise.(徒步旅行是很好的锻炼,也很有趣。)等;故此句应译为:"研制人员认为,开发能像人类那样两腿走路的机器人,除了有助于为事故受害者研制新一代人工假肢,还能帮助科学家更好地理解人类的运动机能。"然而,对于这种表达,几乎没有一个同学意识到;这对于学翻译和英语的同学来讲,不能不说是一大憾事。

参考译文

更好的机器人

亨利·查尔斯

[1] 科学家们正在研制如儿童学步那样用双脚走路的机器人。研究人员说，这项突破将使机器人更日益富有人类特性，并终有一日成为几十年来科幻小说中所描写的那种日常佣人。因为走路须根据地面表层作出敏捷调整，机器人还要考虑所处地面的情况。

[2] 机器人行走耗能的计算表明，其能效相当之高，与步行者走过同等距离时所消耗的热卡量大致相同。研制中所有机器人在运动中所应用的是一种称为"被动动力行走"原理，该原理已在各种行走玩具中应用了一个多世纪。实际上，这些具有可动关节的被动机械装置使得它们在重力作用下可沿斜坡行走。

[3] 将机械化运动的动力源运用于被动动力行走的原理，便能制造出具有非凡能力、像学步儿童那样行走的机器人。研制人员认为，开发能像人类那样两腿走路的机器人，除了有助于为事故受害者研制新一代人工假肢，还能帮助科学家更好地理解人类的运动机能。

21

原 文

Thought and Computer

By J. Krishnamurti

[1] Thought has invented the computer.

[2] You must understand the complexity and the future of the computer; it is going to outstrip man in his thought; it is going to change the structure of society and the structure of government.

[3] This is not some fantastic conclusion of the speaker, or some fantasy, it is something that is actually going on now, of which you may not be aware.

[4] The computer has a mechanical intelligence; it can learn and invent.

[5] The computer is going to make human labour practically unnecessary—perhaps two hours work a day.

[6] These are all changes that are coming. You may not like it, you may revolt against it, but it is coming.

译 析

J. Krishnamurti（1895—1986，J. 克里希纳穆尔蒂，简称"克

氏")是印度著名哲学家,上世纪20年代起主要活跃于美国和欧洲,被称为20世纪最伟大的心灵导师,在西方有着广泛影响。他一生著述60余种,多由演讲和谈话结集而成,译成40多种文字在世界各地出版。本段选自其著作 *The Network of Thought*(1981),尽管是40多年前的言论,但在第五次技术革命的今天,人们仍不得不惊叹于他天才的预见。

具体而言,[1]中,许多人将thought译成"思维/思考/大脑/想法/智慧/想象力"等,不能算错,但要看语境;通观克氏的著作会发现,他的主题是围绕着人类的智慧、社会的发展、人与自然、精神世界与物质世界的关系等展开的,故不妨用更平实、相对应的"人脑"。将invented译成"创造了",欠准确,因该词与created还有区别,故此句不妨译为"人脑发明了电脑"。考虑到这一句与下文的关系,有译文加了"因为……",其实此句可用分号(;)断开,以接下句。

[2]中,you多被译成了"你",其实这里是一种泛指,如You would like them once you got to know them.(不管是谁,只要一认识他们就会喜欢他们。),故不妨译为"人们"或"我们"。对于outstrip,一般都能理解,问题是to outstrip man in his thought,许多参赛者作了过度的发挥,如"它将在思维能力方面将人类远远地甩在后面""计算机将会比人们想象中的发展得更快"等,"超越"了原文。下文中的两个structure,有的分别处理成"社会架构和政府组织""社会结构和政府机制"等,未尝不可,但亦可合并译出,故整句不妨译为:"人们必须对电脑的复杂性和前途有所了解,因为电脑将会超过人类的思想,改变社

会和政府的结构。"

[3] 的译文可谓"异彩纷呈",如"这不是说者之新奇结论或幻想,而是可能被你忽略的,实实在在发生着的事情""这并非发言人妄下结论,而是如今真真切切正在发生的事,只是你并未注意到""这既不是某位演讲者奇妙的推论,也不是某些幻想,而是确有其事的,只是也许你还没有意识到罢了"等。应当说,基本意思都不错,只是颇显笨拙。原因可能是纠结在几个关键词上:1. speaker,鉴于此文为克氏演讲稿,故可译为"我""本人"等。2. conclusion,不一定总是"结论",因该词的原义是to decide that something is true after considering all the information one has,所以,还可译为"判断"等,如:I mean I am really sorry about your conclusion,可译为"我对你的判断真是不敢苟同"。3. fantasy,固然可译成"幻想",但此处还有"推测"的成分。故此,整句不妨译为:"这不是我的臆想论断或幻想推测,却是现时正在发生着的事,而你们对此可能并未意识到。"

对于[4]和[5],大部分译文是按照原文分句处理的,如"计算机拥有机械智能,它既能学习也能够发明创造。这将使人类实际劳动力发挥的余地越来越少——也许仅仅是一天两小时的工作量。""计算机是能自我学习和创造的机械智能体。它减少人类不必要的劳动力——人们可能一天只用工作两小时。"其实,统观两句内容的相关性,可以将其打通考虑。mechanical intelligence,是40余年前的用法,有的参赛者译成"机械的智能",该词后演变成 artificial intelligence (AI)。can 助动 learn 和 invent,译文可稍错落。practically unnecessary 有一种讲话的语气,不可太绝对,如 A debit card makes cash practically unnecessary for students to consume on campus，此句可理解为"银行卡使得学生在校园消费几乎不用现金了"，但要注意不是绝对不用了。而 perhaps two hours work a day 是一种补充说明。故此，不妨将两句合并译为："电脑具有机械智能，会学习能发明，它将使人类劳动变得几乎没有必要（也许每天只需工作两个小时）。"

[6] 中，可能是被单复数（are、it）所困扰，有些参赛者出现理解错误，如"这些都是正在到来的变化。你可能不喜欢计算机，可能厌恶它，但它还是会到来"等。须知，此时计算机早已出现（20世纪40年代问世），故此处还是指 changes。因是演讲，有些口语化的成分，但译者要抓住其中心意思，不被其语言表达的枝节所迷惑；但基本意思把住后，又很容易啰嗦，如"这些都是正在降临的改变。你可能不喜欢，你可能对其反感，但它正向你走来。""所有这些都是即将发生的变化。你也许不喜欢，也许会反感，但是，它的确来了。"其中，revolt against 不一定总是"反感"，还有抵制、反对、反抗之意，如 The novel in essence revolts against any modern warfare.（小说的核心内容是反对任何现代战争。），整句不妨简化为："这些变化，无论人们对此欢迎还是抵制，都正在发生着。"

20世纪四五十年代，科学家们最大胆的设想是，到2000年时，全世界可能只需要几百台计算机（因那时一台计算机价格昂贵，且占用几个车间，约20吨重）。克氏不是科学家，但他的哲思仍然闪耀着智慧的光芒——电脑的发展的确超越了人类想象，改变了社会结构和人们的生活方式，并将加速进行。故该段文字堪称经典,至今值得一译,而且一议。

参考译文

人脑与电脑

J. 克里希纳穆尔蒂

[1] 人脑发明了电脑。

[2] 人们必须对电脑的复杂性和前途有所了解,因为电脑将会超过人类的思想,改变社会和政府的结构。

[3] 这不是我的臆想论断或幻想推测,却是现时正在发生着的事,而你们对此可能并未意识到。

[4] [5] 电脑具有机械智能,会学习能发明,它将使人类劳动变得几乎没有必要(也许每天只需工作两个小时)。

[6] 这些变化,无论人们对此欢迎还是抵制,都正在发生着。

22

原　文

Discovery of Gravitational Waves

[1] But let's step back for a second here and explain what gravitational waves actually are.

[2] According to Einstein's theory, the fabric of space-time can become curved by anything massive in the Universe.

[3] When cataclysmic events happen, such as black holes merging or stars exploding, these curves can ripple out elsewhere as gravitational waves, just like if someone had dropped a stone in a pond.

[4] By the time those ripples get to us on Earth, they're tiny (around a billionth of the diameter of an atom), which is why scientists have struggled for so many years to find them.

—*New York Times*

译　析

本段选自《纽约时报》(*New York Times*)的一则报道，2016年2月11日23时30分，可说是天体物理学史上的一个里程碑，因为人类发现了引力波。

美国国家科学基金会在华盛顿特区国家媒体中心发布了科学家们期待已久的消息：位于美国利文斯顿与汉福德的两座激光干涉仪引力波天文台（Laser Interferometer Gravitational-Wave Observatory, LIGO），首次探测到引力波！这一由距地球13亿光年之遥的双黑洞碰撞产生的引力波信号，被命名为"GW150914"。

[1]中，let's step back for a second here，许多人译得很"实"，如"在这里我们暂时先退一步，解释一下……""我们在此稍作停留""但是我们退一步思考下"等等。其实，这里的step back并非一定要"向后"一下，而是一种舒缓的解释性语气，如Let's take a step back and respect history for a second.（我们可先回顾下过去，对历史表示片刻的尊重。）故此处可译为："这里不妨简略解释一下什么是'引力波'。"

[2]中，对于According to Einstein's theory，稍有物理学科普知识的人都知道，爱因斯坦的理论有"狭义相对论"（special relativity / special theory of relativity / restricted theory of relativity）和"广义相对论"（general relativity / general theory of relativity）之分，后者在物理学上应用更为广泛，显然也是此处所指，但在参赛者中，除极个别外，绝大多数没有使用这一概念；很多甚至译成"爱因斯坦原理"，不能不说是一缺憾。space-time，一般都能译为"时空"；anything massive是一种形容词后置，作定语，如"我想给她买点好东西"，不宜译成I want to buy some good things for her，而为I would like to buy something nice for her

等。对于 fabric，许多人忽略或漏译了，如"宇宙中任何质量大的物质都可能造成时空弯曲""宇宙中任何庞大天体的碰撞都会导致时空弯曲""宇宙中所有重大事件都可能导致时空发生弧形弯曲"等。实则，fabric 源于地质学，如 The sum of all the textural and structural features of a rock（岩石的所有结构和构造特征的总和）等，故以"结构"为宜。如：1. In general relativity, black holes are a consequence of space and time being part of the same fabric.（在广义相对论中，黑洞是空间和时间作为同一结构的不同部分。）2. And so space-time — the malleable fabric whose geometry can be changed by the gravity of stars, planets and matter — was born.（于是，空间—时间的契合，这个可被恒星、行星及其他物质的引力所改变的几何形态的韧性结构诞生了。）。所以，该句不妨译为："根据爱因斯坦的广义相对论，宇宙中的时空结构会因巨大物体而发生弯曲。"

[3] 中，此句的主干结构为 "When cataclysmic events happen, ...these curves can ripple out elsewhere as gravitational waves, ..."，故可顺译，如"当巨变发生时，如黑洞合并、恒星爆炸等，这些曲线便以引力波形态扩散他处，正如有人在池塘里扔入石头"；或者，将句式调整，如"当巨变发生时，可使时空扭曲，引力波扩散他处，如同有人在池塘里扔入石头，'黑洞合并''恒星爆炸'等现象便是如此"。可见中文句子结构的灵活，而少受语法因素的限制。

[4] 中，不少参赛者对词义和语法有些误解，如"而部分经扩散到达地球的引力波，由于它们极其的微小（大约是原子直径

的十亿分之一大小），而这些正是这么多年里科学家们不停地寻找它们的原因"，其中，把those理解成了"部分"；ripples译成"引力波"，其实该词是作者有意对gravitational waves所做的另一表述，将其具体化阐释，而避免同语定义（如不可以Computer is a... computer为定义，而应为Computer is a... machine）；将to find them误解为不定式所表示的持续性动作（仍在不停地寻找），实际根据全文语境，应等同于to have found them。同时，对于ripple的度量单位，有的忽略未译，有的用了"体积""震荡""波段""频率"等，都不准确。在物理学中：Small wave on the surface of a liquid for which the controlling force is not gravity, as for large waves, but surface tension. The velocity of ripples diminishes within creasing wavelength, to a minimum value which for water is 23 cm/s for a wavelength of 1.7 cm. （液面上的小波，控制此波的力不是控制大波的重力而是表面张力。涟波速度随波长增加而减少，对于水其最小值是波长为1.7cm时的23cm/s。）故其单位应为"波长"。所以，整句不妨译为："当这些波纹传送到地球时，因为它们波长极小（大约是原子直径的十亿分之一），科学家们奋斗了许多年才得以发现。"

此次重大科学发现，其实质是一种科学理论的胜利。因为就时间顺序而言，理论走在了前面，而实验室的发现证实了该理论的准确性。早在1916年，爱因斯坦便突破了牛顿力学，而根据广义相对论预言引力波会作为引力放射向外传送能量。在科学史上，这类以科学理论来"预知"科学发现的实例很多。例如，俄国化学家门捷列夫在发明了化学元素周期表后，从该表中的几个空洞预测了新元素的存在。果然，十五年后，其他科学家发现了与预测相符的三种元素。在中国历史上，类似"理论先于实践"的例子也并不罕见。例如，两千多年前老子关于"有"和"无"的论断，就不断被现代许多科学实验所证实。

总之，此次引力波的重大发现，证实了爱因斯坦广义相对论的最后一项重大预测，使人们从此不但可以去观察，而且可以去"聆听"宇宙了，从而进入了宇宙研究的全新时代；而将此段的含义准确翻译出来，对于广大中文读者的理解同样很有意义。

参考译文

发现引力波

[1] 这里不妨简略解释一下什么是"引力波"。

[2] 根据爱因斯坦的广义相对论，宇宙中的时空结构会因巨大物体而发生弯曲。

[3] 当巨变发生时，可使时空扭曲，引力波扩散他处，如同有人在池塘里扔入石头，"黑洞合并""恒星爆炸"等现象便是如此。

[4] 当这些波纹传送到地球时，因为它们波长极小（大约是原子直径的十亿分之一），科学家们奋斗了许多年才得以发现。

——《纽约时报》

23

原 文

The Role of Time

(Excerpts)

By Stephen Hawking

[1] The role played by time at the beginning of the universe is, I believe, the final key to removing the need for a Grand Designer, and revealing how the universe created itself.

[2] Time itself must come to a stop.

[3] You can't get to a time before the Big Bang, because there was no time before the Big Bang.

[4] We have finally found something that does not have a cause because there was no time for a cause to exist in.

[5] In an unchanging universe a beginning in time is something that has to be imposed by some being outside the universe.

[6] One could still imagine that God created the universe at the instant of the Big Bang, or even afterwards in just such a way as to make it look as though there had been a big bang.

[7] An expanding universe does not preclude a creator, but it does place limits on when he might have carried out his job!

译　析

英国著名科学家霍金（Stephen Hawking）于2018年3月14日去世，标志着继爱因斯坦之后，人类又一个物理时代的结束。霍金对于天文学的贡献，改变了人们对于宇宙的认识，特别是颠覆了传统的时间概念，选文就是他有关这方面的一段论述。

[1] 中，the beginning of the universe，许多人译成"宇宙开始之初/诞生/一开始/伊始/混沌初开之际/生成之初"等，并无大问题，但对于客观万物的出现，似有传统译法，如达尔文的 *The Origin of Species* 译为《物种起源》，宇宙也如是。而 play a role，未必总是"所扮演的角色""充当……角色"等，更多的则是"所起的某种作用"。Grand Designer，参赛者多译为"伟大设计师""不朽设计者""宏伟设计师"等，而"神创论""造物主""'世界是上帝创造'的这种说法"则显然有些过度发挥；就茫茫宇宙来讲，不妨译为"宏观设计者"，因有所谓之意，可加引号。对于 removing，许多人译成了"代替"，如"时间是替代伟大设计师以及揭示宇宙如何自发生成的关键所在"，有些莫名其妙；实则其本义为 take it away，即"排除""消除"，如：1. This section shows you how to remove an adapter.（该部分表明如何删除适配器。）2. Remain diligent in your analysis of a company's cash flow statement and you will be well on your way to removing the risk of one of your stocks falling victim to a cash flow crunch.（勤于分析现金流量表，可以很顺利地排除股票陷入现

金流紧张的风险。)。至于 final key，不一定总译成"最后一个关键"，更不是"最后一把钥匙"，而是"最关键""关键作用"，如 The final key is in the integration of a Web site into the real world business processes.（最关键的是把网站整合到现实商业中。）对于 I believe，则可提前，以统领全句。故整句不妨译为："我认为，在宇宙起源中时间所起的关键作用，是排除了创世主的存在，揭示了宇宙如何自我生成。"

[2]中，多被译成"时间是终会停止的""时间本身必须停下来""时间本身不会停止""你不可能接触到时间""时间终将会有尽头"等，但不妨简约译为："时间本身必会终结。"

[3]中，参赛者典型的译法有"在大爆炸之前你无法到达一个时间，因为在大爆炸之前没有时间""你无法追溯宇宙大爆炸发生之前的时间，因为在那之前，一切都是虚无""我们不可能回到大爆炸之前，因为在那之前，时间并不存在""在大爆炸之前，你不可能到达某一个时间，因为在那之前并没有时间"等。问题出在 get to a time，即物理学上"进入时间"的概念，特别是霍金所发现的"时间"概念。在此以前，一般认为既然宇宙在空间上是无边无际的，那么时间也便无始无终，但霍金研究后认为，宇宙诞生于约150亿年前，它从一个"点"开始，聚集能量，向外扩散，到达某一临界点后发生了"大爆炸"，而空间和时间也便由此开始。宇宙的温度最初极高，随着时间的演进冷却下来，而其中的物质与能量之间不断发生复杂反应，形成了星系，并仍在不断膨胀；时间前后都有方向，而按照宇宙的发展规律，时间最终又会消失。在语序上，亦应有所调整，才能

准确表述其意:"因为'大爆炸'之前没有时间,所以也无从进入时间。"

[4]中,若译成"我们终于找到一个不需前因后果的东西,因为这不再拥有时间的概念""我们最终没有找到时间的成因,因为在不变的宇宙中不存在时间的成因",显然理解有误;"有些事物并没有起源,诚然,没有时间,何谈起源?"理解不错,但"起源"过于狭窄,因cause不只是"起源";"最终我们发现一些事物是没有起因的,因为在这些事物存在之前没有时间,即没有时间能够容纳其起因",意思大体不错,但不够简练。其中,something <u>that does not have</u>...下画线部分为后置定语,而中文里的定语一般在主语前面,如"打网球的那些人是我的同事",英译文则将其置后:The people playing tennis are my colleagues. 又如:1. 弃船的命令下达了。(The order to abandon ship was given.) 2. Why invest time and energy in something that we all hate?(为什么投入时间和精力去思考我们都讨厌的事情?)在英译时,要作相应调整。对于something that does not have a cause,不妨借用老子的"天下万物生于有,有生于无",这也被国外学者称之为大智慧,且被科学实践所证实。故此句不妨译为:"我们终于发现了'无中生有'的事物,因为那里没有令原因存在的时间……"

对于[5],译法纷繁,如"在此亘古不变的宇宙中,时间的开端定是宇宙之外的某种化身""在一个不变的宇宙中,时间概念是人所强加的,而不是宇宙中所固有的""时间在不变宇宙中的开始必然是被某些宇宙之外的事物所强加的""时间的开端一定需要某些宇宙之外的强大推力""在一个不变的宇宙中,需要有宇宙外的力量创造时间""在一个不变的宇宙中,时间的起源一定是由某些存在于宇宙之外的人强加于它的"等,多有过度发挥和表述不当之处。其中,an unchanging universe,就宇宙而言,是指"守恒"的,其本质是能量和动量的恒定性;而imposed不一定是"强迫",更不是由"人"决定的,其基本意思是:既然在"大爆炸"之前没有时间,那么时间起点的含义就不能由其自身决定,而是由某种外力决定的。此处不妨使用"赋予"一词,如We don't believe the myth that racial discrimination was imposed by God.(我们并不相信种族歧视是上帝赋予人类的观念。)故此句不妨译为:"守恒状态的宇宙,其时间的起点由宇宙之外的存在赋予意义。"

[6]中,the Big Bang通常译为"宇宙大爆炸"或"创世大爆炸",义为the cosmic explosion that marked the beginning of the universe(引自Merriam Webster's Unabridged Dictionary)。大爆炸理论是霍金所推崇的,现为天体物理学所广泛接受。参赛译文,如"一个猜想就是上帝在宇宙大爆炸的瞬间创造了宇宙,又或者是在后来让宇宙看上去是经历了宇宙大爆炸一样""我们仍然可以想象,上帝在大爆炸的瞬间创造了宇宙,甚至在那之后,用一种方式,让看起来好像存在一场大爆炸""一个人仍然可以设想在宇宙大爆炸的瞬间是上帝创造了宇宙,或是甚至之后以这种方式使其看起来像是这里曾经存在过一次大爆炸""你也可以幻想在'大爆炸'的时候上帝创造了宇宙亦或是上帝创造了宇宙从而使'宇宙大爆炸'像是存在过"等,其中,对One有"一个猜想""一个人""你"等译法,其实"人们"即可;而

or even afterwards 是对 instant 的补充，可在括号中处理；in just such a way as to... as though... 译成"使其看起来像是……"，可简化为"恰似"。故此，该句不妨译为："人们仍然可以想象上帝在大爆炸的瞬间（或稍后时刻）创造了宇宙，恰似发生过大爆炸一样……"

[7] 中，参赛者多译"一个不断膨胀的宇宙不会排斥一个创造者，但是它的确会限制创造者完成他工作的时间""广阔的宇宙并不阻止一位创造者，但它的确会在他本可以进行工作的时候对他加以限制"等，主要是对"place limits on... carried out his job"的处理比较生硬，不妨变通为："膨胀中的宇宙并未排除创世主，不过对其创世的时间加以界定。"

其实，霍金的时间概念，是在之前科学家对于"时间"认识基础上的发挥，例如，美国天文学家惠特罗（Whitrow, G.）说过，"Time is the mediator between the possible and the actual."（时间是"可能"与"现实"之间的调停者。）；英国物理学家邦迪（Bondi, H.）也认为，"Time must never be thought of as pre-existing in any sense; it is a manufactured quantity."（在任何意义上，时间都不是预先存在的，而是人为的参量。）；英国化学家阿特金斯（Atkins, P.）证实，"The experience of time is the gearing of the electrochemical processes in our brains to this purposeless drift into chaos as we sink into equilibrium and the grave."（对于时间的体验，是我们大脑中电化学的过程；当我们进入永久平息状态时，这种任意漂流的时光就会变得浑浊。）。

值得指出的是，有的参赛译文有直接拷贝电脑软件翻译结果之嫌，如将the final key译成"最终的钥匙"、Time itself must come to a stop译成"时间自身必须来终止"、he might have carried out his job译成"他可能已经从事了这项工作"等。对于机器翻译，只可利用，不可照抄，因不可缺少的是译者本人的理解和加工，否则就不是自己的翻译。

霍金不但是一位杰出的科学家，而且是广受大众欢迎的科普作家。他善于将高深的天文学知识以通俗易懂的方式加以表述，语言平实、流畅，这在译文中亦应有所体现。

参考译文

时间的作用

（节选）

斯蒂芬·霍金

[1] 我认为，在宇宙起源中时间所起的关键作用，是排除了创世主的存在，揭示了宇宙如何自我生成。

[2] 时间本身必会终结。

[3] 因为"大爆炸"之前没有时间，所以也无从进入时间。

[4] 我们终于发现了"无中生有"的事物，因为那里没有令原因存在的时间。

[5] 守恒状态的宇宙，其时间的起点由宇宙之外的存在赋予

意义。

[6] 人们仍然可以想象上帝在大爆炸的瞬间（或稍后时刻）创造了宇宙，恰似发生过大爆炸一样。

[7] 膨胀中的宇宙并未排除创世主，不过对其创世的时间加以界定。

Scientific Revolution

By Jerry H. Bentley

[1] Copernicus argued that the sun rather than the earth stood at the center of the universe and that the planets, including the earth, revolved around the sun. Although this new theory harmonized much better with observational data, it did not receive a warm welcome.

[2] Copernicus's ideas not only challenged prevailing scientific theories but also threatened cherished religious beliefs, which held that the earth and humanity were unique creations of God.

[3] In time, though, Copernicus's theory inspired some astronomers to examine the heavens in fresh ways, using precise observational data and mathematical reasoning. Gradually, they abandoned the Ptolemaic in favor of the Copernican model of the universe.

[4] Some also began to apply their analytical methods to mechanics—the branch of science that deals with moving bodies—and by the mid-seventeenth century accurate observation and mathematical reasoning dominated both mechanics and astronomy.

[5] Indeed, reliance on observation and mathematics transformed the study of the natural world and brought about the scientific revolution.

译 析

此段选文摘自 *Traditions & Encounters: A Brief Global History*（Jerry H. Bentley et al），简述了人类科学革命的一个片段。

就题目 Scientific Revolution 而言，有人遗漏未译，值得注意。有的译成"技术革命"显然有误，因那是 technological revolution，实则为"科学革命"。

在[1]中，对于 the sun rather than the earth stood at the center of the universe 有的按字面意思译成"是太阳而不是地球位于宇宙的中心"，似乎不错，但不够通顺，亦不太符合中文的表达习惯；且原文的重点是"宇宙的中心是太阳，而不是地球"。第二个 that 与第一个 that 一样都是 argued 的宾语从句，而 the planets, including the earth, 许多人译成"行星，包括地球……"，是被英文中的后置定语限制住了，在中译文里应将其提前，为"包括地球在内的行星"。对于 ...harmonized... with... 不宜简单译成"与……相和谐"，而更为恰当的词是"吻合"；warm welcome，许多人按词面意思译成"热烈欢迎""热捧"，显然过于表面化，其实作为一个新理论，是个是否被"广泛接受"的问题。

故此段不妨译为："哥白尼认为宇宙的中心是太阳，而不是地球；包括地球在内的行星都围绕太阳运转。这种新学说尽管与观测数据更为吻合，但当时并未被广为接受。"

在[2]中，prevailing固然有"盛行""占优势"之意，但其本义为existing or most common at a particular time，此处可译为"当时权威的"等；cherished有多种含义，如"珍爱的、珍视的、珍藏的"等，但这里因涉及宗教信仰，可稍加变通为"神圣的"等。后面的which held that为宾语从句，有"即认为……"之意。对于the earth and humanity were unique creations of God，一般译成"地球和人类是上帝的特有造物""教会坚信地球和人类是上帝独一无二的创造""上帝是地球和人类独一无二的造物主"，有的还稍作发挥："上帝独一无二的产物，极其珍贵"等，这些都不错，但可精炼，特别是考虑到西方宗教背景。鉴于《圣经》的第一卷书"创世记"叙述的正是宇宙的起源（起初神创造天地）和人类的起源（神创造了亚当和夏娃），故可译为"上帝创世记理论"。整句不妨译为："哥白尼的理念不仅是对当时权威科学理论的挑战，而且也威胁到了神圣宗教的信仰，即上帝创世记的理论。"

在[3]中，此处的In time不是一般意义上的"及时"，而是after a period of time when a situation has changed即"经过一段时间之后……终于"，可译为"随着时间的推移"；而reasoning似乎是名词，但此处应译为动词"……推理加以分析"；inspired有的译成"激励""刺激"等，显然不如"启发"准确；in favor of，许多人译成"拥护""赞成""追随"等，其实就当时的发展情况而言，未必有这样强烈，而"更倾向于……"似更合适。Ptolemaic是希腊天文学家托勒密，进而代表托勒密地心说，有的译成了"普托来梅耶""普托来梅耶天文学"显然不妥。整句不妨译为:"尽管如此,但随着时间的推移,哥白尼的理论启发了天文学家以新方式来研究天体,他们利用准确的观察数据,以数学推理加以分析。他们逐渐地摒弃了托勒密的'地心说',而倾向于哥白尼的'日心说'。"

在[4]中,破折号中间的是对 mechanics 的解释,一般译成"……力学——研究物体运动的科学的分支——到17世纪中期……",其实可用更简略的括号来表述,而有的译成了"——其中一个科学流派解决了机械手臂的问题",显然理解错误。而...dominated 是动词,但在译文中可转换为形容词,却不一定是"主导的",而可为"主要的"。故整句可译为"有的天文学家还将其分析方法应用到力学(研究物体运动的学科),到了17世纪中叶,精确观察和数理分析成为力学和天文学的主要研究方法"。

在[5]中,前半句普遍译成"依靠观察和数学的研究方法改变了对自然世界的研究",似乎没有大错,但应知这里的 observation and mathematics 显然是前文 accurate observation and mathematical reasoning 的略语,强调的则是二者的结合,而 reliance 则未必一定译出(依靠);transform,比一般的 change 更全面,其本义为 to transform something into something else means to change or convert it into that thing,而 transformed the study of the natural world,不宜简单地译成"改变了对自然界的研究",因结合上文可以看到,这里指的是对于自然界的研究方式(in fresh ways)。故整句不妨译为"的确,观测与数理的结合,改变了人们研究自然界的模式,从而引发了科学革命"。

参考译文

科学革命

杰里·宾利

[1] 哥白尼认为宇宙的中心是太阳,而不是地球;包括地球在内的行星都围绕太阳运转。这种新学说尽管与观测数据更为吻合,但当时并未被广泛接受。

[2] 哥白尼的理念不仅是对当时权威科学理论的挑战,而且也威胁到了神圣宗教的信仰,即上帝创世记的理论。

[3] 尽管如此,但随着时间的推移,哥白尼的理论启发了天文学家以新方式来研究天体,他们利用准确的观察数据,以数学推理加以分析。他们逐渐地摒弃了托勒密的"地心说",而倾向于哥白尼的"日心说"。

[4] 有的天文学家还将其分析方法应用到力学(研究物体运动的学科),到了17世纪中叶,精确观察和数理分析成为力学和天文学的主要研究方法。

[5] 的确,观测与数理的结合,改变了人们研究自然界的模式,从而引发了科学革命。

What Is Wisdom?

By Walter Lippmann

[1] If we ask ourselves what is this wisdom which experience forces upon us, the answer must be that we discover the world is not constituted as we had supposed it to be.

[2] It is not that we learn more about its physical elements, or its geography, or the variety of its inhabitants, or the ways in which human society is governed.

[3] Knowledge of this sort can be taught to a child without in any way disturbing his childishness.

[4] In fact, all of us are aware that we once knew a great many things which we have since forgotten.

[5] The essential discovery of maturity has little if anything to do with information about the names, the locations, and the sequence of facts; it is the acquiring of a different sense of life, a different kind of intuition about the nature of things.

译 析

沃尔特·李普曼（Walter Lippmann，1889—1974），美国著名的政论家、作家和学者，传播学的奠基人。他的著作、名言集被翻译成了几十种语言，在世界各地传播。这段文字，体现的是作者对于主观与客观、知识与智慧关系的一种思考——译者对此需有一总体的把握，才不致偏离原意太远。

[1] 中，宾语从句what...中套有定语从句which...，其中的experience forces upon us 修饰 wisdom，但force并非"强加"或"自然力量"之意，如有的译成"经验强加于我们的这种智慧是什么""什么是我们在体验自然力量时获得的智慧"等，而是"具有强烈影响"（having strong influence），如基督教中讲：All this conspired to force upon theologians the need to affirm in new ways that Christ was truly man.（所有这些意念的汇总促使信徒们以新的方式重申基督是真正的人。）。下面的...the world is not constituted可译、可不译，为"世界（的构成）不是我们所……"。故该句不妨译为："若问经验给了我们怎样的智慧？回答必然是：发现了世界的构成并不是我们所想象的那样。"

[2] 中，对于It is not that...，许多人译成了"它不是那些……"，显然是拘泥于字面意思，而没有把握选文的主旨，即如前所述的知识与智慧及人的成长的关系，其意实为：以下这些知识，相对而言，其实并没有那么重要。明白了这一点，对于its physical elements, or its geography, or the variety of its inhabitants,

若译成"关于它的物理元素,或它的地理,或它的居民种类,或人类社会治理的方式""关于世界的物质元素构成,地理状况,生物多样性,或是管理人类社会的各种方法"等,就显得未免"拘谨"。故该句不妨译为:"多学一些具体的事物,如地形地貌、各类生物知识及人类社会的管理方式等,其实并不重要。"

[3]中,问题较多,典型的如"这类知识可以通过不扰乱童心的任何方式教给孩子""这种知识在童年时就被传授给孩子而不以任何方式破坏他的童真""对于这种知识,即使是孩童也能习得,且其童真能毫不受损""这类的知识完全可以在不影响一个孩子的童心的情况下教给他""这样的知识能够在毫不泯灭童心的情况下传授给孩子"等等。显然,问题出在childishness与选文主旨的关系上。前文一直在讲那些干巴巴的"知识",其实跟人的成长没有多大关系,此处则说到孩子和稚气。对于childlike、childish、childishness,在不同的语境中可有不同的解读。如,美国著名教育家亨利·戴克(Henry Dyke)有句名言:The limitations that are childlike in the child are childish in the man.(智能的不足,在孩子身上体现为天真无邪,对于成人则是一种幼稚的表现)。以知识对促进人格发展的影响来看,这一类的教育对于孩子的成长、蜕变其实没有特别大的作用。故该句不妨译为:"这类知识的传授甚至改变不了孩子身上的稚气。"

[4]中,对于knew (a great many things)和(we have since) forgotten一般都可翻译出来,但语气不够准确,如"自己也曾熟知现时已遗忘的许多事物""我们曾经也知道许多这样的知识,只是过后忘了""我们曾经知道很多事情,后来却又都忘记了"

等等。分析起来,"知道了"(knew)是知识层面的,由于没有与个人的思考和感受发生关系,因而没有向智力或性格成熟方面转换,尔后就忘记了(forgotten)。故该句强调的是,已知的未必是有用的:"事实是,我们都知道,许多我们原以为'知道了'的事情,都已不记得了。"

[5] 中则讲得更加明确,即信息(information)类的获得对于人的智力和性格的成熟产生的影响很有限,重要的是与个体的内心发生关系。有的参赛者将 The essential discovery of maturity 反译成"稚气的褪去",似乎是一种创意;而将 a different kind of intuition about the nature of things 译成"一种关于事物本质的完全不一样的直觉"又有失偏颇。有两个地方值得注意:1. has little if anything...,为"几乎没有""微乎其微"之意,如 In terms of technical content, very little if anything has changed at this time.(就技术内容而言,几乎没什么大的改变。)亦可将 little 与 if anything 分开,如 True greatness has little, if anything, to do with rank or power.(真正的伟大是与地位或权力无关的。);2. different,许多人将其译成"不同""不一样的",其实在此更多是"各自"之意,如 Different people reacted in different ways.(人们作出了各自不同的反应。)。故此句不妨译为:"一个人成熟性格的养成与人名、地点等具体事实几乎没有多大关系;重要的是,要获得对于生活的一种自我感悟,一种对事物本质的感知。"

应当说,李普曼的这一论述,对于人们学习什么、如何学习、怎样注重汲取知识与提高自己的关系等,是颇有见地的。

参考译文

什么是智慧?

沃尔特·李普曼

[1] 若问经验给了我们怎样的智慧？回答必然是：发现了世界的构成并不是我们所想象的那样。

[2] 多学一些具体的事物，如地形地貌、各类生物知识及人类社会的管理方式等，其实并不重要。

[3] 这类知识的传授甚至改变不了孩子身上的稚气。

[4] 事实是，我们都知道，许多我们原以为"知道了"的事情，都已不记得了。

[5] 一个人成熟性格的养成与人名、地点等具体事实几乎没有多大关系；重要的是，要获得对于生活的一种自我感悟，一种对事物本质的感知。

26

原 文

What Is Culture?

[1] Culture is a complex matter, including knowledge, belief, morals, custom, capabilities, art and so on acquired by people as a member of society. It is a learned pattern of behavior and ways in which a person lives his or her life. Culture is essential for the existence of a society, because it binds people together.

[2] A people's culture is as important to their survival as food is. Without the guide-posts and direction signs that a culture offers to its adherents, they can soon become disillusioned, confused and easily led into self-detrimental paths.

[3] People learn culture in the course of everyday living by communication with those around them. Culture learning starts at an early age and generally stays with people for the whole of their lives. In turn, people transmit culture to others, especially to their offspring, through direct instruction and the behaviors they consciously and unconsciously encourage and discourage.

[4] The foundation of a culture is its values and norms. Values shape idea about what society believes to be right and wrong; values

also establish the cultural bedrock of a society. They provide the context within which a society's norms are formed and justified. They include a society's attitude toward such concepts as norms of a society; it is also true that the social structure and religion can be influenced by values and norms of a society.

译 析

关于"文化"有着多种定义，选文只是其中的一种。

就题目What Is Culture? 而言，一般译成"何谓文化""何为文化""什么是文化？""文化的含义"，"文化的本质"等，都是可以接受的，但就确切和通顺而言，可译为"文化是什么？"。

[1] 中，Culture is a complex matter, 有的译成"文化是一个复合体""文化是个复杂的事物""文化是个复杂的概念"等；有的将其与后面的合并译出，如"文化是作为社会一员的人所获得的复杂事物，包括知识、信仰、道德、习俗、才能、艺术等""文化是包括知识、信仰、道德、习俗、能力、艺术以及身为社会成员的人所习得的其他方面的复杂整体"等，都有一定道理，但更确切的为"文化是个复杂问题"；对于learned，大都译成"习得的""获得的"，其实该词未必总是这样翻译，如He has ever since learned to look at her with new respect（他就此对她更加尊重了）；"这段时间促进了我们之间的相互了解"（I think we've learned a lot about one another in this session），根据此处具体语境，不妨译为"后天的"；ways in which a person lives his or her life,

实则为the way of life，即"生活方式"；essential固然是"重要的"，但此处更宜为"基础的"；至于从句as a member of society可视情况加入不同的主句中；it binds people together，有的译成"文化能将人们链结在一起""文化使人与人紧密相连""人们因文化而结合在一起""因为它是人与人之间形成联系的纽带"等，意思都不错，只是应作更和谐的搭配，而为了强调"文化"，it此处可不译成"它"。故此，该段不妨译为："文化是个复杂问题，包括人们作为社会成员所具有的知识、信仰、道德、习俗、能力、艺术等。文化是人们后天的行为模式和生活方式，是社会的基础，因为文化将人们联系在一起。"

[2] 中，is as... as...，是"如同……那样……"，对此都能译出，如"一个民族的文化对其人民的生存而言，如食物般重要""一个民族的文化之于其生存，就如同食物一般重要"等，但可更为精练，如A people's culture，实质还是"文化"，而"民以食为天，而文化对人的重要性与食物不分伯仲"，显然有些过度发挥了。Without the guide-posts and direction signs that a culture offers to its adherents, they can soon become disillusioned, confused and easily led into self-detrimental paths，指一种消极情况，即"若没有……会怎么样"，故应尽量保持原貌，而不宜译成"在人生的道路上，文化能为人指明前进的方向，给人前进的信心，驱散迷茫，帮助我们远离人生的弯路"；同时，guide-posts and direction signs that a culture offers to its adherents，若译成"文化是其拥护者的指路牌和方向标"，不免有些过于拘泥字面意思；不妨加以适当变通，如"文化坐标的方向"。因而，整句不妨译

为:"对于人们的生存而言,文化与食物一样重要。丧失了文化坐标的方向,其社会成员便难免感到颓丧和困惑,走上自我毁灭的道路。"

[3] 中,对于 Culture learning starts at an early age and generally stays with people for the whole of their lives,有的译成"文化学习开始于幼年时期,一般又会伴随一生直至死亡",似乎可不必译得这么直白,而"文化学习从幼年开始,伴其一生"即可。对于 In turn, people transmit culture to others, especially to their offspring, through direct instruction and the behaviors they consciously and unconsciously encourage and discourage,典型的译文,如"相反,也有人直接言传身教,将文化传授他人,尤其是授给自己的子孙后代。他们有意或无意鼓励和反对的行为,正是这'身教'",意思固然不错,但分析起来,in turn, 不一定总是"相反",在某种语境下还有"依次""同时"等意,如 There were cheers for each of the women as they spoke in turn(女士们依次发言时,每一位都得到了喝彩);Increased production will, in turn, lead to increased profits(增加生产同时也会增加利润);especially to their offspring、encourage and discourage 在句中的位置也可作适当调整。整段而言,不妨译为:"人们在日常生活中通过与周围人的交往来学习文化;文化学习从幼年开始,伴其一生。同时,人们又通过言行(鼓励和劝勉),自觉或不自觉地将文化传递给他人,特别是自己的后代。"

[4] 中的 values 指的是"价值观",出现在不同位置,为了明确和强调,在译文中数次出现;context,大都译成了"背

景""环境",但这里指的是 within which a society's norms are formed and justified,即"借此……形成判断";it is also true that the social structure and religion can be influenced by values and norms of a society 是被动语态,宜调整为主动语态,同时 social structure 也未必是"社会结构"。因而,该段可译为:"文化的基础是价值观和行为准则。价值观形成社会的是非观,是社会的文化基石;价值观也是社会行为准则的内容和评判参照。价值观同时包括了一个社会对待诸如社会规范等观念的态度。事实上,价值观和行为准则影响着社会制度和宗教信仰。"

关于"文化",著名英国哲学家尼可拉斯·布宁(Nicholas Bunnin)在《西方哲学词典》(*Dictionary of Western Philosophy*)中也有这样的定义:Culture: In its most central sense, culture refers to the forms of life and the tools, symbols, customs and beliefs which are characteristic of a distinct historical group of people. This sense of culture, associated with the notion of society, provides much of the subject matter of sociology and anthropology. The variety of cultures has led some thinkers to endorse "cultural relativism", the claim that the culture of any society must be judged in its own terms and not by standards provided by the culture of another society. Others have accepted the importance of culture while rejecting cultural relativism. Culture may also refer to the system of value and ways of thinking peculiar to society. This amounts to "the consciousness of a society". In its widest sense, culture refers to the totality of human thoughts, behaviors and the products of human activities. Culture in this sense, which stands in contrast to biological nature and has been used to distinguish humans from animals, belongs to the subject of philosophical anthropology. More selectively, culture comprises art, sports, entertainment and other leisure activities. High culture, containing the most significant and accomplished works of visual art, music, dance and literature has often been contrasted with popular culture, although the two in some circumstances influence one another. Culture also means personal cultivation through education and training. The science of culture seeks to understand that which is defined by the creation of values.（文化的核心意义在于表征各历史人群的生活方式、使用工具、象征符号、习俗信仰等；与社会相关的这一文化含义，为社会学和人类学提供了诸多研究课题。文化的多样性使得某些思想家认同"文化相对论"，认为任何社会的文化需由本社会而非其他社会所提供的准则加以评判。另有一些思想家，固然认同文化是重要的，但不承认文化相对主义。文化也是社会特有的价值体系和思维方式，即"社会的良知"。在广义上，文化指人类思想、行为及各种活动产物的总和。在此意义上，文化与生物属性不同，将人类与其他动物区分开来，属哲学意义上人类学的研究课题。在狭义上，文化包括艺术、体育、娱乐及其他休闲活动。高雅文化，与通俗文化不同，包括最富含义的上乘视觉、音乐、舞蹈、文学作品等，尽管二者在某种情况下相互影响。文化亦指经教育、培训获得的个人修养；而文化学旨在对于由价值观所作判断的解读。）

所以，对于学术概念的翻译，既要细致分析，又要综合理解,以求准确、恰当、得体。

参考译文

文化是什么?

[1] 文化是个复杂问题,包括人们作为社会成员所具有的知识、信仰、道德、习俗、能力、艺术等。文化是人们后天的行为模式和生活方式,是社会的基础,因为文化将人们联系在一起。

[2] 对于人们的生存而言,文化与食物一样重要。丧失了文化坐标的方向,其社会成员便难免感到颓丧和困惑,走上自我毁灭的道路。

[3] 人们在日常生活中通过与周围人的交往来学习文化;文化学习从幼年开始,伴其一生。同时,人们又通过言行(鼓励和劝勉),自觉或不自觉地将文化传递给他人,特别是自己的后代。

[4] 文化的基础是价值观和行为准则。价值观形成社会的是非观,是社会的文化基石;价值观也是社会行为准则的内容和评判参照。价值观同时包括了一个社会对待诸如社会规范等观念的态度。事实上,价值观和行为准则影响着社会制度和宗教信仰。

27

原 文

Interpreters and Translators: Good Prospects
By J. Peter

[1] If you are proficient in more than one language, your opportunity for using your skills in an interpreter or translator career will be excellent over the next eight years, to say the least.

[2] "This is a function of the global marketplace. Business is being done on a global scale, and immigration is also at an all-time high. The translation and interpreting industry has proved to be recession-resistant, showing double-digit growth even during the deepest global economic crisis", an American expert says.

[3] This is simply because this service is not a luxury item but rather a communication tool, without which multinational companies and cross-border businesses cannot function.

[4] The need for good translators and interpreters hasn't slowed even after the proliferation of free automated translation tools such as Google Translate or Bing Translator. This does not reduce the need for translators and interpreters, but rather creates a whole new market for their services as world communities become more connected.

[5] Although interpreters and translators typically need a bachelor's degree, the chief requirement is being fluent in English and at least one other language. While there is no universal certification required to become an interpreter or translator, various universities provide certification programs.

译 析

本文（Interpreters and Translators: Good Prospects）选自一份关于美国职业前景的调查报告，对其标题、结构等作了适当调整和改动。

首先要指出的是，有些参赛者的译文是通过某些翻译软件或"在线翻译"完成的，不加修改或很少修改，便递交上来，请看这样的译文：

"笔译和口译行业已被证明是经济衰退的影响，显示两位数增长即使最严重的全球经济危机，一名美国专家说"；

"这仅仅是因为这项服务不是一种奢侈品，而是一种沟通工具，多民族公司和跨越边界企业不可能起作用"；

"口译员和翻译员一般都需要专业的学士学位证明，行政的要求是流利的英语和至少一种其他语言。虽然没有公认证明要求成为一名口译员或翻译员，但各大学都会提供认证程序"，等等。

明眼人一看便知，这是"机器翻译"的，而非人工翻译！什么是"笔译和口译行业已被证明是经济衰退的影响"？什么是"多民族公司和跨越边界企业不可能起作用"？什么是"行政的要求是流利的英语和至少一种其他语言"？不但意思完全相反和错误，而且简直不是在说"人话"。难道这是我们翻译学院的学生应有的水平和态度吗？这样的所谓"翻译"，非但对同学自身翻译能力的提高毫无益处，而且会有误导和危害。故此，对于这样的翻译，下次发现之后，不但没有成绩，而且还要提出批评，甚至影响其学分和毕业成绩。

这里我要向同学们诚恳地告诫：在翻译、外语及语言学习上，没有捷径可走，非下苦功夫不可，否则便是自欺欺人。

就本文标题的翻译而言，应把握这样的原则：既要扣紧原文，又不宜过度发挥，同时要力求简练。归纳同学们的一些典型翻译，例如："机器翻译和人工翻译：美好的前景"——是否有点离谱？"口译和笔译：前程远大、前途无量"——是否有点夸张？"口译译员和笔译译员：前程似锦"——是否有点啰嗦？

其实，可以不受原文的标点符号限制，如有的同学译为"译者好前途""翻译工作者的良好前景"等都不错，参考译文用了"口笔译者，前程乐观"。

[1] 中对于If you are proficient in more than one language，大部分同学译成"精通至少一门以上语言"，固然不错，但考虑到翻译是在两种语言之间进行的，故不妨运用我们在翻译课上学习的"反译法"，译为"精通至少两种语言"；in an interpreter or translator career will be excellent，有同学译成"他的人生机遇将大大增加，前途也会变得更加光明"等，显然都有些太"过"（且不完整）；而对to say the least，又不必单译出来，而只是融合在前面的句子中便可。故此，整句不妨译为："你若精通至少两

种语言,那么起码在今后八年间,在口笔译行业里发挥你才能的机会,十分看好。"

[2] 中对于 "This is a function of the global marketplace. Business is being done on a global scale, and immigration is also at an all-time high. The translation and interpreting industry has proved to be recession-resistant, showing double-digit growth even during the deepest global economic crisis", an American expert says,其中,对于引述别人的话语,英文惯于置后,而这里的翻译则不妨提前;a function of the global marketplace,同学们一般译成"国际市场功能",固然不错,但结合后面所述,整体考虑,是在讲全球化的一种运作现象,故不妨整合为"这是全球化市场的机制——商务在全球范围内展开,移民潮亦创历史新高";...even during the deepest global economic crisis 让步状语从句,英文一般置后处理,为的是强调 showing double-digit growth,而这里的译文则不妨提前,而将结果置后,同样是为了强调:"即便是在世界经济危机最严重的时候,翻译行业也有两位数的增长,足见其不受经济衰退的影响。"至于 recession-resistant,一般都译成了"防衰退""抗衰退"等,固然不错,如 water-resistant watch(防水表),fire-resistant facilities(防火设备)等,但此处读起来稍显别扭,故不妨释意为"不受经济衰退的影响"。

[3] 中对于 This is simply because this service is not a luxury item but rather a communication tool, without which multinational companies and cross-border businesses cannot function,其中的 simply,许多同学译成"这仅仅是因为……",而 without which,

译成"没有翻译工作",固然可以,但还可更简练些:"原因很简单,翻译不是一种奢侈的服务行业,而是一种沟通的工具;舍此,跨国公司及跨境的商务便无法展开"。

[4] 中对于 The need for good translators and interpreters hasn't slowed even after the proliferation of free automated translation tools such as Google Translate or Bing Translator. This does not reduce the need for translators and interpreters, but rather creates a whole new market for their services as world communities become more connected,其中 The need for good translators and interpreters hasn't slowed 和 This does not reduce the need for translators and interpreters 两句的意思有些重叠,若完全跟随原文,便不免重复,故对此可作些"合并"处理,即是将"并未因……的免费自动化翻译工具的广泛使用"提前,而"并未有所减缓"包括了 hasn't slowed 和 does not reduce 两组词汇的含义;world communities,有同学译成"世界群体",是不对的,应为"国际社会";对于"谷歌翻译"等外文词汇,这里可先以中文译出,并将英译文附在括号内,故整段不妨译为"对于优秀口笔译者的需求,并未因'谷歌翻译'(Google Translate)或'必应翻译'(Bing Translator)等的免费自动化翻译工具的广泛使用而有所减缓;非但如此,由于国际社会的联系日益紧密,进而形成了全新的翻译服务市场"。

[5] 中对于 Although interpreters and translators typically need a bachelor's degree, the chief requirement is being fluent in English and at least one other language. While there is no universal

certification required to become an interpreter or translator, various universities provide certification programs，其中，typically 为状语"一般而言"，可提前到句首译出；chief，这里为形容词"主要的""首要的"，而非名词；being influent in English，一般译为"英语流利"，但这里考虑到是"翻译技能"以及 at least one other language，故可译为"熟练地使用英语……"；对于 various universities provide certification programs，很多同学译成了"各种大学提供的认证资格"，其实稍加分析，便会知道，大学提供的不是认证资格，而是"证书课程"，故该句不妨译为"一般而言，口笔译者需要具有学士学位，但其首要条件是能够熟练地使用英语及至少其他另一种语言。尽管目前没有口笔译者的通用证书，但各种大学现都提供相关的证书课程"。

参考译文

口笔译者，前程乐观

J. 彼得

[1] 你若精通至少两种语言，那么起码在今后八年间，在口笔译行业里发挥你才能的机会，十分看好。

[2] 正如一位美国专家所说，"这是全球化市场的机制——商务在全球范围内展开，移民潮亦创历史新高。即便是在世界经济

危机最严重的时候,翻译行业也有两位数的增长,足见其不受经济衰退的影响"。

[3] 原因很简单,翻译不是一种奢侈的服务行业,而是一种沟通的工具;舍此,跨国公司及跨境的商务便无法展开。

[4] 对于优秀口笔译者的需求,并未因"谷歌翻译"(Google Translate)或"必应翻译"(Bing Translator)等的免费自动化翻译工具的广泛使用而有所减缓;非但如此,由于国际社会的联系日益紧密,进而形成了全新的翻译服务市场。

[5] 一般而言,口笔译者需要具有学士学位,但其首要条件是能够熟练地使用英语及至少其他另一种语言。尽管目前没有口笔译者的通用证书,但各种大学现都提供相关的证书课程。

28

> 原 文

Thanksgiving

[1] Although Thanksgiving has historical roots in religious and cultural traditions, it has long been celebrated as a secular holiday as well.

[2] It is a day where everyone should have the opportunity to take just a moment to say thank you, not to a particular religion, but to Mother Nature for the fact that you are alive.

[3] Men are as resentful as they are grateful, but gratitude is the least of virtues; ingratitude the worst of vices.

[4] Gratitude unlocks the fullness of life. It turns what we have into enough, and more. It turns denial into acceptance, chaos to order, confusion to clarity. It can turn a meal into a feast, a house into a home, a stranger into a friend.

[5] The grateful man gets more than he asks.

[6] Therefore, gratitude is the sign of noble souls.

> 译 析

作为一种文化,西方的感恩节已经超越了其原本意义,这也可以通过相关论述和翻译加以理解。

[1] 中，对于 secular，很多参赛者译成了"非宗教的"，实际"世俗"更妥，如英文里通常见到的 ours is a secular society（我们的社会是个世俗社会）、secular and religious music（世俗音乐与宗教音乐）、secular and religious education（世俗教育和宗教教育）等。就词序而言，一般参赛者都按原文译成了"虽然感恩节……，但它也……"，但是，如果将主语"感恩节"提前，便可连贯到下句，而省去后面的"它"字。好的译文应力求字字珠玑，能省即省。

顺便而言，将中文句式"虽然/尽管……，但是……"译成英文 Although..., ... 时，后面并没有 but，如："虽然这套公寓面积很大，但并没有太多房间。"应译为 Although large in area, the flat did not have many rooms.。加 but 是汉译英中易犯的错误。故 [1] 不妨译为："感恩节虽然在宗教和文化传统上有历史渊源，但也长期被当作一个世俗节日来庆祝。"

[2] 很容易译得死板，如"在这一天，每个人应该有机会利用片刻说一声'谢谢你'，不是对一特别的宗教，而是对大自然，因为事实是你还因为它而活着""在这一日人人理应有机会利用一个时刻说谢谢，不是出于特定的宗教，而是出于活着的事实的自然力量""每个人都应该有机会花点时间来说'谢谢你'，不是出于特有的宗教，而是出于你活着这一事实的本性"等。其中，say thank you 不一定是"说谢谢"，而可理解为"表达感谢"，类似的表达如："请代我问候他。"英语说 Please say hello to him for me.。

对于 Mother Nature，参赛者有多种译法，如"大自然""自然的力量""自然环境""那片土地"等，更为兼顾 Mother 和 Nature 二者的，可译为"大自然母亲"；当然，也可译为"上苍""上天""天命""天意"等，因为人是大自然的一部分，中国文化里有"天人合一"的理念，而西方文化里又何尝不是？就英文单词 heart（心灵）和 earth（地球）而言，其中只是 h 的位置有前后的不同，说明古代英文造词者已将地球看作是心灵的家园。还有英文谚语，如：1. He that follows nature is never out of his way.（顺乎自然，不入迷津。/顺天者昌，逆天者亡。）2. He who lives after nature, shall never be poor.（顺天而为，免受贫穷。）。而中英文里都有谚语"天有不测风云"（Man's fortune is as unpredictable as the weather.），即活在世上本身就是一种幸运，由此可把 alive 理解为有幸活在世上、安然无恙，而这都得益于上天的恩赐与眷顾。对于 the fact that you are alive，应当说比较难表达，有参赛者译成"为了你还活着这个事实而感谢大自然""仅仅只是为了你可以依然活着这个不争的事实来说谢谢"等，不免生硬与突兀。

此句不妨借助破折号的作用，译为："每人都应利用这一天来表达感谢，不是对某一宗教，而是对大自然母亲——感恩她对生命的眷顾。"

[3] 中，前半句的参赛译文问题较多，如"人们心怀感激的时候愤愤不平""人们通常在心怀感激的同时也心存怨恨""人们的愤怒就如同感恩一样"等，显然是理解有误；而"人会怨恨，也会感激""人们心怀怨恨的同时也常怀感恩"等，是强调次序

有误。这一类的句式"(subject) be as (adjective)... as (subject) be (adjective)...",强调的是前者,因而翻译出的次序应是相反的,如:1. When hearing the news, he is as worried as he is excited.(得知这一消息后,他既兴奋又担心。)强调的是 worried;2. She is as clever as she is beautiful.(她既漂亮又聪明。)意思是"她不但漂亮而且聪明"。后半句中,the least 不是"最缺的",而是"最起码、最基本的"。将 ingratitude the worst of vices 译成"忘恩负义则是最丑陋的恶习",不能算错,但太拘泥于原文;"不感恩则是最坏的恶行",语气过重;"哀怨是缺点",欠准确且用词过轻;"人是会感激也会怨恨的双向动物"则又有些比喻失当了。故此,该句不妨译为:"人们会感激,也会怨恨,但感恩情怀是基本美德,而忘恩负义则为人不齿。"

[4] 的翻译,参赛译文大都没有太离谱,但用词表达上值得再推敲,比较典型的,如"感恩为我们解锁了生命的完整意义。这样一种情感能使我们已有的变得充盈,甚至更多;也能够把拒绝变为接受,混乱变为有序,困惑变为清醒;还能把一顿普通的餐食变为盛宴,一座空屋变成一个家,一个陌生人变成朋友"等,即着墨应再讲究一些,注重译文的"雅",如词语的变化、对称等。对最后三句,若译成"眼前的粗茶淡饭即是山珍海味,朴实房屋即是温馨家园,萍水相逢即是知己好友"等,好像一切已是既成事实,其实原文强调的是可能发生的过程,即感恩之情可以使那些变成这样。故此,该句不妨译为:"感恩可充分开发生活的潜力——使既有成为富足,抵触变为接纳,动乱化为秩序,混沌显为清晰;在感恩之中,粗茶淡饭即当美妙盛宴,陋

室空堂可作温馨之家，萍水相逢终成手足之交。"

[5] 的翻译，参赛译文如"心怀感恩的人最后得到的往往比他要求的更多""懂得感恩的人总会得到比他乞求的多""感恩之人总有意外的收获"等，固然都不错，但还有更简约的选择："感恩者会求浆得酒"。其中，"浆"是古代一种饮料或可通称米浆，如《孟子·梁惠王》中的名句"箪食壶浆以迎王师"，而《诗经·大东》又有"或以其酒，不以其浆"（有人享用香醇酒，有人则喝不上米浆），二者是一种奢陋的对应。

[6] 的翻译，最一般的译文是"因此，感恩是高尚灵魂的标志"，但也可根据上文语境作些变通："因而，感恩之情尽显高尚风范"。

由此而言，感恩之心虽人皆有之，亦需不断呵护和唤醒，故有人建议吸收西方感恩节中的积极成分，融入中华传统美德，甚至设立有中国特色的"感恩节"。其实，节日只是形式，重要的是对人性中善良成分的发掘，在这一点上，中西方尽管语言不同，但蕴藏在深层的内涵却是相通的。

参考译文

感恩节

[1] 感恩节虽然在宗教和文化传统上有历史渊源，但也长期

被当作一个世俗节日来庆祝。

[2] 每人都应利用这一天来表达感谢，不是对某一宗教，而是对大自然母亲——感恩她对生命的眷顾。

[3] 人们会感激，也会怨恨，但感恩情怀是基本美德，而忘恩负义则为人不齿。

[4] 感恩可充分开发生活的潜力——使既有成为富足，抵触变为接纳，动乱化为秩序，混沌显为清晰；在感恩之中，粗茶淡饭即当美妙盛宴，陋室空堂可作温馨之家，萍水相逢终成手足之交。

[5] 感恩者会求浆得酒。

[6] 因而，感恩之情尽显高尚风范。

29

> 原 文

All Saints' Day

[1] All Saints' Day is a surprisingly old feast. It arose out of the Christian tradition of celebrating the martyrdom of saints on the anniversary of their martyrdom.

[2] When martyrdoms increased during the persecutions of the late Roman Empire, local dioceses instituted a common feast day in order to ensure that all martyrs, known and unknown, were properly honored.

[3] By the late fourth century, this common feast was celebrated in Antioch, and Saint Ephrem the Syrian mentioned it in a sermon in 373. In the early centuries, this feast was celebrated in the Easter season, and the Eastern Churches, both Catholic, and Orthodox, still celebrate it then, tying the celebration of the lives of the saints in with Christ's Resurrection.

[4] The current date of November 1 was instituted by Pope Gregory III (731-741), when he consecrated a chapel to all the martyrs in Saint Peter's Basilica in Rome. Gregory ordered his priests to celebrate the Feast of All Saints annually.

译 析

在西方，到了10月底、11月初都少不了要过万圣节，但10月31日是"万圣节之夜"（Halloween），11月1日才是"万圣节"（All Saints' Day）（或译"诸圣节"）。关于此节有着各种传说，构成西方传统文化的一部分。

[1] 中，许多人将 a surprisingly old feast 译成"一个令人惊讶的古老节日""一个古老而又奇幻的节日""历史出乎意外地悠久""令人惊奇的神秘而古老节日""一个令人惊讶的古老盛宴"等，似乎忠实原文，但读来不免有些佶屈。这里需要了解一些相关的背景，笔者因在西方生活多年，有点儿切身体会。每到这个日子前后，便有成群结队装扮成各种可爱鬼怪的小朋友们拎着南瓜灯提篓敲门来要糖果，并喊着"Trick or Treat！"（不给糖就捣乱！），街上更有年轻人的化装舞会。据说，这一传统来自古西欧国家（主要是爱尔兰、苏格兰、威尔士等）的德鲁伊特人（Druids），村民们相信在万圣节前夜鬼魂会群集于居家附近，并接受设宴款待，而"宴会"后村民们就自己扮成鬼魂精灵，游走村外，引导鬼魂离开，避邪免灾，故称"鬼节"；同时，村民们又在屋前院后摆布些水果、食品，喂足鬼魂，而不遵规者，便被孩子们取笑为不慷慨之家。显然，如今的年轻人已视万圣节为一通俗的娱乐节日，故该文作者才有 surprisingly 的感叹；而 feast 一词，亦有多种含义，此处应理解为一种 religious festival，更恰当的表述可为"万圣节竟然是个古老的宗教节日"（现在的青年

一代可能大都有所不知）。

对于"It arose out of the Christian tradition of celebrating the martyrdom of saints on the anniversary of their martyrdom.",一般理解上没有大问题,但在选词造句上可更加讲究。比较典型的参赛译文有:1."它源于基督教的传统,即在烈士周年纪念日庆祝烈士",其中显然将martyr与martyrdom混淆了;2."它起源于基督教传统,在圣人殉道纪念日庆祝他们的殉道",其中saints应为"圣徒"而非"圣人",且"庆祝"(celebrate)亦不准确(见[4]分析);3."它源自于在纪念日纪念圣徒殉难的基督教传统""他源于基督教徒在殉难周年纪念日赞美殉难圣徒的基督教传统",其中的"他"不恰当,且重复了太多的"纪念""基督教"等;Christian tradition未必要译成"基督教传统",而可将其分开表述。

因而,此部分不妨译为:"万圣节竟然是个古老的宗教节日,源于基督教在殉道日敬仰其殉道圣徒的传统。"

对于[2],一般译成"在罗马帝国晚期的残酷统治时期,殉道人数上涨,为此,地方教区设立了一个常用宗教节日,以确保所有已知和未知的殉道者都得到合适的纪念""当殉道者在罗马帝国后期的迫害中增加,当地教区设立了一个共同的节日,以确保所有殉道者(无论是已知的还是未知的),都能得到应有的荣誉""罗马帝国晚期因宗教迫害而殉难的人数增加,各地的主教教区于是设立了一个共同的宗教节日,以确保无论是有名的还是无名的殉道者皆能得到应有的尊重"等,其中下画线部分为笔者所加,以示问题之处。首先,martyrdom的原义是the suffering or death of a martyr,可见指的不是"人"而是"事件";其次,common feast译成"共同的节日""常用宗教节日""共同的宗教节日"不如"公共纪念日";再次,honor有多种含义,可用作名词或动词,如:1. It's a tremendous <u>honor</u> and a privilege for me to be here with all of you.(能与大家在这里相聚我感到万分<u>荣幸</u>。);2. A memorial tablet was established by the local people to <u>honor</u> their death for the country.(当地居民建立了一座纪念碑,以<u>铭记</u>他们为国捐躯。);3. This time it's quite possible to <u>honor</u> her with the award.(这次她<u>获奖</u>的可能性很大。);4. Rontgen called these new rays X rays, which were named Rontgen rays by other scientists in <u>honor</u> of him.(伦琴把这种新射线称为X射线,其他科学家为纪念他而把这种射线命名为伦琴射线。);5. They should not promise too many things to people; otherwise, they would not be able to <u>honor</u> these things.(他们不要对老百姓许愿太多,否则不能兑现。)。该词译法也要灵活变通,此处则不妨译作"缅怀",其意是以敬仰的心情追忆逝者。故该句不妨译为:"罗马帝国末年,迫害愈烈,殉道日增,于是地方教区设立了公共纪念日,以缅怀那些已知和未知的殉道者。"

[3] 中,this common feast was celebrated in Antioch, and Saint Ephrem the Syrian mentioned it in a sermon in 373,参赛译文有:1."它成为了安提阿地区主要节日,叙利亚的以法莲在公元373年的一次布道中提到过它",哪里可以看出它是"主要节日"?且没有译出Saint;2."这个共同的节日才在安提俄克(Antioch古叙利亚首都)庆祝,并且373年,叙利亚的圣徒厄弗冷

（Ephrem）曾在布道中提到过它"，此处的Saint不宜译成"圣徒"，而是其姓名的一部分，如Saint John（圣约翰）、Saint Louis（圣路易斯）、Saint Paul（圣保罗）等；3. "人们在安提俄克庆祝万圣节，在373年的布道中，古叙利亚的圣埃弗雷姆就提到了这一节日"，似乎人们去到那里庆祝，而不是万圣节开始成为当地的节日，同时漏掉了a sermon。此外，Catholic和Orthodox并提，二者都属Eastern Churches（东方教会派）而lives of the saints，字面意思是"圣徒的生命"，但实质指圣徒们以身奉教，即"殉道"。

故此，这部分不妨译为："四世纪末，安提俄克（古叙利亚首都，现土耳其南部城市）开始庆祝万圣节，叙利亚人圣埃弗雷姆也在373年的一篇布道文中有所提及。在早期数个世纪里，这种仪式会在复活节期间举行，而那时东方教会派，即天主教和东正教也会庆祝，并且将圣徒的殉道与基督的复活相关联。"

[4] 中，he consecrated a chapel to all the martyrs，其中的consecrate有多重含义。就世俗意义而言，是"奉献"，如：1. A doctor's life is consecrated to curing sick people.（医生献身于医治病人。）；2. She consecrated herself to art.（她献身于艺术事业。）。而就宗教意义而言，则有"使神圣化"之意，如：1. The churchyard is consecrated ground.（教堂墓地是圣地。）；2. He was consecrated Archbishop last year.（他于去年就任大主教之圣职。）；3. The church was consecrated in 1853.（这座教堂于1853年祝圣。）。所谓"祝圣"，是指通过牧师或神父的祷告，使某样物品从普通的东西变为圣洁之物，故应为此处之意。许多人将

chapel 译成"小教堂",而到了罗马圣彼得大教堂便会发现,那其实是其中的一部分(a part of a church which has its own altar and which is used for private prayer),故可译为"……教堂里的一座礼拜堂"。

至于 celebrate,如前所述,是这段文字中用得最多的一个词汇。通常,该词译"庆祝",但亦需根据具体语境而定,如:1. Odysseus's heroic exploits are celebrated in *The Odyssey*. 可译为"歌颂"(《奥德赛》史诗中歌颂了奥德修斯的丰功伟绩。);2. On this day, we celebrate our love for this sweet and spoil ourselves. 又可为"表达"(在这一天,我们表达对巧克力的热爱,无节制地享用巧克力。);3. For centuries we've prayed for you and our world, every hour of every day, whenever we celebrate the Mass. 还可为"举行"(几个世纪以来,我们一直举行弥撒圣祭,无时无刻不为你们大家和我们的世界祈祷。)。而前面[1]中的 celebrating the martyrdom of saints 译为了"敬仰"。在《圣经》中,亦有许多 Celebrating Death 的表述,恐怕都不能译成"庆祝死亡"。正如语言学里的一种说法,"在新语境里,每个词都是新词"。(Every word is a new word when used in a new context.)。

综合而言,这部分不妨译为:"如今每年11月1日的'万圣节'是罗马教皇格列高利三世(Pope Gregory III, 731-741)规定的,他在那一日将罗马圣彼得大教堂里的一座礼拜堂祝圣给所有殉道者,并要求牧师们每年祭奠这一日子。"

须知,翻译好每一句的基础,在于对原文宏观和微观背景(语境)的透彻理解。

参考译文

万圣节

[1] 万圣节竟然是个古老的宗教节日，源于基督教在殉道日敬仰其殉道圣徒的传统。

[2] 罗马帝国末年，迫害愈烈，殉道日增，于是地方教区设立了公共纪念日，以缅怀那些已知和未知的殉道者。

[3] 四世纪末，安提俄克（古叙利亚首都，现土耳其南部城市）开始庆祝万圣节，叙利亚人圣埃弗雷姆也在373年的一篇布道文中有所提及。在早期数个世纪里，这种仪式会在复活节期间举行，而那时东方教会派，即天主教和东正教也会庆祝，并且将圣徒的殉道与基督的复活相关联。

[4] 如今每年11月1日的"万圣节"是罗马教皇格列高利三世（Pope Gregory III, 731—741）规定的，他在那一日将罗马圣彼得大教堂里的一座礼拜堂祝圣给所有殉道者，并要求牧师们每年祭奠这一日子。

30

Looking for an Honest Person

[1] It was the famous Greek philosopher and cynic Diogenes who went around the streets of Athens, lantern in hand, looking for an honest person. [2] This was over two thousand years ago, but I presume that Diogenes would have as little success in his search today. [3] Lying seems to be an integral weakness of mortal character—I doubt that few human beings would be so brash as to claim that they have never in their lives told at least a partial untruth. [4] Indeed, one philologist goes so far as to theorize language must have been invented for the sole purpose of deception. Perhaps so. It is certainly true that animals seem somewhat more honest than humans, maybe because they are less gifted mentally. [5] Why do people lie? To increase their sense of importance, to escape punishment, to gain an end that would otherwise be denied them, out of long-standing habit, or sometimes because they actually do not know the differences between fact and fancy.

译 析

公元前500年前后，被中外学者称为"轴心时代"（the Axial Age），那时在古希腊、以色列、印度和中国同时出现了伟大的思想家，如苏格拉底、柏拉图、孔子、老子、释迦牟尼、犹太教的先知们等，以及一些有信念而特立独行的人，选文所提及的第欧根尼正是生活在这样年代里的"怪人"。

就题目Looking for an Honest Person而言，许多参赛者译成"寻找一个诚实的人"，其实此处可理解成一种泛指，即不定冠词an可省略，译为"寻觅诚实人"。

[1] 中的cynic源自Cynics，指古希腊的犬儒哲学，由苏格拉底的学生安提西尼（Antisthenes）所创立，而最著名的代表人物则是第欧根尼。对此，有一段广为流传的记载：Diogenes held that the good man was self-sufficient and did not require material comforts or wealth. He believed that wealth and possessions constrained humanity's natural state of freedom. In keeping with his philosophy, he was perfectly satisfied with making his home in a large tub discarded from the temple of Cybele. This earthen tub, called a pithos, and formerly been used for holding wine or oil for the sacrifices at the temple. One day, Alexander the Great, conqueror of half the civilized world, saw Diogenes sitting in this tub in the sunshine. So the king, surrounded by his entourages, approached Diogenes and said, "I am Alexander the Great." The philosopher

replied rather contemptuously, "I am Diogenes, the Cynic." Alexander then asked him if he could help him in any way. "Yes," shot back Diogenes, "please don't stand between me and the sun." A surprised Alexander then replied quickly, "If I were not Alexander, I would be Diogenes."（第欧根尼认为好人是自给自足的，不需要物质享受和财富，而财富、财产束缚了人们天生的自由状态。为践行这一哲学，他从自然女神庙里捡得一大桶，以桶为家，心满意足。这只陶制大桶之前在祭祀中用于盛油或酒，他称之为"圣桶"。一天，征服了半个文明世界的亚历山大大帝看见第欧根尼坐在桶里晒太阳，于是在随从簇拥下走到第欧根尼跟前说："我是亚历山大大帝。"第欧根尼不屑一顾地答道："我是第欧根尼，犬儒学者。"然后，亚历山大问他是否需要什么帮助。"需要，"第欧根尼回道，"请躲开些，不要站在我和太阳之间。"亚历山大惊讶不已，当下表示："我要不是亚历山大，必做第欧根尼！"）这个故事足以显出第欧根尼桀骜不驯的个性。

对于 lantern，参赛者大都译成"灯笼"，但这一称呼容易让人联想到中国的"大红灯笼"，故不如译为"提灯"。

streets 是复数，由于中文字词本身形式的局限，这时可用增译词语来表述，如 The <u>dishes</u> were passed and emptied, as were the <u>jugs</u> of yellow cider.（<u>一盘盘</u>菜肴端了上来，上一盘吃光一盘；<u>一瓶瓶</u>苹果酒也是一样，上一瓶喝光一瓶。），此处为表现第欧根尼到处寻找的情景，不妨用"踏遍……大街小巷"。

故整句可译为："古希腊著名哲学家、犬儒学派代表人物第欧根尼手持提灯，踏遍雅典大街小巷，寻觅诚实人。"

对于[2]，参赛译文有"这一切发生在2000年以前，但是我擅自揣测一下，戴奥真尼斯在每一次探索中都收效甚微""这虽然已经是两千多年前的事了，但我敢说，即便是在今天，第奥奇尼斯同样也难以找到这样一个人""若在今日，他的这番寻找很可能和二千多年前一样，无所收获"等，其中下画线部分显然都有"过度翻译成分"（something over translated）。关于这种"诚实人"到底找到没有，文中没有说，但其实并不重要，重要的是这一动作本身的象征意义。

至于presume的本义，为to suppose that something is true, although you do not have actual proof，故有"倘若"之意。

此处的little不是small or of less than average size，故little success不是"一点儿/一些成功"，而是hardly or not at all，类似little chance、little hope等，如：1. The doctors agreed to let the illness run its course, rather than prescribe drugs which had little chance of success.（医生认同此病只能顺其自然，不用那些几乎没有什么疗效的药。）2. He told me that he held out very little hope for this experiment.（他告诉我，他对这次试验不抱什么希望。）。因而，该句不妨译为："此为两千余年前之事，若在当今，料他会空手而归。"

[3] 中的mortal不是moral，此处含义为a human, not a god or spirit，即"普通人""一般人""世人"，mortal character可译为"人的特点""人性"等。

而an integral weakness，若译成"完整的弱点""人的品性中不可分割的弱点"等，则显然过于拘泥，而译为"每个凡人骨子里的弱点"便生动很多，此处实则指性格的一部分。

　　brash一般英汉词典解释为"无礼的、傲慢的、仓促的、性急的"，但不宜照搬，应加变通，如"敢于"。

　　partial untruth，是"部分的真相"？"一部分真实"？意思似乎不错，但还不免有些翻译腔。

　　同时，对于其中的标点符号，也不必原封照搬："撒谎似乎已成普遍人性缺陷。我不禁怀疑，是否有人敢坦言生活中从未说过假话，哪怕是遮遮掩掩？"

　　[4] 中，theorize是动词，为to conceive of something in a theoretical way，即对某事从理论上找原因，如：1. The sleeping brain, they theorize, is vastly capable of synthesizing complex information.（他们的理论根据是，睡眠的大脑对合成复杂信息具有非常强的能力。）2. Some scientists now can theorize that endocrine-disrupting chemicals in the environment also can reduce fertility.（现在一些科学家可用理论说明，环境中存在的扰乱内分泌的化学成分还会降低怀孕几率。）。

　　Perhaps so.看起来是陈述句，但其中也不乏疑问因素。

　　而so far as to不是到很远的地方（去建立语言学说），而是"甚至""以至于"之意，表程度，如：1. Actually, the techniques should not only be studied systematically, I'd go so far as to call it a science.（事实上，这门技艺不但应系统地学习，我甚至认为它是一门科学。）2. He went so far as to say that he would give up his life for the poor girl.（他甚至说他愿意为这可怜的姑娘献出生命。）。

对于"It is certainly true that animals seem somewhat more honest than humans, maybe because they are less gifted mentally.",大都按其顺序翻译,比如"动物看似比人类更诚实,也许是因其智商不如人类""动物似乎比人类更加诚实,这可能是因为它们的智力不如人类""动物往往比人类更诚实,大抵是因为智力水平不如人类"等,其实可将其因果关系调整,以示强调,如"正因……,所以……"。因而,该部分不妨译为:"更有语言学家探究其理论依据,认为语言的发明实乃为行骗——大概如此?或许,正因动物不及人类智力发达,所以比人更加诚实。"

[5]中的主要问题有两个。一是end,此处为目的,如同aim、goal、purpose、target、object、objective等,如:1. But that was not the end of the matter for him.(然而,那并非他的最终目的。)2. Many families struggle to make ends meet.(许多家庭只能勉强维持生计。)。二是denied,许多人译成了"拒绝""否定",但该词还有其泛化的意思,如:1. The opportunity has denied him.(他失去了这一机会。)2. Kids are denied to enter.(儿童免入。)故to gain an end that would otherwise be denied them意思是,(说谎人)不说谎就达不到目的。

对于do not know the differences between fact and fancy,似乎难以译得比较得体,如"分不清现实与幻境之间的差距",到底指的是什么?其实,此处不妨将思路拓展一些,例如,考虑到并非所有谎言都是恶意的。在社会心理学(social psychology)里有一种"善意谎言"(white lies),即不是为了自己利益而是出于善待对方而说出(做出)的与事实不符的话(举动),有时需富想象力。例如,对于患有绝症的病人,并未突然告知其真实病情,以顾及其精神承受力;告诉小朋友们"小猫咪终于回家找妈妈去了",以避免在不适当的年龄段和孩子们讨论死亡的话题;给家里老人买礼物,把价钱说得很低,以免他们心疼,等等。就此,让人自然联想到美国著名作家欧·亨利(O. Henry)在《最后一片叶子》(The Last Leaf)里描述的一个情节:生病的穷学生望着窗外凋零的树叶,认为当最后一片叶子掉落时,便是自己生命的终结,于是那位充满爱心的老画家每天精心画一片绿叶挂在树上,以期维持那盏即将熄灭的生命之光……这可说是一种极致的美丽谎言了。但是,这当中有着微妙的界限(fine line)。在利人与损人之间,有时只有毫厘之差。

有感于此,该部分不妨译为:"人们为何要说谎?——为了突显自己?躲避惩罚?舍此无以为计?习惯成自然?抑或,难以把握真假分寸?"

翻译,有时看似只言片语,但深入下去,可思接千载,视通万里,有一种时空穿越的感悟。

参考译文

寻觅诚实人

[1] 古希腊著名哲学家、犬儒学派代表人物第欧根尼手持提

灯，踏遍雅典大街小巷，寻觅诚实人。

[2] 此为两千余年前之事，若在当今，料他会空手而归。

[3] 撒谎似乎已成普遍人性缺陷。我不禁怀疑，是否有人敢坦言生活中从未说过假话，哪怕是遮遮掩掩？

[4] 更有语言学家探究其理论依据，认为语言的发明实乃为行骗——大概如此？或许，正因动物不及人类智力发达，所以比人更加诚实。

[5] 人们为何要说谎？——为了突显自己？躲避惩罚？舍此无以为计？习惯成自然？抑或，难以把握真假分寸？

31

> 原 文

A Year

By Adhish Mazumder

[1] A lot can be changed in a span of a year. A thousand lives can be moulded, a lot many lessons can be learnt and life can show its unpredictability.

[2] Even so, one year is enough to prove to yourself that you are worth the struggle that you undertake just to reap a momentary fruit of that labour.

[3] If fighting a new fight keeps us motivated each year, so be it.

[4] Here is wishing every fighter, struggling to make a break and succeed in life a memorable New Year.

[5] Do what you do best and don't trade your passion for fame but rather earn the fame through your passion.

[6] May your fight be fruitful this year and your name engraved in hearts of horde in the form of your work.

> 译 析

阿迪施·马宗达（Adhish Mazumder）是印度学者和专栏作

家,该选文以格言式的话语表达了一份祝愿,鼓励青年人在新的一年有所作为。

对于[1],参赛者一般译得比较"实",如"在一年的时间里,很多东西都可以改变。一千条生命可以被塑造,可以学到很多很多的教训,生活也可以显示出它的不可预见性。""诸多事物皆可在一年之内被改变。千万生灵可以被塑造,很多教训可以被学到,生活会显示它的不可预知性。""一年之际,很多东西会发生变化。上千条生命能得以塑造,能得到很多教训,而生命则向我们展示了它的变幻莫测。""一年光阴可带来巨变。成百生命塑造成形,上千课程得到学习,生活的多变性显露无遗。",等等。其实,这里强调时间是一种相对的变量;一年虽短,但仍会发生许多事情,甚至不可预测,言简意赅,表明即可。该部分不妨译为:"一年之中,会有许多变化;千般生活,万种教训——事事难以预料。"

[2]中,许多人将struggle译成"斗争""战斗""争战"等,实际这里可变通为"努力",如It's a constant struggle to try to keep them up to par.(要让他们达标,需不断努力。)。而momentary,参赛者一般译成了"暂时的""片刻的""瞬间的",但此处指经过个人辛劳所取得的那份成果,所以不必过于拘泥,故整句不妨译为:"即便如此,一年时间也足以证明你为获得那份转瞬即逝的劳动果实所付出的努力是值得的。"

[3]中,fighting a new fight,许多人译成了"进入/参加一次新的战斗"等,其实就一般人的日常生活而言,"投入新的任务"更宜;而整句多被译成"如果每场新的战斗让我们每年都有动

力，那就这样吧"等，其中的 ...so be it 因具体语境的不同，会有多种意思，特别是语气，如：1. If he doesn't want to be involved, then so be it.（他要是不想参与，就随他便吧。）2. If this is also commercialization at a remove, so be it.（如果这也是该阶段的商品化过程，那就顺其自然吧。）3. You destroyed our barracks. So be it. I will destroy yours.（你毁了我们的兵营，好吧，我也会毁了你们的。）4. Now to God our Father be glory for ever and ever. So be it!（愿荣耀归于我们的父神，直到永永远远，阿门！）5. Budget deficits will end at levels previously considered unimaginable. So be it.（最终预算赤字将升至以前被认为不可想象的水准，那又何妨。）。

对于 ... keeps us motivated，有参赛者译成"使我们年年保持动力""让我们斗志昂扬"等。motivate 固然可以译成"（使有）动力"，如 People will be expecting to learn something from us and this will keep us motivated.（人们期待从我们这里学到一些东西，这将成为我们的动力。），但有时也可变通，如：1. Now more than ever, organizations must be proactive and have the right strategies in place to keep employees motivated.（对机构来说，现在比以往任何时候都需要发挥积极主动性，并制定正确的策略激励员工。）2. 最好找一个能激励你坚持锻炼的时间。(It is best to find the time of day that is going to keep you motivated.)。有时未必出现"激励"一词，只是含有其意，如：明确最终目标，才能干劲十足。(Focusing on the end goal can keep you motivated.)。故此句语气不妨强烈一些："如果每年投入新的任务可以激励我们的

话，那何乐不为！"

[4]中，接续前面而言，fighter不一定是"战斗者""斗士"等，而宜译为"奋斗者"。... to make a break，有近似breakthrough的意思，如：1. Meet the challenge, and make a breakthrough.（迎接挑战，有所突破。）2. They wish he would make a break for it so that the problem could be sold out.（他们希望他能打破僵局，从而使问题迎刃而解。）。同时，succeed和memorable也可作相应的变通："在此祝福那些努力在生活中有所作为、有所建树的奋斗者，新年有成！"

[5]中，许多人将do what you do best与do your best相混淆，后者是"尽力而为"之意，如：1. Do your best to come to me quickly.（你要赶紧到我这里来。）2. 我会尽力帮助你的。（I will do my best to help you.）而前者则为"做你拿手、擅长的"，如：1. Do what you do best and outsource the rest!（做你最擅长的，其余的外包！）2. What do you do best?（什么是你最拿手的？）。

对于don't trade your passion for fame but rather earn the fame through your passion，应当说比较难译，因为很容易译得自相矛盾或分辨不明，如有的参赛者译成"不用自己的热情换取名声，而是用自己的热情博取名声"，其中"博取"意为"用言语、行动取得（信任、重视等）：博取欢心、博取同情"（《现代汉语词典》），也并非褒义词；还有的译成"不要用你的激情去交换名望，而要通过你的激情去获得名望"，其实广义而言，"获得"也是一种"交换"（如以时间、劳动、努力等获得的），故还应有更大程度的区别。问题出在对两个fame的处理，如可将前一个译为"虚名",后一个译为"美誉",同时将两个passion作相应调整。在英汉翻译中,这种对于同一词语的交错、变通处理,也是"动态等值"的一种技巧。如You may have troubled yourself when there are actually no troubles,其中后面的troubles是名词,意为"烦事""险事""问题"等,而前面的troubled为动词,有"烦扰""扰乱"之意,故该句可译为:"天下本无事,庸人自扰之。"再如He is simply adding numbers to years but not years to numbers.(他不过是在经年累月地混日子,而并未使生活更有意义。),其中两个numbers和years都译成了不同的词。在汉译英中,例如毛泽东的一句诗词"不爱红装爱武装",其中的"红装"与"武装",既要注重原意,又要顾及双关语和音韵的效果,应当说翻译起来有相当难度。有翻译家认为可选择powder,因为该词作为名词有"火药"之意,如The smell of powder was in the air there.(那里充满了火药味——寓意要开战了。)作为动词,powder又有涂粉、化妆之意,如It takes ages to powder her face before going out.(她出门前且要打扮一番呢。)。该句诗词若译为"They prefer to face the powder but not to powder the face.",可较为巧妙地吻合原文。故此,句[5]不妨译为:"做你所擅长的;莫以激情求虚名,但凭热忱得美誉。"

[6]中,参赛译文大都译得比较冗赘,如"希望这一年,你的奋斗有所收获,你的名字以你的作品的形式铭记在众人心中""在新的一年里,愿你的奋进能硕果累累,愿你名字能因你的成就而为众人铭记""祝愿你今年硕果累累,你的名字因你的努力而镌刻在人们的心中"等。其实,如前所述,因该段是表

达"祝愿",难免有些套词赘语,不必"一一兑现",而重在传情达意:其中的May表心愿,如May I wish you every success for the future.(祝你前途无量,马到成功!)。而in the form of your work指其未来工作,亦为"业绩",但不必"具体落实",如They received a benefit in the form of a tax reduction.(他们获得了减税优惠。),不必译成"以减税形式获得了优惠"。your name engraved in hearts of horde字面意为"你的名字会铭记于大众之心",但实际为"长留下来"。至于有的参赛者译成"愿你非凡表现艳惊世界——扬名中外""名留青史"等,显然有些用力过猛,不是祝愿每个人时都需这样高调,以致会有适得其反的效果。故此,该句可简化为:"愿你今年硕果累累,业绩长留!"

可见,原文的"言"为其表,"意"为其里,译者只有善于"得其意而忘其言",才能让译文更加准确、恰当。

参考译文

一年之中

阿迪施·马宗达

[1] 一年之中,会有许多变化;千般生活,万种教训——事事难以预料。

[2] 即便如此,一年时间也足以证明你为获得那份转瞬即逝

的劳动果实所付出的努力是值得的。

[3] 如果每年投入新的任务可以激励我们的话，那何乐不为！

[4] 在此祝福那些努力在生活中有所作为、有所建树的奋斗者，新年有成！

[5] 做你所擅长的；莫以激情求虚名，但凭热忱得美誉。

[6] 愿你今年硕果累累，业绩长留！

32

原 文

What You Learn from the Games

[1] The Olympic Winter Games are a major international sporting event held once every four years for sports practiced on snow and ice.

[2] The Winter Games have evolved since their inception. Sports and disciplines have been added and some of them, such as Alpine skiing, luge, short track speed skating, freestyle skiing, skeleton, and snowboarding, have earned a permanent spot on the Olympic programme.

[3] Some others, including curling and bobsleigh, have been discontinued and later reintroduced.

[4] Canadian champion rower Silken Laumann once said, "It's important to know that at the end of the day it's not the medals you remember. What you remember is the process—what you learn about yourself by challenging yourself, the experiences you share with other people, the honesty the training demands—those are things nobody can take away from you whether you finish twelfth or you're an Olympic Champion."

译 析

奥运会（包括冬夏两季）是最著名的国际运动会，其意义和影响其实已经超过体育赛事本身，这使得有关内容的阅读和翻译别有意义。

[1] 中，有 international sporting event、once every four years、snow and ice 等要素，译文要考虑如何将其合理、通顺地组织起来，参赛译文中较为典型的，如"冬奥会是每四年举办一次的冰雪运动的重要国际体育赛事""奥林匹克冬季运动会是每四年举办一次的在雪和冰上进行的国际主要赛事"等，其中似乎具备所有要素，但读起来过于冗长，难以通顺，主要问题出在定语。众所周知，英文多长句，中文善短句，特别是对于定语的处理，要注意"分化"。如 The police are concerned for the safety of the 12-year-old boy who has been missing for three days，若译成"警方对那个已失踪三天的12岁男孩的安全感到担忧"，便会读来不畅，不如根据中文表述习惯，将其分解、调整为"那个12岁的男孩失踪三天了，警方对他的安全感到担忧"。就本句而言，其语法结构为：The Olympic Winter Games（主语）are（谓语）a major international sporting event（宾语），后面的 held once every four years for sports practiced on snow and ice 均为定语，不宜刻板地按原文语序排列翻译，而不妨将其变通为："冬季奥林匹克运动会是一项重要的国际冰雪体育赛事，每四年举行一次。"同时，又要注意另一个极端，如"冬季奥运会是一个重要的国际运动

赛事，并于每四年举办一次，以在冰雪上运动为主""冬奥会每隔四年举行一次，它是国际上的体育盛事，是冰与雪上的体育盛会"等，显然又过于零碎，且多赘语（如下画线部分）。

此外，应注意的是，专业名词（如 The Olympic Winter Games）第一次出现时应以正规的全称形式（如"冬季奥林匹克运动会"，而不是"冬奥会"），以后再次出现可简略。

[2] 中，since their inception 是时间状语，以中文习惯，一般放在前面。对于 evolved，有参赛者译成了"演化""进化""推断"等，显然是拘泥于词典的解释，而实际是指一种"发展变化"；earned a permanent spot，许多人译成了"永久的位置""不变的项目"等，其实，这里应根据体育赛事来理解，如 Wayne Rooney smashed home a penalty to spark a second-half comeback against Arsenal, and says he'll now take the role of permanent spot kick taker.（韦恩·鲁尼下半场打进点球，点燃了主队的反攻浪潮，最终逆转阿森纳；现在他将成为曼联正式的点球手。）。特别是结合后面的 the Olympic programme，便不难看出，这里指的是"冬奥会的永久项目"，故此句不妨译为："自建立之日起，冬奥会便不断发展变化，比赛项目不断增加，其中的一些，如高山滑雪、雪橇、短道速滑、自由式滑雪、钢架雪车、单板滑雪等，成为冬奥会的永久项目。"

补充说明一点，[2] 中的 sports and disciplines 有不少参赛者翻错，多数错在把这里的 disciplines 理解成了"规则"。请看这段摘自维基百科 Olympic sports 条目的英文解释，一目了然：The International Olympic Committee (IOC) establishes a hierarchy of sports, disciplines, and events. According to this hierarchy, the Olympic sports can be subdivided into multiple disciplines, which are often assumed to be distinct sports. Examples include swimming and water polo (disciplines of aquatics, represented by the International Swimming Federation), or figure skating and speed skating (disciplines of skating, represented by the International Skating Union). In their turn, disciplines can be subdivided into events, for which medals are actually awarded. 故而，这里直接译作"比赛项目"即可。

[3] 中，将 discontinued and later reintroduced 译成"时断时续""被停赛后又重新引进了""它们曾一度被中止比赛，现今又重新被纳入比赛项目"等，严格讲，都有不确切之处；同时，这里还应体现出 have been... and later 的先后顺序。故此句不妨译为："有些项目，如冰壶和雪车，曾一度取消，后又恢复。"

[4] 中，许多参赛者似乎被 It's important to know 所困扰，如译成"重要的是要知道""知道这些是非常重要的"等，特别是其中的 important，是否一定要译成"重要的"？其实未必，例如：1. It's important to know that the three days you spend checking stats add up, and you end up not getting much done.（要知道花费三天时间查阅数据会是什么代价！到头来你会觉得得不偿失。）2. Even if you hire someone else to handle the low-level implementation, it's important to know what you're getting into.（即使你雇人处理这些低端事务，你也要对此有所掌控。），可见其意在强调，可以用相关词语和标点符号体现，如"须知"即可；但若译成"要知道，其实到最后重要的不是你记得的那些奖牌，而是你记住的那些过

程"则意思又有些变化,成了"你应当记住……"的教诲口吻。

对 at the end of the day,若译成"在最后一天""在一天末了""在结束的时候""在赛程的最后一天"等,显然过于拘泥,其实该短语为"最终""最后"之意,如:1. At the end of the day, he'll still have to make his own decision.(最终,他毕竟还得自己拿主意。) 2. So we cannot cheat death because at the end of the day death always wins.(所以,我们并不能愚弄死亡,因为在生命的尽头,死亡会战胜一切。)。

对 the honesty the training demands 中的 honesty,许多人译成了"(培训所要求的)诚实",似乎没错,但读来别扭;其实该词(包括其形容词 honest)有多种含义,如 by honest labor(下笨功夫)、an honest countryside(地道的乡村)、honest work（认真工作)等,所以这里也不妨相应作些变通;而 nobody can take away from you,很容易译成"没人从你这里夺走""这些东西都是没人能够从你身上拿走的"等,都过于字面化,这里可更自然地译为"非你莫属"。后面的 twelfth,参赛者大都译成"第十二""第十二名",其实这是一个笼统的说法,因第十名之后的成绩可谓"出局"了,当然也不是"最后一名",故可不必译得那么实。就句式而言,许多人按原文译成了两句,如"……不是你所记住的奖牌。你所记住的是……""你记住的不是你的奖牌。你记住的是……"等,其实这里可以打通处理。类似的,如美国前总统尼克松在1972年访华时说过一句名言:What we say here will not be long remembered. What we do here will change the world. 这看似两句话,在中文里实为一句,宜用

"不是……，而是……"的句式，译为："我们在这里所讲的话人们不会长久记住，我们在这里所做的事却能改变世界。"这样处理更加自然、通顺。

故此，该段不妨译为："加拿大赛艇冠军西尔肯·劳曼曾说：'须知，最终留在记忆中的不是你所获得的奖牌，而是拼搏奋斗的历程，其中既有挑战自我引发的感悟、与他人分享的经历，也有认真艰苦的训练——这些才非你莫属，无论你是获得奥运冠军还是榜上无名'。"

体育是生活的一部分，其中蕴含了对生命的磨炼与体验；而其相关的论述，尽管短小，亦体现出翻译中某些普遍性问题。

参考译文

运动所得

[1] 冬季奥林匹克运动会是一项重要的国际冰雪体育赛事，每四年举行一次。

[2] 自建立之日起，冬奥会便不断发展变化，比赛项目不断增加，其中的一些，如高山滑雪、雪橇、短道速滑、自由式滑雪、钢架雪车、单板滑雪等，成为冬奥会的永久项目。

[3] 有些项目，如冰壶和雪车，曾一度取消，后又恢复。

[4] 加拿大赛艇冠军西尔肯·劳曼曾说:"须知,最终留在记忆中的不是你所获得的奖牌,而是拼搏奋斗的历程,其中既有挑战自我引发的感悟、与他人分享的经历,也有认真艰苦的训练——这些才非你莫属,无论你是获得奥运冠军还是榜上无名。"

33

原 文

The Sunrise

By Miriam C. Daum

[1] My friend Bill and I shivered in the predawn of a frigid winter day. We stood on a high cliff edge, facing east to watch the sunrise. A few stars still twinkled in the black sky when we arrived, but soon the first hints of lighter blue proclaimed that night was, indeed, retreating. Slowly, the blues were joined by soft pinks that found wispy clouds drifting by.

[2] Across the lower sky were faint peach and lavender brush strokes, as if some celestial painter were experimenting and not quite sure which pigments to choose. We watched the horizon intently, trying to guess where the sun would emerge. Suddenly, Bill pointed to one small area of brilliant orange-red.

[3] First, a bright tip appeared. The tip became an arc crowing a definite sphere as if that celestial painter had decided, "Yes, this is what I want". Now the glowing ball expanded quickly, rising like a helium balloon. Other colors diffused away like those of ethereal dreams chased off by awakening day. Finally, orange-red became an

intense yellow-gold—too brilliant to look at. It was full-fledged day in all its shiny brightness.

译 析

本文节选自 Nature Raises and Lowers the Curtain，原刊载于 2005 年 2 月 2 日的《基督教科学箴言报》(*The Christian Science Monitor*)，作者为米丽亚姆·C. 多姆（Miriam C. Daum）为该报撰稿人，擅长景物散文创作，著有 A Tree as Old as Honest Abe, Dandelions: Cheery Signs of Spring 等。

该文笔调清新、自然、细腻，娓娓道来，看似平常，但翻译好了并不容易。这里的"好"，首先是对文章基调的把握，其次是形容恰当，再次是精练。以下是简要分析。

[1] 中 My friend Bill and I shivered in the predawn of a frigid winter day，对英文的状语 in the predawn of a frigid winter day 应根据中文表达习惯作相应调整，否则就很别扭，如有同学所译"我和朋友 Bill 在一个冰冷的冬日黎明前夕瑟瑟发抖"（其中人名 Bill 亦应翻译出来）；A few stars still twinkled in the black sky when we arrived, but soon the first hints of lighter blue proclaimed that night was, indeed, retreating，其中 twinkle 原意为 a rapid change in brightness; a brief spark or flash，可译为"闪烁"；proclaim，一般为"宣告、公布、声明、表明、赞扬"等，但在此处不宜硬套，而应作适当变通，如"昭示""暗示""预兆"等又不够准确，不如"标示"；retreating，意为 moving away，有的译为"撤

退""隐去"等,但就"夜色"而言,"褪去""离去"更恰当;同时,语序也要作些调整,故该句不妨译为"我们刚到那里时,黑蒙蒙的天空中还闪烁着些星星,不一会儿,便露出了淡淡的蓝色,标示着夜色的离去"。Slowly, the blues were joined by soft pinks that found wispy clouds drifting by, 此句并不难,一般都可译出,但缺文采者多,如"慢慢地,这些浅蓝色与漂浮过来的粉红色云层相融合""慢慢地,那蓝色的微光中融进些许柔和的粉,映着朵朵飘过的薄云"等,不妨参阅:"渐渐地,蓝色中有了柔和的粉色,几抹青云也飘然而过。"

[2] 中 Across the lower sky were faint peach and lavender brush strokes, as if some celestial painter were experimenting and not quite sure which pigments to choose. 其中,across是介词或副词,有的译成"低空""地平线之上"等都不够准确;因中文里有成语"横空出世",故不妨译为"横空之下";faint peach and lavender brush strokes应作为整体看待,为"几笔略带桃红色和紫色的油彩";experimenting表面意思是"实验",但此处语境与画家作画有关,故可译为"(画家正在)调试颜料",整句不妨译为"横空之下,出现了几笔略带桃红色和紫色的油彩,像是天边的某位画家正在调试颜料,还没打定主意用哪种色彩"。

[3] 中 First, a bright tip appeared. The tip became an arc crowning a definite sphere as if that celestial painter had decided, "Yes, this is what I want." 有同学译成"一开始这小片橘色只露出了明亮的顶端,随后便成了一道弧线,明显能看出是球形,仿佛一切在那位神仙画家的计划之中。'太棒了,这正是我想要的理想效

果！'"似乎没有大错，但不够简练，不妨改为"起初，露出了一个亮尖，接着变成了拱形，勾画出了轮廓分明的球体形状，似乎天边画师已经打定了主意：'对，这就是我要的效果！'" Now the glowing ball expanded quickly, rising like a helium balloon. Other colors diffused away like those of ethereal dreams chased off by awakening day. 有同学译成"此时，<u>光球</u>快速膨胀，像氦气球般上升。其他颜色<u>弥散</u>开去，就像<u>觉醒</u>时散去的那些虚无缥缈的梦"，其中加下画线处为不够恰当、明确的词语，故可参考："这时，闪光的球体迅速膨胀，像一只氦气球冉冉而起；其他的颜色随之纷纷退去，像是苏醒了的白日驱散了朦胧的梦境。" Finally, orange-red became an intense yellow-gold—too brilliant to look at. It was full-fledged day in all its shiny brightness, 其中 too brilliant to look at, 是句型 too ...to 意为"太……以至于不能……"，但有些同学没有译出来，如"最后，橙红色的球体变成了明亮耀眼的金黄色。这是一个光线十足的白昼的开端"，且标点符号也有可改进之处，可参考："终于，橘红色变成了浓烈的金黄色，如此耀眼，不可正视——一个光彩四射的白日到来了！"

此次，有两位同学用了文言文，虽有可取之处，但亦多少有点不够准确（由文言文特点所决定），故对此并不提倡。须知，中国近代以来，在文化建设领域，最伟大的进步有两项，即20世纪初"五四"新文化运动中由胡适、陈独秀倡导完成的白话文写作（至今已过百年），和1949年以后，由共产党成功领导的汉字的简化，使得中国文字和文化大大普及了，所以，不能走回头路。作为个人爱好，可以，但作为标准译文，还应以规范的白话文来写作，同时应该避免"半文半白"。相反，对于文言文翻译成英文，倒是应当提倡的；那属于典籍英译专业。

参考译文

日出

米丽亚姆·C.多姆

[1] 在一个寒冷冬天的黎明，我和朋友比尔冻得瑟瑟发抖。我们站在高高的悬崖峭壁旁，面对东方，等着看日出。我们刚到那里时，黑蒙蒙的天空中还闪烁着些星星，不一会儿，便露出了淡淡的蓝色，标示着夜色的离去。渐渐地，蓝色中有了柔和的粉色，几抹青云也飘然而过。

[2] 横空之下，出现了几笔略带桃红色和紫色的油彩，像是天边的某位画家正在调试颜料，还没打定主意用哪种色彩。我们目不转睛地盯着地平线，试图猜出太阳会从哪里升起。霎那间，比尔指向了一小块发出耀眼的橘红色的地方。

[3] 起初，露出了一个亮尖，接着变成了拱形，勾画出了轮廓分明的球体形状，似乎天边画师已经打定了主意："对，这就是我要的效果！"这时，闪光的球体迅速膨胀，像一只氦气球冉冉而起；其他的颜色随之纷纷退去，像是苏醒了的白日驱散了朦胧的梦境。终于，橘红色变成了浓烈的金黄色，如此耀眼，不可正视——一个光彩四射的白日到来了！

34

原 文

The Sunset

By Miriam C. Daum

[1] In the early afternoon Bill phoned. "Can you make it for sunset?" That was an opportunity too good to miss. We were both able to carve out a chunk of time again. A brief climb along a nearby wooded trail brought us to a hilltop that faced west.

[2] Once again we had front-row seats—this time for nature's closing. Slowly daytime brightness muted, changed to softer light. Lavenders, dusky pinks, and blues stained the gauzy clouds. Copper layered into bronze behind winter-bare trees. The sun eased its way downward, melting into the horizon until only a final red arc remained. We watched in silence as day dissolved into nocturnal repose. Remaining bits of bronze sank away from sight. A star or two began twinkling. "The sun moves so quickly now in the short days of winter", I said. "The sun isn't moving", Bill replied. "We are". Of course; I knew that.

[3] Every child learns how Earth rotates toward the sun and away from it. But often we tend to view events relative to ourselves,

with everything revolving around us. Yet it is we, inhabitants of Earth, who traverse the days and seasons of our lives as we rise above the horizon and sink below it, through each dawn and dusk.

译 析

本文节选自"自然的更替"(Nature Raises and Lowers the Curtain),原载于美国《基督教科学箴言报》(*The Christian Science Monitor*)。作者米丽亚姆·C.多姆(Miriam C. Daum)。

总的来讲,大部分同学都能把握描写段落的画面感,形容词与动词方面的词汇量比较丰富,可看出用词造句时作了一定的斟酌和选择。

主要问题是,大都对[1](可能出于语感和思维方式的原因)和[3](未能认真思考文章的逻辑关系)的理解不太到位,从而显得死板;有的则"发挥"过度,不够忠于原文,个别的漏译比较严重,亦有错别字。故建议同学们还要认真、细致地阅读、理解原文,勤查字典,锤炼文字功夫。

具体而言,在[2]中,Once again we had front-row seats—this time for nature's closing,这一句看起来简单,但一落到译文,便会有不少问题,如有同学译成:"我们再一次有了个前排位置,只不过这次是为了与大自然亲近""我们又一次抢占前排,观赏大自然一天的闭幕式""我们又坐在了头排坐席——但这次是为了看自然是如何敛息",等等。这里需要有亲历其境的感觉——在旷野里、山头上、悬崖旁,不是在剧场、电影院,故没有"雅座""前排"之类的；而这里的closing不是亲近，而是concluding section，是结尾、收关之作，故不妨译为："我俩又坐在了悬崖之前，来一睹大自然的落幕。"

接下来，Slowly daytime brightness muted, changed to softer light. Lavenders, dusky pinks, and blues stained the gauzy clouds. Copper layered into bronze behind winter-bare trees. The sun eased its way downward, melting into the horizon until only a final red arc remained，这一段写得很美，译文应尽力再现其"顺"与"雅"，有的同学，看得出来是做了努力，如"彼时，白天耀眼的日光渐渐褪去，傍晚淡淡的柔光悄悄地透迤开来。淡紫色、暗粉色和深蓝色的丝线编织着如烟似雾的绸缎，在那巨幅的紫铜色天幕下摇曳着冬日里光秃秃的枝桠。夕阳沉入了地平线，只留下一抹妖艳的红"，但行文还不够通畅，用词不够准确，如"彼时""光秃秃的枝桠""妖艳的红"等，需进一步自然、精道。参考译文为："日光渐渐暗淡，愈显柔和；紫色、蓝色、暗红色染上了如纱的薄云。透过冬天光秃的树木，黄铜色的云团一层层地变成了青铜色。太阳缓缓下落，融入地平线，只剩最后一道红弧。"

对于We watched in silence as day dissolved into nocturnal repose. Remaining bits of bronze sank away from sight. A star or two began twinkling，有同学译成"我们静谧地凝视安睡的夜。青铜色的余晖无影无踪，唯余稀星闪烁"，意思大致不错，但经不住推敲和玩味，如"静谧地"是形容客观事物的，而不用来形容人或人的感情，同时"唯余……"显得文白夹杂，不够自然流畅。

其中 in silence 是状语,中文里不妨放置句前,译为:"寂静里,我们目送着日头消失在黑夜的睡梦中。青铜色的余辉也逸去了踪影,寥落的星辰开始闪烁。"

在[3]中,Every child learns how Earth rotates toward the sun and away from it. But often we tend to view events relative to ourselves, with everything revolving around us. Yet it is we, inhabitants of Earth, who traverse the days and seasons of our lives as we rise above the horizon and sink below it, through each dawn and dusk,这是作者的借题发挥,引申含义,也是本文的点睛之笔。对此,重要的是须理解正确,然后通顺表达。然而,大部分同学对此不够到位,譬如:"每个孩子都知道地球如何绕着太阳时远时近地旋转。但我们通常更愿意以一种万物都围绕着自己的眼光看待身边的事物。然而正是我们这群地球的居民,不断从地平线升起又落下,随着日出和日落度过我们生命中的每一天,每一个季节,昼出夜伏,寒来暑往"。分析起来,how Earth rotates toward the sun and away from it 并不是指一天中"地球如何绕着太阳时远时近地旋转",这是地理知识的问题,而是指"地球有时面向、有时背向太阳而转动";"昼出夜伏"是指什么?太阳?人?文理不通了。而且,dawn and dusk 指的是"每日的黎明和日暮"这里漏译了;重点词是 seasons of our lives 即"人生的四季",故参考译文为:"每个孩子都明白地球有时面向、有时背向太阳而转动;然而,我们往往认为生活中的事情都同自己相关,一切都围绕着自我转。其实,是我们——地球的居民,爬升到地平线之上,又回落到地平线之下,经历着每日的黎明和日暮,周而复始,度过着人生的四季。"

这里只是作了重点评析,请同学们加以比较、总结,从而有所提高。

参考译文

日落

米丽亚姆·C.多姆

[1] 下午一两点时,比尔打电话来:"你能有时间去看日落吗?"这个好机会岂能错过?我俩自然能再次挤出时间酿成此行。沿着附近的林中小路,向上攀登不久,我们便到达了朝向西面的山顶。

[2] 我俩又坐在了悬崖之前,来一睹大自然的落幕。日光渐渐暗淡,愈显柔和;紫色、蓝色、暗红色染上了如纱的薄云。透过冬天光秃的树木,黄铜色的云团一层层地变成了青铜色。太阳缓缓下落,融入地平线,只剩最后一道红弧。寂静里,我们目送着日头消失在黑夜的睡梦中。青铜色的余辉也逸去了踪影,寥落的星辰开始闪烁。"在昼短夜长的冬天,太阳移动得真快。",我说。"不是太阳在移动,是我们在动。"比尔回答道。我当然知道这一点。

[3] 每个孩子都明白地球有时面向、有时背向太阳而转动;

然而，我们往往认为生活中的事情都同自己相关，一切都围绕着自我转。其实，是我们——地球的居民，爬升到地平线之上，又回落到地平线之下，经历着每日的黎明和日暮，周而复始，度过着人生的四季。

Understanding Travel

By Alain de Botton

[1] If our lives are dominated by a search for happiness, then perhaps few activities reveal as much about the dynamics of this quest—in all its ardor and paradoxes—than our travels.

[2] They express, however inarticulately, an understanding of what life might be about, outside the constraints of work and the struggle for survival. Yet rarely are they considered to present philosophical problems—that is, issues requiring thought beyond the practical.

[3] We are inundated with advice on *where* to travel to; we hear little of *why* and *how* we could be more fulfilled doing so—though the art of travel seems naturally to sustain a number of questions neither so simple nor so trivial and whose study might in modest ways contribute to an understanding of the Greek philosophers beautifully termed *eudaimonia* or human flourishing.

[4] To this end, the tourist industry has become one of the most important economic influences of modern times. Tourism has been

one of the fastest growing industries in recent years. In fact, the growth rate of tourism, including that of both international tourism and internal tourism or domestic tourism, has generally exceeded the growth rate for the worldwide economy. Sometimes it seems as though a new resort area springs up everyday wherever there are sun and sea.

译 析

该文部分取材于 *The Art of Travel*，但有改写。关于题目的翻译，Understanding Travel，参赛者给出了各种译文，如"领悟旅行""感知旅行""旅行之我见""小议旅行""对旅行的认识""旅行浅解"等，都有一定道理。但是，要找到最确切的答案，还应对作者和作品有所了解。对此，与其去找现成的译文，不如去找些相关的背景材料。例如，关于该书的介绍：The Art of Travel is a philosophical look at the ubiquitous but peculiar activity of travelling 'for pleasure', with thoughts on airports, landscapes, museums, holiday romances, photographs, exotic carpets and the contents of hotel mini-bars. The book mixes personal thought with insights drawn from some of the great figures of the past. Unlike existing guidebooks on travel, it dares to ask what the point of travel might be—and modestly suggests how we could learn to be less silently and guiltily miserable on our journeys. 而该书作者阿兰·德波顿（Alain de Botton）原是一名大学哲学教师，善于逻辑推理，

爱好旅游，可谓读万卷书，行万里路，这使他的旅行作品富有哲理性和思辨性。故该题目不妨译为"对旅行的理解""旅行之我见"等。

在[1]中，对dominated一词，许多参赛者译成"主宰""统治""控制"等，如"对幸福的求索主宰着我们的生活"等，显然是太囿于字典含义了，而翻译时应根据具体语境来处理。如It wasn't a real library, of course, it was just a small den dominated by a television set（当然，它只是一个放电视的小房间，并不是一个真正的图书馆）；Many Europeans have grown up in corporatist systems, dominated by trade unions, employers' groups and politicians（许多欧洲人成长都离不开社团体制，比如工会、雇主协会及政客们）等，都没有死板地翻译。

接下来，perhaps few activities reveal as much about the dynamics of this quest—in all its ardor and paradoxes—than our travels，实际是将句子有意识拆开了，若还原成这样可能更好理解一些：perhaps few activities reveal as much about the dynamics of this quest than our travels in all its ardor and paradoxes，所以这样写，是一种个人的表达方式，也是为了强调某一部分。而许多同学为此被迷惑了，翻译得很别扭或有错误，如："几乎没有其他活动能够像旅行一样体现出寻求幸福的动力——这一过程中的热情和矛盾""那也许没有什么活动——在同样的热忱和矛盾方面，比旅行更能揭示这种需求的力度了""那么可能几乎没有什么活动可以像旅行一样充满热情与矛盾地让我们去追求动态感"等。其实，可以将整句在准确理解的基础上，前后连贯起来翻译:"如果说生活的目的在于追求幸福的话,那么很少有其他活动能像旅游那样焕发出我们的热情,同时也暴露出矛盾。"

在[2]中,They express, however inarticulately 指对这一题目的相关论述是不尽如人意的(inarticulately),如被译成"它们十分清晰地表达了除去工作的约束以及生存的挣扎外是怎样理解人生的""旅行能够清晰地表达出一些认知""然而人们言之凿凿地表达自己对生活的理解"等,显然意思是相反了。结合后面的,其整句不妨译为:"无论表述得多么含混,旅游仍可理解为在紧张工作和辛苦谋生之外的另一种生活。"下句中又出现了破折号,于是许多同学翻译成"然而人们很少将其上升到哲学层面上来——哲学问题对思考的要求比实践更甚""很少人把旅行上升为一种哲学问题——一种需要思考,并超越现实的问题"等。其实,由于中英两种语言的不同,翻译中可不必保持对等的标点符号,而应根据译文的表达习惯,尽量自然、通顺,如"还是很少有人能考虑一些超越现实的哲学意义上的问题"。

在[3]中,对于 inundated 许多译成了"淹没""埋没"等,实际是"大量""过多""充足"之意,如 People are inundated with a myriad of information each day. (人们每天被大量信息充斥着。); If you try sitting silent for a while, you will probably be inundated with thoughts. (如果你试着安静地坐上一会儿,就可能会沉浸在思维里。)此处,要前后连贯起来考虑:We are inundated with...; we hear little of..., 形成对比,故可译为"我们经常会得到应该

去哪里旅游的建议,但却很少有人告诉我们为什么及怎样才能有更充实的旅行"。后面的 the Greek philosophers beautifully termed *eudaimonia* or human flourishing,其中 or 不是"或者"之意,而是解释前面的词,如 We have to do our best to promote *guo xue re* or "Fever of Studies of Chinese Ancient Culture". (我们要大力促进国学热。)。而 human flourishing 大都被译成"人类昌盛""人类繁荣""人类兴旺"等,不觉得有些怪怪的吗?如前所述,作者善于从哲学角度来思考生活、幸福感等,故不妨译为"……称之为'eudaimonia'的概念,即'人类生活的幸福四溢'"。

在[4]中,许多同学没有理解 To this end,而翻译成"到此为止""直到最后""至此"等,实则为"为此""因此""为此目的",如 To this end, we had accumulated over the years the funds for our daughter to go abroad for preparation. (为此我们多年积累资金,为女儿出国作准备。); China appreciates such a position and is also ready to work with Japan to this end. (中方对此表示赞赏,也愿与日方为此作出共同努力。)等。

对于 Sometimes it seems as though a new resort area springs up everyday wherever there are sun and sea,大都能理解其意,但译文往往不够完整,如"有时好像只要有太阳和大海,每天就会有新的度假区出现",其中"有太阳和大海"后应加上"的地方",而且表明这是在世界各地,尽管没有出现 in the world,但其意尽含其中,故该句不妨译为"有时仿佛在世界各地,只要有阳光和海水的地方,每天便会出现一个旅游景点"。

参考译文

懂得旅行

阿兰·博顿

[1] 如果说生活的目的在于追求幸福的话,那么很少有其他活动能像旅游那样焕发出我们的热情,同时也暴露出矛盾。

[2] 无论表述得多么含混,旅游仍可理解为在紧张工作和辛苦谋生之外的另一种生活;然而,还是很少有人能考虑一些超越现实的哲学意义上的问题。

[3] 我们经常会得到应该去哪里旅游的建议,但却很少有人告诉我们为什么及怎样才能有更充实的旅行,尽管"旅游艺术"涉及一些并不简单或无所谓的问题,但对此的研究仍可在一定意义上帮助人们理解希腊哲人美妙地称之为"eudaimonia"的概念,即"人类生活的幸福四溢"。

[4] 出于这样的理解,旅游业已经成为当今最具经济影响力的行业之一,近年来得到了飞速的发展。实际上,旅游业(包括国际和国内旅游业)的增长率已经超过了世界经济的平均增长率。有时仿佛在世界各地,只要有阳光和海水的地方,每天便会出现一个旅游景点。

36

原 文

A Green Hill Far Away

(Excerpts)

By John Galsworthy

[1] Was it indeed only last March, or in another life, that I climbed this green hill on that day of dolor, the Sunday after the last great German offensive began?

[2] Each day this thought of Peace becomes more and real and blessed. I can lie on this green hill and praise Creation that I am alive in a world of beauty.

[3] And the flight of birds, the gulls and rooks and little brown waving things which flit out and along the edge of the chalk-pits, is once more refreshment to me, utterly untempered.

[4] But if one could gather the deep curses breathed by man and woman upon war since the first bugle was blown, the dirge of them could not be contained in the air which wraps this earth.

[5] It is happiness greater than I have known for four years and four months, to lie here and let that thought go on its wings, quiet and free as the wind stealing soft from the sea, and blessed as the sunlight

on this green hill.

译 析

该文节选自 A Green Hill Far Away，其语来自古希腊诗人忒俄克里托斯（Theocritus）的诗歌，此处有明显的象征意义，用以代表一切美好、没有战争与灾难的理想世界。作者约翰·高尔斯华绥（John Galsworthy，1867—1933），英国小说家和剧作家，1932年获得诺贝尔文学奖。进入牛津攻读法律，毕业后从事文学创作。其主要作品有《法利赛人岛》(The Island Pharisees)、《福尔赛世家》(The Forsyte Saga)、《白猿》(The White Monkey)、《天鹅曲》(Swan Song) 等。

在[1]中，Was it indeed only last March, or in another life, that I climbed this green hill on that day of dolor, the Sunday after the last great German offensive began? 依然是上书的作者将其译成"不仅仅是在那刚刚过去的三月里（难道已恍同隔世），在一个充满痛苦的日子——德国发动它最后一次总攻后的那个星期天，我还登上过这座青山吗？"下画线是问题所在："不仅仅……吗？"问句太长，特别是中间隔有括号、破折号等，难以形成完整意思；而将 in another life 译成"难道已恍同隔世"并在括号中处理，显然没有必要，应尽量避免这种特别方式的表达；同样，后面的"它"亦应删去。故此，该句不妨译为"那是刚刚过去的三月，便恍如隔世！在德国发动了最后总攻后的那个星期天——一个充满痛苦的日子，我还登上过那座青山，不是吗？"

在 [2] 中，Each day this thought of Peace becomes more and real and blessed. I can lie on this green hill and praise Creation that I am alive in a world of beauty. 被译成"这种和平<u>之</u>感正在一天天变得愈益真实<u>和愈益</u>与幸福<u>相连</u>。此刻<u>我已能</u>在这座青山上为自己还能活在这样一个美好的世界而赞美<u>造物</u>"，其中的"之""和愈益""相连""我已能"均可删去，而大写的 Creation，用来特指《圣经》中的"创世记"，如 The Creation of the universe as told in Genesis Chapter One（"创世记"第一章中讲述的上帝创造天地万物），此处可译为上帝所创造的"万物"，而非"造物"。故此段不妨译为："这种和平感每天变得愈加真实与幸福。现在，躺在这座青山上，为自己还能活在这个美好的世界而赞美万物！"

在 [3] 中，将 And the flight of birds, the gulls and rooks and little brown waving things which flit out and along the edge of the chalk-pits, is once more refreshment to me, utterly untempered 译成"天空中各种禽鸟的飞翔，海鸥、白嘴鸦以及那往来徘徊于白垩坑边的<u>棕色小东西再一次成了我的欣慰，它们</u>是那样的自由自在，<u>不受拘束</u>"，其中对于 little brown waving things、refreshment 都译得过"实"，可将其变通为更加通顺、朴实的"棕色水鸟""倍感"等；"它们"可删去；utterly untempered 若译成"自由自在"或"不受拘束"，则可删去其一，避免重复，同时，由于其描述的是那些主语，宜调整词序，将其置前。故此，不妨译为"天空中的鸟群、海鸥、白嘴鸦，还有那徘徊于白垩坑边的棕色水鸟，自由自在，令我倍感欣慰"。

在 [4] 中，But if one could gather the deep curses breathed by

man and woman upon war since the first bugle was blown, the dirge of them could not be contained in the air which wraps this earth 译成"但是如果我们能自那第一声战斗号角之后一切男女对战争所发出的深切诅咒全都聚集起来，那些哀怨之多恐怕连笼罩地面的高空也盛装不下"，其中，man and woman 是"一切男女"？应为"人们"；"深切"意为"深挚而亲切"，故可以"深切怀念"，但不宜"深切诅咒"（deep curses），应为"积怨"；the air which wraps this earth 指的不只是一片笼罩地面的"高空"，实则为整个苍穹（文学夸张形容），而"盛装"亦欠推敲。故此，不妨译为"然而，若能把自那第一声战斗号角吹响后，人们对于战争的积怨汇拢起来，恐怕连苍穹也容纳不下"。

在[5]中，It is happiness greater than I have known for four years and four months, to lie here and let that thought go on its wings, quiet and free as the wind stealing soft from the sea, and blessed as the sunlight on this green hill 译成"这是四年零四个月来我从没有领略过的幸福，现在我躺在草上，把心头的那点不快尽量驱掉，那安详有如海面上轻轻袭来的和风，那幸福有如这座青山的晴光"，其中，依词序"我""现在""我"均可删去，中文里无主语即是指第一人称，如"看到这情景，不禁激动万分"，指的当然是"我"，而"现在""这座"为赘语，应删去；"草""把……驱掉""晴光"过于粗糙，值得打磨。故此，不妨译为"这种幸福，是四年四个月以来从未感受过的。躺在这草坪上，让心头的那点郁闷随风飘去；那份安详有如海上轻抚的和风，那种幸福恰似青山上的一缕霞光"。

显然，译者应当特别注重的是译入语的地道程度与表达效果。

参考译文

远方的青山

（节选）

约翰·高尔斯华绥

[1] 那是刚刚过去的三月，便恍如隔世！在德国发动了最后总攻后的那个星期天——一个充满痛苦的日子，我还登上过那座青山，不是吗？

[2] 这种和平感每天变得愈加真实与幸福。现在，躺在这座青山上，为自己还能活在这个美好的世界而赞美万物！

[3] 天空中的鸟群、海鸥、白嘴鸦，还有那徘徊于白垩坑边的棕色水鸟，自由自在，令我倍感欣慰。

[4] 然而，若能把自那第一声战斗号角吹响后，人们对于战争的积怨汇拢起来，恐怕连苍穹也容纳不下。

[5] 这种幸福，是四年四个月以来从未感受过的。躺在这草坪上，让心头的那点郁闷随风飘去；那份安详有如海上轻抚的和风，那种幸福恰似青山上的一缕霞光。

原 文

The Philosopher

By William Somerset Maugham

[1] And here lived a philosopher of repute, the desire to see whom had been to me one of the incentives of a somewhat arduous journey.

[2] He was the greatest authority in China on the Confucian learning. He was said to speak English and German with facility.

[3] On certain days in the week, however, all through the year he opened his doors to such as sought after knowledge, and discoursed on the teaching of Confucius.

[4] He had a body of disciples, but it was small, since the students, for the most part, preferred to his modest dwelling and his severe exhortations the sumptuous buildings of the foreign university and the useful science of the barbarians: with him this was mentioned only to be scornfully dismissed.

[5] From all I heard of him I concluded that he was a man of character.

译 析

该文选自英国现代著名作家毛姆（William Somerset Maugham，1874—1965）的游记《在中国屏风上》（*On A Chinese Screen*），出版于1922年。写的是"清末怪杰"辜鸿铭（1857—1928），他学贯中西，精通英、法、德、日、俄、意、拉丁、希腊、马来九门外语。毛姆慕名而来，对他作了精彩描写。为了增加神秘色彩，作者将访问地点想象成某一山林之处，实则为北京东椿树胡同18号院。

关于题目The Philosopher，一般译成"哲学家"，有的译为"中国哲学家——辜鸿铭"证明是做了功课，而"中国贤人"则相差过远。

[1] 中，repute译为"有名、著名、大名鼎鼎、颇有名望"等都可以；the desire to see whom had been to me one of the incentives of a somewhat arduous journey译成"正是因为想要拜访他，我才会不辞辛劳来到这里"，似乎未尝不可，但作者用了one of the incentives是有意图的，因1920年他一到中国便听人说"可以不看三大殿，一定要见辜鸿铭"，于是他就托朋友写了一封信给辜鸿铭，但不见回复，便几经周折前来拜访，故此意还应有所表示；然"要去拜见他是我此次艰辛之旅中有刺激的愿望之一""前去拜谒这位先生也是我此番略微艰难的旅行的动机之一""前去拜访也是我这段略显艰苦之旅的目的之一"，又显突兀。因而，此段不妨译为："这里住着位著名哲学家，前去拜谒

他，是我此行不计旅途辛劳的一大目的。"

[2] 中，the greatest authority 有的译成"大权威"，过于拘泥于文字，而"……研究领域最有权威的人"又显啰嗦，不如"泰斗、大师"等（但未必是"第一人"）；with facility，一般译成了"精通"，但该词更多是一种能力（ability to learn or do things easily），如 have a great facility for languages（具有语言的天赋），He plays the piano with surprising facility.（他弹奏钢琴神乎其技。），The training has prepared him to fill any post with credit, and to master any subject with facility.（培训使他可胜任任何职位，轻松自如地掌握任何科目。）等，特别是此处与 speak 相结合，应有（可说）"流利……"之意，即 fluently、glibly、spiel off 等，类似的，如 Jane mingled French with English in her conversation, for she used both languages with equal facility.（简说话的时候一会儿用法语，一会儿用英语，两种语言讲得同样流利。）。同时，该两句可合并一句为："他是中国儒学大师，据说可讲流利的英语和德语。"

[3] 中，许多人漏译了 all through the year，只译成"在一周的某些日子里"；discourse，大都译成"谈话""讨论"，一般情况下固然不错，但具体语境亦有不同，如 He made a stirring discourse.（他作了一个激动人心的演讲。），Hegel is the sublime representative of the discourse of knowledge and of university knowledge.（黑格尔是知识的真理论述，以及大学知识的最崇高的代表。），And as Ms. Dubow's book makes plain, public discourse has had an impact on how the courts, at every level, have approached

the fetus.（因为杜博在其书中解释得很清楚，公众舆论已对各级法院如何处理胎儿案产生了影响。）, Much bored by this moral discourse, Georges appeared in his mothers presence with heavy heart and downcast head.（乔治对这种道德教育很反感，他回到母亲身边时，忧心忡忡，耷拉着脑袋。）。所以，此处可译为"教"或"教授"（动词）。

同时，the teaching of Confucius 被译成"孔子的教育"，显然对于 teaching 一词理解片面；该词在此为 a doctrine that is taught，如 the teachings of Jesus（耶稣的教义）、the teachings of Lenin（列宁的学说）、the teachings of the Church（教会的教规），而"孔子的教义"又是什么呢？就是儒学。故此，该句不妨译为："然而，每年他总是在一周的某日，向那些渴求知识的人打开宅门、教授儒学。"

[4] 中，a body of 本义是 a group of persons associated by some common tie or occupation and regarded as an entity，此处指"一群弟子""一批门徒"；it was small, 固然是"人数不多"，但 since the students, for the most part, preferred to his modest dwelling and his severe exhortations the sumptuous buildings of the foreign university and the useful science of the barbarians 被译成"原因是绝大多数的学生，在简朴的居室、严格的劝勉与国外大学华丽的建筑、实用的科学之间，他们更喜欢后者，更偏爱这种野蛮的形式"，显然是受到某些误导。其中，有几个问题：preferred to... 明明是 give a preference to something，怎么会是"更喜欢后者"？如 I prefer to read than watch television.（比起看电视，我更

愿看书。), We prefer cooperation over competition with them.（我们更愿意与他们合作，而不是竞争。), They prefer to bargain with individual clients, for cash.（在现款方面，他们更愿意同散户打交道。）等；severe exhortations 译成"严格的劝勉"属词语搭配不当——"劝勉"是用事理说服、勉励别人，怎么会是"严格的"？当然更不是"严厉的批判"；结合辜鸿铭的性格，此处不妨译为"尖刻词语""激愤之辞"等。同时，将 barbarians 译成"野蛮的"亦不准确，因该词在此不过是泛指西方人（洋人）。当年，有人曾把"夷人"译成 barbarian，但著名汉学家马礼逊（Robert Morrison, 1782—1834）在其编纂的中国最早的《华英字典》(*A Dictionary of the Chinese Language*)中却译为 foreigner。

众所周知，辜鸿铭虽精通西学，却更重国学，认为中国文化更有深度，他在英文著作 *The Spirit of the Chinese People*（《中国人的精神》）前言中写道："... the American people if they will study the Chinese civilization, will get depth; the English, broadness; the Germans, simplicity; and all of them, Americans, English and Germans by the study of the Chinese civilization, of Chinese books and literature, will get a quality of mind which, I take the liberty of saying here that it seems to me, they all of them, as a rule, have not to a preeminent degree, namely, delicacy. The French people finally, by the study of the Chinese civilization, will get all, —depth, broadness, simplicity and a still finer delicacy than the delicacy which they now have. Thus the study of the Chinese civilization, of Chinese books and literature will, I believe, be of benefit to all the people of

Europe and America."(若学习中国文明,美国人会变得深沉,英国人会博大,德国人会质朴。通过学习中国文明、典籍、文学,此三国人可得到一种精神升华——恕我冒昧,在我看来,他们通常还未能达到如此"优雅"程度。至于法国人,他们若学习中国文明,除获得上述所有素质外,他们的优雅将更加得体。所以,在我看来,研究中国文明、典籍、文学将使所有欧美人士受益匪浅。)可作为理解此段文字的注脚。

综合而言,此段不妨译为:"他有些弟子,但人数不多,他们大都喜欢他那简朴的住宅、他对外国大学豪华建筑及那些洋人'实用科学'的激愤之辞;而每每谈及这些,他又会不屑一顾地淡而处之。"

对于[5],典型的翻译,如"从我所听到的一切来看,我断定他是一个有品格的人""从我听闻的一切中,我可以断定,他是一个有骨气的人""通过这些传闻,我断定:他个性非凡""从我打听到的消息来看,我认为他并非寻常人物""从我了解到关于他的一切消息中,我断定他是一个品格高尚的人"等。其中,heard of 不一定永远是"听说",如 I haven't heard of it.(我对此不得而知。),My mother heard of this school through Leslie.(我母亲是从莱斯利那里知道这所学校的。),After his beating Colin ran away and hasn't been heard of since.(科林被他打了一顿后就离家出走了,从此杳无音讯。)等;a man of character,在不同的语境会有不同的意思,此处结合辜氏性格,宜译为"有个性的人"。类似的,如"从相貌看他很有个性"(From his looks, I'd say he's a man of character)。因而,此句不妨译为:"从各方面对他的了解，我认为他是个有个性的人。"

辜鸿铭的确是中国近代史上的一个奇才，据说当年在李鸿章接见外宾的招待会上，他一个人为七国公使当翻译。1928年去世后，当时的内阁总理唐绍仪说，没能为辜举行国葬是件憾事。

对于此次翻译，有的同学认真查找资料，并作注释，值得称道。其实，翻译的过程也是学习、研究的过程，从而使自己在知识和技能上都有所提高。

参考译文

哲学家

威廉·萨默塞特·毛姆

[1] 这里住着位著名哲学家，前去拜谒他，是我此行不计旅途辛劳的一大目的。

[2] 他是中国儒学大师，据说可讲流利的英语和德语。

[3] 然而，每年他总是在一周的某日，向那些渴求知识的人打开宅门、教授儒学。

[4] 他有些弟子，但人数不多，他们大都喜欢他那简朴的住宅、他对外国大学豪华建筑及那些洋人"实用科学"的激愤之辞；而每每谈及这些，他又会不屑一顾地淡而处之。

[5] 从各方面对他的了解，我认为他是个有个性的人。

原文

An Invisible Hand

By Adam Smith

[1] Every individual is continually exerting himself to find out the most advantageous employment for whatever capital he can command. It is his own advantage, indeed, and not that of the society, which he has in view.

[2] By generally, indeed, neither intends to promote the public interest, nor knows how much he is promoting it.

[3] By preferring the support of domestic to that of foreign industry, he intends only his own security; and by directing that industry in such a manner as its produce may be of the greatest value, he intends only his own gain, and he is in this, as in many other cases, led by an invisible hand to promote an end which was no part of his intention.

[4] Nor is it always the worse for the society that it was no part of it. By pursuing his own interest he frequently promotes that of the society more effectually than when he really intends to promote it.

译 析

选文摘自英国古典经济学家亚当·斯密（Adam Smith）的名著《国富论》（*The Wealth of Nations*），该书全称为《国民财富的性质和原因的研究》（*An Inquiry into the Nature and Causes of the Wealth of Nations*），首版于1776年。该文提出了经济学中的一个重要论点：人的本性是利己的，追求个人利益是人们从事经济活动的唯一动力；同时，作为理性的经济人，经由价格机制中"看不见的手"的作用，人们不仅会实现个人利益的最大化，还会推进公共利益。

关于题目An Invisible Hand，不少参赛者译成"一只看不见的手"，其实英文中的这种不定冠词，许多情况下不必刻意译出，如Try to get a feeling for the people who live there（试着去理解生活在那里的人们）；The room with a view of the sea（有海景的房间）；It is used to make a smoke screen or to mark a position（这用来制造烟雾或标志位置）（下画线均为笔者所加）。故该标题译为"看不见的手"即可。

[1] 中，exert的本义是to make a great physical or mental effort, or work hard to do something better，而exert himself，为"尽其所能"，如He must exert himself to subdue so proud a display of resentment.（他必须尽可能地克服这种因忌恨而产生的骄傲。）；It thus stimulates everybody, within the system of the social division of labor, to exert himself to the utmost.（因此这个社会分工体系会

激励每个人去尽其所能。)。文中的employment，不是"雇佣"，而是"用途"；command并非"指挥"，而是"掌握""掌控"；in view很多人译成"他所看到的""他眼中的""其心中所想的"等，显然表述得不够确切，不如"所考虑的"。典型的参赛译文，如"每个人都一直在尽自己最大的努力为自己所擅长的领域寻找最有利的事业，这的的确确是他的个人优势，而不是他所看到的，泛滥在社会群体上的本领""每个人都在不断努力寻求最佳工作，实现利益最大化。确切来说，人们所考虑的是个人利益，而非社会利益"，其中都漏掉了capital（须知该文出自经济学著作），而advantageous也不必译成"优势"，因其意不表自明；同时，还可更加精炼。故此段不妨译为："每个人都不断使自己的资本得到最佳的利用；他考虑的是自己的而非社会的利益。"

对于[2]，大都译成"一般来说，他这么做实际上并不是为了促进社会利益，且同时他并不能意识到自己的行为能在多大程度上促进社会利益""总的来说，他实际上既没有促进公众利益的打算，也不知道自己到底促进了多少公众利益""简而言之，实际上，他既无心去促进公共利益的发展，也并不知道自己促进了多少""实际上，一般来说，他既没打算促进这种社会利益，也不知道他已经促进了多少"等，应当说，意思都不错，但在表述的准确和简练上，似乎还有改进的空间。简而言之，此句可译为"的确，总的来讲，个人既不为公众利益、也不知能贡献多少"。

参赛者对于[3]的典型翻译，如"为了仅仅确保自己的生存安全,比起得到国外工业的支持,他更倾向于得到国内工业的支持。为了仅仅确保自己的利益,他用某产业里最具价值的产品生产方式来指导该产业发展。在这种情况下,就像在其他很多情况下一样,他为一只无形的手所引领以达到某种目的,而这最终的结果并不是他设想中的一部分"。其中,support 不一定译成"支持",如 Fit hinge bolts to give extra support to the door lock.(安上铰链插销,让门锁更牢靠。),此处主要是就安全而言,指在国内投资比在国外投资更有保障,而 led by、part of 亦非总是"引领"和"一部分",即无须照搬词典,而可根据具体语境更灵活处理。同时,...and he is in this, as in many other cases,显然是对前句的补充说明,故不妨放在括号之中,如(如同在许多其他经营中一样);对于 led by an invisible hand to promote an end which was no part of his intention,大都作了多句处理,如"他被一双看不见的手引导着,往一个目标前进,而这个目标往往并非其本意""但在他这样做时,这总有一只看不见的手引导他去实现另一个目标,而这个目标本非他所追求的东西"等,实可并为一句。故整段不妨译为"个人倾向于投资国内而非国外企业,考虑的是自身资本的安全;其管理企业的方式是追求产品价值的最大化,其本意也只是自身利益。在这种经营逐利中(如同在许多其他经营中一样),他受到的却并非是其本意而是一只看不见的手的支配"。

[4] 中,对于 Nor is it always the worse for the society that it was no part of it,许多人译成"对于社会来说,缺少人们的参与也不总是坏事""对于社会来说,不参与并不是一件坏事""对于

社会来说，它不属于社会，这不总是最糟糕的"等，显然是对 no part of it 理解有误；该短语实际上是前面 no part of his intention 的简化，即不经意而为的；而 By pursuing his own interest he frequently promotes that of the society more effectually than when he really intends to promote it，有的译成"与刻意的促进社会利益相比，追求自身的利益反而能更加有效地促进社会利益"，意思固然不错，但在表述上似乎有些"过"了；作者所要强调的是，人们在追求自身利益过程中无意识地带来尚佳的客观社会效果，而并没有与"刻意的促进社会利益"相比较。此句较好的译文，如"这一无心之举，对社会并没什么坏处。但在追求个人利益的同时，无意中促进了社会利益，这样往往比有意为之更加有效""也不会因为这并非他的本意就对社会有害。他追求自己的利益时，相较于真正出于本意的情况，往往能更有效地促进社会的利益"等。因而，本段不妨译为："然而这种非本意的支配，对社会又并非总是有害的；在为自己谋利的过程中，人们往往能够对社会起到超乎其本意的促进作用。"

"看不见的手"，是亚当·斯密贯穿其名著《道德情操论》和《国富论》的一个重要思想，比起"毫不利己，专门利人"的理论，更为当代经济学所广泛接受、引用和阐释。显然，对于原著和作者的全面而深入的理解，是准确、精道翻译的前提。此次参赛的几十名同学，总体上态度认真、行文规范、表述清晰，尽管还有若干不足，但这是初期翻译中不可避免的。

参考译文

看不见的手

亚当·斯密

[1] 每个人都不断使自己的资本得到最佳的利用；他考虑的是自己的而非社会的利益。

[2] 的确，总的来讲，个人既不为公众利益、也不知能贡献多少。

[3] 个人倾向于投资国内而非国外企业，考虑的是自身资本的安全；其管理企业的方式是追求产品价值的最大化，其本意也只是自身利益。在这种经营逐利中（如同在许多其他经营中一样），他受到的却并非是其本意而是一只看不见的手的支配。

[4] 然而这种非本意的支配，对社会又并非总是有害的；在为自己谋利的过程中，人们往往能够对社会起到超乎其本意的促进作用。

39

New World Order

By George Herbert Walker Bush

[1] The United States' war on terror, which legitimized the invasion of Iraq in 2003, offered a telling testament to the emergence of a new world order.

[2] By the turn of the twenty-first century, empires had given way to a multiplicity of national states, and the collapse of the Soviet system had destroyed the bipolar world.

[3] Even the name of the conflict—the war on terror—does not feature nation-states or locations: rather, it denotes a more far-reaching, extensive conflict that could be anywhere, at any time.

[4] It implies connections between civilians all over the world who could be victims of terrorism in their home countries, while moving from place to place, or even on their computers. It is a global conflict in an increasingly globalized world.

译 析

　　New World Order，是美国总统布什于1990年9月11日对国会两院联席会议正式提出的，主要目的是建立一个"稳定而安全"的世界，有力保持同苏联军事力量的抗衡，同时按照美国的价值观，在全球巩固和推进"自由"与"民主"，促进"政治多元化"和"自由市场经济"。就该题目的翻译而言，有的按原文词序译成"新世界秩序"，实际若理解该词组背景，便知"世界"还是原来的，不同的只是"秩序"，故宜为"世界新秩序"或"国际新秩序"。

　　[1] 中，有的译成"美国在2003年入侵伊拉克的反恐战争证明了新世界秩序的出现"，漏译了 legitimized the invasion；而"美国发起的所谓'反恐战争'，合法化了其在2003年入侵伊拉克的'罪行'，也正是新世界秩序出现的强有力证据"，又有些言过其实了；"美国的反恐战争将2003入侵伊拉克合法化，有力证明了世界新秩序的产生"，在时间顺序上，似乎是"入侵"在前，"反恐"在后，其实不然。相对而言，"2013年，美国开展反恐战争，将入侵伊拉克的行为合法化，这充分表明了世界新秩序的萌芽"（其中年代有误）、"美国的反恐战争为2003年入侵伊拉克提供了合理借口，有力地证实了世界新秩序的出现"等，比较合理，但同时应更加明确该句的主语（"反恐战争"）。因而，此句不妨译为："2003年美国以'合法方式'入侵伊拉克的反恐战争，着实宣告了世界新秩序的出现。"

[2]中，By the turn of the twenty-first century，许多人译成"到20世纪末21世纪初""到20世纪、21世纪之交"，而更准确的应为"……之初"，如By the turn of the century, it had become apparent that the value of content was plummeting as more and more media were digitized.（到本世纪初，内容的价值急转直下，随之而来的媒介越来越被数字化了，这种现象已经十分明显。），So by the turn of the year, apparently, you could buy a high-quality portfolio of those loans at 70−75 cents on the Euro.（因此，到今年年初，很明显，你能够以7到7.5折的欧元价格购买那些贷款的优质组合。）等。对于multiplicity，许多人译成"多民族国家""民族主义"，其实该词原义是a great number and variety of something，一般情况下是"多样性"，如We are all amazed at the multiplicity of the nature.（大自然的多样性令我们大家惊奇。）；但在不同语境中要有所变通，如How could he cope with a multiplicity of duties？（他怎能应付这繁多的职责？）、A true study of history is sure to be multiplicity.（真正的历史研究必须是多元化的。）、Multiplicity is the force base to construct new world order.（多极化是建立世界新秩序的实力基础。）等，特别是考虑到其背景是要促进"政治多元化"，故此处以"多元体制"为宜。有人将the Soviet system译成"苏维埃政权"，是不够确切，因该词是俄文совет的音译，即会议或代表会议，是指俄国无产阶级在1905—1907年革命时期创造的领导群众进行革命斗争的组织形式，1917年俄国十月革命后，通称"苏联"；bipolar world为两个超级大国主宰的"两级格局世界"。故此，该句不妨译为：

"21世纪初,帝国体制让位给了多元体制的民族国家,而苏联的解体,也结束了两极格局的世界。"

[3] 中,the name of 许多人都译成"名称",但其实未必总是这样,如 Friedman would likely have objected strongly to any attempt by the Fed to increase the money supply <u>in the name of fighting a recession</u>.(弗莱德曼应该会强烈反对美联储通过增加货币供应量<u>来对抗经济衰退</u>。)、This may look a bit verbose compared to other book introduction, but I've spread things out a bit <u>in the name of readability</u>.(比起其他书介,这看起来有点冗长,但为了便于阅读我适当展开了一些。)等,此处可为"内涵"等;其中的破折号部分— the war on terror —,在中文里用括号更显自然;nation-states,许多人没译出来,实则为"国家、民族";同时,其他标点符号也可作相应调整:"甚至于'冲突'(反恐战争)的含义并非以国家、民族或地区为特征,而是指可随时随地发生的、更为全面、意义深远的冲突。"

[4] 是一个长句,在词意和语序的把握、表述上,有些难度,如"这显示出世界各地深受祖国恐怖主义之害的公民之间的联系,他们可能于<u>现实生活颠沛流离</u>,或是于<u>网络世界众说纷纭</u>。在全球化日益加快的时代,这已是一场全球性的冲突""例如,全世界人们<u>在自家境内的搬家途中</u>,甚至在<u>使用电脑这一过程中</u>,都有可能遭到恐怖分子的袭击。而这场冲突正是表明了这<u>一受害人群之间的联系</u>。如今,随着世界全球化日益加深,这一冲突也就成了全球性的问题",其中有下画线的为问题部分。结合其背景(建立一个"稳定而安全"的世界),该段整体意思,

首先讲面对恐怖主义威胁，世界人民已被联为一体（connections between civilians all over the world），其次是空间和地域上的可能性（moving from place to place, or even on their computers），最后总结为全球性的冲突（global conflict in... globalized world）。在将清线索的基础上，注意语言表述的准确和简练。该段不妨译为："这意味着全世界的公民连结成了一体，他们都可能成为恐怖主义的受害者，无论是在本国或在旅途中，甚至在自己的电脑里！这是在日益全球化世界里的一种全球性冲突。"

此篇选文看似容易，没有太生僻的词汇，但仍需在充分理解其背景上融会贯通，才能表达准确、通畅。

参考译文

世界新秩序

乔治·赫伯特·沃克·布什

[1] 2003年美国以"合法方式"入侵伊拉克的反恐战争，着实宣告了世界新秩序的出现。

[2] 21世纪初，帝国体制让位给了多元体制的民族国家，而苏联的解体，也结束了两极格局的世界。

[3] 甚至于"冲突"（反恐战争）的含义并非以国家、民族或地区为特征，而是指可随时随地发生的、更为全面、意义深远的

冲突。

[4] 这意味着全世界的公民连结成了一体，他们都可能成为恐怖主义的受害者，无论是在本国或在旅途中，甚至在自己的电脑里！这是在日益全球化世界里的一种全球性冲突。

The Persuaders

By Jo Carlowe

[1] We have long lived in an age where powerful images, catchy soundbites and too-good-to-miss offers bombard us from every quarter. All around us the persuaders are at work. Occasionally their methods are unsubtle—the planting of a kiss on a baby's head by a wannabe political leader, or a liquidation sale in a shop that has been "closing down" for well over a year, but generally the persuaders know what they are about and are highly capable.

[2] Be they politicians, supermarket chains, salespeople or advertisers, they know exactly what to do to sell us their image, ideas or produce. When it comes to persuasion, these giants rule supreme. They employ the most skilled image-makers and use the best psychological tricks to guarantee that even the most cautious among us are open to manipulation.

[3] Just think about how you are persuaded by supermarkets. We normally spend more time in them than we mean to, we buy 75 percent of our food from them and end up with products that we

didn't realize we wanted.

[4] Right from the start, supermarkets have been ahead of the game. For example, when Sainsbury introduced shopping baskets into its 1950s store, it was a stroke of marketing genius. Now shoppers could browse and pick up items they previously would have ignored. Soon after came trolleys, and just as new roads attract more traffic, the same applied to trolley space.

译 析

作者乔·卡罗维（Jo Carlowe），英国著名自由撰稿人，为多家报刊撰写稿件。本文摘自她的一篇短文，略有改写。

就题目 The Persuaders 而言，许多同学译成"说服者""推销员""营销者""控制者""劝说家""说客"等等，但鉴于全篇讲的是各色各样的说客（"说"应读 shuì），故不妨译为"说客种种"。

[1] 中，We have long lived in an age where powerful images, catchy soundbites and too-good-to-miss offers bombard us from every quarter，其中的介词 where 将前后两句连接起来，在中文里可作相应的处理（如采用冒号、破折号等），而 bombard，不宜照搬其原意，如有许多同学译成类似这样的句子："我们长期生活在这样一个时代，有震撼力的形象、吸引人的言论，以及难以回绝的提议，从四面八方轰炸着我们"等；而其引申含义实则为"大量面对"，英文释为 If you bombard someone with something, you

make them face <u>a great deal of it</u>. 如 The new journal is bombarded with letter of criticism from the subscriber.（订阅者纷至沓来的批评信，使该新杂志感到措手不及。）; HK was fun as well, I met up with sweet fans who constantly bombard me with tidbits.（香港相当有趣，一直有许多贴心的歌迷给我一些好吃的食物。）等。所以，此句不妨译为"我们生活在这样一种时代已经很久了——妩媚的形象、动听的警句、'机不可失'的呈现，从四面八方涌向我们"。

将 All around us the persuaders <u>are at work</u> 译成"我们周围的说客们都在<u>不停工作着</u>"，显然太过于表面化，实际此处讲的是一种效果、功效等。此处"——"之后是对前面的具体说明，故不必照搬，而可用"诸如""例如"等，the planting，似乎是一个难点，因为字典上好像没有特别对应的解释，如：种植、栽种、栽种物、an act of planting something、something that has just been planted 等；此处实为由其意象所引申的含义，有的译成"蹩脚地"似乎有些靠谱，但许多译成了"在婴儿的额头上印下一吻""通过给婴儿的额头亲吻就想要成为政治领导人物"等显然都不确切；而 "closing down" for well over a year 不是"在关闭一年多的商店里做大甩卖"，而是"以'closing down'为诱饵来招揽顾客，但已经一年多了，故技不灵了"。故此句不妨译为"他们的方式有时也并不精妙，诸如志为政治领袖者，着实地亲住婴儿的额头，或是'清仓大甩卖'的店铺，一年多了还在那里等等"。

对于 generally the persuaders know what they are about and are highly capable，一般都可译出意思，但比较啰嗦，如"但大体上，说客知道自己在干什么，他们也做得很好""但是通常说客们都了解他们自己，知道自己有很强的能力"等，其实不妨译为"总体而言，说客们目的明确，身手不凡"。

[2]中，Be they... 为"无论何人、何事、何物"之意，如Laws treat all people alike, be they foreign visitors or local VIPs.（法律面前人人平等，即使是外国旅客、达官贵人，也不能例外。）；As for your payment term, be they down payment or unasked payment?（贵公司的付款条件是下定金呢还是远期付款？）；All magnets behave the same, be they large or small.（所有磁体，不论大小，其性质都相同。）等，但许多同学没有译出来，如"作为他们那样的政客、连锁超市拥有者、销售员或者广告商""身为政治家、连锁超市（管理者）、销售人员和广告商的他们都……"等。其实，此句不妨译为"无论是政客、连锁超市、推销员或广告商，都知道如何恰到好处地推销其形象、理念或产品"。

对于When it comes to persuasion, these giants rule supreme，大都译得比较死板，如persuasion这里指的不是一般的"说服"，而是"说服力"；giants rule supreme 不宜译为"巨人的统治至高无上"，而不妨译为"这些'高手们'技艺不凡"等。对于... are open to manipulation许多译成"受制于他们""受人摆布""难逃他们的操控"等，固然不错，但可更口语化些，如用时下的流行词"被忽悠"等。

[3]中，Just think about how you are persuaded by supermarkets.

We normally spend...，此两句之间是有因果关系的，但大部分同学只是原封不动地翻译，如"就想想你自己是怎么被超市说服的。通常我们耗在超市里的时间都比……""想想你是如何被超市说服的吧。我们常常不必要地在超市花费更多的……"等；其实，其内在关系是："只是想一想我们是怎样被超市所左右的，便不难发现：我们通常待在超市里的时间比……"。至于are persuaded 并不一定永远是"被说服"，亦可变换表述方式；而we buy 75 percent of our food from them，并非是"但只买到我们购物清单上75%的食物"，而是指我们有大约这么多的食物买自超市。

[4] 中，Right from the start, supermarkets have been ahead of the game，指的是"诱惑顾客购物"而言的，故不妨加上"在这方面，……"；ahead of the game，许多人译成"在这场游戏中就已经取得领先"等，有些死板，不妨译为"超市在营销伊始便占了上风"。

对于just as new roads attract more traffic, the same applied to trolley space，其中二者的比喻关系不难理解，但trolley space 的含义一般没有翻译出来，如"手推车也会被越来越多的商品填满""购物车会增加顾客的购买量""购物手推车出现不久也会吸引顾客购买更多的商品"等，实则应该突出"手推车<u>空间的便利</u>，……"，以形成类似的比喻关系。

同时，通过翻译此篇，让我们对销售心理学方面的知识，也或多或少有所了解了。

参考译文

说客种种

乔·卡罗维

[1] 我们生活在这样一种时代已经很久了——妩媚的形象、动听的警句、"机不可失"的呈现，从四面八方涌向我们；说客们的功效无所不在。他们的方式有时也并不精妙，诸如志为政治领袖者，着实地亲吻婴儿的额头，或是"清仓大甩卖"的店铺，一年多了还在那里等等。但是，总体而言，说客们目的明确，身手不凡。

[2] 无论是政客、连锁超市、推销员或广告商，都知道如何恰到好处地推销其形象、理念或产品。就说服力而言，这些高手们可谓绝技缠身。他们雇用顶级的形象设计师，采用最佳的心理策略，令那些即使最谨慎的人也难免不被忽悠。

[3] 只是想一想我们是怎样被超市所左右的，便不难发现：我们通常呆在超市里的时间比我们预想的要长，我们大约四分之三的食物买自超市，但最后发现有的并不是我们想要的。

[4] 在这方面，超市在营销伊始便占了上风。例如，在20世纪50年代，森宝利（Sainsbury）连锁超市便引进了购物篮，此为营销的一个绝招。这样，顾客们便可悠闲采购，随手拿起以前不大留意的东西。不久又有了手推车，正如新道路可吸引更多的车辆，手推车空间的便利，也招徕了更多的顾客。

Theatre

By Melvin Howards

[1] What is theatre? Actors telling a story in words and actions on a stage, a director, and us, an audience. Why has theatre been so intriguing to people all over the world and throughout history? Theatre in the West began in Greece in 534 BC in the celebration of the cult of Dionysius.

[2] The relationship between religion and theatre is not accidental nor incidental: they both include ceremony, ritual, and spectacle that create drama which engages our emotions and intellect because they tell stories that are universal. In prehistoric times, ceremonies and rituals helped people explain such awe-inspiring, dramatic events as birth, death, and powerful natural forces. Man needs a way to cope with his deepest fears and concerns so he creates dramatic situations that express and mimic these feelings.

[3] The costumed participants in the ceremony (with a script), like the actors on stage, pretend they are driving out demons or propitiating their God, or resolving their fears and concerns. This is

what Aristotle called catharsis: the purgation of powerful emotions such as fear and pity that offers the release from tension that we experience as we empathize with the actors facing their conflicts (and our own) and work toward resolving them. Theatre and religion touch us not only emotionally and intellectually, but spiritually. Shakespeare was right when he said that all the world's a stage and we but actors playing our parts.

译　析

关于题目Theatre，一些同学译成了"剧院"，该词固然有此意，但此处却不是，如I want to work in theatre并不是"我要到剧院工作"，而是"我想从事戏剧工作"，所以应为"戏剧"。有的译成了"论戏剧""戏剧漫谈"等，又有些画蛇添足了。

在[1]中，介词in (words and actions) 在此转化为动词，意为"通过""运用"等，与后面的成分构成状语从句，类似的如He is walking in the park with an umbrella.（他拿着把伞在公园散步。）等。故此句应为"戏剧就是演员在舞台上通过语言和动作来讲述故事"。对于a director, and us, an audience，许多人不知如何处理，如"背后还有导演、我们和观众"等；其实，us, an audience是同位语，此处应增加"参与"，即为"还有导演和我们观众的参与"。关于all over the world and throughout history，有的译成"古今中外"，未尝不可；亦可变通为"放眼世界，综观历史"。Dionysius，一般译为"狄俄尼索斯"，古希腊神话中的酒神，即古希腊色雷斯人信奉的葡萄酒之神，不仅握有葡萄酒醉人的力量，还以布施欢乐与慈爱，在当时成为极有感召力的神，而celebration of the cult又不宜译成"狂欢""赞美诗"等，应为"庆典""祭奠"等活动；同时应注意人名表述的一般规范，故该句不妨译为"西方的戏剧始于公元前534年希腊的狄俄尼索斯（Dionysius）的祭奠活动"。

在[2]中，对于accidental nor incidental，许多同学译得很唐突，如"衍生物""附属品""既非偶然也不是彼此相互附属"等；其实，这里指的是宗教与戏剧之间的关系，"既非偶然也非附带性的"，而是相互间有着必然的内在联系。

其中create drama，不是"创作剧本"，而是"戏剧效果"；engages不是"从事""进行"等，而是与艺术创作相关的"投入"；that后是从句，修饰stories。

其中的man，为不可数名词，即humans as a group or from a particular period of history，泛指"人"，或"人类"，如The damage caused by man to the environment（人类给环境带来的破坏）等；而此处的creates则为有关戏剧情节的创作。

在[3]中，The costumed participants不一定是"乔装打扮的参与"，而为"着装参与者"即可；而将in the ceremony (with a script),译成"在仪式上（有程序）/（有着固定流程）"等，显然是理解错误。同时，括号中的(script)亦可作些灵活处理，即不一定还有括号；这里的concerns不是动词，而是名词。

对于catharsis，许多人译成了"宣泄""卡塔西斯"等，不很恰当，考虑到与purgation的搭配，不妨将此句处理为"这就是亚里士多德所说的'精神净化'（catharsis），即对于恐惧、怜悯等强烈感情的一种陶冶",即是以"净化"和"陶冶"将catharsis与purgation区分开。

在touch us not only emotionally and intellectually, but spiritually中，一个动词搭配后面的三个副词，翻译时可将touch扩展为三，如"触动……，启迪……，升华……"，充分显出中文一词多表的优势。

对于we but，许多人没有翻译出来，应为"我们不过是……"，类似的，如He is but a child（他只不过是个孩子）、This scene lasted but a few seconds（这情景不过延续了几秒钟）、"我不过开个玩笑而已"（I speak but in jest）等；而将actors playing our parts译成"众生皆是戏子"等，贬义色彩过重，不妨译为"我们不过是在其中扮演各自的角色"。

参考译文

戏剧

梅尔文·霍华兹

[1] 什么是戏剧？戏剧就是演员在舞台上通过语言和动作来讲述故事，还有导演和我们观众的参与。放眼世界，综观历史，戏剧为什么对人们会有如此的吸引力？西方的戏剧始于公元前

534年希腊的狄俄尼索斯（Dionysius）的祭奠活动。

[2] 宗教和戏剧的关系，既非偶然也非附带性的：二者都包含制造戏剧效果的典礼、仪式和场面，令人们投入心智与情感，因为戏剧中所讲述的故事具有普遍性。在史前期，典礼和仪式有助于人们解释那些令人敬畏、戏剧性的事情，如生、死及强大的自然力。人们需要某种方式来应对自己内心深处的恐惧与关注，因而创作出戏剧情节，用以表达和模仿这些情感。

[3] 仪式上的着装参与者，如同台上的演员，根据脚本，在假扮中驱逐魔鬼、息怒上帝、消除恐惧、释解担忧。这就是亚里士多德所说的"精神净化"（catharsis），即对于恐惧、怜悯等强烈感情的一种陶冶。演员面对他们的（也是我们的）冲突时，我们与他们心系一处，想努力化解，因而产生紧张情绪，而这种"净化"可以使之得以释然。戏剧和宗教对于我们，不仅触动感情、启迪智慧，而且升华精神。诚如莎士比亚所说，整个世界是个舞台，我们不过是在其中扮演各自的角色。

42

原文

Power and Discourse

[1] The discourse power is used when it comes to differentiating the levels of power due to cultural and social characteristics that come about through societal upbringing.

[2] The ways we think and talk about a subject influence and reflect the ways we act in relation to that subject.

[3] We should examine the link between power and discourse and propose a framework for understanding the complex relationship between them. Our framework grows out of the observation that power and discourse are mutually constitutive: at any particular moment in time, discourses-structured collections of texts and associated practices of textual production, transmission and consumption shape the system of power that exists in a particular context by holding in place the categories and identities upon which it rests.

[4] In other words, the distribution of power among actors, the forms of power on which actors can draw, and the types of actor that may exercise power in a given situation are constituted by discourse

and are, at a particular moment, fixed.

[5] Over time, however, discourses evolve as this system of power privileges certain actors, enabling them to construct and disseminate texts.

译 析

就标题而言，power这里不是"能力""力量""权利"等，而是"权力"；discourse也不是一般词典上的"论文""演说""讲述""著述"，而是语言学和传播学专业上的"话语"。

[1] 中，discourse power与discourse right有所区别，一般将前者译为"话语权"，后者为"话语权利"。如Discourse power and discourse right are two sides of one fact. （话语权与话语权利是一个事物的两个方面。）；There is a certain kind of intension between the discourse power of the teacher and the discourse right of the student, the latter leading to the transformation of the former. （教师话语权和学生话语权利之间有着一种制约；后者会改变前者。）；In the urgency of modernization, reforming peasant culture and their personality becomes a subject of our era, and the discourse right of modernization brings oppression on the peasant. （鉴于现代化的迫切需求，改造农民文化和人格成为我们时代的一个课题，现代化话语权利给农民造成一定压力。）。整句比较长，其中through societal upbringing为状语"由社会教养而……"，动词come about 为"产生""发生"；The discourse power is used when it comes

to…，此处的 discourse power 不是简单的"话语权"，而应是指其概念。故整句不妨译为："当区分由社会教养而形成的具有社会文化特征的不同权力水平时，便需要使用'话语权'的概念。"

[2] 中，subject 一般译成"主题""题目""学科"等，但这里可理解为泛指的"问题"；influence and reflect，可按中文表达习惯，将其词序调整为"反映、影响"。此句不妨译为："我们思考和谈论某一问题的方式，反映并影响我们的相关行为方式。"

[3] 中，framework 可有多种翻译，如"构架""结构""梗概"等，此处不妨译为"理论框架"，而 Our framework，与前句相关联，在译文中可不必断开，但可稍加省略，如将"理论框架"变为"框架"；observation，一般译为"观察"，但此处可引申为由观察得出的"认识"；mutually constitutive 直译是"相互构建"，实则为"相互关联"。破折号后面，是对前面的补充说明，故可用"即……"；by holding in place the categories and identities upon which it rests 原文是状语，修饰 shape the system of power，但译文若按原句式译出，便会冗赘，故不妨将 by holding… 部分放入括号中，用作对 a particular context 的补充说明。整段可译为："我们应该审视权力与话语之间的联系，并提出理解这一复杂关系的理论框架，而这种框架基于对权力与话语间相互关联的认识，即在任何特定时刻，文本汇集的话语结构及文本产生、传递和消费形成了某一特定语境（其赖以存在的种类与身份）中的话语体系。"

[4] 中，…in a given situation 可能会有歧义，似乎既可以修饰 that may exercise power，也可修饰整句，但根据表述习惯，以前

者为宜。该句不妨译为"换言之，行为者中权力的分配、权力运用的形式及在某种情景下运用权力的类型，是由特定时段的话语决定的"。

[5] 中，privilege 的本义为 a special right or advantage that only one person or group has，但此处是动词，即 to treat someone or something better or differently than other people or things rather than treat them all equally; as 为"随……（而产生）"。故该句不妨译为："然而，随着时间的推移，话语随着此种权力体系赋予某些行动者以特权而演变，使其能建构和传播文本。"

参考译文

权力与话语

[1] 当区分由社会教养而形成的具有社会文化特征的不同权力水平时，便需要使用"话语权"的概念。

[2] 我们思考和谈论某一问题的方式，反映并影响我们的相关行为方式。

[3] 我们应该审视权力与话语之间的联系，并提出理解这一复杂关系的理论框架，而这种框架基于对权力与话语间相互关联的认识，即在任何特定时刻，文本汇集的话语结构及文本产生、传递和消费形成了某一特定语境（其赖以存在的种类与身份）中

的话语体系。

　　[4] 换言之，行为者中权力的分配、权力运用的形式及在某种情景下运用权力的类型，是由特定时段的话语决定的。

　　[5] 然而，随着时间的推移，话语随着此种权力体系赋予某些行动者以特权而演变，使其能建构和传播文本。

43

原 文

Conflict Management

By Jerry H. Bentley et al.

[1] Conflict is part of the human condition. A conflict arises whenever the interests and desires of one differ from the interests and desires of another in some social or business setting. Humans are social creatures—human has no meaning except in relation to other individuals or groups.

[2] At the same time, to be human is to be an individual with interests and desires that may be different from those of another. Managing conflict, balancing the interests and desires of individuals and groups is also part of the human condition.

[3] There are many methods for managing conflicts. When conflicts are not managed properly, there is a need to develop new methods to aid in conflict management and the resolution of disputes. In the United States, the general field is called Conflict Management.

[4] In short, conflict management is the process of limiting the negative aspects of conflict while increasing the positive aspects of conflict.

译 析

本文摘自杰瑞·H. 本特利等人（Jerry H. Bentley et al.）著的《管理学》（*Management*）。就题目Conflict Management而言，参赛者一般都译成"冲突管理""冲突管控"等，但也有相当数量漏译的，故没有成绩，很可惜。

在[1]中，对于the human condition，参赛者有多种译法，如"人类条件""人类生活""人类状况"等，其实condition一词在不同语境中有多种含义，如He was concerned with the enhancement of the human condition（他关心人类生存环境的改善）、Her condition took a sharp turn for the worse（她的病情突然急剧恶化）、He was too out of condition to clamber over the top（他体质太差，爬不到山顶）等，但此处根据其管理内容，可译成"人类社会"；而Conflict is part of the human condition，许多人译成"冲突是人类社会的一部分""冲突是人类状况的部分内容""冲突是人类社会的常态""冲突乃人之常事"等，固然不错，但考虑到下面所讲内容，不妨将语气转换为"人类社会总免不了冲突"。对于A conflict arises whenever the interests and desires of one differ from the interests and desires of another in some social or business setting，有的译成"当一个人的利益和愿望与另一个人的利益和愿望不同时，便会产生冲突"，意思不错，但下画线部分有问题：one不宜译成"一个人"，而为"一方"（利益）；第二个"利益和愿望"属重复，可删去，该句可译为"在社交或商业场合，一方利益、愿望与另一方不同时，就会发生冲突"。而 Humans are social creatures—human has no meaning except in relation to other individuals or groups，其中的前半部分大都译成了"人类是群居动物""人类是社交动物""人是社交性的动物"等，但推敲起来并不太确切，如"群居""动物"，在这里都是有所特指的，不宜照搬过来，故不妨变通为"人是'社群动物'"。句式 has no meaning except... 可以正译"只有……才有意义"，也可反译"如果不这样……就没有意义"，如 Life has no meaning except in terms of responsibility（不讲责任，人生便会失去意义）、History has no meaning except what the winners give to it（历史除了胜者赋予的意义外别无他意——历史永远是胜利者书写的）、Evaluation of product quality has no meaning except with reference to the customer's needs（只有关照顾客需求，评判产品质量才有意义）等；就此处的后半句而言，较为典型的参赛译文，如"只有与其他的个人或群体互相联系，人类才有其意义""个人如果没有和其他个体或群体来往，那么他就没有存在的意义""人类的意义就在于和其他个体或集体产生联系""只有在与他人或团体的关系中，才能体现出人的涵义"等，但是这些都不免太拘泥于原文的词面意思、不乏翻译腔；其实，该句的实质意思，是人类的本性体现在与他人的关系之中。因而，此句不妨译为："人类社会总免不了冲突；在社交或商业场合，一方利益、愿望与另一方不同时，就会发生冲突。人是'社群动物'，而人类的本性就体现在与他人（个人或团体）的关系之中。"

在[2]中，to be human is to be an individual with interests and

desires that may be different from those of another，有的译成"身为一个人，我们就要做好与众不同的准备。没有人的利益是完全一致的"，显然，在理解上有偏差；而"人是有利益和需求的个体，而每人的利益与需求各不相同"又有些啰嗦，可简化。至于 is also part of... 一般都译成了"一部分"，固然不错，但也可变通，如 He says the emergence of new websites covering science <u>is also part of</u> the problem because they often fail to check the veracity of information they publish（他认为新出现的各种报道科学的网站<u>也很成问题</u>，因为它们经常没有核实自己发布信息的准确性）、The China trip <u>is also part of</u> his first to Asia as president（此次中国之行<u>也是</u>他当选总统后的首次访问亚洲）等，但若译成"也是人类的天性"，则又偏颇了，即对 human condition 理解有误。综合而言，该句不妨译为"同时，人是有利益和需求的个体，且各不相同，于是管控冲突、平衡个人和群体的利益与需求，也是人类社会所必需的"。

在[3]中，When conflicts are not managed properly 译成"当我们无法恰当处理好冲突时""当冲突没有得到妥善的处理""当冲突得不到合理解决时"等，都是可以接受的；而 to develop new methods to aid in conflict management，有的译成"开辟新途径去协助冲突管理""就有必要用一些新的方式解决冲突与争端"等，其实这里不妨把 to develop new methods 分开，译为"需研究新方法"，后面的另译，故整句为"管控冲突的方法多种多样。当管控不利时，就需研究新方法，协助管控、化解纠纷。在美国，这一领域称为'冲突管控'（Conflict Management）"。

在[4]中，the negative aspects of、the positive aspects of词面意思为"消极方面""积极方面"；前者不言而喻，后者体现在监督、制约等方面的作用，故可变通为"消极、积极因素"；句子conflict management is the process of... 的宾语为process，但有的译文没有把握住，如"冲突管理是指采用一定手段以发挥冲突益处而抑制其害处""冲突管理的目的就是增加冲突的积极作用，并把其消极影响降到最低""冲突管理是在限制消极影响的同时产生积极的作用"等，虽然意思不错，但考虑到本句具有定义的性质，故应比较严谨地译为"简言之，所谓'冲突管控'即是限制冲突的消极因素而增加其积极因素的过程"。

可见，翻译是个复杂的过程，有的需严谨，有的需变通。

参考译文

冲突管控

杰瑞·H.本特利等

[1] 人类社会总免不了冲突；在社交或商业场合，一方利益、愿望与另一方不同时，就会发生冲突。人是"社群动物"，而人类的本性就体现在与他人（个人或团体）的关系之中。

[2] 同时，人是有利益和需求的个体，且各不相同，于是管控冲突、平衡个人和群体的利益与需求，也是人类社会所必

需的。

[3] 管控冲突的方法多种多样。当管控不利时，就需研究新方法，协助管控、化解纠纷。在美国，这一领域称为"冲突管控"（Conflict Management）。

[4] 简言之，所谓"冲突管控"即是限制冲突的消极因素而增加其积极因素的过程。

44

原 文

Early Capitalist Society

[1] While the Protestant Reformation and the emergence of sovereign states brought religious and political change, a rapidly expanding population and economy encouraged the development of capitalism, which in turn led to a restructuring of European economy and society.

[2] Technologies of communication and transportation enabled businessmen to profit from distant markets, and merchants and manufacturers increasingly organized their affairs with the market rather than local communities in mind.

[3] Although capitalism generated considerable wealth, its effects were uneven and sometimes unsettling. Even in Western Europe, where development and prosperity were most noticeable, early capitalism sometimes required painful adjustments to new conditions.

译 析

对于题目Early Capitalist Society，一般都译为"早期资本主义社会",没有太大问题。

在[1]中,Protestant Reformation是指始于欧洲16世纪基督教自上而下的宗教改革运动,它瓦解了从罗马帝国颁布基督教为国家宗教以后由天主教会所主导的政教体系,奠定了新教的基础,因而也可译为"新教改革运动"。该运动可视为文艺复兴在宗教领域的继续,有利地推动了西方早期资本主义社会的发展。

对于a rapidly expanding population and economy encouraged the development of capitalism,很多参赛译文据字面意思译成"人口和经济迅速扩张,鼓励了资本主义的发展",其中"扩张"的原义是扩大势力、范围等,如"日本这种领土扩张的欲望,在历史上是有渊源的"等,所以用在此处不够确切。而且,动名词expanding后面有两个宾语population和economy,在翻译时要注意动词与宾语搭配的问题,如"急速发展的人口和经济"就不够恰当,因为"发展经济"可以,但不宜"发展人口",可改为"急剧增长的人口及飞速发展的经济""人口和经济的迅速膨胀与增长"等。把encouraged译成"鼓励了",显然太拘泥于字典的定义了,而此处不妨译为"促进了"等。

其中的in turn,一般都翻译成"反过来""反之"等,其实不必刻意译出,尽管其中有转折的语气,如They, in turn, were charmed by the famous author's cultured and civilized outlook(他们呢,则为那位著名作家有教养的、开化的见解而折服),One of the members of the surgical team leaked the story to a fellow physician who, in turn, confided in a reporter(手术小组的一名成

员把这个消息泄露给了在一起工作的一个内科医生，而这个医生又透露给了一位记者）等；而将 led to a restructuring of European economy and society 译成"领导了欧洲经济社会的改革"显然是将 led 拘泥于其字面意思，而同时对 restructuring 作了过度发挥。"改革"是指把事物中旧的不合理的部分改成新的、能适应客观情况的，如"技术改革""改革经济管理体制"等，是一种主观能动行为（特别是加之"领导"），而此处主要讲的是由于前面那些事物的出现，而带来了后面的客观后果，所以应选用更确切的词语。同时，将 restructuring 译成"结构调整""重组"等，亦都不如"重塑"。故此，该段不妨译为"新教改革和主权国家的出现，带来了宗教与政治的变化。人口、经济的迅速膨胀与增长，促进了资本主义的发展，从而也重塑了欧洲的社会与经济结构"。

在[2]中，profit 在此处不是名词，而是动词，即"获利"。参赛译文，如"交通运输技术的进步让商人们从远销商品到海外来获利"，方位似乎表述的不是很清楚，似乎作者是站在海外；而"商人们得以在距离很远的市场上去做生意"，又有些不够简练。对于 merchants and manufacturers increasingly organized their affairs with the market rather than local communities in mind，一般译成"批发商和厂商们也会更多地根据对大的市场的判断来安排生意生产计划，而不是仅考虑本地区的小市场"（下画线为笔者所加，下同）等，固然不错，但分析起来，还可进一步推敲：with the market 是处处从市场出发，in mind 是考虑，但有时不一定译出，因其已包括在"从……出发"之中。在词序上，也应作些相应的调整，将 local communities in mind 提前，把要强调的放在后面，而 increasingly 也未必在原来的位置。故此，整句不妨译为"交通运输技术使得生意人可以从遥远的市场中获利，商人和制造者不再局限于本地，而是日益以市场为导向、组织规划其业务"。

在[3]中，对于 Although capitalism generated considerable wealth, its effects were uneven and sometimes unsettling，参赛译文，如"尽管资本主义的发展带来了可观的财富，但它产生的影响却并不总是积极的，有时这些结果更会让人不安""尽管资本主义制度创造了相当多的财富，其带来的影响却是不均衡的，有时甚至令人混乱不安"等。对于uneven，一般可译成"不平衡""不均匀"，如党的十九大文件中指明"我国社会主要矛盾已经转化为人民日益增长的美好生活需要和不平衡不充分的发展之间的矛盾"，可译为 The principal contradiction facing Chinese society has evolved—what we now face is the contradiction between uneven and inadequate development and the people's ever-growing needs for a better life. 其中的"不平衡"可用uneven，该词主要指客观现象，如 He staggered on the uneven surface of the car park（他摇摇晃晃地行走在停车场凹凸不平的地面上）等。与之相关的是unbalanced，该词主要是指主观方面的，如 He was shown to be mentally unbalanced（他被证明精神有问题），An unbalanced article（持论偏颇的文章）等，翻译时应有所甄别。

对于unsettling，许多人译成了"使人不安""使人感到混乱"等，但查看其原意，为 If you describe something as unsettling, you mean that it makes you feel rather worried or uncertain; making you feel upset, nervous or worried (*Collins Dictionary*)，但这些都是就个人而言的，如His bad habit was really unsettling（他的坏习惯确实令人感到不安）等；对一个社会而言，则是更严重的，可译为"动荡"等。在where development and prosperity were most noticeable，其中的noticeable不是一般意义上的easy to see or notice or clear or definite，而应与前面的prosperity相结合理解，即是"相当繁荣的"。

故此，该段不妨译为："尽管资本主义创造了可观的财富，但其效益不均，有时引起动荡。即使在资本主义繁荣发展的西欧，其早期资本主义也经历了适应新情况的艰难过程。"

总之，从上文翻译中可以看出，词语的选择不能仅限于词典中的解释，而是要根据其历史和社会的语境加以具体辨析。

参考译文

早期资本主义社会

[1] 新教改革和主权国家的出现，带来了宗教与政治的变化。人口、经济的迅速膨胀与增长，促进了资本主义的发展，从而也重塑了欧洲的社会与经济结构。

[2] 交通运输技术使得生意人可以从遥远的市场中获利，商

人和制造者不再局限于本地,而是日益以市场为导向、组织规划其业务。

[3] 尽管资本主义创造了可观的财富,但其效益不均,有时引起动荡。即使在资本主义繁荣发展的西欧,其早期资本主义也经历了适应新情况的艰难过程。

Global Exchanges

[1] European explorers and those who followed them established links between all lands and peoples of the world. Interaction between peoples in turn resulted in an unprecedented volume of exchange across the boundary lines of societies and cultural regions.

[2] Some of that exchange involved biological species: plants, food crops, animals, human populations, and disease pathogens all spread to regions they had not previously invited.

[3] These biological exchanges had differing and dramatic effects on human populations, destroying some of them through epidemic disease while enlarging others through increased food supplies and richer diets.

[4] Commercial exchange also flourished in the wake of the voyages of exploration as European merchants traveled to ports throughout the world in search of trade. Indeed, by the mid-eighteenth century they had established globe-girdling networks of trade and communication.

译 析

　　就题目而言，有的译成"全球交流"，是过于拘泥原文了，实则可为通常的"国际交流"。

　　[1] 中的第二句Interaction between peoples...许多人译成了独立的句子"在不同人之间……"，其实可用连词等将其译为一句。volume，固然有"大量、体积"等意，但此处不宜硬性转述，可变通为"（空前）规模"。

　　[2] 中invited不是一般意义上的"邀请、请求、引诱、招致"，而此处不妨译为"涉及"；they had not previously invited是省略了that的从句，在译文里则可作定语。

　　[3] 中的biological exchanges，许多人译成了"生物交换"，显然有误，实则是指"生物意义上的交流"；dramatic effects，不宜译为"戏剧化的影响"，而应译为"强烈的、不同凡响的"。对于destroying some of them through epidemic disease while enlarging others through increased food supplies and richer diets，不妨以中文"先扬后抑"的表述习惯，将词序调整："有些因食物供应的增加和更有营养而健壮起来，有些则因流行病的泛滥而死亡。"

　　[4] 中对于长句Commercial exchange also flourished in the wake of the voyages of exploration as European merchants traveled to ports throughout the world in search of trade，要从as European merchants traveled to...入手理解，即"欧洲商人的航船到达各地港口"，接着"在世界遍寻贸易机会"，而其结果则是"带来了商

业贸易的繁荣";globe-girdling networks 为"环球……网络"。

参考译文

国际交流

[1] 欧洲探险家及其追随者与世界各地的人们建立起了联系，而不同人群之间的互动又产生了跨越社会、文化边界的空前规模的交流。

[2] 其中有生物种群方面的交流，如植物、粮食作物、动物及人口等，而病菌也随之传播到了以前未曾涉足过的地方。

[3] 这些生物意义上的交流，对人类产生的效应是剧烈而不同凡响的；有些因食物供应的增加和更有营养而健壮起来，有些则因流行病的泛滥而死亡。

[4] 欧洲商人的航船到达各地港口，在世界遍寻贸易机会，这种航海探险带来了商业贸易的繁荣。实际上，到了18世纪中叶，人们业已建立起了环球贸易和交通网络。

Individual Engagement

By John Dewey

[1] We cannot better Plato's conviction that an individual is happy and society well organized when each individual engages in those activities for which he has a natural equipment, nor his conviction that it is the primary office of education to discover this equipment to its possessor and train him for hits effective use.

[2] But progress in knowledge has made us aware of the superficiality of Plato's lumping of individuals and their original powers into a few sharply marked-off classes; it has taught us that original capacities are indefinitely numerous and variable.

[3] It is but the other side of this fact to say that in the degree in which society has become democratic, social organization means utilization of the specific and variable qualities of individuals, nor stratification by classes.

译 析

约翰·杜威（John Dewey, 1859—1952），美国著名的教育家、思想家、心理学家，曾于1919年5月至1921年7月来华讲学两年多，胡适曾为他当翻译。他的实用主义教育思想，对中国的知识界和教育界产生了很大影响。选文摘自他的《民主主义与教育》(*Democracy and Education*)，言简意赅，翻译起来有些难度。

关于题目Individual Engagement，有的漏译了，有的理解错误，如"社会参与度""自雇人士""个人贡献"，individual的本义是being or characteristic of a single thing or person，是"单个的"，而engagement为an arrangement that you have made to do something at a particular time; employment for performers or performing groups that lasts for a limited period of time，其实质是"从事""参与"，相对来说，译成"个人参与""个人契约"等似更接近原文。但是，根据全文的意思，这里主要讲个人与社会运作的关系，故不妨译为"各尽所能"。所以这里建议，题目可在理解、翻译全文之后再翻译。

在[1]中，对better一词的处理是个难点。有的漏译，有的译成"我们不能提高Plato的信心"（其中如此著名的古希腊哲学家的名字都没有译出）、"绝妙之最""这没有什么可以诟病的""非常认同""不置可否""他的论断极好""既不能升华、也不能改变""令人无从置喙""他的这一论述实在是绝妙极了"等，显然不妥或不够准确。该词通常用作形容词或副词,如 There must be a better way to do this(一定还会有更好的办法来做这事)、He sings better than I do(他唱得比我好)等;有时也用作名词,如 Which is the better of these two pens?(这两支钢笔哪一支更好?)。但这里却用作动词,即"超过""比……更好"之意,类似的,如 We should do our best to better the relations between the two countries(我们应尽力改善两国关系)、The university has tremendously bettered the living conditions of students(学校已经大大改善了学生的生活条件)、His performance as Hamlet could not have been bettered(他把哈姆雷特演得不能再好了)等。所以,此处意为"……不能比柏拉图认为的……更好"。

接下来,便是句子结构问题。比较典型的参赛译文:"我们不能优化柏拉图的信念""我们不可能提出比柏拉图更好的观点了""我们超越不了柏拉图的思想——……;也超越不了他的信仰——……"等,主要意思固然表达出来了,但欠准确和精练。其实,此处有"句中句",即"不能比柏拉图认为更好"的内容是 conviction that 后的从句,其中又有两项内容,故不妨对其结构中的前后次序作一大调整,这就需要在充分理解原文的基础上,分辨不同成分,准确加以把握。典型的类似句子,如 <u>The reform</u> that met the technical requirements of the new age by engaging a large number of professionals and preventing the decline in efficiency that so commonly spoiled the fortunes of family firms in the second and third generation after the energetic founders, effectively enabled the family firms to survive the harsh competition.

（聘请大批专业人士、预防通常导致"富不过三代"的效率低下问题，从而满足新时期的技术需求，<u>由此进行的变革有效地帮助家族企业在激烈竞争中生存下来</u>。），即在诠释了 engaging a large number of professionals and preventing the decline in efficiency 之后，把 The reform 调整到句末译出，从而避免了曲解原文和蹩脚的译文。

同理，此处可先译出柏拉图所深信的是什么，然后增一句概述"不能比他更好""……在这两点上，我们都没能超过柏拉图"。

其中还有几点值得一提。有人将 the primary (office) 译成"小学"，其实该词本义为 of first rank or importance or value; direct and immediate rather than secondhand，如 the primary function（主要功能），primary task（头等任务），a primary interest（最感兴趣的）等，这里根据上下文可译为"教育的首要任务"，而"小学"（primary school）只是后来引申出的一种。同时，有的将 equipment 照搬译成"设施""装备"等，殊不知该词还有"素质、才能"之意，如 He does have the equipment for the new job（他确实具备了从事这项新工作的才能）；她是个唱歌的材料（She has the vocal equipment of a singer）等。再者，对于 train him for its effective use，有的译成"更好的使用""不断放大长处""强化它"等，都措辞欠佳，且有语法错误。

在[2]中，将 progress in knowledge 译成"教育的发展""不断的学习""在知识这方面所取得的硕果""随着知识的增加"等似都欠妥，实则为"知识方面的进步（积累）"。对于

superficiality，有的没有将其与柏拉图的观点很好地融合在一起，如"使我们意识到柏拉图把个人和他们的原始力量集中在少数尖锐、肤浅的等级中"等。同时，lump一般作名词，其本义为a large piece of something without definite shape, "a lump of bread", "a lump of coal"（一大块没有确定形状的东西，如"一块面包""一块煤"等），但这里用作动词to put together indiscriminately，即笼统地归类；如if we lump all our money together, we should be able to purchase that property［我们把所有的钱（可能包括定期、活期、股票、外币等）都凑在一起，就可以买下那栋房子］；他把所有问题都归结为"种族主义"（He lumped the whole problem under one label "racism"）等；a few，原意为a small number，即少数，如I've got a few books on gardening（我有几本园艺书），In a few words she had put him in his place（她简单几句话就杀了他的威风）；他平时是个沉默寡言的人（He is a man of few words in his daily life）等，但有的将a few sharply marked-off classes译成"鲜有明显划分的阶级"则又有问题了，因根据Collins字典解释：When talking about amounts, you use "a few" with plural countable nouns, and a little with uncountable nouns，即a few与可数名词连用，而a little与不可数名词连用，所以在此是误将其当成不可数之词了，实则强调的是仅"若干个"。值得指出的是，分号"；"之后的it是progress in knowledge的代主语，仍需点明（必要的"重复"）。

在[3]中，in the degree in which society has... 许多同学译成"……我们的社会在一定程度上变得民主了"，或"从当今社会的民主程度上来看"等都欠准确，实则，这里是指（假设）"社会发展到……程度"；而social organization means utilization of the specific and variable qualities of individuals, nor stratification by classes，许多人译成"事实恰好相反，个体独特而多样的品质正是社会多元化的原因，而非阶级的划分""另一面是说在社会已经成为民主的学位，社会组织是利用特定的和可变的个人品质，还是分层的类""在民主的社会，……不是不同的人群划分，而是社会团体依赖对每个个体自身与众不同的特质的使用"等，显然，都有对原文关键词语和句子结构的误解。实则，"……如果社会是民主的，社会组织就应利用个人特殊而多样的品质，而不是将其划分成阶级"。

诚然，杜威的语言有些古雅，与当代用法稍有差异，但只要潜心领会，便不会成为好译文的障碍。

参考译文

各尽所能

约翰·杜威

[1] 柏拉图深信，若每人都能从事自己具有天赋的活动，个人则会觉得愉快，社会组织亦会日臻完善；他又认为，教育的首要在于使人发现其天赋，并训练其有效地利用这种天赋。在这两

点上,我们都没能超过柏拉图。

[2] 但是,知识的进步使我们认识到,柏拉图把个人和其本来的能力分成若干不同的阶级,却是肤浅的。知识的进步还告诉我们,人的最初能力是无限多样、变化多端的。

[3] 事实的另一面,是说如果社会是民主的,社会组织就应利用个人特殊而多样的品质,而不是将其划分成阶级。

47

原 文

The Asking Animal

[1] Caught between two eternities—the vanished past and the unknown future—human beings never cease to seek their bearings and sense of direction.

[2] We inherit our legacy of the sciences and the arts—the works of the great discoverers and creators, the Columbuses and Leonardos—but we all remain seekers. Man is the asking animal...

[3] Western culture has witnessed at least three grand historical epochs of seeking—each with a dominant spirit, enduring spokesmen and distinctive problems. We have gone from "Why?" to the "How?", from the search for purpose to the search for causes.

[4] First was the heroic way of prophets and philosophers seeking answers—salvation or truth—from the God above or the reason within each of us. Then came an age of communal seeking, pursuing civilization in the liberal spirit.

[5] And most recently there was the age of the social sciences, in which man was ruled by the forces of history.

[6] We can draw on all these ways of seeking in our personal

search for purpose, to find meaning in the seeking.

译 析

该篇题目 The Asking Animal 似乎有些费解，参赛者译得多种多样，如"探索的动物""追问的动物""求知若渴的动物"等，虽不算错，但过于直白。通读全文，会发现，其内容是人类对于自身奥秘的不断询问和探究，因而有人译成"人类是探索的动物""求知的动物——人类""寻找答案""人类——生命不息、探寻不止"等，但又多少有些离原文过远。人类毕竟不同于一般的动物。比较而言，不如"不断探究的物种"。

[1] 中，Caught between two eternities—the vanished past and the unknown future—...，许多人译成"在已消逝的过去与未知的未来的夹缝中"，似乎符合原意，但翻译体太明显；seek their bearings，译成"探究人生意义"，有些宽泛；sense of direction，实为"方向感"。此句不妨译为："在永远消失的过去与永远未知的将来之间，人类从未停止过探究自己的位置、失去方向感。"

[2] 中，We inherit our legacy of the sciences and the arts—the works of the great discoverers and creators, the Columbuses and Leonardos—...，是一长句，典型的参赛译文，如"我们继承了无尽的科学财富——伟大的发现者的成就：哥伦布发现了新大陆；我们继承了无尽的艺术宝藏——天才创造者的作品：列奥纳多创作的惊世名画""我们继承了科学和艺术的遗产——伟大的发现者和创造者——哥伦布和列奥纳多的作品……"，虽颇费周折，

但未必表述清楚了。这里，不妨将句子断开，同时增加必要的词语，特别是后半句，译为"<u>受益于</u>哥伦布们和达芬奇们的……"。整段不妨译为："我们继承了前人的科学和艺术遗产，受益于哥伦布们和达芬奇们的伟大发现和发明，但我们仍然是探究者——人类就是这样一种探究的物种。"

[3] 中，Western culture has witnessed at least three grand historical epochs of seeking—each with a dominant spirit, enduring spokesmen and distinctive problems，较为典型的参赛译文："西方文明在历史上已经见证了至少三次<u>人类之问</u>——每一次都伴随着一种<u>核心的精神</u>，<u>一群孜孜不倦的先驱</u>和<u>一些空前绝后的问题</u>"，除句子结构外，其中下画线部分属用词不妥；同时，还有将enduring spokesmen译成"持久、忍耐的发言人"，distinctive problems译成"鲜明的问题"等，都有推敲的余地。对于We have gone from "Why?" to the "How?", from the search for purpose to the search for causes，一般参赛译文没有大问题，如"我们已经从'为什么'步入'怎么做'，从探求目的到追根溯源""我们不再是探索'为什么'，而是探索事情的缘由""我们最初只注重探索结果，而现在我们更注重探索原因"等，但在用词、表述上可更加准确、简练、完整。综合来看，此段不妨译为："西方文化至少经历了三个人类探究的伟大历史时期，每个时期都有各自的主导精神、留名于史的代言人和独具特色的问题。我们已经从探究'为何'到探究'如何'，从探究目的到探究原因。"

[4] 中，对于communal (seeking...)，大都译成"共同探索的时代""集体求索的时代"等，然而分析起来，该词的一般

意思是"公用、公共的、公社的、公民的",如 The toilets and other communal facilities were in a shocking state(厕所及其他公共设施的状况极其糟糕), Sometimes social conditions spawn great numbers of communal groups(有时社会状况酿成了一批共同群体), To the ancient Greeks she was known as Themis, originally the organizer of the "communal affairs of humans, particularly assemblies"(古希腊人认为的正义女神是西弥斯,她最初是"人类共同事务,特别是公民大会"的组织者)等,但对应前面的 prophets and philosopher,此处不妨译为"大众的"。故此,该段不妨译为:"最初,是先知和哲学家们大无畏的探究方式,即从上帝或各自理性探究救赎和真理。之后,是大众探究的时代,即以自由的精神追寻文明。"

[5] 中, man was ruled by the forces of history,其中的 forces 是一种历史向前发展的内在动力。参赛译文,如"最近的一个时代是社会科学时代,在这个时代,人类被历史的<u>力量所统治</u>""而现在,我们处于社会科学时期,历史动力规约着人类""至于近代,社会科学初见,人类历史得<u>以凭科学样貌示人,规诫与引领人类社会发展</u>"等,其中下画线部分显然不准确,甚至不靠谱。该句不妨译为:"最近处于社会科学时代,此时人们被历史的内在动力所驱使。"

[6] 中, draw on 不是绘画,而是"利用、得到", During the writing of this article, he can draw on his own experience(他可以利用自己的经历,写好这篇文章), In trying to resuscitate Doha, Mr. Bush will be able to draw on support from business lobby groups(通

过努力挽救多哈回合贸易谈判，布什将可以赢得商业游说团体的支持）等，此处不妨译为"借鉴"；同时，对于 find meaning in the seeking，许多参赛者有所忽略，未能准确译出。该句可译为："在我们个人探究答案的过程中，可以借鉴所有这些探究方式，从而找到探究的真谛。"

总之，词语的选择、搭配都要在具体语境下斟酌，在语篇中考量。

参考译文

不断探究的物种

[1] 在永远消失的过去与永远未知的将来之间，人类从未停止过探究自己的位置、失去方向感。

[2] 我们继承了前人的科学和艺术遗产，受益于哥伦布们和达芬奇们的伟大发现和发明，但我们仍然是探究者——人类就是这样一种探究的物种。

[3] 西方文化至少经历了三个人类探究的伟大历史时期，每个时期都有各自的主导精神、留名于史的代言人和独具特色的问题。我们已经从探究"为何"到探究"如何"，从探究目的到探究原因。

[4] 最初，是先知和哲学家们大无畏的探究方式，即从上帝

或各自理性探究救赎和真理。之后，是大众探究的时代，即以自由的精神追寻文明。

[5] 最近处于社会科学时代，此时人们被历史的内在动力所驱使。

[6] 在我们个人探究答案的过程中，可以借鉴所有这些探究方式，从而找到探究的真谛。

48

原 文

The Gifted Children

By Kate Hilbun

[1] Why let them walk when they can fly? This is a question that is being asked by more and more parents in the UK who believe their children to be "gifted" or child prodigies. Among the calls received by the National Association of Gifted Children (NAGC) are many who claim their offspring demonstrate remarkable ability across all subjects, often with problem-solving and verbal skills way beyond their years. Then there are those who say their children are gifted in specific areas such as maths, or that they are exceptionally talented in non-academic fields such as art, sport or music.

[2] The present British government's focus on provision for the crème de la crème in UK schools is doubtless significant. Among today's statutory requirements are for secondary schools to identify between 5% and 10% of their pupils as "gifted and talented" and to encourage them to sit General Certificate of Secondary Education (GCSEs) early if possible.

[3] The optimist's view is that this has increased the likelihood

of tapping into the potential of more young geniuses; the cynic's is that it has contributed to such labels being used far more loosely.

[4] Bright children often, of course, have ambitious parents behind them. Even Ryde College, famed for its proportion of students taking exams early, argues that its high achievers are not exceptional necessarily—"but children who have been given the opportunity to achieve".

译 析

就题目 The Gifted Children 而言，有的参赛者译成"天资聪颖的儿童""天选之子""神童"等，而"天才神童"，则属前后重复；其实，按原文平实地译为"天才儿童"即可。

在[1]中，对 Why let them walk when they can fly? 参赛者一般译成"为什么让他们在他们可以飞的时候行走？""当他们能够张开双翅飞翔的时候为什么还只让他们用双脚行走呢？""为什么在他们有能力飞的时候让他们走路？"等，意思不错，但有些啰嗦，可通过断句、省略等，译得更简练，如"既然可以飞翔，为什么还让他们行走？"同样，This is a question that is being asked by more and more parents in the UK who believe their children to be "gifted" or child prodigies，大都译成"这是一个被越来越多的英国父母询问他们相信自己的孩子是'天才'还是'神童'的问题""这是越来越多那些认为自己的孩子是'天才'或神童的英国家长所提出的问题""越来越多认为自己的孩子'天赋异禀'

或认为自己的孩子是奇才神童的英国家长纷纷抛出这个疑问"等，分析起来，question是宾语，但它后面又带个从句，若将其译成定语，就会出现上面这些译文，读来不免冗赘；办法是，把从句中的主语抽出来，调整到前面，转化成状语，从而断开句子，使后面的谓语和宾语更为简化："在认为自己的孩子是天才或神童的英国父母中，有越来越多的人提出了这样的问题。"

National Association of Gifted Children可译为"国家天才儿童联合会"（或类似的），但有的译成"全美资优儿童联合会"，便有问题——这里明明讲的是英国的事，怎么出现了"全美"？可见没有认真理解原文背景。同时，across all subjects不是"跨学科"（为大学研究学科），而是"各门功课"（为中小学的课程）；verbal skills不是简单的"口头技巧"，而为"言语能力"（不同于概念更宽泛的"语言能力"）；这里的way (beyond)是far的意思，即"远"（超过）……。故此句不妨译为："在国家天才儿童联合会（简称NAGC）接到的电话中，许多家长称他们的子女在各门功课上均显出超人的能力，往往在解决问题和言语能力方面大大高于他们的生理年龄。"

[2]中的crème de la crème是法语，为"精英"；而The present British government's focus on provision for the crème de la crème in UK schools is doubtless significant中的provision，大都被译成了"条款""规定""供给"等，如"目前英国政府把重点放在英国学校超级精英的有关条款""当今的英国政府十分关注学校里的精英人才的相关规定""英国政府目前着重对校内英才学习资源的供给"等，其实该词还有"服务""提供"之意，如Local

authority nursery provision covers only a tiny minority of working mothers（当地政府提供的保育服务只有少数上班族母亲才能够享受到）；The government is responsible for the provision of health care（政府负责提供医疗服务），而此处宜译为"培养"："现在英国政府无疑十分重视对学校中拔尖学生的培养。"

对于to encourage them to sit General Certificate of Secondary Education，一般译成了"鼓励他们尽早取得普通中等教育证书（GCSEs）、并可尽可能地提前授予他们普通中等教育证书"等，其中都忽略了sit exam的用法，即"参加……考试"。而其中的GCSEs恰是"普通中等教育证书考试"。类似的，如It is laid down that all applicants must sit a written exam（根据规定，申请者一律需经笔试），A number of students came up last week to sit for the university entrance exam（上星期有许多学生来参加大学入学考试）等；而statutory requirements才是现行法规，故该句不妨译为："按现行法规，中学须将其5%至10%的在校生确认为'天才'学生，并鼓励他们在可能的情况下，尽早参加普通中等教育证书考试。"

对于[3]中的The optimist's view is that this has increased the likelihood of tapping into the potential of more young geniuses; the cynic's is that it has contributed to such labels being used far more loosely，参赛者一般译成"对此，乐观主义者认为这增加了挖掘更多年轻天才潜力的可能性；然而一些愤世嫉俗者则认为这导致了此类标签的含金量低了许多""乐天派认为这样做会增大激发更多青年人才潜能的可能性，然而讽世派觉得这样做则会导致对像'神童'这类词语的定义过于随便及过于标签化""对此持乐观态度的人认为,这有利于开发更多天才儿童的潜能;而持消极态度的人则认为,这只会导致'天才'的定义更加宽泛"等,即都将optimist译成"乐观主义者""乐天派""持乐观态度的人"等,而将cynic译成与之相反的意思。其实,此处对于optimist和loosely都不必过于死板,而不妨稍加变通,如 I am very optimist about our education(对我们的教育我很有信心); Don't use the word too loosely(这个词不要用得太随便)等,故此句不妨译为:"积极支持者认为,这增加了发掘天才儿童潜力的可能性;而持怀疑态度者则认为,这将导致'天才儿童'标签的使用过于随意。"

[4] 中的ambitious parents,一般被译成了"雄心壮志/雄心勃勃的父母",其实此处形容父母,不同于青少年,更适宜的为"望子成龙",即"聪明孩子的背后自然是望子成龙的父母"。较难处理的,是 Even Ryde College, famed for its proportion of students taking exams early, argues that its high achievers are not exceptional necessarily—"but children who have been given the opportunity to achieve". 参赛译文差异很大,如"澳大利亚莱德中学的很多学生在入学后早期就被安排开始考试了,这也是这所学校出名的原因";如上所述,这里明明讲的英国的事,怎么又出现了"澳大利亚"?且该句所要说明的并不是"学校出名的原因""即使莱德中学——因为相当比例的学生提前参加考试而声名在外,也认为高成就者不一定都是神童——而往往是那些被给予机会去努力获取成功的孩子",尽管是译文用了很复杂的句式,

但也未必把句子意思重点讲清楚了，特别是but的转折语气，应为"不过是"；而children who have been given the opportunity并不是"孩子"，而是"机会"。同时，若将第一句中的定语整合起来，又不免冗长，如"甚至以提前参加普通中学教育证书考试比例居高而闻名的莱德公学，（也认为……）"，故不妨采取分译法，如"莱德公学以提前参加普通中学教育证书考试比例居高而闻名，甚至该校也认为他们那些成绩优异的学生，并不一定是才能出众的，而不过是得到了取得优异成绩的机会"。

参考译文

天才儿童

凯特·希尔本

[1] 既然可以飞翔，为什么还让他们行走？在认为自己的孩子是天才或神童的英国父母中，有越来越多的人提出了这样的问题。在"国家天才儿童联合会"（简称NAGC）接到的电话中，许多家长称他们的子女在各门功课上均显出超人的能力，往往在解决问题和言语能力方面大大高于他们的生理年龄。还有家长说，他们的孩子在诸如数学之类的特定领域有天赋，或是在美术、体育、音乐等非普通文化课具有特殊才能。

[2] 现在英国政府无疑十分重视对学校中拔尖学生的培养。

按现行法规，中学须将其5%至10%的在校生确认为"天才"学生，并鼓励他们在可能的情况下，尽早参加普通中等教育证书考试。

[3] 积极支持者认为，这增加了发掘天才儿童潜力的可能性；而持怀疑态度者则认为，这将导致"天才儿童"标签的使用过于随意。

[4] 聪明孩子的背后自然是望子成龙的父母。莱德公学以提前参加普通中学教育证书考试比例居高而闻名，甚至该校也认为他们那些成绩优异的学生，并不一定是才能出众的，而不过是得到了取得优异成绩的机会。

> 原 文

Be Ordinary

By William Martin

[1] Do not ask your children to strive for extraordinary lives. Such striving may seem admirable, but it is the way of foolishness.

[2] Help them instead to find the wonder and the marvel of an ordinary life. Show them the joy of tasting tomatoes, apples and pears. Show them how to cry when pets and people die. Show them the infinite pleasure in the touch of a hand.

[3] And make the ordinary come alive for them. The extraordinary will take care of itself.

> 译 析

美国文学家威廉·马丁（William Martin）写于上世纪初的这首散文诗经常被人引用。美国教育家丹尼尔·施瓦茨（Daniel Schwartz）对此说过一段有名的话："Society often measures success by material possessions, salaries paid, and degrees earned. In schools, success typically means high grades, strong test scores, and awards and recognition. Yet in the rush to achieve, we can lose the whole child, pursuing a two-dimensional view of success."（对于"成功"，社会通常以物质占有、薪金和学位来衡量；在学校，则以高分数、考得好、获得奖励和赞誉为标志。然而，在这种对于肤浅成功理念的不懈追求中，我们可能会失去整个孩子。）。可以说，这对于一般家长的教育理念是一种反传统。

对于[1]，参赛者一般译成了"不要勉强你的孩子们为非凡的人生而苦斗，这种奋斗看似令人羡慕，但实则为一种愚蠢的办法""不要让你的孩子刻意追求非凡的人生。这种奋斗也许看上去令人钦佩，但实际上是一种愚蠢的做法""不要苛求你的孩子们去争取过非凡的生活，这种努力看似令人钦佩，但其实是一种愚笨的方式"等，似都不错，但太囿于原文的词语。有的则更加离谱："不要让你的孩子力争特别的生活。这样的战争似乎是可爱的。但是它是愚蠢的方式。"对此，我真要怀疑是否是机器翻译的。比较好的，作了些变通："切莫苛求你的孩子出人头地：他为此付出的努力看似值得钦佩，实则愚昧荒唐""不要让你的孩子去追求非凡的人生。追求非凡看似令人欣羡，但却是愚蠢的"等。其实，现代西方文化的核心价值理念是尊重人性和个性；据我在西方生活、工作十余年的体会，那里的家长很少有"不让孩子输在起跑线上"的想法，而更多的是让孩子自然成长。如果孩子有某方面的特长，去参加某项比赛，夺冠也未必是唯一的目标，更重要的是 enjoy（享受）和 do your best（尽力），可以说，这是经过实践证明了的比较成熟的教育和生活理念。此句，不妨译为："不必要求你的孩子追求非凡的生活；那似乎令人羡慕,但却是愚蠢的。"

在理解上文基础上,应当不难体会,[2]是向其相反方面的进一步发挥。许多人翻译得比较"实",如"请帮助他们找到平凡生活中的奇迹。请向他们展示品尝西红柿、苹果和梨的快乐。请让他们明白,当宠物和人们逝去时应该如何哭泣。请让他们感受到亲手触碰的无尽快乐"等。显然,似乎其中的每一词都能"对号入座",但读起来却不免死板、佶屈;而有的,又过于笼统、发挥,如"告诉他们并非珍馐才能带来喜悦,带着他们感受死别带来的悲泣。让他们明白哪怕只是手心的触碰,也会感到温暖"等。其实,此处的 instead 原本可以放在句首(Instead, help them to...),即强调相反的情况,而 tomatoes, apples and pears 不过是信手拈来的比喻,而此处要译出的是"实质",即让孩子们得到享受生活的乐趣。故此,不妨译为:"相反,应当帮助孩子发现平凡生活中的奇迹与美妙——让他们学会享受如品尝西红柿、苹果、梨子的乐趣,体会对人们、宠物逝去的悲伤,感受到抚摸的无限慰藉……"

[3] 的问题较多,如"并且为了他们而使平凡活跃起来。非凡会照顾自己""让平常日子都变得灵动活力,让那些不平凡的日子随风而逝吧""让他们平凡的生活充满活力与激情,而这个层面上的非凡便是——关爱自己""让平凡为他们绽放精彩,大可对那非凡不予理睬""非同凡响的生活不必苦苦追寻,它不来也不去"等。显然,主要问题出在对 come alive 和 take care of itself 的理解。前者,在此处是"有意义",如 Instead of wandering about, you should now consider what makes you come alive.(不要再游荡了,你现在应该考虑下,怎样使生活过得有意义。)后

者，有"自然而然"之意，如：1. If you make a good investment, the money will take care of itself.（投资对了，赚钱不成问题。）2. Focusing on your bottom line and the rest will take care of itself.（解决了基本问题，其他便会迎刃而解。）3. Concentrating on the present; the future will take care of itself.（集中精力做好现在的事，将来就不用担心了。）而And在此不只是起连接作用，而且还有归总之意。故此，不妨译为："总之，使平凡具有意义，非凡就在其中了。"

澳大利亚心理学家曾做过调查，了解人们成年后回忆儿时对家庭最怀念的地方，大部分人的回答并不是学习、励志的时刻，而恰恰是日常生活中的点点滴滴，如一起烧烤、躺在海滩上闲聊之类的"无所事事"。路遥的《平凡的世界》写的也是一群平凡人的平凡故事，但却激励了千百万人。关于平凡与不平凡之间的异同与关系（the differences and relations between ordinary and extraordinary），是社会心理学中的一个研究课题，有兴趣者，不妨找来一阅。

参考译文

安于平凡

威廉·马丁

[1] 不必要求你的孩子追求非凡的生活；那似乎令人羡慕，

但却是愚蠢的。

[2] 相反，应当帮助孩子发现平凡生活中的奇迹与美妙——让他们学会享受如品尝西红柿、苹果、梨子的乐趣，体会对人们、宠物逝去的悲伤，感受到抚摸的无限慰藉……

[3] 总之，使平凡具有意义，非凡就在其中了。

原　文

Studying Abroad

[1] Every year hundreds of thousands of Chinese students leave the comfort of their homes to study overseas, either wooed by the exotic pleasure such a journey brings, or convinced that an extended stay in another country can create lifelong memories and give them prestige in their homeland.

[2] The most important reason for participating in a study abroad program is the opportunity to see the world through a different cultural lens. The powerful, transformative experiences will serve you well in business and in life.

[3] Studying abroad, like higher education, is an investment in your future, which requires planning, careful management, perseverance and commitment. The personal, academic and professional rewards, however, will last a lifetime.

[4] Educational and cultural exchanges will elevate our ideals, deepen our tolerance, sharpen our appetite for knowledge, and make us more sensitive and wiser international citizens throughout our careers.

[5] Personally, I think the best way to explore a new foreign place is to wander about on foot and talk to as many locals and other foreigners living there as you can, which will provide you with a plethora of different views and experiences.

译 析

对于题目 Studying Abroad，有的译成"出国留学""求学海外""国外留学"等；其实，所谓"留学"是指某人去母国以外的国家去接受一段时期的教育，所以不必词语重复，只需"留学"即可。至于"向西方取经"则偏离更远。

[1] 中，either wooed by the exotic pleasure such a journey brings, or convinced that an extended stay in another country can create lifelong memories and give them prestige in their homeland 是一长句，有的译成"这些留学生要么是被留学之旅中感受异域风情带来的愉悦所吸引，要么是坚定地认为，能在异国他乡住上如此长一段时间，定是一段终生难忘的回忆，<u>也能提升祖国在他们心中的威严</u>"，对 either... or... 一般都能把握，但下画线部分显然理解错误；而更多的是理解对了，但表述欠佳，如"要么是因为向往异国求学之旅的别样风情，要么是因为坚信，长居在异国他乡的体验定是一段终生难忘的回忆；<u>留洋经历也能让自己在祖国更添声望</u>""他们或是被求学旅程中的异国情调所吸引，或是深信长期生活在异国会留下终其一生的回忆，<u>并使他们归国后声誉卓著</u>""他们或是为这场旅程中的异国风情所吸引，或是相信

在另一个国家长住的经历能给他们带来长足一生的回忆,<u>并且让他们在祖国享有名誉</u>"等;其中,prestige 的本义是 the respect and admiration that someone or something has because of their social position, or what they have done,而此处又不宜机械地译成"声誉卓著""享有名誉"等,而是指获得某种别人没有的感觉。因而,该段不妨译为:"每年都有成千上万的中国学生离开舒适的家庭去海外留学。他们要么被出游的异国情调所吸引,要么相信在他国的一段生活会留下终生难忘记忆,而回国后又具有某种优越感。"

[2] 中,cultural lens 不宜译成"文化镜头""文化透视"等,powerful,不是"有力的",transformative,亦不是"变形的",即不可照搬字典,而应根据此处的具体语境加以适当变通;如可分别译为"文化视角""深刻的""令人触动的"等。同时,serve you well in business and in life,其中的 you 是一种泛指,若译成"无论是在事业上,还是在生活中,……都会对你有所益处",颇显死板;如 You don't have to be a pessimist to realize that we're in trouble(不是悲观论者也能意识到我们有了麻烦);In all actuality, you don't have to be in a theater hall, concert hall or anything(事实上,这种行为不必非要发生在剧院礼堂、音乐大厅或别的什么特定地方);You don't have to be feline to study the feline(人不必变成猫来研究猫科动物)等。故此,可将两句合成为:"参加留学项目最重要的理由,是想有机会从不同文化视角看待世界;深刻而令人触动的个人经历,对一个人今后的职业、生活都大有益处。"

对于[3]，较为典型的译文，如"出国留学，比如在海外接受高等教育，是对未来的一笔投资。这个过程需要我们的恒心与毅力，合理规划，悉心经营。但我们在个人、学术和专业方面所能获得的回报，足以让我们受益终生""出国留学，比如在海外接受高等教育，是对未来的一笔投资。这个过程需要我们的恒心与毅力，合理规划，悉心经营。但我们在个人、学术和专业方面所能获得的回报，足以让我们受益终生""出国留学，比如接受高等教育，是一项对未来的投资，需要你做好规划、用心经营，还要坚持不懈、投身其中。而无论是个人的，还是学业或专业上的收获，都将让你终生受益"等；应当说总体意思都不错，但在词序上似可作些调整，如将状语 like higher education 提前，以使主语 Studying abroad 直接谓语、宾语 is an investment；对于 perseverance and commitment 两个名词，若处理成动词，需作某些增译，如"富有毅力，敢于担当"。同时，如上所述，慎用"你"。整句不妨译为："如同高等教育，出国留学是对未来的投资，需要精心规划、管理，富有毅力，敢于担当。于是，个人可在学术和专业方面终身受益。"

[4] 中，elevate our ideals 若译成"让我们在事业生涯中树立更崇高的理想""能促使人们提高个人理想境界""可以让我们在自己的职业生涯里获得更高远的理想""使我们树立远大的理想"等，显然不够简练，不如"提升我们的理想"，尔后采用同样的句式，如"加深……，增强……"等；throughout our careers 不必译成"我们在整个职业生涯"，而 international citizens 是一种特指，不妨加上引号。因而，该句可译为："教育和文化方面的

交流,将提升我们的理想,加深我们的容忍度,增强我们的求知欲,使我们在事业中成为更敏感、明智的'国际公民'"。

[5] 是个长句,其中Personally,释为used to show that you are giving your own opinion about something,即"就本人而言、个人意见",如Personally, I prefer the second option(就个人而言,我倾向第二种选择);wander about表面意思是闲逛、漫步、徘徊等,但此处是指the best way to explore,即"最好的方式是……",便不妨译为"到处走走";plethora的本义为an amount that is greater than is needed or can be used,但不必译成"过度的",而为"丰富的"。故此,整句不妨译为:"个人而言,我认为熟悉异国他乡的最好方式,是到处走走,与尽可能多的当地人和那里的外国人交流,从中了解到不同的观点和丰富的经历。"

参考译文

留学

[1] 每年都有成千上万的中国学生离开舒适的家庭去海外留学。他们要么被出游的异国情调所吸引,要么相信在他国的一段生活会留下终生难忘记忆,而回国后又具有某种优越感。

[2] 参加留学项目最重要的理由,是想有机会从不同文化视

角看待世界；深刻而令人触动的个人经历，对一个人今后的职业、生活都大有益处。

[3] 如同高等教育，出国留学是对未来的投资，需要精心规划、管理，富有毅力，敢于担当。于是，个人可在学术和专业方面终身受益。

[4] 教育和文化方面的交流，将提升我们的理想，加深我们的容忍度，增强我们的求知欲，使我们在事业中成为更敏感、明智的"国际公民"。

[5] 个人而言，我认为熟悉异国他乡的最好方式，是到处走走，与尽可能多的当地人和那里的外国人交流，从中了解到不同的观点和丰富的经历。

II. 汉译英部分

1

> 原 文

汤显祖与莎士比亚

[1] 今年是明代戏剧家汤显祖逝世400周年,也是英国戏剧大家莎士比亚逝世400周年。

[2] 汤显祖和莎士比亚是两位同时期的世界级戏剧家,在不同的文化背景与生活环境下,同样都创作出了脍炙人口超越时空的剧作。

[3] 我们是否可以假设,如果400年前也有今天一样发达的通讯和交通,说不定两人会看到彼此的作品,甚至会一见如故,相见恨晚,成为最好的朋友。

——叶长海《人民日报》

> 译 析

汤显祖与莎士比亚,两位东西方戏剧大师,原本并无关系,却因同在400多年前(1616年)去世而联系在了一起,以至联合国都发起了对他们的系列纪念活动。

两位的才华难分伯仲,但作品数量却相差很大。汤氏活了66岁,只有戏剧5部,而莎翁52岁早逝,却留下37部戏剧及154

首十四行诗等。原因很简单：前者心系官场，视戏剧为末节；后者身在梨园，把此职当正事。然而留给后世的，哪个更有价值？年代越久，看得越清楚。

[1]中，"400周年"应为序数词（-th），而非一般数字；"戏剧家"许多人用了playwright，该词原本与dramatist意思相近，但近年多用于电影剧本作家，而后者则保留了传统含义（而且与dramas相对应）；"逝世"指的是二位，故可合并译出；而中国历史朝代后面应注明年代，以使读者有时间概念。下面为一典型参赛译文：This year {2016} is the 400 [th] anniversary of [the] Ming dynasty playwright Tang Xianzu's death {and also the 400 anniversary of} the British dramatist [William] Shakespeare's {death}.（注：{ }内为可删去或不应重复的，[ ]内为应增加的部分。）。实则，不妨译为：This year marks the four hundredth anniversaries of the deaths of both Chinese Tang Xianzu of the Ming dynasty (1368-1644) and British William Shakespeare.

[2]中，"同时期的"，许多人用了the same period、of the same historical period、in the same time等，其实contemporary不只是"当代的"，而且是"同代的"（alive or existing at the same time as a particular person or event）；"在不同的文化背景与生活环境下"，许多人译成Under different/diverse cultural backgrounds and living environments，固然不错，但略显死板（如"在……下"不一定总是under...，"不同"亦非永远为different、diverse等）；"生活环境"，有的用了ecological setting，似乎很合现在的环保理念，但此处似有过之，而ambience可以考虑，该词从法

语ambiant（surrounding）而来，有古典色彩；"脍炙人口"，译成enjoy great popularity、appeal to most people等固然不错，但考虑到两位跨东西方的界度，win universal praise似更切宜。另外，在语序上，此句翻译时亦不妨根据中文的习惯有所调整。

考察历史，发现最早将汤氏和莎翁相提并论的，竟然是20世纪30年代的日本汉学家青木正儿在其《中国近世戏曲史》中的表述："东西曲坛伟人，同出其时，亦一奇也……"翻译出来："两位伟人虽同时出现于东西方戏剧界，（素昧平生，）却共为人类文化的奇葩……"——这可谓为二人安排的首次跨时空"握手"。

在英汉对比研究中，学术界一般将英语定义为"形合"（Hypotactic），即其句子成分之间主要靠语言形式手段（如关联词等）相连接；中文是"意合"（Paratactic），即词语或子句之间不用语言形式，而是通过逻辑关系和内在含义相整合。于是，在翻译上便有了明显的增、减、整的现象。典型的例子如：1. When the pressure gets low, the boiling point becomes low. 译成中文时，可省去介词、动词等——"气压低，沸点就低。"；2. "求职者，会说英语的优先录取。"译成英文时，则需加上代词、助词、介词等——"Job applicants who can speak English would receive preference over those who can't."。

故此，不妨将[1] [2]以语言形式（如同位语、代词、动名词、介词等）整合起来：This year marks the four hundredth anniversaries of the deaths of both Chinese Tang Xianzu of the Ming dynasty (1368-1644) and British William Shakespeare, two contemporary world class dramatists who created their dramas that have been winning universal praise transcending time and space, based on their own living ambiences and cultural backgrounds.

[3]中,见到"假设",很多人用了 assume,但仔细推敲,该词的原意为 to accept that something is true without checking or confirming it; accept without verification or proof,即是一种推测,现更多用于学术上未经证实的个案或命题;而"如果"很容易与 if 联在一起。其实,表示虚拟语气,还可将谓语中的过去式 had、should、were 等移至主语前,如:1. Had he been in your position, he would probably have done the same.(他若处在你的位置,也会这样做的。)2. I will go, should it be necessary.(有必要的话,我会去的。)3. Were you to argue, object, and annoy me for a year, I would not agree with you.(你就是争吵、对抗、烦扰我一年,我也不会同意的。)。故此句起码可以用这三种表现形式,如 had they... / should they have / were they provided with... 等。更确切而言,这里的"假设"实为"想象"(imagine),如 We can well image that、Imaging that、It catches imagination of... 等。语气更强的则为 fire imagination(激发想象),如 Stories of adventure fire Tom's imagination.(冒险故事激发了汤姆的想象力。)。故此处不妨译为 It should fire our imagination that...。

"相见恨晚",此处的"恨"不是现代汉语的"憎恨",而是古汉语的原意,"恨,怨也"(《说文》),即"遗憾、悔恨",英文为 regretful、regret deeply、pity、sorry 等。有参赛者译成 they regretted not to have known each other much earlier、the two masters would have hit it off and regretted their missing、were only feeling regretful not to have met much sooner等，都不乏创意，问题是如何更好地将其整合在句子和篇章之中。的确，如果先译出了"一见如故"，似乎又不好加入regret之意，但将其置后，补充说明，不失为一种表达技巧。例如参赛译文：Shall we assume that {400 years ago}, if there had been telecommunications and {means of} transportation as advanced as those in modern time, {Tang Xianzu and Shakespeare} might have chance to read each other's works and even become fast friends at their first meeting {as if they had known each other for quite along time}, only to regret meeting each other too late.

应当说，隔离来看，此段译文大体可以接受，但结合篇章，{ }里的内容似有可精简或改进之处。

故此，综合考虑，该段不妨译为：It should fire our imagination that had they communication and transportation as advanced as we have today, the two giants might have read each other's works, or even become old acquaintances and best friends at their first meeting—regrettably, they didn't.

此外，参赛译文中还有一些语法错误，如过去式、完成时、虚拟语气的运用等，属基本功问题，不妨做些针对性补课，以利日后参赛。

顺便而言，两位戏剧大师的创作精神其实极其相似：汤氏褒扬个性，痛挞腐朽摧残；莎翁悲天悯人，极富人文情怀。然而，他们在世界上的影响却不可同日而语。除了其他因素，显然也与翻译有关。

参考译文

Tang Xianzu and Shakespeare
By Ye Changhai

[1] [2] This year marks the four hundredth anniversaries of the deaths of both Chinese Tang Xianzu of the Ming Dynasty (1368–1644) and British William Shakespeare, two contemporary world class dramatists who created their dramas that have been winning universal praise transcending time and space, based on their own living ambiences and cultural backgrounds.

[3] It should fire our imagination that had they communication and transportation as advanced as we have today, the two giants might have read each other's works, or even become old acquaintances and best friends at their first meeting—regrettably, they didn't.

——*People's Daily*

2

> 原 文

过年

[1] 又到岁末年初了。

[2] 中文"年"的本义是指丰收,俗语说"人寿年丰"。

[3] 在古代,由于稻禾一年收获一次,所以又引申出了"岁"的意思,代表一年四季,后来又表示一个人的年龄。

[4] 在西方,人们通常有"新年许愿",即希望在新的一年有所进步。

[5] 其实,这种许愿不必太多,能做到一两件小事就好。例如,最简单的,保证在与人交谈时不再看手机,等等。

> 译 析

新年是一个新起点,总给人带来希望,中外皆然。但知其缘由,辨其含义,方可寄语情怀。

[1] 中,"岁末年初",许多人译成"It's time again for us to see the old year out and welcome the new year in.","We have come once again to the time of bidding farewell to the old year and welcoming the new."等,似乎可以,但有些过"实"。固然,习

近平主席在新年贺词中有"在这辞旧迎新的美好时刻",可译成"At this beautiful moment to bid farewell to the old and usher in the new." 或 "At this happy moment of ringing out the old year and ringing in the new.",但那是在特定的除夕时刻讲的,就一般表述而言不妨简化些:New Year is once again approaching.

[2] 中,对于"年"的解释、翻译,参赛者有着各种各样的表述。一般而言,以英文解释中文词语时,可先用拼音(斜体)以便能读出,最好附以汉字(括号内)以知原字,但对于颇长的原文句子,可酌情略去中文,再以"or..."加以释译。"本义",可用 original meaning、literally、in a literal sense 等,如 This word should not be taken in its literal sense.(该词不能按本义去理解。)。在语序上,亦可根据语境作些灵活处理。"人寿年丰",有的译成 people live a long life and have good harvest、people long for longevity and the harvest is extraordinarily abundant 等,其实,"寿"与"年丰"结合,这里可理解为泛指过好日子。故该句不妨译为:Originally, the character *nian* (年) in Chinese denoted the amount of crops gathered. There is a saying *ren shou nian feng*, or "people enjoy good health and the land yields bumper harvests".

[3] 中,"稻禾",许多人译成了 rice、grain,其实这里所丰收的是泛指"作物",故可用 crops;而这里的"岁"实则指的是 year,其主语仍然是"年";"年龄"则是 the age of a person,故此句不妨译为:Since the crops were reaped once a year in ancient times, the word also came to mean "year", referring to the four seasons, and consequently the age of a person.

[4] 中,"新年许愿",许多人译成了 New Year wishes、make a good wish for New Year 等,其实英语中固定用语为 New Year's resolutions 或者 start the New Year right;"即希望……"是对前面的进一步说明;而这里"新的一年"可避免再用 New Year,不妨变通一下,如 the coming year。故此句不妨译为:In the West, people are likely to make "New Year's resolutions", wishing for self-improvement in the coming year.

[5] 中,"小事"可谓时下流行说的"定个小目标",一般译成了 small goal / target / change、little thing、tiny adjustment 等,似乎都可。做好"小事",已经成为一种西方文化,如英文常说的:"Forget the overreaching, hard-to-achieve goals. Just think small."(放弃那些自不量力、难以实现的大目标,考虑一些小目标就好了。)。美国心理学家罗伯特·莫伊雷尔(Robert Maurer)还写过一本很有影响的书《小事改变人生》(*One Small Step Can Change Your Life*),其中极力推崇日本的 kaizen 的概念,书中解释道:Kaizen is the art of making great and lasting change through small, steady increments. Kaizen is the tortoise versus the hare.(Kaizen 是通过小事产生大的持久变化的艺术;一种龟兔赛跑。),意思是"以慢胜快""以小拨大"。而根据有关日文辞典,kaizen 是"改善",其本义为"物事のむだなこと、悪いことを取り除いて、よりよいものにかえること",即"去掉无用无益的东西而变得越来越好",这是一个渐进的过程,如"体質の改善を図る"(to gradually improve one's health),很符合英文的 improvement、betterment,其实质是 a change for the better、

progress in development，所以很容易被战后的美国所接受，作为一种指导理念，在日后的经济恢复中也卓有成效，故其"小"意亦不妨译为 the simplest thing。同时，此书还引用了老子的"The journey of a thousand miles begins with a single step."（千里之行，始于足下。），属同一哲理。故此，不妨译为：The idea of what should change, in fact, doesn't have to be broad, one or two of the simplest things will do—for example, promising not to check your smartphone when talking to others and so on.

对于岁月的流逝，各个年龄段的感觉是不同的；但对于新日子的期许总是好的，特别是在汉英两种语言之间的转换，也算是一种跨越时空的感悟吧。

参考译文

Celebrating the New Year

[1] New Year is once again approaching.

[2] Originally, the character *nian* (年) in Chinese denoted the amount of crops gathered. There is a saying *ren shou nian feng*, or "people enjoy good health and the land yields bumper harvests".

[3] Since the crops were reaped once a year in ancient times, the word also came to mean "year", referring to the four seasons, and

consequently the age of a person.

[4] In the West, people are likely to make "New Year's resolutions", wishing for self-improvement in the coming year.

[5] The idea of what should change, in fact, doesn't have to be broad, one or two of the simplest things will do—for example, promising not to check your smartphone when talking to others and so on.

3

原　文

岁月的流逝①

（节选）

林清玄

[1] 我们在人生里，随着岁月的流逝而感觉到自己的成长（其实是一种老去），会发现每一个阶段都拥有了不同的朋友。

[2] 友谊虽不至于散失，聚散却随因缘流转，常常转到我们一回首感到惊心的地步。

[3] 比较可悲的是，那些特别相知的朋友往往远在天际，泛泛之交却在眼前，因此，生活里经常令我们陷入一种人生寂寥的境地。

译　析

岁末年初，最容易让人感叹日月消长、时光不复。随着年龄的增加，对此可能更会有不同的感受。

关于题目"岁月的流逝"，有各种译法，有的用了 Time

---

① 编者注：原名为《怀君与怀珠》，现标题为作者所加。

Flies，看似不错，但细加分析，该短语主要是感叹时光飞逝、岁月如梭，如：1. Time flies by, and a world of changes has occurred.（光阴荏苒，世事沧桑。）2. These five years have seemed to me like 5 months. Time flies!（这5年对我来说就像5个月一样，时光飞逝！）3. How time flies! Here you are graduating from high school and planning to attend State University in the fall.（时间过得真快，转眼间你就将中学毕业，并拟于秋季进入州立大学了！）。然而，该文着意"随着岁月的流逝"，即强调的是"过程"，而非"速度"，类似的如经典歌曲《卡萨布兰卡》（*Casablanca*）中唱道："I love you more and more each day / As time goes by"（时光流逝，对你的爱恋却与日俱增。）。夏丏尊的名篇《中年人的寂寞》中有："不消说，相识的人数是随了年龄增加的，一个人年龄越大，走过的地方当过的职务越多，相识的人理该越增加了。"著名翻译家张培基的译文为：Needless to say, the number of acquaintances increases with one's age. The older one gets, the more widely traveled one is and the more work experience one has, the more acquaintances one is supposed to have. 这些表达都有"随着岁月而发生……"之意，故此处不妨用：As Years Go By...

对于[1]，许多人都按部就班地依原文译成 In our lives, we could realize that we grow up (a kind of aging, actually), In our lifetime, we feel certain inner growth with the flow of years (which, in essence, is a sign of ageing), In our life journey, we witness our growth as time marches on (actually we get older as the years rolled by), We, in our life, feel our own growth (an aging in disguise) as time goes by 等,其实,中英文的语序在译文里不必刻板,而可根据要表达或强调的意思相当灵活地加以处理,特别是状语。例如:"有时候在外面玩儿到半夜才回家睡觉,于是又梦见玩儿的情景",若循规蹈矩地译成 Sometimes, I played outside till midnight, and then sent to sleep. So I dreamed again of how I played. 不免显得呆滞,不如调整语序译为 Not until midnight did I go home to sleep, and then I dreamed what happened during the day. 更符合英文表达方式。有的调整幅度甚至很大:1. 在这个国家,一直以来,我最喜欢的地方其实很多。(The most loved place, for me, in this country has in fact been many places.) 2. 西洋人究竟近乎白痴,什么事都只讲究脚踏实地去做,这样费力气的勾当,我们聪明的中国人,简直连牙齿都要笑掉了。(Because of their earnest and down-to-earth approach to work, Westerners are, in the eyes of Chinese smarties, next door to idiot.)。同时,亦可不必受制于原文的标点符号(如其中的括号),而在译文中加以展开,更显平实、自然。故此,该部分不妨译为:As years go by, we can feel our growth, as a kind of ageing. At every stage of life, we make friends with all sorts of people.

[2]中,"聚散却随因缘流转"是个焦点,表层意思固然是 its (in terms of friendship) gathering or departure is transferred by fate、many of them come and go by such an uncertain twist of fate、makes our friends and us gather and separate by karma、gatherings and partings are steered by our destinies 等,但其深层含义是,经过世态炎凉,友谊经过了各种测试、拣选、考验,分流出了下文所讲

的"特别相知的朋友"和"泛泛之交",故应有the friendship has been tested by various turbulences之意。

"回首",一般译成as we look back、when looking back、call to mind、recollect、turning round等,固然都不错,但hindsight别有含义(understanding the nature of an event after it has happened; the ability to understand and realize something about an event after it has happened, although you did not understand or realize it at the time),故用该词,似更为恰当。

至于"惊心",有的用了shock,其实该词强调的是suddenly、accidentally (something <u>suddenly</u> happens which is unpleasant or upsetting; the feeling of distress and disbelief that you have when something bad happens <u>accidentally</u>),而surprise强调的是unexpected、unanticipated (the astonishment you feel when something totally <u>unexpected</u> or <u>unanticipated</u> happens to you)。二者比较,显然后者占优。

因而,该部分似可译为:While friendship may not be easily lost, various turbulences do test its endurance, to a point which may surprise us in hindsight.

[3]中,"特别相知的朋友",显然不只是those who know us particularly well,而是"相互理解的"bosom friends、soul mates等;"泛泛之交",一般可用general friends、nodding / bowing / casual acquaintances等。较为典型的译文,如The more grief is that friends whom we know from the bottom of our hearts are poles away and whom we know skin deep are in front of ones' eyes,

consequently we fall into a solitary situation in our life., We scarcely lose our most prominent friendship, but couldn't be with our friends for long. With the glimpse of the looking footprints, things are barely recalling the permanent terror and regrets., The sad thing is those who intimate with each other live far away while who is on hand-shaking terms is close to me. Therefore, life often puts us in a lonely position. 等。就此，上文提到的夏丏尊亦有类似论述："可是相识的人并不就是朋友。我们和许多人相识，或是因了事务关系，或是因了偶然的机缘——如在别人请客的时候同席吃过饭之类。见面时点头或握手，有事时走访或通信，口头上彼此也称'朋友'，笔头上有时或称'仁兄'，诸如此类，其实只是一种社交上的客套，和'顿首''百拜'同是仪式的虚伪。这种交际可以说是社交，和真正的友谊相差似乎很远。"张培基的译文为：But not all acquaintances are friends. We come to know many people either in the way of business or by mere chance—say, having been at the same table at a dinner party. We may be on nodding or hand-shaking terms, call each other "friend", sometimes write to each other with the salutation of "Dear So-and-So", etc. All these are, in fact, nothing but civilities of social life, as hypocritical as the polite formula *dunshou* (kowtow) or *baibai* (a hundred greetings) used after the signature in old-fashioned Chinese letter-writing. We may call them social intercourse, but they seem to have very little in common with genuine friendship.这段译文虽用词平淡，却深浅有度，叙述平实，仍情理之致，在某种程度上，可作为此段译文的注脚和参照。

故此，该部分不妨译为：Sadly, we often find that bosom friends are far away and casual acquaintances widely present, frequently trapping us in loneliness.

悠悠岁月，芸芸众生，实在有写不完且译不尽的精彩、感叹与无奈，这也正是生花妙笔的用武之地。

参考译文

As Years Go By...

(Excerpts)

By Lin Qingxuan

[1] As years go by, we can feel our growth, as a kind of ageing. At every stage of life, we make friends with all sorts of people.

[2] While friendship may not be easily lost, various turbulences do test its endurance, to a point which may surprise us in hindsight.

[3] Sadly, we often find that bosom friends are far away and casual acquaintances widely present, frequently trapping us in loneliness.

4

> 原　文

老家的端午节

[1] 小时候，端午节随清风吹送，风度翩翩地来了。林家的老屋顿时沸腾起来。每一户人家都会买一些肉，更重要的是，大人们一起包粽子。

[2] 传统的节日里，粽子却很朴素，料子就单纯一色一样的糯米。心灵手巧的老家的亲人们，一边有说有笑，一边手里忙个不停，艺术般的手，炉火纯青地包着粽子。

[3] 宽大的竹叶，经过细心地清洗，折成特别的形状，包着平时难得一见的糯米。棕树的细长的叶子做牢固的"线"，捆绑着弄好的棱角分明的粽叶，恰当到极点。

[4] 粽子，经过较长时间的水煮，一个个分外迷人。吃在嘴里，香在心头，妙在竹叶包装里的独特的形状。

[5] 于是，每一年的端午节，吃粽子成为一种渴望，一种等待，一种难得的记忆。

> 译　析

就题目"老家的端午节"而言，其中的"老家"有的参赛者译成the old house，即使用翻译软件，也未必会这样翻译吧？而Dragon Boat Festival又显然不完整；Reminiscences of My Hometown Dragon Boat Festival、Some Memories about the Dragon Boat Festival in My Hometown则过犹不及。应当说，hometown与native place在多数情况下可以互换，但后者更强调"籍贯"，如What is your native place?（你是哪儿的人？）。因而，标题不妨译为：The Dragon Boat Festival in My Hometown。

[1]中，"小时候"一般译成when I was a child、when I was little、In my childhood等，但纵观全文，看得出写的是作者儿时对端午节的记忆，故可用in my childhood memory。

"端午节随清风吹送，风度翩翩地来了"，是一种拟人的文学笔法，若译成the Dragon Boat Festival came along with the breeze未免过于简单，而...came home with the breeze, elegantly又有些狭窄，特别是elegantly，其"雅"常与"俗"相对应，如While you all do things elegantly, I do things crudely.（好吧，你们都是雅范儿的，我偏要来点儿俗的。）。而端午节是大众的"俗节"，用"风度翩翩"是指会给百姓带来恩惠，故不如用grace/gracefully，即不只具有表面的美，而是有更多的含义，如A born elegance, she even aged gracefully.（她天生丽质，甚至老去也优雅。）。

"林家"是指其家族，如"克林顿家族"（the Clintons），故可用the Lins（而不必是the Lin clan）。

"沸腾起来"固然可以用was very excited、suddenly bustling、full of jollification等，但cheer up更为简单、明快，该短语具有"fill with gladness, hope, high spirits, comfort"之意。

"更重要的是",大都译成more importantly。其实就"对等"而言,可有多种,如more to the point、what is more、what's more、above all等,而在此处日常随和的语境下,甚至可以不用这些,而在其具体行动中表现出来,即家家户户都把"包粽子"作为一件不可或缺的大事(serious business)来做,如:

1. Now Americans don't really think marriage is a business deal. But marriage is serious business in people's live.(虽然今天美国人并不真正认为婚姻是一宗商业交易,但婚姻确实是件人生大事。)
2. Since the Covid-19 pandemic, handheld and mobile devices have steadily become serious business for various teaching and seminars.(自新冠病毒流行以来,手持和移动设备已逐渐成为各种教学、研讨会的重要平台。)。

故此,该部分不妨译为:In my childhood memory, whenever the Dragon Boat Festival arrived, it came gracefully in the breeze and instantly cheered up the old house of the Lins. At that time, every family bought some meat and the grown-ups would soon engage in their serious *zongzi* (rice dumpling) packing business.

[2] 中,"很朴素"用simple即可,如"朴素生活"(simple life)、"朴素的人"(a simple man)。

"单纯一色一样的"不是the simple and pure of the same color,而是指"单一颜色",即a single color。

为使"传统的节日"与"粽子的朴素"产生联系,可用"As reflected in the traditional festival, ..."。

"老家的亲人们",许多人译成ingenuity relatives of my old

house、the ingenious kinsmen of the hometown 等，似乎有些复杂，而 the grandpas and grandmas、the relatives of my hometown 又过于简单，不如 close family members。

至于长句"心灵手巧的老家的亲人们，一边有说有笑，一边手里忙个不停，艺术般的手，炉火纯青地包着粽子"，若按原文词序，很容易译得冗长、中式，如 The family members of ingenuity in my hometown, talking and laughing, are busy packing *zongzi* proficiently in ingenious hand., Ingenious relatives in the hometown were busy on their hands over talking and laughing with the dexterous hands making *zongzi* perfectly., The family members of the ingenious hometown, talking and laughing at the same time, are busy with their hands, artistic hands, wrapped with *zongzi*. 其实，遇到这种句式，不妨将原文中的状语或定语提前译出，如：1. 他认真热情，一字不漏地记下了所说的话。(Conscientious and eager, he took down what was said, careful not to miss a word.) 2. 她，一个瘦弱多病的女子，以坚强的毅力拿到了博士学位。(A thin and weak girl susceptible to diseases, she has obtained her PhD degree with her strong will.) 故此处可用"While talking and laughing, ..."。相应地，对于"艺术般的手，炉火纯青地包着粽子"也要作些词序调整，以融入句中。

因而，该部分不妨译为：As reflected in the traditional festival, *zongzi* was very simple: wrapped pure glutinous rice of a single color. While talking and laughing, close family members would skillfully use their artistic hands to make *zongzi* with a high degree of proficiency.

[3]中,"宽大的竹叶,经过细心地清洗,折成特别的形状,包着……",可用"Wrapped in broad bamboo leaves..."。注意此处的 wrapped in... 是指"用……包着……",而上文的 wrapped (pure glutinous rice) 是指"包着……东西"。

对于"难得一见的糯米",一般照字面意思译成 the sticky rice rarely seen in daily life、the glutinous rice that was not common in ordinary days 等,然而还可在具体语境中作些变通。

这部分不妨译为:Wrapped in broad bamboo leaves, carefully cleaned and specifically shaped, together with slender threads of the "firming line", the sharp-edged unusual glutinous rice dumplings in this way formulate perfect *zongzi*.

[4]中,"经过较长时间的水煮",若按字面译成 after a long time boiling in water,显然冗赘,因 boil 本义为 to cook something by submerging it in boiling liquid for a period of time。

而将"吃在嘴里,香在心头,妙在竹叶包装里的独特的形状。"译成"Eating in the mouth, fragrance in the heart, wonderful in the unique shape of bamboo leaf packaging."亦有同样问题。此处不妨"合并同类项",将对于粽子形状、特色的描述归到一起,而将"吃"和"香"的感觉留在后面。

同时,此处的"香"不是一般意义的 fragrant、aroma、incense、appetizing 等,而实际是一种"味道""滋味""甜美",故宜用 taste、flavor、relish 等,作为动词,此处 flavor 更确切,如:
1. With discoveries in methods to preserve food, almost every kind of food can be frozen and yet keep its original flavor.(发明食品保存

方法之后，几乎每种食品都能冷冻，并且能保持原味。) 2. All of them are excellent both in color and flavor. No wonder our people like China's Tea than any other kind. （所有产品都色纯香浓，难怪我们那儿的人都喜欢中国茶。) 3. 女人的一生中，若没有尝过被人默默暗恋的滋味，也算是一种憾事。(In a woman's life, if she did not taste this flavor of being loved stealthily, she shall feel so regretful.)。

因而，该句不妨译为：After lengthy boiling, every one of them became a uniquely attractive figure and so tasty in the mouth, flavoring the heart.

[5] 中的"于是"，一般都译成了 Therefore、Thus、Hence、So 等，但就作者儿时对于粽子的记忆而言，这里更多指的是"从那以后"便有了一种渴望、等待、记忆。所以，该句不妨译为：Ever since then, eating *zongzi* during the annual Dragon Boat Festival has been a kind of aspiration, longing and precious memory.

可见，翻译中对于原文的语序，需作灵活处理，即在融会贯通之后，以译入语的表达习惯再现出来。

参考译文

The Dragon Boat Festival in My Hometown

[1] In my childhood memory, whenever the Dragon Boat

Festival arrived, it came gracefully in the breeze and instantly cheered up the old house of the Lins. At that time, every family bought some meat and the grown-ups would soon engage in their serious *zongzi* (rice dumpling) packing business.

[2] As reflected in the traditional festival, *zongzi* was very simple: wrapped pure glutinous rice of a single color. While talking and laughing, close family members would skillfully use their artistic hands to make *zongzi* with a high degree of proficiency.

[3] Wrapped in broad bamboo leaves, carefully cleaned and specifically shaped, together with slender threads of the "firming line", the sharp-edged unusual glutinous rice dumplings in this way formulate perfect *zongzi*.

[4] After lengthy boiling, every one of them became a uniquely attractive figure and so tasty in the mouth, flavoring the heart.

[5] Ever since then, eating *zongzi* during the annual Dragon Boat Festival has been a kind of aspiration, longing and precious memory.

5

原　文

心与脑

林巍

[1] 中西方文化里,"心"和"脑"有着不同的含义。

[2] 中国人自古就认为"心之官则思";在西方,若家长告诉孩子"做事要用心",则是指"跟着感觉走",而思维处于大脑之中。

[3] 在科学上,西医的"心"与中医的"心"并非是一个概念:前者是建立在解剖学、生理学和神经学等基础上的纯粹生物概念;后者则不仅限于医学,而且还是一种文化、哲学、宗教,甚至玄学的理念——"心者,神之舍也"。

译　析

本段文字以"心"和"脑"的概念为截面,简要分析了二者在中西文化里的不同含义。参赛者大都能翻译出基本意思,但在遣词用语(diction)方面似还有提高的空间。

所谓diction,在翻译中可理解为the proper choice and use of words and phrases to express meaning on the basis of accurate understanding of the original 等。以此而论，只是大概翻译出来是不够的。

[1]中，对于"含义"，大部分参赛者用了 meanings、implications、definitions 等，固然有一定道理，但更为准确的应为 connotations，其原意是 a feeling or an idea that a word makes you think of that is not its actual meaning，即深层隐含之意，同时词序也应随英文习惯调整，故整句不妨译为："Heart" and "brain" have different connotations in Chinese and Western cultures.

[2]中，"心之官则思"是孟子所说（有的译文指出了这一点），因而自古形成共识，对此有多种译法，如：The heart is the organ for thinking., The heart's function is to think., The office of the mind is to think.（《新英汉大词典》）。而 the heart is controlled by thinking 则过于偏颇。为了强调，不妨译为：The heart is the very organ generating thought. "做事要用心"，有的译成 to work hard with minds，则又混淆了 heart 和 mind 在中西文化中的区别，故可译为 to do things with their hearts 或 do it with your heart 等。"跟着感觉走"，译成 follow their / your feeling / instinct / nose 似都可以，但要注意直接引语与间接引语在标点符号上的区别；同时，有"不是根据理性思考"（not follow their minds）之意，可适当增译。紧接的"而思维处于大脑之中"，许多人没有翻译出来，或是忽略了；而译成 thought exists in the brain 亦有缺陷，因 exist 是一种客观静态，此处不妨译成动态。具体而言，thought 是 the content of cognition，而 thinking 则是 the process of using your mind to consider something carefully。一般来讲，I thought about it 是指

"我过去以为是那样",而通常的"思维""考虑"为thinking。同时,原文是分开的,但考虑到英文"形合"的特点,可将其并为一处,整句不妨译为:Since the ancient times the Chinese believe that "the heart is the very organ generating thought". In the West, when parents tell their children to do things with their hearts, they mean to follow their feelings not their minds, for thinking is taking place in the brain.

[3] 中,"在科学上",译成 In science / scientifically speaking / scientifically 都是可取的。将"西医的'心'与中医的'心'并非是一个概念"译成 It isn't the same concept of heart between western medicine and Chinese traditional medicine,本身便没有区分出 heart 与 xin 的不同性质;同时,Traditional Chinese Medicine 一般在第一次出现后缩写为 TCM,Western Medicine 为 WM,便于之后的表述。"心者,神之舍也"出自《黄帝内经》(这一点亦应以适当方式在译文中体现),其中的"心"还是中国传统文化意义上的,不应理解成 mind,故仍为 heart;"舍"似可为 home、house 等,而 sanctuary、dwelling place 则更准确。在句式上,该句既可整合表述,如:Scientifically, "heart" in the Western Medicine (WM) and "xin" in Traditional Chinese Medicine (TCM) are different things: the former refers to a purely biological concept based on anatomy, biology and neurology; while the latter denotes to not only a medical concept, but an idea of culture, philosophy, religion and even metaphysics—"heart is where the spirit lives" as it is believed in TCM. 也可分句处理,如 Scientifically speaking,

there are different understandings of heart (*xin*) in Western Medicine (WM) and Traditional Chinese Medicine (TCM). Heart in WM is purely a biological concept based on anatomy, biology, neurology and so on. TCM is much more holistic, everything being rooted in culture, philosophy, religion or even metaphysics, so that heart is regarded to be the "dwelling place of the spirit".

总之，词语的辨析是基本功，由此建立不同的句式。

参考译文

Heart and Brain

By Lin Wei

[1] "Heart" and "brain" have different connotations in Chinese and Western cultures.

[2] Since the ancient times the Chinese believe that "the heart is the very organ generating thought". In the West, when parents tell their children to do things with their hearts, they mean to follow their feelings not their minds, for thinking is taking place in the brain.

[3] Scientifically speaking, there are different understandings of heart (*xin*) in Western Medicine (WM) and Traditional Chinese Medicine (TCM). Heart in WM is purely a biological concept based

on anatomy, biology, neurology and so on. TCM is much more holistic, everything being rooted in culture, philosophy, religion or even metaphysics, so that heart is regarded to be the "dwelling place of the spirit".

6

> 原 文

知识结构

林巍

[1] 知识在人的大脑里，只有被编织在网络结构中，才能产生效用；否则，一盘散沙，互不相连，便形不成功能。每个人的知识结构不同，便形成了不同的能力和专长。知识结构似乎是看不见的，但却很重要。会不会学习，其重要标志之一，就是这种结构的质量。

[2] 建立结构的首要条件是分类，即是将新获取信息与原有信息的对比、印证、连接，需要的时候，可随时提取。有的人读了很多书，经历了许多事，但仍显无知与幼稚。他们其实不是缺乏"材料"，而是缺乏"加工"，以至于该用的时候用不上。

[3] 所以，在整个求学过程中，并不仅仅在于你读了多少书，而是在于你是否和怎样建立起了自己的知识结构。

> 译 析

该文谈及学习中的一种现象和规律，涉及教育学和心理学的有关问题。

主要问题：1. 词汇用法混淆，如用weave来翻译"编织"，将其过去分词形式写为weaved；若查字典便知，该词在"迂回穿行"这个意思下，过去分词才是weaved，其他意思情况下，过去分词形式为woven。问题虽小，但很能体现出英文功底和翻译态度。2. 时态、单复数、双谓语等错误，如Otherwise, it will lacking spirit of cooperation., Classification are contrast, confirm and connect the new getting information with the original information., Therefore, the importance of your study is not merely lies on..., Will learn, one of the important symbols, is the quality of this structure. （完全难以理解will learn是在翻译什么……），They actually don't lack the "material", but the lack of "processing", so that when use but lose.（when use but lose可以这么用吗？这是no zuo no die的节奏……），Everyone have different knowledge structure., Otherwise, knowledge will like a state of lacking spirit of cooperation., Knowledge structure seems be invisible, but it counts a great deal., Knowledge can be used flexibly only is a part of the large thinking net.等等。3. 逻辑关系不明确，缺少应有的衔接词（如otherwise，therefore，in this way等词或词组），以中文式的逻辑关系表述，而不符合英语思维方式和表达习惯。4. 标点符号问题，如没有空格，使用中文的顿号等。

具体而言，关于题目"知识结构"，同学们有多种翻译，如Knowledge Structure、Intellectual Structure、Knowledge Construction、The Constitution of Knowledge等，参考译文用了The Knowledge Structure，对此同学们可以查阅一下有关的

书籍。

[1]中"知识在人的大脑里，只有被编织在网络结构中，才能产生效用；否则，一盘散沙，互不相连，便形不成功能"，其中，对"一盘散沙，互不相连"，有的同学译得很"实"，如with all bits and pieces separated from each other like a tray of sand、… if it is a dish of loose sand、it shall turn disjointed like a heap of loose sand、it will be just like a heap of loose sand without connection to each other and finally become useless、otherwise, as a heap of loose sand, knowledge could be too fragmented to form function、… or it will be sinking into the sand等，在某种情况下，形象的比喻是有必要的，但此处似不必要按字面意思译成a sheet of loose sand 及unrelated parts等，而更主要的是将其主要含义翻译出来，如 otherwise, the scattered knowledge will fail to play its function、… it cannot be at work in a state of disunity等，或以fall apart简言之；对于"形不成功能"亦无需实译为cannot form function，而可简化为with little use，以利其简约、通顺的英文表达方式。故参考译文为：Knowledge can be fully functional in the cerebral cortex only if it has been woven into a network of previous knowledge, otherwise it will fall apart with little use.

"每个人的知识结构不同，便形成了不同的能力和专长"，可以有两种理解，一为"每个人的"，如Everybody's knowledge structure is different, so different capacity and expertise is developed., The knowledge structure of each person is different, so as to form different capacity and expertise., Because of the difference of everyone's knowledge, there are different abilities and advantages.、Knowledge structure varies from person to person and thus form various capabilities and specialties. 等；另一种笼统地认为"人们"如此，如 Different people have different structures of knowledge, which lead to different capacities and specialties.、Because of the differences of structure of knowledge among people, everyone has different abilities and specialties.、Different ability and expertise derived from different people's knowledge structure等，参考译文采用了后一种，即 People have different knowledge structures that functionalize various capacities and specialties.

"知识结构似乎是看不见的，但却很重要。会不会学习，其重要标志之一，就是这种结构的质量"，其中的"看不见"，有同学译成cannot be seen、unseen等，其实有个常用词invisible / invisibility；而如 ... it seems to be invisible, but very important...、Whether one can learn or not, ... which is one of important indications, ...等，这样在字面上似乎比较"对等"了，但却是中文的思路，译出来的英文就不够地道。从英文角度思考，则要注重"形合"上的连贯性：knowledge structure前面已有，故后面不再重复，而以its代替；将"会学习与不会学习"释译为differentiating a competent learner from the rest，即以具体代抽象，英文里类似的有Jack shall have Jill（有情人终成眷属）等，故不妨译为：A knowledge structure, though invisible, is crucially important for learning and its quality differentiates a competent learner from the rest.

[2] 中"建立结构的首要条件是分类,即是将新获取信息与原有信息的对比、印证、连接,需要的时候,可随时提取",对于"首要条件",许多同学译成 the first condition、priority、first requirement 等,实则 prerequisite 更佳。"分类",主要有三个词,即 Classification: the act or process of putting people or things into a group or class; Categorization: the act of putting people or things into groups according to what type they are,也可用动词 to categorize...; Sorting: the act of separating things of one type from others. 而"对比、印证、连接"中的"印证"(通过对照比较,证明与事实相符)可理解为 clarify (to make something clearer or easier to understand)、verify (to check that something is true or accurate)、confirm (to state or show that something is definitely true or correct, especially providing evidence)、demonstrate (to show something clearly by giving proof or evidence)。对于"原有的信息",有同学译成 the original information、the information before,实则为 previous knowledge,而"对比、印证、连接"则不妨以从句来处理,故参考译文为:The prerequisite for a knowledge structure is categorization, where new information is compared, clarified and linked with previous knowledge, becoming available for future retrieval when needed.

"有的人读了很多书,经历了许多事,但仍显无知与幼稚。他们其实不是缺乏'材料',而是缺乏'加工',以至于该用的时候用不上",其中的"幼稚",可考虑三个词:childish (behaving in a stupid or silly way)、naive (lacking experience of life, knowledge or good judgment and willing to believe that people always tell you the truth）、immature（behaving in a way that is not sensible and is typical of people who are much younger）；而"材料"和"加工"，主要有两个词：material (information or ideas used in books, etc.)和information (facts or details about some body or something)，但译文却不必完全囿于原文，如In fact, what they lack is not the "material" but "processing" their material, for this reason, they are disable to use their knowledge when they need it等，而可作些更灵活地变通，故整句不妨译为：Someone may have read and experienced a lot, and yet still seems ignorant and naive. The phenomenon may be explained this way: what they lack is not the information itself but information-processing, resulting in failure to retrieve information when it is required.

[3] 中"所以，在整个求学过程中，并不仅仅在于你读了多少书，而是在于你是否和怎样建立起了自己的知识结构"，如有同学翻译的，With all that being said, it's not how many books you have read but whether and how you build your own constitution of knowledge that matter more during the whole learning process., In conclusion, throughout the process of study, the most important things is not how many knowledge you gain but how to build your own structure of knowledge., Therefore, the process of learning, is not only about how many books you have read, but also about whether you know the way to build your own structure of knowledge., Therefore, what is important throughout the study is not limited to how many

books you read, but depends on whether and how you build your own knowledge construction. 等，似乎都没有大错，但还可更强调、明确些，如 What matters most, concerning a learning process, therefore, is not how many books you have read, but whether and how well your knowledge structure has been established.

总之，在翻译中，不必每字对译，而是在一个相对"单位"内（如一段落），找到功能上的对应关系；即有时又不需拘泥于具体的描述，而可概括化。要在充分理解的基础上，整体考虑，再以恰当的表达方式译出。

参考译文

The Knowledge Structure

By Lin Wei

[1] Knowledge can be fully functional in the cerebral cortex only if it has been woven into a network of previous knowledge, otherwise it will fall apart with little use. People have different knowledge structures that functionalize various capacities and specialties. A knowledge structure, though invisible, is crucially important for learning and its quality differentiates a competent learner from the rest.

[2] The prerequisite for a knowledge structure is categorization, where new information is compared, clarified and linked with previous knowledge, becoming available for future retrieval when needed. Someone may have read and experienced a lot, and yet still seems ignorant and naive. The phenomenon may be explained this way: what they lack is not the information itself but information-processing, resulting in failure to retrieve information when it is required.

[3] What matters most, concerning a learning process, therefore, is not how many books you have read, but whether and how well your knowledge structure has been established.

7

原　文

注意力的分配

林巍

[1] 学习知识、获得技能，都需要注意力。然而，注意力是有质量的，这就需要合理分配。同样的信息，对于不同的人，所吸引的注意力是不同的。我们似乎都有这种经历，即有时会过目不忘，有时则又视若罔闻；有的细节会记忆深刻，有的部分却又全无印象。原来，人们所接收的事物，都是经过注意力筛选的。

[2] 一个人的注意力，在一定时段内，其总量是有限的，是个"常数"；但在具体的环节上，又是可以相对集中的，是个"变数"，可"以局部优势"解决问题。所以，我们常可以见到，智力看似平平的人，可以在某些方面有着超群的表现。

[3] 有人认为，做翻译主要是学好外语；这固然不错，但还只是注意力分配中的一部分。其实，还有另外两部分，即母语的质量和在两种语言间转换的质量。特别是在口译中，注意力合理分配的作用就更加突出。

[4] 令人欣慰的是，在生理学上讲，人的注意力是可以塑造、训练和加强的。所以，不断提高我们注意力的分配质量，对我们的学习和工作都大有裨益。

译 析

对于题目"注意力的分配",有的译成 Allocation of Attention、Assignment of Attention 等,但分析起来,allocation: an amount of something, especially money, that is given to a particular person or used for a particular purpose(尤指经费)配置; assignment: a piece of work that is given to someone as part of their job 等。而 distribution 本义为 an arrangement of values of a variable showing their observed or theoretical frequency of occurrence, 故该题目不妨译为 The Distribution of Attention。

在[1]中,对于"学习知识、获得技能"许多参赛者都直译成了 learning knowledge and obtaining skills,这里有英语词语搭配问题,knowledge 是个抽象名词,与其搭配的有 absorb、accumulate、acquire、apply、obtain、advance、assimilate、broaden、enlarge、enrich、brush up、improve、build up、correct、amplify、communicate、diffuse 等,但不可有 learning knowledge,故此处不妨译为 acquire knowledge and obtain skills,或 obtain knowledge and skills 等。

同时,对"有时会过目不忘,有时则又视若罔闻;有的细节会记忆深刻,有的部分却又全无印象",比较典型的参赛译文,如 Most of us have the experience that sometimes we seemed gifted with an extraordinary retentive memory but at other times we just ignored it. Some details may leave a profound impression, while we may have no recollection on other parts. 似乎没有大问题，但由于视角来回转换（we... sometimes... some details... we... ），令行文不够顺畅。其实，可将 experience 作为动词，如 we may all have experienced times when... 以使语势更加连贯；同时，对"同样的信息，对于不同的人，所吸引的注意力是不同的"的译文加上（may attract different）forms and levels（of attention），以使"注意力"具体化。对于"（经过注意力）筛选的"，许多人用了 allocated、absorb、carefully receive 等，其实 screen、filter 更为合适。同时，需加上必要的介词、连词等，使其更加通顺：We may all have experienced times when information has been photographically retained, or completely ignored. As a matter of fact, all the information we received have been screened and filtered by our attention.

在[2]中，"一个人的注意力，在一定时段内，其总量是有限的，是个'常数'；但在具体的环节上，又是可以相对集中的，是个'变数'，可'以局部优势'解决问题"，很容易译得零碎，如 A person's attention, in a certain period of time, is limited and is a "constant", but in specific links, it can be relatively centralized, a "variable", and a "local advantage" to solve the problem. 其中，"具体的环节"并非其字面的 specific links，而是就"解决具体问题而言的"，如 in dealing with certain issues；而"集中"可用 concentrate、focus 等。"局部优势"，许多人译成了 local advantage，实则此处是指"相对优势"而言的，故可考虑 comparative advantage、relative advantage、relative potency、comparative edge

等。同时，可不必受原文标点符号的限制，而将其译为两个独立句子：A person's attention capacity as a "constant" is limited within a certain time-span. In dealing with certain issues, however, it can be organized as a "variable", concentrating on a targeted area by its comparative edge.

对于"我们常可以见到，智力看似平平的人，可以在某些方面有着超群的表现"，一般译成：We can often see that the seemingly flat intelligence of people, can in some ways have a superior performance., We can always find out that people with mediocre intelligence have superior performance in certain aspects., We always find some people who are seen to have ordinary intelligence can have a super performance in some ways. 等，其中，除了 flat intelligence，似无大问题，但推敲起来，这里的"看见"固然有一般意义上的 often see、always find、constantly find out 等，但还可强调其作为有意观察的一种现象；而"在某些方面有着超群的表现"的原因是什么？结合注意力的应用，这里不妨作些补充，即"增译"：Therefore, it is not surprising to observe that people with average intelligence can have outstanding performance in certain fields by rationally distributing their attention.

在[3]中，对"有人认为，做翻译主要是学好外语；这固然不错，但还只是注意力分配中的一部分。其实，还有另外两部分，即母语的质量和在两种语言间转换的质量"，其中，"有人认为"是谁不重要，故笼统处理为 has long been regarded as...，"但还只是注意力分配中的一部分"可以译为 which is only part of it,

但为了与前面的 is not wrong 相吻合，可将此译为 is not enough 或 is not in itself adequate；而在下一句"还有另外两部分"前加上 Concerning the quality of attention，为的是使论述句式更加清晰。对于"特别是在口译中，注意力合理分配的作用就更加突出"，可打破 specially in oral interpreting, ... is more important 的句式，而将其变通为 When it comes to oral interpretation, rational attention distribution plays an even more crucial role，其中 even more 便涵盖了 specially 之意。故该段不妨译为：Learning translation has long been regarded as learning a foreign language, which is not wrong, but is not in itself adequate. The package should also include the mother tongue and the convertibility between the two apart from the foreign language. When it comes to oral interpretation, rational attention distribution plays an even more crucial role.

在[4]中，关于"欣慰"有几种选择，如 gratified, pleased, contented, satisfied 等，但这里指的都不是这种情感，而是有"发现""获知"之意，故译为 the good news，同时增加了 by effective exercises 和 with that in mind，以使意思更加完整。令人欣慰的是，在生理学上讲，人的注意力是可以塑造、训练和加强的。所以，不断提高我们注意力的分配质量，对我们的学习和工作都大有裨益。因而，此段可译为：The good news is that biologically speaking, a person's attention can be shaped, trained and strengthened by effective exercises. With that in mind, finding ways of constantly improving the quality of our distributed attention can benefit our study and work in a substantial way.

可见，确切的译文需以相关的知识为语言背景。

参考译文

The Distribution of Attention
By Lin Wei

[1] Attention is required in obtaining knowledge and skills. However, the function of attention is based on its quality of rational distribution. The same information may attract different forms and levels of attention from different people. We may all have experienced times when information has been photographically retained, or completely ignored. As a matter of fact, all the information we received have been screened and filtered by our attention.

[2] A person's attention capacity as a "constant" is limited within a certain time-span. In dealing with certain issues, however, it can be organized as a "variable", concentrating on a targeted area by its comparative edge. Therefore, it is not surprising to observe that people with average intelligence can have outstanding performance in certain fields by rationally distributing their attention.

[3] Learning translation has long been regarded as learning a foreign language, which is not wrong, but is not in itself adequate. The

package should also include the mother tongue and the convertibility between the two apart from the foreign language. When it comes to oral interpretation, rational attention distribution plays an even more crucial role.

[4] The good news is that biologically speaking, a person's attention can be shaped, trained and strengthened by effective exercises. With that in mind, finding ways of constantly improving the quality of our distributed attention can benefit our study and work in a substantial way.

8

> 原　文

系统的功能

（上）

林巍

[1] 现代意义上的"系统"一词，转译自日文，从西方而来，如希腊文的 systema，英文的 system，其功能大于各个部分相加之和。

[2] 世界上的事物不是随意堆加在一起的，而是有着内在规律，即形成了系统。一切事物都是复杂的系统集合，有宏观亦有微观的，包括天体、地理、社会、人体、思维等等。

[3] 然而，人类取得这样的认识，却经历了几千年。特别是四百年前的牛顿发现了万有引力，一百年前爱因斯坦创立了相对论，使我们的这种认识有了科学的依据——事物各系统之间、各层次内部，发生着永无休止的相互影响；只有从系统的角度，才能真正认识事物、把握事物的实质。

[4] 人们对于世界的认识，之所以要分门别类，是出于理解的便利，而非事物本身的面目。在古希腊，最初并没有"分科"的学问，而只有唯一的"学问"——哲学，因为那里概括了人类对世界的所有认识。在中国，对学问的分类，也是到了汉代司马

谈的《论六家要旨》才出现的。所以,"学问"是人为的,是人做出来的;而人的认识系统与客观世界的系统之间永远有着差距。在这个意义上讲,学问应当永远让位于真相。

译 析

就标题"系统的功能"而言,绝大多数同学的翻译是可以接受的,如 The Function of System,注意这里因是泛指,故 function 和 system 之后都不需加 s。

问题比较多的是[1]中,"现代意义上的'系统'一词,转译自日文,从西方而来,如希腊文的 systema,英文的 system,其功能大于各个部分相加之和",一般译文,如 The modern sense of the word "system", which is translated from the Japanese, coming from the west, just like the Greek *systema*, means it is greater than the sum of the parts in English., In the modern sense the word "system", translated from Japanese, comes from the west, for example, Greek word "systema" and English word "system", whose function is greater than the sum of parts. 等,不能算错误,但太拘泥于中文的思路,应作适当的句式结构调整,以适应英文的表达习惯;同时,"转译"一般没有翻译出来,而且中文意思的"系统"最好标出原文来。"大于各个部分相加之和"指的是"其功能"(效果),不妨将其增加为 functional effectiveness;"之和"用 sum, aggregation 等,而不用 wide range, large part 等,因这里讲的是质量,不是面积。故参考译文为: The Chinese character *xitong*

(系统) in the modern sense is a transplanted term from the West, such as "systema" in Greek and "system" in English, retranslating from Japanese. The functional effectiveness of a system is supposed to be greater than the aggregation of its individual parts.

在[2]中，这里的"事物"，不是一般意义上的everything，而应为matters, objects；后面的"一切事物"，则宜用everything；"随意"许多同学用了casual, at will, accidentally等，都不够确切，而不妨选用random，其意为done, chosen, or occurring without an identifiable pattern, plan, system, or connection等。

在[3]中，"人类取得这样的认识，却经历了几千年"，同学典型的翻译，如human beings have eventually gained this knowledge through thousands of years，这是典型的中文思维，实则应该调转过来：it took several thousand years for human beings to reach this realization；"特别是四百年前的牛顿发现了万有引力，一百年前爱因斯坦创立了相对论，使我们的这种认识有了科学的依据——事物各系统之间、各层次内部，发生着永无休止的相互影响"，一般翻译成Especially, the universal gravitation had been observed by Newton 400 years ago and Einstein created the theory of relativity 100 years ago. These are the scientific bases to cognition that mutual effects happened among systems and interior relation in different levels permanently，固然都可以接受，但不妨再加以"整合"一下，如In particular, Newton's Law of Universal Gravitation (400 or so years ago) and Einstein's Relativity (100 or so years ago) laid a scientific foundation for us to grasp the essence of everlasting interactions among different systems at various levels. 等。"只有从系统的角度，才能真正认识事物、把握事物的实质"，固然可以译成 Only from the systematical aspect, can we know a thing and grasp the nature，但考虑到这一句是总结性的，故不妨译为 In short, the best realization about our world comes from a systematic approach.

在[4]中，"之所以要分门别类，是出于理解的便利，而非事物本身的面目"，比较典型的同学译文，如 The reason why people know the world severally is out of the convenience of comprehension rather than the object itself., The reason why people classify the cognition of the world is that it is convenient for people to understand, rather than out of the things themselves 等，应该说是不错的，但参考译文没有以否定的方式译成 is not the true appearance of the matter，而是以肯定的方式处理为 ... has blurred its originality。这里的 blur 意为 to smear or stain something but not to efface，类似的，The framed reality shown in movies blurred the unframed reality（电影里所表现的是经过加工过的现实，而非现实本身）。同时，"对学问的分类，也是到了汉代司马谈的《论六家要旨》才出现的"，在译文中不但加入了 Similarly，以便接续，同时在"司马谈"后增添了生卒年代"（？-BC110）"，以使西方读者对此有一时代的概念，故整句为：Similarly, in China the disciplines did not occur until "On the Theme of the Six Scholarships" was written by Sima Tan (?-BC110) in the Han dynasty. "而人的认识系统与客观世界的系统之间永远有着差距"，若将其径直翻译为 There is always a gap between human conceptional system and the world system，固然是"形近"了，但

并未揭示出该句的主旨——人们的主观认识与客观世界无限性之间的矛盾，故经提示后，有的学生将其译为 (Knowledge of any kind is after all designed and produced by man), whose revealing of the world may never match his objective totally, 显然是进了一步，但根据其语境，便知应更准确地挖掘出其中所蕴含的 totality 之意，故其后半句不妨译为：... who may fail to reveal the totality of the world. 在文字形式上看似差距大了，但实际离原意却更近了。

在同一段中，"学问应当永远让位于真相"，似可译为 knowledge should always give away to the truth，或 knowledge should always be led by the truth。然而，分析起来，这里的"学问"不是一般意义上的 knowledge，而是人们为了研究学问而对其所作的分门别类的学科，故可为 branch of learning, discipline, school subject, course of study，但更准确的，此处宜为 scholarship；而"让位"，不是一般意义上的 give away——该词更多的是"失去"之意，如：法国哲学家加缪（Camus）的名句 It is normal to give away a little of one's life in order not to lose it all. （生活中有时失去一部分，是为了不失去全部。），而这里又有其特殊含义，即不可与事实相冲突（conflict, contradict），故不妨译为：scholarship is always vulnerable when confronted with newly revealed truth. 其中，两个词值得一述——vulnerable 和 revealed。这里的 vulnerable，可引申之 open to attack or damage。例如，The man who can read legal documents is far less vulnerable to cheat（可以看懂法律文件者就不易上当）。进而言之，其含义 susceptible to criticism or persuasion or temptation，例如：an argument vulnerable to refutation（一个可被轻

易驳倒的立论）。又如：A country losing touch with its own history is like an old man losing his glasses, a distressing sight, at once vulnerable, unsure, and easily disoriented.（一个国家若丢弃了自己的历史，就如同老翁失去了眼镜，顿时会变得弱视、彷徨、不堪一击，没了方向感。）。相应地，其中的"（学问应当永远让位于）真相"，不是一般意义上的reality、fact或truth，而是相对"学问"而言的"已知事实"。英国著名物理学家戴维斯（Davies）有一段精辟论述：In spite of the fact that religion looks backward to revealed truth while science looks forward to new vistas and discoveries, both activities produce a sense of awe and a curious mixture of humility and arrogance in their practitioners.（尽管宗教是向后探寻已知的真理，而科学是向往前景、有所新的发现，但宗教与科学活动都让人同时产生由卑微与高傲两种素质相揉的敬畏与好奇感。）。故此，不妨译为newly revealed truth；当然，这也只是其中的一种选择。

参考译文

The Function of System

（Ⅰ）

By Lin Wei

[1] The Chinese character *xitong*（系统）in the modern

sense is a transplanted term from the West, such as "systema" in Greek and "system" in English, retranslating from Japanese. The functional effectiveness of a system is supposed to be greater than the aggregation of its individual parts.

[2] Matters on earth are arranged not by random collection but by inner laws, namely a systematic mechanism. Everything exists in a complex system consisting of macro-cosmos and micro-cosmos, including cosmology, geography, society, human beings, thinking mode and so on.

[3] However, it took several thousand years for human beings to reach this realization. In particular, Newton's Law of Universal Gravitation (400 or so years ago) and Einstein's Relativity (100 or so years ago) laid a scientific foundation for us to grasp the essence of everlasting interactions among different systems at various levels. In short, the best realization about our world comes from a systematic approach.

[4] Categorization of the world into academic disciplines has blurred its originality, for no purpose other than easy understanding. In Ancient Greece, there was no such thing as different branches of learning except "philosophy", which was believed to embrace all human knowledge of the world. Similarly, in China the disciplines did not occur until "On the Theme of the Six Scholarships" was written by Sima Tan (?–BC110) in the Han dynasty. Knowledge of any kind is, after all, designed and produced by man, who may fail to reveal the totality of the world. In this way, scholarship is always vulnerable when confronted with newly revealed truth.

9

原文

系统的功能

（下）

林巍

[1] 人无论多么复杂，都是一个有限系统，而认识的对象——世界，却是一个无限系统，这就要求人在信息处理方面要具有以简驭繁、以有限形式去容纳无限内容的能力。在生理结构和功能上，人的感觉器官并不比其他高等生物更敏锐，但却可以在本质上认识无限的物质世界，这主要得益于人的抽象思维能力和与之配套的语言系统。

[2] 人的所谓"预知"或"触类旁通"，其实都是系统功能的作用。俄国化学家门捷列夫，在发明了化学元素周期表后，从该表中的几个空洞，预测了新元素的存在。果然，十五年后，其他科学家发现了与预测相符的三种元素。理论物理学家狄拉克研究电子的性质，认为"真空"正如充满电子的海洋，那里其实没有电子的"泡泡"，却预测了正电子的存在。在物理学上，许多基本粒子的发现，都是先用对称理论预测，然后通过复杂试验找寻出来的，从而弥补了主观与客观间的差距。

[3] 系统的核心是结构；不同的结构决定了不同的性质与功

能。金刚石和石墨，都是由碳元素组成的单质，但由于其碳原子排列顺序的不同，形成了世界上最硬和最软的物质。人的认识体系、知识结构也是如此。同样的信息量在不同人身上会产生不同的效果。所以，学习"系统"，搭建"结构"，有时比学习"零件"更重要。

译 析

就参与的译文而言，在[1]中，"人无论多么复杂，都是一个有限系统，而认识的对象——世界，却是一个无限系统"，许多同学有"顾此失彼"的现象，如 No matter how complex is a finite system, object and understanding of the world, it is an infinite system，其中的"人"哪儿去了？语法对应吗？可参考 No matter how complicated a human is as a system, it is a limited one compared with the unlimited world that he tries to understand. "这就要求人在信息处理方面要具有以简驭繁、以有限形式去容纳无限内容的能力"，对此若逐字翻译，有些困难，如 It requires us to make it simplify on processing information. And the ability to have a capacity of unlimited content using a restricted format., It demands that in the aspect of information processing, men should possess abilities that are handling complexity with simplicity as well as holding infinite content by finite forms., This requires us to form an ability of managing complex information in the simplest way and the ability of holding unlimited content in limited forms 等等，显得臃肿、晦涩，

不如将其中的难点变通、概括为 highly efficient approaches，故整句不妨译为 In handling the overwhelming information that human beings are confronted with, highly efficient approaches have thus been developed.

"在生理结构和功能上，人的感觉器官并不比其他高等生物更敏锐，但却可以在本质上认识无限的物质世界，这主要得益于人的抽象思维能力和与之配套的语言系统"，有同学译得过于零散，如 Human's sensory organs are not more sensitive than other higher animals in terms of physical structure and function. But human can understand the nature of the physical world. This phenomenon is attributed to abstract thought and its well-suited language system. 而有的同学则又译得过于冗长，如 Owing mostly to the ability of abstraction of human as well as the matching capacity for language, we can know about the infinite material world in essence though our sensory organs of biological structures and function are not so acute as that of other high organisms，而且未能突出"在生理结构和功能上"；不妨参考：In terms of biological structure and functions, the sensory organs of human beings are in fact no more developed than other highly evolved creatures, and yet humans can catch more of the essence of the world, mainly due to their abstract thinking capacity and their language systems.

在[2]中，"人的所谓'预知'或'触类旁通'，其实都是系统功能的作用"，其中的"功能"，很多同学都译成了 function / functional 等，然而该词是从客观的"系统作用"而言的，而原文实际指人通过该系统所作出的分析与结果，是从主观角度着眼的，故应用 systematic analysis，整句为 is essentially generated by systematic analysis. 同时，"从而弥补了主观与客观间的差距"，其中的"弥补"并非通常意义上的 make up, remedy, make good, make up for weaknesses, fill in the shortage，等等，而实则是 bridge the gap；而且"主观""客观"指的是主客观世界。故整句不妨译为 What is so-called "prediction" or "knowing the rest by analogy" is essentially generated by systematic analysis.

接下来，需要同学们查找一些资料，而有的同学不够认真，如将"门捷列夫"译成 German chemist 等。同时，"俄国化学家门捷列夫在发明了化学元素周期表后"，该句在中文里的衔接不显唐突，甚是紧凑，为了使英文连贯，则不妨在此之前插入 Taking chemistry for example，以示过渡。同样，在下文"理论物理学家狄拉克研究电子的性质……"，为了衔接，亦不妨加入 Similarly, ... 等。

"在物理学上，许多基本粒子的发现，都是先用对称理论预测，然后通过复杂试验找寻出来的，从而弥补了主观与客观间的差距"，比较典型的同学译文，如 In physics, the discovery of a number of elementary particles is by the predication of Symmetry Theory first, and then work out through complex experiments so that the differences between subjective and objective are compensated. 似无大错误，但过于死板，拘泥于原文的表述方式，不妨做些相应的变通，如 In physics, many basic particles are found by way of repeated experiments based on a symmetrical theory, thus bridging the gap between the subjective and objective worlds. 等，以求更为顺达。

在[3]中，"系统的核心是结构；不同的结构决定了不同的性质与功能"，有同学译成 The key of system is structure and different structure makes different properties and functions，而大多数同学将"核心"译为 core 是可取的，试比较：The core of a system is the structure which determines its nature and functions.

接下来，"金刚石和石墨，都是由碳元素组成的单质，但由于其碳原子排列顺序的不同，形成了世界上最硬和最软的物质"，许多同学译成 Diamond and graphite which are both comprised of carbon, come into being the hardest and the softest substances in the world due to the various marshalling sequences of carbon atom. 等。其中，很少有人用到 allotrope，即"同素异形体"，其原意为 one of many forms in which a chemical element occurs, each differing in physical properties, e.g. diamonds and coal as forms of carbon，如 Naturally occurring transparent, colorless crystalline allotrope of carbon（天然存在的透明、无色、结晶的碳的同素异形体）等，故该句不妨译为 Diamond and graphite, for example, are two allotropes of carbon. 而"碳原子排列顺序的不同"，不可依字面译为 the difference of arranging order of carbonaceous atoms，可依化学教科书上的表述 their different arrangements of carbonaceous atoms. 同时，"学习'系统'，搭建'结构'，有时比学习'零件'更重要"，在中文词汇里搭配得当、错落有致，然而若照样译成英文，如 study the system, establish the construction... 则重复、冗

赘；同时，"更重要"，也不必译为more important，而可整合、甚至简化。"人的认识体系、知识结构也是如此。同样的信息量在不同人身上会产生不同的效果。所以，学习'系统'，搭建'结构'，有时比学习'零件'更重要。"此句可正译，如有同学译成Because the same amount of information has different effects on different people, learning "system" and forming "structure" weigh more than learning "component"，同时也可反译，如In this way, one could say that learning "parts" sometimes may not be as effective as mastering a "system" or a "structure"，以示强调。

参考译文

The Function of System

(II)

By Lin Wei

[1] No matter how complicated a human is as a system, it is a limited one compared with the unlimited world that he tries to understand. In handling the overwhelming information that human beings are confronted with, highly efficient approaches have thus been developed. In terms of biological structure and functions, the sensory organs of human beings are in fact no more developed than

other highly evolved creatures, and yet humans can catch more of the essence of the world, mainly due to their abstract thinking capacity and their language systems.

[2] What is so-called "prediction" or "knowing the rest by analogy" is essentially generated by systematic analysis. Taking chemistry as an example, some gaps in the Periodic Table discovered by the Russian chemist Mendeleyev predicted several new chemical elements; three of which were found by other chemists fifteen years later. Similarly, the theoretical physicist Diac revealed that there were no electronic "bubbles" in a vacuum during his research into the nature of electrons, and then predicted that something called a positron might exist. In physics, many basic particles are found by way of repeated experiments based on a symmetrical theory, thus bridging the gap between the subjective and objective worlds.

[3] The core of a system is the structure which determines its nature and functions. Diamond and graphite, for example, are two allotropes of carbon. However, their different arrangements of carbonaceous atoms result in the hardest and softest substances in the world. The same principle applies to our perceptual and knowledge systems, where the same amount of information may cause different effects. In this way, one could say that learning "parts" sometimes may not be as effective as mastering a "system" or a "structure".

10

> 原　文

痛苦也是财富

（上）

林巍

[1] 人生固然有欢乐，但也一定不乏痛苦。有这种认识和思想准备是非常必要的，因为这样会使你的生活增加欢乐而减少痛苦。

[2] 鸟瞰人生，可略有领悟。上学时，有获得知识的乐趣，便有做功课、考试、排名次的危机与痛苦。同时，也有同学间的相处的融合与纠结。青年时，春心萌动，幻想联翩，难以实现，亦难免陷入困扰。

[3] 结婚之后，实际进入了更多的矛盾之中：思想的落差、相处的困难、子女的教育、财物的争执等等，也会陷入婚姻危机。随后，年龄愈大，健康愈差，事业、家庭中的许多潜在矛盾会日益突出，因而又会有中年危机和老年危机，直至步入死亡。

> 译　析

关于标题"痛苦也是财富"的翻译，同学们做了各种尝试，如The pain is also the wealth, Pain is Fortune、Pain, treasure as well、Misery: Your Lifetime Treasure、Hardship is Also a Kind of Fortune、Torture is Another Kind of Treasure, Bitterness Is Wealth As Well、Suffering Is Also A Kind of Treasure等等，都有可商榷、改进之处。分析起来，"痛苦"可有pain, 其原意为a symptom of some physical hurt or disorder, emotional distress等，多用于一般意义上的疼痛，而torture，则是the infliction of intense pain (as from burning, crushing, wounding) to punish or coerce someone，多用在惩罚行为；misery: a state of suffering and want that is the result of poverty or other external conditions; a state of ill-being due to affliction or misfortune or a feeling of intense unhappiness；然而，suffer: to submit to or be forced to endure the infliction or imposition; Hardship: a particular instance or type of suffering or privation; Bitter: distasteful to the mind，所以，suffering, hardship, bitterness是最可取的。关于"财富"，许多同学都用了wealth, 该词为large possessions; abundance of things that are objects of human desire; abundance of worldly estate; the state of being rich and affluent; having a plentiful supply of material goods and money，多用于有形的财富方面；而fortune为: a hypothetical force or power that unpredictably or capriciously determines events and issues favorably or unfavorably for persons or causes，多是一种命运或运气；而asset: a quality, condition, or entity that serves as an advantage, support, resource, or source of strength，既可以是物质的，也可以是精神的，如Your savings are a liability to the bank even though those same savings are an asset to you（你的储蓄对银行来说是一种债务，虽然这些储蓄也是你的一种资产）; Is uniqueness an asset or liability? Can you accept others when they behave differently from what you consider to be the norm? Do you love your own uniqueness?（与众不同到底是种优点还是种羁绊？你能接受那些在你看来与你的行为准则相左的人吗？你喜欢你自己的独特之处吗？）等，故此，该标题不妨译为 Suffering Is Also an Asset，同时请注意：在形式上，标题中的实词都应大写。

[1]中，"人生固然有欢乐，但也一定不乏痛苦"，同学们大都译得很"实"，如Life is joyful, but painful as well., It is true that life is full of pleasures, but life is also plagued by all kinds of pains., Life is full of happiness, of course, but of bitterness as well., There is no doubt that we have happiness in our life but pain also exists., Besides delight, misery is another major part of your life., While life has happiness, it certainly has painfulness., 等等；其实，这里不妨"超脱"一些，如引用英文的谚语There's no rose without a thorn, 可更为简练、生动。

"有这种认识和思想准备是非常必要的……"，其中的"认识"似可为cognition，意为the mental process or faculty of knowing, including aspects such as awareness, perception, reasoning, and judgment（思想过程或认识才能，包括意识、知觉、推理和判断等），而"思想"为thought，其意为the act or process of thinking or cogitation（思考的行为或过程，亦或思索），在此，二者的英文意思不免重复之处，故可将其合并为thought；同时，

将"准备"译为动词prepare，整句为This thought is absolutely necessary to prepare you to...。因这里是讲人生，故将"生活"扩展为your journey of life；类似的英文表述有很多，如On your journey of life, everything may turn old, only years remaining fresh.（你的生命旅途上，一切都变得陈旧，只有岁月常新。）; Please follow these rules to make the journey of your life a journey of joy.（那就请你遵循这些原则，让你的生活旅途充满欢乐吧。）; As you continue your journey on this stage of life, we hope that you too will try new steps and find the strength and courage to carry on the dance of life!（当您在生命舞台奋斗的时候，我们希望您找寻生命之舞的勇气和力量，走好人生的每一步！）等；同时，有许多诗歌和文章都以此为主题，如The journey of life is like a bus trip / We all know that a bus trip has its origin and its final destination. But what we cannot predict are the experiences along the way / Some people have longer journeys, while others have shorter ones / Some people are very relaxed and they can enjoy the scenery as it rolls by / Some are always crowded and must push and struggle for room, always feeling disconcerted...（人生，就像坐一辆公交车。/我们知道它有起点和终点，却无法预知沿途的经历。/有的人行程长，有的人行程短。/有的人很从容，可以欣赏窗外的景色。/有的人很窘迫，总处于推搡和拥挤之中……）等。

[2] 中，"鸟瞰人生，可略有领悟"，这里只取其"鸟瞰"之意：bird's-eye view；"略有领悟"，something meaningful。将"……排名次的危机与痛苦"，分为两句处理：...and ranking. You

face crises and agony, 以示清晰。可见，在中译英里，并不总是将短句合并为长句的过程，有时亦可相反。"……春心萌动，幻想联翩，难以实现，亦难免陷入困扰"，未作一一对译，而是概括、综述为...puberty may fill you with unrealized desires and send you into deeper perplexity. 在翻译中，这是化繁为简的方法，类似的如："人无论多么复杂，都是一个有限系统，而认识的对象——世界，却是一个无限系统，这就要求人在信息处理方面要具有以简驭繁、以有限形式去容纳无限内容的能力"不妨译为：No matter how complicated a human is as a system, the human system is a limited one compared with the unlimited world that he tries to understand. In handling the overwhelming information that human beings are confronted with, highly efficient approaches have thus been developed. 等。

[3] 中，"……实际进入了更多的矛盾之中；思想的落差、相处的困难……"，其中"更多的矛盾"，未按字面意思译成 more contradictions，而是为 in the center of all the contradictions；"思想的落差"，这里指的是夫妻间性格的磨合，故为 the matching of different personalities；"相处的困难"，也主要是指家庭成员之间的，故为 enduring of family members。"年龄愈大"，将 age 用为动词，类似的有：As we age our appetite would slough.（随着年龄的增长，我们的食欲会减弱。）；These buildings are aging, and some are unsafe now.（这些建筑已经老化，有些不安全了。）等。

"潜在矛盾会日益突出"，因 emerge 已有显露、呈现之意，故未将"潜在矛盾"译成 potential contradictions，而仅为 various troubles。"中年危机和老年危机",合译为mid-life and old-age crises,而(直至步入)"死亡",未译成通常的death,而为讳语eternity;类似的有,We laid him to rest for all eternity.(我们安葬了他。);I want to be with you through eternity.(我愿来世与你同在。)等。

此外,书写(打字)形式上,提醒同学们注意:格式要规范,标点要确切(如逗号紧跟前面的词,后词空一格等),拼写要准确,不能满篇标红(错误格式或拼写的符号)就上交,那是一种极不认真的学习态度;同时,建议使用Times New Roman,12号字,1.5倍行距。希望遵守统一格式。

参考译文

Suffering Is Also an Asset

(Ⅰ)

By Lin Wei

[1] There's no rose without a thorn. This thought is absolutely necessary to prepare you to experience less pain and more joy in your journey of life.

[2] With a bird's-eye view, you may realize something meaningful. During your school years, while joyfully acquiring

knowledge you are also under the pressure of homework, examinations, and ranking. You face crises and agony. Meanwhile, all sorts of intricate affairs may happen between you and your classmates. In your youth, puberty may fill you with unrealized desires and send you into deeper perplexity.

[3] Entering marriage, you are actually in the center of all the contradictions—the matching of different personalities, enduring of family members, children's schooling, financial management and so on, you may also fall into marriage crisis. As you age, your health may deteriorate and various troubles in your career and family may gradually emerge. Mid-life and old-age crises will follow, leading you to your eternity.

11

原 文

痛苦也是财富

（下）

林巍

[1] 所以说，人生在世，如意的事不足一二，不如意的则十有八九。但这"八九"不是负担，而是有用的，因为人在痛苦中所学到的，要比在欢乐中所学到的多得多。

[2] "自古欢愉酿糟糠，从来痛苦出杰作。"对此，司马迁早在两千多年前便有精彩论述："盖西伯拘而演《周易》；仲尼厄而作《春秋》；屈原放逐，乃赋《离骚》；左丘失明，厥有《国语》；孙子膑脚，《兵法》修列；不韦迁蜀，世传《吕览》；韩非囚秦，《说难》《孤愤》。《诗》三百篇，大抵贤圣发愤之所为作也。此人皆意有所郁结，不得通其道，故述往事，思来者。"

[3] 所以，让我们把人生每一阶段上的痛苦，都当做自己的宝贵财富吧。

译 析

本期继续"痛苦也是财富"的后半部分的翻译。

[1]中，对于"如意的事不足一二，不如意的则十有八九"，有的同学按其字面意思译为 In one's life less than 10-20% of what one experiences is satisfactory, but over 80-90% isn't., That is to say, unhappy events occupy nine-tenths of one's life while happy events occupy one-tenth of one's life. 等，翻译得过"实"，其实不妨将其浓缩、提炼，如 in one's lifetime, rainy days are far more than sunny days，进而概述为 ...conclude that much of our life may not be spent in contentment. 其中的 contentment，本义为 the state of being contented; satisfaction；如 In gerocomium, the old men spent his old age in contentment.（老人们在敬老院晚年过得很称心。）；She found great contentment in reading novels.（读小说，使她得到极大满足。）等。

[2]中，"自古欢愉酿糟糠，从来痛苦出杰作"实为谚语，故以 As the saying goes 启始，而此句亦不宜死板对应；"自古""从来"本为一意，故以 perpetual 述之，"糟糠"这里难以具体落实，而泛指不成功的艺术作品，故用了 flop，其意为 utter failure；"欢愉"则指得意洋洋与略带轻浮，故用了副词 elatedly，意指 exultantly proud and joyful. 这也可说是一种"互文"，如"论大功者不录小过，举大美者不疵细瑕"（《汉书·陈汤传》），可合并而译为：In evaluating one's merits and virtue, his trivial faults and minor flaws should be neglected.

接下来司马迁的论述精彩而富有文采，用词错落有致，翻译成英文时，亦应尽力保持其原有风格，但似乎又很难完全存其韵味。不妨将其分解为 ...was arrested, ...while he was experiencing adversity; ...during his exile等，以求变化、不重复，又多少体现原文的韵律。"左丘失明，厥有《国语》；孙子膑脚，《兵法》修列"，则两句并列译为When Zuo Qiu lost his sight and Sun Zi had his feet chopped off, they edited their writings and stratagems，都试图使译文变化错落而不显呆板。

[3] 中，对于"都当做自己的宝贵财富"，...as assets且加上which can only do us good以示强调。Can do ...good，意为"对……有好处"，如Stop smoking now can only do you good.（现在戒烟，只会对你有好处。）；One enemy can do more harm than ten friends do you good.（十个朋友对你做的好事，抵不上一个敌人造成的危害。）等，故该句不妨译为Let's treat all the sufferings at every stage of life as assets which can only do us good. 当然，同学们做了许多其他的尝试，也是有益的，请加以比较。

参考译文

Suffering Is Also an Asset
（II）
By Lin Wei

[1] We may therefore conclude that much of our life may not be spent in contentment. However, the things that discontent are, in fact,

not useless since you may learn more from them than from the things that cheered you up.

[2] As the saying goes, "It seems to be a perpetual rule that flops are produced elatedly and masterpieces painstakingly". To put it vividly, the great historian Sima Qian had a view even two thousand years ago: "When Emperor Wen of Zhou dynasty was arrested, he produced the classic *Zhou Yi Jing*; Confucius wrote the *History of Spring and Autumn* while he was experiencing adversity; Qu Yuan produced his monumental long poem, *On Encountering Sorrow*, during his exile. When Zuo Qiu lost his sight and Sun Zi had his feet chopped off, they edited their writings and stratagems. After Lü Buwei was forced to live in Shu, the valuable *The Book of Lü* was fortunately handed down to posterity. Similarly, when Han Feizi was imprisoned in Qin, *On Difficulty* and *On Resentment*—two precious books—were written by him. Three hundred *Classic Poems* were also produced in roughly the same way, where the writers' hearts were smouldering in the doldrums with no way out: they therefore conveyed everything in words, narrating the past and contemplating the future".

[3] Let's treat all the sufferings at every stage of life as assets which can only do us good.

12

> 原 文

丝绸之路

林巍

[1] "丝绸之路",一般指陆上丝绸之路,广义上讲又分为陆上丝绸之路和海上丝绸之路。

[2] 陆上丝绸之路起源于西汉(前202年—208年)汉武帝派张骞出使西域开辟的以首都长安(今西安)为起点,经甘肃、新疆,到中亚、西亚,并连接地中海各国的陆上通道。它的最初作用是运输中国古代出产的丝绸。

[3] 海上丝绸之路是古代中国与外国交通贸易和文化交往的海上通道,该路主要以南海为中心,所以又称南海丝绸之路。海上丝绸之路形成于秦汉时期,发展于三国至隋朝时期,繁荣于唐宋时期,转变于明清时期,是已知的最为古老的海上航线。

> 译 析

1877年,德国地质地理学家李希霍芬(Richthofen, Ferdinand von,1833—1905年)在其著作《中国——亲身旅行和据此所作研究的成果》(*China: The Results of My Travels and the*

Studies Based Thereon）一书中，把"从公元前114年至公元127年间，中国与中亚、中国与印度间以丝绸贸易为媒介的西域通道"命名为"丝绸之路"，该词为学术界和大众所普遍接受，流传至今。

就题目而言，有的将"丝绸之路"译成Silk Road，显然前面应加定冠词The，因其是个专有名词；而有的译成The Ancient Silk Road of China，又有些冗长、繁琐了，因其本身特指古时中国与中亚细亚间的以丝绸为主的贸易之路，故可不必有ancient和China，而The Silk Road即可。

[1]中，"'丝绸之路'，一般指陆上丝绸之路"，有的译成The general Silk Road refers to the land one，不如按原文将主语置前，即"Silk Road" generally refers to...；同时the land one，过于省略；有的则译成onshore Silk Road、the overland silk road、land silk road等，而考虑到后面的"海上丝绸之路"（the sea-based Silk Road），此处不妨译为land-based Silk Road。"广义上讲"，可有多种译法，如broadly speaking、in its broad sense、in a wide sense of the word、in broad terms、broadly等等。

顺便而言，"一带一路"，在中国英文媒体上最初译成"One belt and one road" strategy，但strategy本义为an elaborate and systematic plan of action，容易引起西方的警觉和反感，后有的改为Land Silk Road and Maritime Route Initiative，收到较好效果。

故[1]不妨译为："Silk Road" generally refers to the land-based Silk Road. In a broad sense, however, it is divided into the land-based Silk Road and the sea-based Silk Road.

[2]中,"起源于",译成can be traced back to、dated back to 都是可以的,而This is the origin of the Silk Road、The overland Silk Road originated in... 就多少有些"翻译腔"了,不如将状语提前,如Originating in...。接续的句子,参赛者大都按原文语序译成Emperor Wu of the Han dynasty sent Zhang Qian to the western regions to open a land route from the capital Chang'an (now Xi'an), to central and western Asia through Gansu province and Xinjiang which linked Mediterranean countries., ...when Emperor Wu of the Han dynasty sent Zhang Qian on a diplomatic mission to the western region. Starting from Chang'an (now Xi'an), the capital of the Han dynasty, it went through Gansu and Xinjiang to Central Asia and West Asia, and connected the Mediterranean countries with the overland passage., ...Emperor Wu sent Zhang Qian, a diplomat and explorer, to open up a thoroughfare starting from Chang'an (Now Xi'an, Shaanxi province), the capital of Western Han dynasty, through Gansu and Xinjiang, to the Central Asia and West Asia, connecting the Mediterranean countries. 等,意思固然也表述出来了,但经过调整和语态变化,会使句子更加紧凑、通顺。如,由张骞"开辟的""汉武帝派张骞出使西域"都可用被动语态(the land-based Silk Road) was explored by Zhang Qian、as an envoy to the Western Region sent by Emperor Wu, 而"以……为起点",可用动名词"starting from..."。"它的最初作用是……"原文是另起一句,于是一般都译成At that time, the road primarily was designed for transporting China's silk to other nations., Its primary

function was to transport silk from ancient China., Its earliest role was to transport silk from Ancient China.等，不能算错，但可加以整合，以使句子更加简练、连贯。该段不妨译为：Originating in the Western Han dynasty (201-208 BC), the land-based Silk Road was explored by Zhang Qian as an envoy to the Western Region sent by Emperor Wu, starting from the capital Chang'an (today's Xi'an) and passing through Gansu, Xinjiang, Central Asia and Western Asia, connecting to the Mediterranean countries, with the initial function of transporting silk from ancient China to these places.

同样的问题出现在[3]中，比较典型的参赛译文，如The Maritime Silk Road was the passage on the sea through which transportation, trades and cultural exchanges took place between China and foreign countries in ancient times. <u>Mainly centered in the South China Sea, it is also called the South China Sea Silk Road.</u> Formed in the period of Qin dynasty and Han dynasty, developed between the Three Kingdoms and the Sui dynasty, prosperous in the period of the Tang dynasty and Song dynasty and transformed in the Ming dynasty and Qing dynasty, the Maritime Silk Road is now the oldest sea lane around the world., The maritime silk road is an ancient maritime channel for communication, trade and cultural exchanges between China and foreign countries. <u>It is centered on the South China Sea, so it is also called the South China Sea Silk Road.</u> The maritime silk road was formed in the Qin (221BC-207BC) and Han (202BC-220AC) dynasties, developed from the Three Kingdoms

(220AC–280AC) to the Sui (581AC–618AC) dynasty, flourished in the Tang (618AC–907AC) and Song (960AC–1279AC) dynasties, and transformed in the Ming (1368AC–1644AC) and Qing (1616AC–1912AC) dynasties. It is the oldest maritime route we have known. 应当说，都是可接受的译文，但其中下画线部分可作调整。这里涉及"语篇意识"的问题，即翻译不只是简单地翻译句子，而是要在语篇统领下，在对原文透彻理解上，有时可能需将句子重新编排。著名语篇学家冯·戴伊克（Van Dijk）指出，"话语和篇章中，不仅在线性的句子和句子之间存在着各种微观的连贯关系，从话语的整体和全局来看，也存在着宏观结构，而这种结构又决定了话语和篇章的整体连贯和组织"（Dijk Van, *Macrostructures: An Interdisciplinary Study of Global Structure in Discourse, Interaction and Cognition*. New Jersey: Lawrence Erlbaum, 1990, p. 3），其中的关键词是"整体""全局""连贯"。就该段而言，原文富有中文表述特征，但在英译时，不妨将其理解为"海上丝绸之路是……海上通道，……形成于秦汉时期，发展于……，繁荣于……，转变于……，是已知的最为古老的海上航线"，一以贯之，同时可将最后部分置前处理：The Maritime Silk Road, the oldest sea route known today, was primarily formed in the Qin and Han dynasties, developed in the period of the Three Kingdoms, flourished in the Tang and Song dynasties and was transformed in the Ming and Qing dynasties. 而"该路主要以南海为中心，所以又称南海丝绸之路"是对其意的补充说明；即若将其删去，并不妨碍其中心意思，故可置后处理：Centered in the South China Sea, it is also called the "Silk Road in the South Sea". 其中,"主要以……为中心"一定要译成Mainly centered in... 吗? 未必,因为center只有一个(the middle point),故多余词可省。

该段不妨译为: The Maritime Silk Road, the oldest sea route known today, was primarily formed in the Qin and Han dynasties, developed in the period of the Three Kingdoms, flourished in the Tang and Song dynasties and was transformed in the Ming and Qing dynasties. Centered in the South China Sea, it is also called the "Silk Road in the South Sea".

总之,翻译中既要谨慎,又需大胆;二者若以忠实为基础,并不矛盾。

参考译文

The Silk Road

By Lin Wei

[1] "Silk Road" generally refers to the land-based Silk Road. In a broad sense, however, it is divided into the land-based Silk Road and the sea-based Silk Road.

[2] Originating in the Western Han dynasty (201−208 BC), the land-based Silk Road was explored by Zhang Qian as an envoy to

the Western Regions sent by Emperor Wu, starting from the capital Chang'an (today's Xi'an) and passing through Gansu, Xinjiang, Central Asia and Western Asia, connecting to the Mediterranean countries, with the initial function of transporting silk from ancient China to these places.

[3] The Maritime Silk Road, the oldest sea route known today, was primarily formed in the Qin and Han dynasties, developed in the period of the Three Kingdoms, flourished in the Tang and Song dynasties and was transformed in the Ming and Qing dynasties. Centered in the South China Sea, it is also called the "Silk Road in the South Sea".

13

> 原　文

孟子的"性善论"

林巍

[1] 关于孟子的"性善论",长期以来人们有种误解,认为他主张人性是天然、永远善良的。

[2] 其实,孟子并不认为人人生而尽"舜尧";人的本性中,也有些东西是无所谓善或恶的,人也会堕落,也有与兽相同的本能。

[3] 但是,孟子的高明之处,在于他指出了,那并非"人性",而是与禽兽无异。

> 译　析

中国传统文化的特色之一是孟子的"性善论",迥然不同于西方的"性恶论";而对其的理解和翻译,历来不乏争议。

[1] 中,这里的"性",指的是"人性",即 human nature;而"性善论",若译成 the mankind-hearted、virtue of human thought、kind-hearted by nature、the innate goodness theory 等,似有一定道理,但不够准确。其中的状语"长期",多数

人习惯性译成了For a long time ...、For the long run...、...since very long ago等，但考虑到英语"形合"的特点，宜将其融入句子之中。"误解"，有misunderstanding、misconception、be misunderstood、misconstrued等，但实质是其含义被曲解了，所以可用be mistakenly interpreted等。故该句不妨译为：Mencius' theory of the original goodness of human nature has long been mistakenly interpreted to mean that humans are innately and perpetually kindhearted. 或更直译些的：Concerning the theory of original goodness by Mencius (372–289 BC), it has long been misunderstood that human nature is naturally and eternally good.

[2] 中，上半句所涉及的内容根据的是：《孟子·滕文公章句上》，"孟子道性善，言必称尧舜"；《孟子·告子章句下》，"曹交问曰：'人皆可以为尧舜，有诸？'孟子曰：'然'"。很多人译为：It is said that all men may become Yaos and Shuns. 化用为"尽舜尧"后，又有了不同翻译，许多人译成："...is born to be Yao and Shun." 这么译似有不妥。首先，born good / evil 即可，如：1. I believe that the normal human heart is born good. （我相信一般人生来心都是善的。）2. Criminals are never born evil, and, in the case of corruption, it is quite clear that social factors play an important role. （罪犯并非生来就是恶的，在腐败案例中，很明显，社会因素起了很大作用。）。其次，单纯地译成Yao and Shun，恐难为英文读者尽知，故可添同位语或稍加诠释。"与兽相同的"，很多人译成了 same to other animals、have same instinct as animals、of the instinct similar to creatures等，似乎可以接受，但是更为准确的

"兽",应为 beasts,该词的本义是 a living organism characterized by voluntary movement。animal 固然也可以,但该词原意是 a living organism that is distinguished from plants by independent movement and responsive sense organs,主要是指与植物的区别。creature 则为 any living person or animal,其中包括"人"(除非以 other 来区分)。

关于"有些东西是无所谓善或恶的,人也会堕落",孟子在《告子章句上》中针对人性如水、"决诸东方则东流,决诸西方则西流"的观点,指出"今夫水,搏而跃之,可使过颡;激而行之,可使在山。是岂水之性哉?其势则然也"(就水而言,拍打溅起来,可以高过额角;屈水使之倒流,可以引上高山。这难道是水的本性吗?是形势使其那样)。所以,他认为,正如水本性往低处流,受外力作用才会变向,人也只有在外部条件的影响下才会变坏,这种改变不是人的本性使然。这里的"坏",许多人用了 bad、corrupt、brutish、degenerate、immoral、unethical 等,实际上 good 与 evil 是一对概念。同时,应将"人也会堕落"的暗含条件作为状语补充上去,如 ... if ... 、under... condition 等,故此句不妨译为:In fact, Mencius did not hold that every man is born Yao or Shun, the two sages in ancient China; he also identified other attributes, resembling beasts, which may be either good or bad in themselves, but which can lead to evil if not duly controlled.

[3] 中,对孟子的"高明",许多人译成 Mencius' genius 或 wise / brilliant / excellent / super as Mencius is 等,未免有些过分,实则不妨译为 judiciously / sensibly (points out) 等。而那样便并

非"人性"，是"与禽兽无异"之意，朱熹在《孟子集注》解释道："事物之理，莫非自然，顺而循之，则为大智；若用小智而凿以自私，则害于性而反为不智。"所谓"害于性""不智"便是有别于人性了，不过朱老夫子说得更文雅些，但在中国传统文化里，若用到"禽兽不如""形同禽兽""行若狗彘"等，已经是对人最不齿的形容了，所以需加些"反人性""屈同于"之类的贬义词，如defy、go against、contrary to及downgrade、demean、abase等，故该句不妨译为：However, Mencius judiciously pointed out that when a man does evil he is actually defying human nature and abasing himself to the level of other living creatures.

正巧，近日看到黄永玉刚刚出版的《给孩子的动物寓言》，开篇便讲"动物比人好……"，其中当然不乏哄逗孩子的成分，但这种对于动物（禽兽）在感情上的转变，却是有悖于中国传统的，也体现了一种人性的变化，更接近于西方。

参考译文

Mencius' Original Goodness of Human Nature

By Lin Wei

[1] Mencius' theory of the original goodness of human nature has long been mistakenly interpreted to mean that humans are innately

and perpetually kindhearted.

[2] In fact, Mencius did not hold that every man is born Yao or Shun, the two sages in ancient China; he also identified other attributes, resembling beasts, which may be either good or bad in themselves, but which can lead to evil if not duly controlled.

[3] However, Mencius judiciously pointed out that when a man does evil he is actually defying human nature and abasing himself to the level of other living creatures.

14

原　文

适应自然的能力

[1] 人生于自然。自然赋予的资本不少，可见者为肉体，不可见者还有本能、资质之类。

[2] 但为了能活并且活得好，他或她就还要取得适应环境的多种能力。这多种能力，可以概括为两个方面：知和德。

[3] 人生来都是野的，为了能在自然的社会中生活，而且活得好，就必须变野为文。变野为文，要靠身外的力量以文明化之。

译　析

[1] 中，"人生于自然"，很容易译成 Man is born in nature，似乎不错，但分析起来，其实质是什么？是 Man is part of nature；"资本"一般是 capital，但此处讲的是自然意义上对人的价值（a useful or valuable quality），故宜为 asset。"可见""不可见"可用 visible、invisible 但要分别辨析，而"肉体"不是一般意义上的 flesh、clay、body 等，而是物理学上与 nature 相对应的 physical beings。

[2]中,"为了"可用in order to、for the sake of、by way of、in the interest of等;"多种能力"在原文中出现两次,在译文里不应重复,而"可以概括为两个方面"似可译成"can be summarized into two aspects: ...",但可采取相应简化方式。

[3]中,"野"这里不是wild、rough等,而是相对"文"而言的,故可用uncivilized;此处的"而且活得好"的译文要避免与前面的"而且活得好"相重复,故不宜再用In order to... live a better life,而要选择其他更适宜的词。"人生来都是野的",若译成All men are born uncivilized,单独成句,未尝不可,但要考虑如何与其他句子成分相结合,且要简练,故不妨用插入语的形式"people—born uncivilized—...";而所谓"身外的力量"实则是指"外界的文明、教化"等。

参考译文

Abilities to Cope with the Environment

[1] Man is part of nature, which endows us with quite a lot of assets both visible and invisible. Visibly these are manifested in our physical beings; invisibly they are innate instinct and intelligence, among many other things.

[2] In order to survive and live a better life, he or she has to

acquire various abilities (mainly knowledge and virtue) to cope with the environment.

[3] To live in a natural society, or even more so, decently, people—born uncivilized—have to be civilized by way of external cultivation.

15

原 文

可爱的中国

（节选）

方志敏

[1] 朋友，我相信，到那时，到处都是活跃的创造，到处都是日新月异的进步，欢歌将代替了悲叹，笑脸将代替了哭脸，富裕将代替了贫穷，康健将代替了疾病，智慧将代替了愚昧，友爱将代替了仇恨，生之快乐将代替了死之忧伤，明媚的花园将代替了暗淡的荒地！

[2] 这时，我们民族就可以无愧色的立在人类的面前，而生育我们的母亲，也会最美丽地装饰起来，与世界上各位母亲平等的携手了。

[3] 这么光荣的一天，决不在辽远的将来，而在很近的将来，我们可以这样相信的，朋友！

译 析

选文摘自方志敏于1935年在狱中写就的《可爱的中国》，作者概述了自己艰辛的革命经历，讴歌了"生育我们的祖国母亲"，深切之情溢于言表。

文章标题参赛者一般译成Lovely China、The Lovable China、Beloved China (Excerpts)、Adorable China (Excerpts) 等，似乎合理，但仔细品味，发现此语亦可出自外国人之笔，而更为确切的译法可以是：My Beloved Motherland—China (Excerpts)。

[1] 中的排比部分"欢歌将代替了悲叹……明媚的花园将代替了暗淡的荒地！"，不少参赛者译成：...Cheerful sound of singing will replace mournful lament. Smiling face will replace crying face. Wealth will replace poorness. Health will replace disease. Wisdom will replace ignorance. Friendly affection will replace enmity. The happiness of life will replace the sadness of death. Brilliant garden will replace dim wasteland!, ...where sad sighs are replaced by merry songs, weeping faces are replaced by smiling faces, poverty is replaced by wealth, illness is replaced by health, ignorance is replaced by wisdom, hatred is replaced by friendship, sadness of death is replaced by happiness of birth and barren lands are replaced by beautiful gardens., ...There will be joyful songs instead of lament, smiling faces instead of crying faces, richness instead of poverty, health instead of disease, wisdom instead of ignorance, friendship instead of hatred, the happiness of living instead of the sadness of death, bright gardens instead of bleak wasteland! 下画线均为笔者所加，可见其中重复部分。应当说，"文似看山不喜平"是条普遍规律；除非有特殊表述，一般应避免重复。

例如,"<u>向</u>促改革要动力,<u>向</u>调结构要助力,<u>向</u>惠民生要潜力,既扩大市场需求,又增加有效供给,努力做到结构调优而不失速。"(We <u>promoted reform</u> to gain impetus for development, <u>made structural adjustments</u> to produce support for development, and <u>improved living standards</u> to increase the potential for development. We both expanded market demand and increased effective supply, working to ensure that structural adjustments were made without compromising the growth rate.),其中的三个"向……要"分别采用了不同的词语和句式,既避免了重复,又使语势产生波澜。再如,朱自清的名篇《匆匆》:"洗手的时候,日子从水盆里<u>过去</u>;吃饭的时候,日子从饭碗里<u>过去</u>;默默时,便从凝然的双眼前<u>过去</u>。"可译为:Thus the day <u>flows away</u> through the sink when I wash my hands; <u>vanishes</u> in the rice bowl when I have my meal; <u>passes away</u> quietly before the fixed gaze of my eyes when I am lost in reverie. 原文中三个分句都重复了"过去",译文则分别采用 flows away、vanishes、passes away 三个同义词组进行对应,既构成了和原文相似的、平行的句法结构,又避免了完全的重复。有时,即便是一短句,高超的译者也会避免重复,如老舍的《月牙儿》中有一句"妈对我很好,而且有时候极庄重的说我:'念书!念书!'"著名翻译家沙博理的译文:She was so good to me, always urging, "Read your books, study hard!" 即以字面的变形体现了内在的忠实。

当然,也有一些参赛者意识到了这个问题,采取了种种"避免"措施,如 Paean will <u>overwhelm</u> the lament, smile will displace the tear, prosperity will eliminate the privation, health will vanquish the disease, wisdom will enlighten the folly, love will transform the hatred, the joy of life will dilute the sorrow of death, vigorous garden will spring the bleak wasteland!, We will sing joyful songs rather than sad sighs, our smiles spread but our tears dissipate, our people are well off instead of poor, health drives illness far away, people hold wisdom and abandon ignorance, friendships replace hostilities, the pleasure of life dispels the sorrow of death, the bright garden turns into gloomy wasteland! 等,显出不同的译文质量。

其实,领悟原文,这是一幅泼墨山水画,写意大于写实,主要讲将来比现在更好,美丽会战胜丑恶,光明必取代黑暗;故可不必过于拘泥细节上的对等,而不妨采取"肢解""重组""合并同类项"等技法,以求"神似"。具体而言,"到那时"是指中国总有改天换地的那一天,见证着"日新月异的进步"(China will one day truly transform itself, witnessing its rapid progress);而新天地的总体蓝图是"生之快乐将代替了死之忧伤,明媚的花园将代替了暗淡的荒地"(where a joyful life will replace the netherworld; bright gardens will supplant bleak wastelands),不妨提前译出,统领该段;"悲叹""哭脸""贫穷""疾病""愚昧""仇恨"这些象征旧社会的面容将被新时代所荡涤,成为历史(sadness, grief, poverty, exhaustion, ignorance, hatred will all have become things of the past);而"活跃的创造""欢歌""笑脸""富裕""康健""智慧""友爱"指的是在美好愿景中新人的风貌(people, instead, will be innovative, cheerful, happy, rich, healthy, intelligent and kind)。故整段不妨译为：Dear friends, I believe that China will one day truly transform itself, witnessing its rapid progress, where a joyful life will replace the netherworld; bright gardens will supplant bleak wastelands; and sadness, grief, poverty, exhaustion, ignorance, hatred will all have become things of the past; people, instead, will be innovative, cheerful, happy, rich, healthy, intelligent and kind. 从而力求与原文的"整体对等"效果。

[2] 中，"无愧色的立在人类的面前"（因那时还不分"的""地"，此处实则为"地"），参赛者一般译成 can stand up unashamedly at the front of the human、we can stand in front of all mankind without shame、can be truly worthy of taking a stand before mankind，其中的"无愧色"既可如原文"反说"（without shame），亦可"正说"（be truly worthy of、proudly）；"而生育我们的母亲，也会最美丽地装饰起来，与世界上各位母亲平等的携手了"，许多人译成：And, our motherland, which give birth to us, will be best decorated and join hands with those of other nations as equals、and the mother who gives birth to us will be decorated most beautifully and will work hand in hand with the mothers of the world、so our great mothers, who gave birth to us, will get beautifully dressed and join hands together with all other mothers in the world 不免有些过"实"。应当说，"无愧色的立在人类的面前"和"与世界上各位母亲平等的携手"是一种并列表述，故可将"我们民族"和"我们的母亲"联系起来；"最美丽地装饰"，若修饰

人，不宜用decorate，该词的本义是to make something look more attractive by putting things on it，如：1. They decorated the room with flowers and balloons.（他们用花和气球装饰了房间。）2. The cake was decorated to look like a car.（这蛋糕装饰得像一辆汽车。），即该词多用来修饰物，而少用于人，不如dress、clothe等更适宜。此句不妨译为：By that time, our nation can proudly stand in front of mankind, and our elegantly clad motherland will join hands with others on an equal footing.

对于[3]，较为典型的译文有：How glorious that day would be! It will never be far away but in the foreseeable future. We can all believe in that way, my friend!, Such a glorious is not hidden far away, but lies just in the near future. We can believe that, my friends!, So glorious will the day not be far away, yet in a near future. We can have faith in it, my friend! 这类译文几乎与原文句式丝丝相扣，但未必是通顺、优质的译文。其中，再次出现了"朋友"，有进一步强调、加深之意，而"相信"也可不再用believe that。此句不妨译为：My fellow countrymen, we should all have faith that such a glorious day is not in the distant future but is as imminent as you can imagine.

总之，中英文里都有足够的词汇和表达方式来变换多样地描述、形容、议论同一事物、情景和感受，而译者此方面储备的丰富程度会直接影响其翻译质量。

My Beloved Motherland—China

(Excerpts)

By Fang Zhimin

[1] Dear friends, I believe that China will one day truly transform itself, witnessing its rapid progress, where a joyful life will replace the netherworld; bright gardens will supplant bleak wastelands; and sadness, grief, poverty, exhaustion, ignorance, hatred will all have become things of the past; people, instead, will be innovative, cheerful, happy, rich, healthy, intelligent and kind.

[2] By that time, our nation can proudly stand in front of mankind, and our elegantly clad motherland will join hands with others on an equal footing.

[3] My fellow countrymen, we should all have faith that such a glorious day is not in the distant future but is as imminent as you can imagine.

16

原 文

陈独秀在法庭上的抗辩

林巍

[1] 1932年10月，国民党当局因危害民国罪逮捕了陈独秀。

[2] 对此，陈独秀在法庭上据理抗辩："我只承认反对国民党和国民政府，却不承认危害民国。

[3] "因为政府并非国家，反对政府，并非危害国家。

[4] "我之所以反对政府，因为：一是人民不自由，二是贪官污吏横行，三是政府不能彻底抗日。"

[5] 最后他提出，检察官之控告根本不能成立，应当庭宣判无罪。

译 析

[1] 中的"国民党"可用 National Party，但此处是"国民党当局"，可为 the Kuomintang authorities；"因……罪而逮捕"，这里的"罪"不是 sin 而是 crime，即 arrested by... for...，整句不妨译为：In October 1932, Chen Duxiu was arrested by the Kuomintang authorities for crimes against the country.

[2]中,"抗辩",其中"抗"为抗争、抗议;"辩"为辩解、辩驳,该词组意为"为不接受责难而做辩护"。许多人译成plea、appeal等,固然不错,但分析起来,plea的本义为an urgent emotional request,且多用于名词,如The Judge told him that if he failed to enter a plea, he would almost inevitably be found guilty.(法官告诉他如果这次不进行抗辩,他将无法避免被定罪。);appeal可为名词、动词,词语也更为宽泛:to make an earnest or urgent request for something,如He has four weeks in which to lodge an appeal.(他有四个星期的时间提出上诉。);The Party shall ensure the right to appeal by the supplier to an impartial such an authority if it is not the first instance review body.(参加方应确保供应商拥有向一个公正的、非初审查机构的机构提出上诉的权利。)。然而,相对而言,defended更符合陈独秀此时据理力争的语境;而"承认……,却不承认……",可用一个admit that... 不必重复。"危害民国"为动宾结构,其动词有harm、damage、endanger等,但亦可以形容词detrimental作定语。整句不妨译为:In this case, Chen defended himself in court: "I admit only that I am opposed to the Kuomintang and the national government, but I have done nothing detrimental to the Republic of China".

在[3]中,两个"并非"的译文应有区别,可用 ...is not...、not be confused with,类似的如,Translators should be fully aware of the commercial terms of the context dependency, do not be confused with the general vocabulary.(译者应充分认识到商务词汇对语境的依赖性,而非做一般词汇使用。);For this discussion, type safety specifically refers to memory type safety and should not be confused with type safety in a broader respect.（在本讨论中，类型安全特指内存类型安全，而并非范围更广类型的安全。）。整句可译为：Since the government is not the state, being anti-government should not be confused with jeopardizing national security.

对于[4]中的"一是""二是""三是"，可不必遵循原文译成the first, second, third等，而是融合在整句之中：The reasons why I object to the government are as follows: People do not have freedom, corrupt officials are rampant and the government has not totally committed itself in fighting against the Japanese invasion.

[5]中的"根本不能成立"似可译成can never be established，而在法律语境，就无根据的指控而言，groundless更为有力；"宣判无罪"，通常可译成pronounced not guilty、declared innocent等，但此处更确切的应为acquit sb. of a crime，类似的，如It can decide to proceed, to convict or to acquit.（法院可以决定是要继续审理、宣判有罪或无罪。）；Although the Iranian nation has the authority and legal right to put on trial the British military people, Iran will instead acquit them.（尽管伊朗有权力、也有权利去审判这些英国军人，但伊朗将赦免他们。）；However, Zenger's attorney, Andrew Hamilton, convinced the jury to acquit Zenger on the grounds that what he had published was true.（但是，曾格的律师，安德鲁·汉密尔顿说服陪审团定曾格无罪，理由是，曾格所发表的情况属实。）等。该句不妨译为：Finally, he pointed out that the prosecutor's accusation was therefore groundless and the

court should acquit him.

Chen Duxiu's Objection in Court
By Lin Wei

[1] In October 1932, Chen Duxiu was arrested by the Kuomintang authorities for crimes against the country.

[2] In this case, Chen defended himself in court: "I admit only that I am opposed to the Kuomintang and the national government, but I have done nothing detrimental to the Republic of China.

[3] "Since the government is not the state, being anti-government should not be confused with jeopardizing national security.

[4] "The reasons why I object to the government are as follows: People do not have freedom, corrupt officials are rampant and the government has not totally committed itself in fighting against the Japanese invasion."

[5] Finally, he pointed out that the prosecutor's accusation was therefore groundless and the court should acquit him.

17

原　文

一条公益广告

美德成于心，
诚信见于行，
文明贵于恒。

译　析

本期原文是一条公益广告，即以社会公众利益为目的而设计的一种普及、非营利的广告，具有效益性、现实性和号召性三大特点。在翻译上，又可归为"公示语翻译"，既有普遍性，又有特殊性。

普遍性，是指其具有一般翻译的性质；特殊性，则指其特有的言简意赅，捉人眼球。例如，"热烈欢迎外国朋友来我校参观指导！"，许多人会翻译成"Warmly welcome foreign friends come to our school for inspection!"，实则，可以大大简化为"Welcome to our school!"或"Our school welcomes you!"。而"美食天堂，异彩平添"不必按字面意思译成Delicious heaven; Extraordinary splendor in riotous profusion，而Food Paradise即可解决。至于"生

意兴隆通四海，财源茂盛达三江"，若译成 Business is thriving, reaching out to the five continents of the world; Revenues are accruing, flowing in from the four corners of the earth，则难以吸引大众的注意，故不妨精练为 Business booms far and near, profits net there and here。

可能因本次原文看似简单，所以参赛者人数剧增。然而，"言简意不简"，许多译文又过于简单，典型的，如：1. Virtue forms in mind; Honesty shows in behavior; Civilization lies in persistence. 2. Virtue is established in souls, Integrity is seen in actions, Civilization is valued in perseverance.

其中，一些关键字眼值得认真推敲。如"成于心"，将"成"译成 form、establish、shape、produce、become 等都略显简单；这里表述的是一种心智的历练过程，故不如用 nurture、foster、cultivate 等。至于"心"，如以往所述，有 mind、heart、soul 等之分。西方文化里，mind 一般代表理智，heart 则多为情感，如英语说：My mind tells me "no", but my heart tells me "yes".（我的理智对我说不，但我的情感却令我屈从。）。希拉里（Hillary）在回忆录中说，她嫁给克林顿（Clinton）主要是 followed her heart but not her mind，言外之意，若依理性而非情感，可能就不会嫁给他了。当然，实际运用中 heart 亦可包括理性成分，如：1. 若有人提出批评意见，我会非常在意的。(If someone says something critical I take it to heart.) 2. 他告诉她，自己所做的一切都是为了她好。(He told her that he only had her interests at heart.)，所以，heart 比 mind 的含义更广。而 soul 则更多强调 deep feeling or emotion, the spiritual part of a person, believed to exist after death,

不乏宗教色彩，如 He believed his immortal soul was in peril.（他认为他不死的灵魂有堕入地狱的危险。），故应慎用。

"见于行"，将"见"译成 see、exist、show 亦略显肤浅，不如 manifest、evidence、reveal 等贴切，而"行"又有 behavior、action、conduct、deed 等选择。分析起来，1. behavior: the reaction of something under specified circumstances，即具体环境中的行为；2. action: something done (usually as opposed to something said)，即主要相对"言"的实际行动；3. conduct: manner of acting or conducting yourself, namely a person's way of behaving (behavioral attributes), the way a person behaves toward other people，即侧重于人际关系方面的行为；4. deed: a notable achievement，即多为褒义举动。综合考虑，似以 action 为宜。

最后一句中的"文明"，参赛者大都按字面意思译成了 civilization，但其实经不住推敲。该词的基本含义为：A society in an advanced state of social development (e.g., with complex legal and political and religious organizations); the fact of becoming or state of being highly developed socially, with a system of government, methods of education etc. 即主要是对社会整体进步程度而言的，如 In 20 years they have reached the level of civilization which took our society a century to reach.（他们用二十年达到了我们社会花了一个世纪才达到的文明程度。），而这里指的主要是个人行为。类似的，有的用了 culture，其实该词本质上也是集体行为（all the knowledge, values and customs shared by a society or a group of people in a society）。容易误译的，如将一个人的"文化水平"

译成cultural level，实际应为educational background或schooling等。细加分析，这里的"文明"指的是个人素质，于是quality、quality people、good qualities便应进入首选范畴，如：1. Quality people are essences in our quest for quality service.（优秀人员是提供高素质服务的先决条件。）2. Those are good qualities that we would want in every employee.（这些都是我们想要每位员工都具备的良好素质。）3. 他有许多好的品质，其中最好的就是善良。(He has many good qualities, but his best quality is his kindness.)。有的译者采用了这样的句式：

He who has great virtues has rooted his righteous behaviors in his heart deep.

He who is a man of integrity only reveals himself from his acts followed.

He who is a civilized citizen only shines in his persistence in behaviors related.

显示其阅读范围和素养，其思路也值得肯定；不足之处，在不够确切和工整，故不妨作些修改。

就本质而言，"公示语"是一种在公众场合看的语言，负载着某种社交的特殊使命，因而又要注重通俗、易接受。这就不能不涉及之前论述过的汉英"意合"与"形合"的特点。简言之，汉语是"意合"（paratactic），即句中及句间的语法意义是靠其内在含义和逻辑关系来表达的（The grammatical relations are conveyed by the connotations and logic contained within or between the sentences），而英语在性质上是一种"形合"（hypotactic）的语言，即句中及句之间的成分是靠语言形式相连接（The dependent or subordinate construction or relationship of clauses are linked with connectives）。典型的例子，如"早知这样，我就不来了"，译为英文则要加上许多"零碎"：If I had known it earlier, I would not have come 等。

据此，该三句也可融合为：While virtue is nurtured in the heart, credibility has to be attested by one's actions, and time ultimately proves good qualities. 在许多情况下，同样可以收到公益广告的宣传效果。

参考译文

A Public Service Advertising

He who is virtuous has his righteousness rooted in the heart;
He who is honest has his credibility manifested in actions;
He who is civil has his quality attested in persistence.

18

> 原　文

开始写作[1]

（节选）

谢冰莹

[1] 我开始写小说，是在进了女师的第二年，那时刚满十五岁。

[2] 有一天，我和两位小学时代的同学，去一个同乡家里吃饭，主人刚刚买了一个十三岁的丫头来，那女孩长得面黄肌瘦，身材短小，满脸现着泪痕；倒是一双乌溜溜的大眼睛，非常惹人怜爱。

[3] 女主人是一位师长太太，她命令女孩走路给我们看，并请我们批评她的一举一动的姿势，是否合于一个师长公馆用的丫头。

[4] 那两位同学真的将视线集中在女孩的身上；可是我的眼里却正燃烧着不平的火焰！我恨那位女主人太不人道了，简直把人当做畜生看，我当时气得饭也吃不下，借故回到学校，立刻写了一篇《刹那的印象》。

---

[1] 编者注：原名为《刹那的印象》，现标题为作者所加。

译 析

　　本文节选自著名现代作家谢冰莹的一篇回忆文章，虽寥寥几笔，但形象生动，有真情实感。

　　关于题目"开始写作"，参赛者大都译成了 Begin Writing、Started Writing、The Beginning of My Writing Journey、Initiate of Writing 等，其实这里讲了一个小故事，说明作者自己是如何开始写作的，故不妨译为：How I Start to Write。

　　[1] 中，"女师"指的是女子师范学校，似可译成 Union Normal School for Women、the Women's Normal school、Women Teacher's Training School 等，但更为通俗的，可为 the Female Normal School。但在行文中，有的译得过于"零碎"，如 I started writing novels, and I was in the second year of entering the female teacher, when I was just fifteen years old.、I was just fifteen years old when I decided to write novel, the second year I studied in Women's Normal School.、It was on my second year in the women's normal school that I started to write a novel, when I was just fifteen years old. 等。原文固然是三句，但根据英文形合的特点，可用介词、代词等连成一句，如 I began to write novels in my second year at the Female Normal School when I was just fifteen years old.

　　[2] 中，"同乡"是一个很宽泛的概念，可指来自同一个村、县城、省市的认识或不认识的人，英文可有 countrymen、fellow、fellow townsman 等，鉴于作者那时是个小学生，可译为

fellow student；"丫头"是那时做佣人女孩子的一种称呼，可译为 servant girl；对于"面黄肌瘦，身材短小，满脸现着泪痕"不宜"一一对应"，如 who had a thin face, a short figure and tears all over her face、She was short and slight in build, with a tear-stained face that showed an air of sickness 等，而可概述为 She was small, thin, emaciated with sallow complexion；而"非常惹人怜爱"似不必单句译成 but her a pair of big, black eyes were very affectionate / attractive，而可与前面"大眼睛"相结合，译成 big adorable black eyes。故此，整句不妨译为：One day, I, together with my two primary school classmates, went to a fellow student's home to eat. The hostess, a teacher's wife, had just bought a 13-year-old servant girl. She was small, thin, emaciated with sallow complexion but a pair of big adorable black eyes.

[3] 中，比较典型的参赛译文，如 As the wife of a division commander, the hostess ordered the girl to walk for us guests to see whether the way the girl walk match her family status before we criticizing on that., The hostess was a teacher's wife in Woman's Normal School. She orders the girl to show us her position to walk. Then asked us to judge the girl's position of her gait. Therefore, we can judge the girl is available or not to be a maid in the residence of hostess's house., The hostess, the teacher's wife, ordered the girl to walk and show us. Moreover, she asked us to criticize her every move and gesture, whether it was suitable for a girl of the master's residence. 等，意思似乎译出来了，但某些词语和表述不够准

确（下画线标出）。其中，"师长"是旧时教师的尊称，"师长太太"（a teacher's wife）已在前面译出，此处可省略，"走路给我们看"就是摆 posture；"是否合于"，即"是否符合……的标准"，而这里的"批评"不是一般意义上的 criticize，且宜结合下面的内容译出。故此，该句不妨译为 The hostess ordered her to walk and posture to show us whether she fit the criteria to be a girl serving in the teacher's mansion.

[4] 中，其中有些语义、语气的转合。对于"将视线集中在……身上"参赛者一般译成 The two classmates really focused on the girl、the two classmates actually put their eyes on her、those two classmates of mine did fix their eyes upon the girl 等，固然没有错，但根据上文说的"批评"，此处应有所体现，即可意译为 In forming their judgment，以产生语境上的衔接；"把人当做畜生看"，不宜照字面意思译成 looked at people as animals、treat people as animals、I hated the hostess for being so inhuman that she treated people like animals、I held an intense grudge against the inhumanity of the hostess who went so far as to regard human as brutes 等，而可通述为 treating people with indignity，在句子中作主语，"我当时气得饭也吃不下"，是对比她同学的态度而言的，可用 verb + object + adjective + that 的句式译出：... made me so angry that I found it difficult to eat anything；"借故"，可另起一句为 On an excuse；"刹那的印象"，一般译成了 Momentary Impression、The Sudden Impression、Impression of the Moment，而 flash 在此似更确切，该词的本义为 a sudden brilliant

understanding。故此段不妨译为：In forming their judgment, my two classmates mainly concentrated on the girl's body; my eyes, however, burned with a flame for the injustice. I hated the hostess, and her inhuman way of treating people with indignity made me so angry that I found it difficult to eat anything. On an excuse, I went back to school and immediately wrote a piece of work entitled "The Flash on My Mind".

总之，翻译中词语的选择和句式的表述，既要尊重字典上的含义，又要根据具体语境作灵活的变通。

参考译文

How I Start to Write

(Excerpts)

By Xie Bingying

[1] I began to write novels in my second year at the Female Normal School when I was just fifteen years old.

[2] One day, I, together with my two primary school classmates, went to a fellow student's home to eat. The hostess, a teacher's wife, had just bought a 13-year-old servant girl. She was small, thin, emaciated with sallow complexion but a pair of big adorable black

eyes.

[3] The hostess ordered her to walk and posture to show us whether she fit the criteria to be a girl serving in the teacher's mansion.

[4] In forming their judgment, my two classmates mainly concentrated on the girl's body; my eyes, however, burned with a flame for the injustice. I hated the hostess, and her inhuman way of treating people with indignity made me so angry that I found it difficult to eat anything. On an excuse, I went back to school and immediately wrote a piece of work entitled "The Flash on My Mind".

19

原 文

我的小说写法[①]

（节选）

鲁迅

[1] 所写的事迹，大抵有一点见过或听到过的缘由，但决不全用这事实，只是采取一端，加以改造，或生发开去，到足以几乎完全发表我的意思为止。

[2] 人物的模特儿也一样，没有专用过一个人，往往嘴在浙江，脸在北京，衣服在山西，是一个拼凑起来的脚色。有人说，我的那一篇是骂谁，某一篇又是骂谁，那是完全胡说的。

[3] 不过这样的写法，有一种困难，就是令人难以放下笔。一气写下去，这人物就逐渐活动起来，尽了他的任务。

[4] 但倘有什么分心的事情来一打岔，放下许久之后再来写，性格也许就变了样，情景也会和先前所豫想的不同起来。

---

① 编者注：原名为《我怎么做起小说来？》，现标题为作者所加。

译 析

鲁迅是中国现代史上著名的文学家、思想家、革命家，但他首先是一位出色的小说家。本文所选是他关于怎样写小说的一段著名论述。

关于题目"我的小说写法"，有的译成 The Way of Writing 似过于笼统；The Way I Write My Stories、The Way I Write Novels、My Style of Novel Writing 好些，而 My Way of Writing a Novel 即可。

[1] 中，"但决不全用这事实"，其中的"事实"不是 truth、reality 等，而是指与 fiction (a type of literature that describes imaginary people and events, not real ones) 相对应的 factual (based on or containing facts)；"只是采取一端，加以改造，或生发开去，到足以几乎完全发表我的意思为止"，一般译成 I will just take a part of them to adapt or extend to the point where I can almost completely express what I mean., I will partly or even completely change the reality until I can express myself very well., I just took one end to transform it or create a story until it was almost enough to express my thoughts totally 等，其中下画线部分值得进一步斟酌。该段不妨译为：The stories emerging from under my pen were generally what I had seen or heard, but not entirely factual. I normally took one happening and modified or magnified it to the extent that my idea was almost fully expressed.

[2] 中，"拼凑起来的脚色"，大都译成 their images blending

characteristics of people from...、they are jointed in one figure、the role was pieced up等，都有可取之处，但he or she is a conglomerated role，则有不妥，因该词多指a large business firm consisting of several different companies，即大企业集团，如the world's second-largest media conglomerate（世界第二大传媒集团）。"完全胡说的"，若译成which is absolutely nonsense，显得有些过重了，因为这里的意思是"搞错了""没根据""没道理"，故可用makes no sense、rootless等；同样，"骂谁"也尽量不用scold、rebuke、reproach等。因而，整段不妨译为：My character models were produced roughly in the same way. Instead of picking on specific individuals they were often a mixture of a mouth from Zhejiang, a face from Beijing and clothes from Shanxi. Rumors about certain of my writing discrediting someone are thus simply rootless.

对于[3]，较为典型的译文，如However the difficulty falls on the fact that once I get my writing started, it would be hard to lay down my pen. Gradually, the character becomes vivid and is able to complete its due mission.、However, there is one problem of writing novels this way: once you start, you'd better not drop your pen in the middle. Only if you write nonstop will your characters come to life and carry out their missions.、But then, such a writing method can inevitably bring about a difficulty in putting down my pen, since the character would be gradually brought alive so long as I let the pen take its course. 大致上都不错，但在一些关键词上，如"困难""难以放下笔""活动起来""任务"等，都不宜根据其字面意思翻译，而要从小说创作的角度来考虑

问题，作出某些变通：The trouble with this kind of writing, however, is how it lingers on your pen since the characters become so active once they start playing their roles to the full.

[4] 中，"分心的事情"，固然可以译成there is something distracting，但这里更多的是从作者角度讲的，即the author is distracted for something；"性格"，似乎是the personality of the character，但实则the character即可；"先前所豫想的"，若译成the initial plans，便没有译出写作中的"构思"之意。因而，综合考虑，不妨译为：But as soon as you are distracted for some reason and unable to go back to the story for a lengthy time, you will lose the clue to portraying the character, which may turn out quite differently from what you initially conceived.

总之，就该段的翻译而言，应更多地从文学创作来选择英文词汇，而不是字典上一般词义的表述。

参考译文

My Way of Writing a Novel

（Excerpts）

By Lu Xun

[1] The stories emerging from under my pen were generally

what I had seen or heard, but not entirely factual. I normally took one happening and modified or magnified it to the extent that my idea was almost fully expressed.

[2] My character models were produced roughly in the same way. Instead of picking on specific individuals they were often a mixture of a mouth from Zhejiang, a face from Beijing and clothes from Shanxi. Rumors about certain of my writing discrediting someone are thus simply rootless.

[3] The trouble with this kind of writing, however, is how it lingers on your pen since the characters become so active once they start playing their roles to the full.

[4] But as soon as you are distracted for some reason and unable to go back to the story for a lengthy time, you will lose the clue to portraying the character, which may turn out quite differently from what you initially conceived.

20

原 文

其他侧面[①]

（节选）

冰心

[1] 一地同志关于这些地方的描写，由于时代和注意点的不同，使我看到了那些地方的许多其他的侧面，也扩大了我的知识。

[2] 我应该说一地同志这本回忆童年和旅游的散文集子，不但是青少年最好的读物，大人们也应当拿来看看。

[3] 因为这是一本写情真挚、写景鲜明；流畅、健康、引人向上的散文作品。

译 析

选文摘自著名作家冰心为王一地的散文集写的一篇书介，寥寥数语，言简意赅。

关于题目"其他侧面"，有的译成 Some Other Reflections，更多的是 Other Side(s)，但 side 本义是 either of the two halves of

---

① 编者注：原名为《旧梦重温》，现标题为作者所加。

a surface, an object or an area that is divided by an imaginary central line，即由想象的中线分出的一边、一侧，而从本文看又不只如此；aspect 则为 the parts of its character or nature，同时注意用复数；当然，features 也有其道理。故可译为 Other Aspects。

对于[1]，许多参赛译文雷同，如 Owing to the different times and perspective, Yidi's description of these places has brought their other aspects to my attention and broadened my knowledge., Owing to the different times and perspectives, Yidi's description of those places has brought their other aspects to my attention and broaden my knowledge., Owing to the difference of the epoch and the limelight, Yidi's description of those place made me know many other aspects and expanded my knowledge., Owing to the different ages and perspectives, Yidi's description of those places has helped me to find other aspects of them and broadened my knowledge. 等，显然有"复制"他人（包括网上的）译文（也包括其中的语法错误）之嫌，今后应予杜绝。

分析起来，"注意点"是什么？就是作者因关注而所写的东西，所以其实只有时间的不同，故 the profiles captured by... in different times 即可；"扩大……知识"，可用 broaden / expand knowledge，同时转换相应的时态。故该句不妨译为：The profiles captured by Mr.Yidi in different times, enabled me to see many other aspects of these places and expand my knowledge.

[2]中，"我应该说"，若译成 I should say that、I must say that 等，但语气欠佳，不如 It's fair to say that、I would recommend that 等；"散文集子"，一般译成了 pose collection、prose corpus

等，但essay也是散文，且更具纪实性（an analytic or interpretive literary composition），在此为宜。"回忆童年和旅游的散文集子"，有的特意强调为which has written the reminiscence of his childhood and the past traveling experiences，似乎有些太复杂了；其中"旅游"，有的译成voyage，但该词多用于航海，即an act of traveling by water，却又不是一般意义上的tourism，而是颇具游记（travel notes）的意味。"大人们也应当拿来看看"，不宜按字面意思译成adults should also take it over and read，而应释译为 ...worth reading by adults as well，或简略为should also be read by adults。

对于[3]中的"因为这是一本……的散文作品"，许多人单译一句，如Written in fluent words, it is really positive and inspiring with sincere feelings and lucid descriptions., Because this book contains sincere feelings and vivid scenery description. It's indeed a collection of readable, beneficial and inspiring prose works., It is worthwhile to read this book, because this is a smooth, healthy and inspiring book with sincere love and vivid scenery., It is an essay that expresses emotion sincerely and describes scenery vividly, with fluent, positive and inspiring contents等。其实，该句紧密衔接上文，可用介词等连接，与上段合成一体，如少数参赛译文"I must say that Yidi's collection of essays recalling his childhood and past travel experiences is not only the best choice for teenagers but also worth reading for adults as well, as it is a healthy and inspiring prose work that is fluent in language, sincere in emotions and vivid in scenery descriptions."实属难得。

"最好的读物"可译成 the best reading、a best choice、first class reading 等;"……写情真挚、写景鲜明;流畅、健康、引人向上的……",其中有的译成 sincere in feeling and lucid in description,其实 sincerity 就是一种 feeling,而 lucid 是形容词,不如改为 lucid description 或 lucid writing 等;有的如 ... is a book with sincere feelings, a vivid picture, fluency, nutrition and uplift... 则是更好的表述;同时,若用从句,如 ...prose works that are sincere,... 会使译文更加紧凑。

因而,[2][3]可合译成 It is fair to say that this collection of essays, composed of the recollections of his childhood and travel notes, is not only first class reading for teenagers, but should also be read by adults, since they present the reader with prose works that are sincere, vivid, fluent, healthy and uplifting.

可见,翻译中的分解与整合是个时时值得留意的问题。

参考译文

Other Aspects

(Excerpts)

By Bing Xin

[1] The profiles captured by Mr. Yidi in different times,

enabled me to see many other aspects of these places and expand my knowledge.

[2][3] It is fair to say that this collection of essays, composed of the recollections of his childhood and travel notes, is not only first class reading for teenagers, but should also be read by adults, since they present the reader with prose works that are sincere, vivid, fluent, healthy and uplifting.

21

> 原　文

我住处的景色[①]

（节选）

苏雪林

[1] 我现在居住的地方，风景并不坏。

[2] 从扶疏绿柳中望过去，可以看见旭日下黄浦江闪射的金色光辉，水上常有船驶过，白帆映着荡漾水光，有如银浦流云。

[3] 打开窗子，可以听见风送来浩渺宏壮江涛激石的声响。

[4] 宇宙是静谧的，但跳跃着永久生命的脉搏，唱颂着永久生命的歌声。

[5] 不过在我烦闷的时候，这些景色，都成了灰暗的一片，所给我的只有一种漠然的感觉。

> 译　析

该文选自苏雪林的散文《烦闷的时候》，寥寥数笔，朴素无华，寓情于景，别有味道。

---

① 编者注：原篇名为《烦闷的时候》，现标题是作者所加。

就题目"我住处的景色"而言，一般译成 The View of Where I Live、The View of My Dwelling、The View Around My Dwelling、Looking Around Where I Live、The View of My Place，但通读全篇，会发现此处讲的是周围的景色，故不妨译为 The Scenery Surrounding My Place。

[1] 中，"风景并不坏"，大都译成 the view around my place is not bad、doesn't look bad、it's not too bad，但作者这里更多是欣赏的口气，用"正说"更好，同时在 place 后应加介词 where: The place where I live now has fairly good scenery.

[2] 一般译成，Through the luxuriant but well-spaced green willows, the golden glow can be seen flickering on the Huangpu River bathed in the rising sun, where glittering white-sail ships sail as if clouds float on the silver water. / The Huangpu River, hiding behind the curtain-like green willows, sparkled in the morning sun. Sloops are often seen to trickle on the water, with whose white sails reflecting the rippling light of the water, which reminds me of the drifting silver clouds in the Milky Way./ From the luxuriant but well-spaced willows, the rising sun brings the Huangpu River of Shanghai shining golden rays. There are often ships passing by on the river, whose white sails reflect the rippling water like the flowing clouds of the Milky. 应当说，都大体可以接受。具体而言，"扶疏"是一种文雅的表述，可用 the luxuriant and well-spaced；"有船驶过"，似可用 boats glide，但 boats regularly travel 更确切；同时，"金色光辉"和"荡漾水光"有重叠之处，如可用 glittering 概述。该句不

妨译为：Looking through the luxuriant and well-spaced willows, I can see the golden glow from the Huangpu River under the rising sun, through which boats regularly travel with their white bulging sails glittering like silver clouds.

[3] 的译文，大都译成 When I open the window, the wind brings the great and solid sound of waves lapping on the rocks. / Open the window, you will hear the wind carrying the roar of surging waves beating rocks. / The laps of the waves brought by wind can be heard from the windows now and then. 等，有可取亦有可斟酌之处，如 open，宜用动名词；"浩渺宏壮江涛激石的声响"是一种渲染，如闻其声，不妨用 the powerful sound of the torrential rain thrashing the stones 等，故考虑译为 Opening the window, I can hear the powerful sound of the torrential rain thrashing the stones.

[4] 中，重点而言，"跳跃……脉搏"，译为 pulse rate / blood beat 等；"永久生命的"要结合前面的"宇宙"，可译为 the eternal pulse of the universe，因而整句可考虑译为：Being tranquil, the eternal pulse of the universe is also beating and singing its everlasting song of life.

对于[5]，比较典型的译文，如 However, when I am bored or anxious, these scenes will become dim and blank, which only gives a sense of indifference. / However, when I sank into irritancy, these sceneries all became gloomy, only giving me a feeling of detachment. / Yet all these views appear grey and gloomy to me when I'm unhappy, producing only a feeling of indifference 等等。其实，"灰暗的一

片",未必都是dim、blank、gloomy,而可用动词pale,其义为to become paler than usual, 如The blue of the sky paled to a light grey(天空的蓝色渐变成了浅灰色),其中还有心情的成分;"一种漠然的感觉",许多人用了indifference,多用于对人的冷漠,如What she said is a matter of complete indifference to me(她的话对于我来说完全无关紧要),He treated others with indifference(他对他人的事情漠不关心)等;而apathy则这种感觉更强烈,如Apathy is the long-standing curse of democracy(冷漠是民主的长期祸根),They told me about isolation and public apathy(他们向我讲述了孤立感与公众的冷漠)等。因而,该段不妨译为:And yet, when I am bored all this scenery pales, leaving me with only a feeling of apathy.

总之,还需根据具体语境,注重不同词语之间的细微差别,从而能更贴切地转述原文。

参考译文

The Scenery Surrounding My Place

(Excerpts)

By Su Xuelin

[1] The place where I live now has fairly good scenery.

[2] Looking through the luxuriant and well-spaced willows, I can see the golden glow from the Huangpu River under the rising sun, through which boats regularly travel with their white bulging sails glittering like silver clouds.

[3] Opening the window, I can hear the powerful sound of the torrential rain thrashing the stones.

[4] Being tranquil, the eternal pulse of the universe is also beating and singing its everlasting song of life.

[5] And yet, when I am bored all this scenery pales, leaving me with only a feeling of apathy.

22

原　文

白雪与青草[①]

丰子恺

[1] 自然景色中，青草与白雪是最伟大的现象。

[2] 造物者描写"自然"这幅大画图时，对于春红、秋艳，都只是轻描淡写。

[3] 到了描写白雪与青草，他就毫不吝惜颜料，用刷子大块地涂抹，使屋屋皆白，山山皆青。这是何等泼辣的画风！而草色青青，连天遍野，尤为和平可亲，大公无私的春色。

[4] 花木有时被关闭在私人的庭园里，草则到处自生自长，不择贵贱高下。人都以为花是春的作品，其实春工不在花枝，而在于草。

[5] 看花的能有几人？草则广泛地生长在大地的表面，普遍地受大众的欣赏。一年好景，无过于此时。自然对人的恩宠，也以此时为最深厚了。

---

① 编者注：原名为《春》，现标题是作者所加。

译 析

就题目而言,许多人将"白雪"译成White Snow,其实大可不必,因通常来讲,雪还有其他颜色吗?而该词组让人更多联想到的是"白雪公主";故译为Snow and Grasses即可。

对于[1],较为典型的参赛译文,如Snowfield and grassland are two greatest works in nature、White snow and green grass are the greatest views among the natural scenery、In nature, green grasses and white snow are the two greatest beauties等;分析起来,"自然景色中"似乎是in nature或in the natural colorful world,但更确切的应为in the natural landscape,因landscape的本义为an expanse of scenery that can be seen in a single view;而"最伟大的现象",显然不宜用greatest works in nature,而为the greatest / grandest phenomena。因而,该句不妨译为:Grass and snow are the grandest phenomena in the natural landscape.

[2]中,"造物者"可译为God或the Creator;(造物者描写"自然"这幅大画图时,对于春红、秋艳,都只是)"轻描淡写",可用touch on lightly、adumbrate、a light sketch and simple writing等,但若用paints... 便不妨用with a light brush。故该句可译为:In portraying the big picture of nature, the Creator paints spring and autumn with a light brush.

[3]中,"到了描写白雪与青草,他就毫不吝惜颜料,用刷子大块地涂抹,使屋屋皆白,山山皆青",若译成While portraying

the snow and the grass, he sweeps his brush over the picture and paints without restraint, so that all the roofs become white and all the mountains turn green. / However, when he draws snow and grass, he paints with patches of thick and heavy colors, making all the houses white and all the mountains green. / The snow and grass, however, are painted passionately. The white snow-capped houses and green grass-covered mountains constitute most of the splendid picture scroll. 似还没有译出"毫不吝惜"之意，比较而言，不如When it comes to snow and grass, he lavishes his paint and daubs all of the roofs with white and mountains with green. / But when it comes to the portrayal of white snow and green grass, he takes back all his parsimony and becomes extremely generous to use colors, painting in thick stroke with a brush, whitening all the houses and greening all the mountains. / When it came to painting the white snow and green grass, he spared no dye to wave his brush, making all the houses white and all the hills green 等；同时，该句似还可译成To describe the snow and grass, he did not hesitate to paint with a large brush daubing so that all houses are white and all mountains are green；然而，若与前面的译文相呼应，则可不妨变通为He is so generous in daubing the pigment, making every house white and every mountain green；"这是何等泼辣的画风！"一般译成How bright and bold the picture is! / What a stimulating drawing style it is! / How strongly amazing his painting style is! 其实，就其对比描写而言，此处更多的是一种sharply contrast，而"连天遍野"是一种渲染描述，可不必直译

为 connecting the heaven and allover the wildness；同时，对"和平可亲""大公无私""春色"也要做相应变通，以融合在句式中。因而，整句不妨译为：When it comes to snow and grass, however, he is so generous in daubing the pigment, making every house white and every mountain green. What a sharply contrasting painting style! The vast grassland seemingly connecting the heaven and earth is so amiable, embodying the selfless spring scenery.

[4] 中，"花木有时被关闭在私人的庭园里，草则到处……"两句有对比、转折关系，故不妨用 While..., grasses can... 的句式；"不择贵贱高下"，有的译成 without the affection for nobleness or prejudice against humbleness，似乎过于复杂，同时亦不是 regardless of dignity，而是指 regardless of the status of the place they grow；"人都以为花是春的作品"，实际是一种习惯上的感觉，故不妨用 conventionally；"不在……而在于……"可用句式 not so much in... as in...。故此，这两句不妨译为：While flowers and trees are sometimes enclosed in private gardens, grasses can flourish everywhere regardless of the status of the place they grow. Conventionally, flowers are seen as the works of spring; in fact, spring is reflected not so much in flowers as in grasses.

对于[5]，一般都按原文的语气和句式译成 How many people can appreciate flowers? But grass grows widely across the fields, generally accepting appreciation. The scenery at this time is the greatest of the year. And nature's favor to man is the deepest. / How many people could watch flowers blooming? Meanwhile grass grows everywhere on earth and widely appreciated by us. This is the best time of the year to see such wonderful scene which is also the most fascinating present given by the nature. / How many people can enjoy flowers? But grass grows all over the fields, and is generally accepted and admired. The scenery at this time of the year is the best while the nature bestows its deepest kindness to humans. 然而，分析起来，"看花的能有几人？"看似问句，实则作者的语气是肯定的，故可用句式 one thing is for sure that...；"自然对人的恩宠"可用 the grace of nature with man，但为句式表达通顺，亦可用 people are favored by nature... that...。因而，整段不妨译为：One thing is for sure that only a few people can really appreciate flowers compared with grass which spreading out everywhere, can be enjoyed by the wider public. People are favored by nature so greatly that no time is better than now.

总之，对于原文的理解不应止于字面意思，而应争求"力透纸背"，从而使译文更加准确、完整。

参考译文

Snow and Grass

By Feng Zikai

[1] Grass and snow are the grandest phenomena in the natural

landscape.

[2] In portraying the big picture of nature, the Creator paints spring and autumn with a light brush.

[3] When it comes to snow and grass, however, he is so generous in daubing the pigment, making every house white and every mountain green. What a sharply contrasting painting style! The vast grassland seemingly connecting the heaven and earth is so amiable, embodying the selfless spring scenery.

[4] While flowers and trees are sometimes enclosed in private gardens, grasses can flourish everywhere regardless of the status of the place they grow. Conventionally, flowers are seen as the works of spring; in fact, spring is reflected not so much in flowers as in grasses.

[5] One thing is for sure that only a few people can really appreciate flowers compared with grass which spreading out everywhere, can be enjoyed by the wider public. People are favored by nature so greatly that no time is better than now.

23

> 原　文

旧梦重温

（节选）

冰心

[1] 意大利是我最喜欢的一个欧洲国家。

[2] 罗马是建在七山之上的城市，拥有大小500座教堂，我几乎都去过了。最大的是圣彼得。

[3] 梵蒂冈就是在圣彼得教堂附近，是罗马教皇的宫殿，这是一个"国中之国"！我进去看了，只记得门警是瑞士兵士，穿着黄色制服，别的没有印象了。

[4] 佛罗伦萨给我留下的，除了美术馆里的雕像和壁画之外，还有一座座府第墙壁上的灯座，每座灯下都有一只拴马的铁环，是聚会或宴会时拴马用的，十分别致！

> 译　析

该文节选自《冰心全集》（第八卷）中的《旧梦重温》。著名作家冰心不但以儿童文学著称，而且散文写得清新隽永、寓意深邃、构思灵巧、行文流畅、独具魅力，弥漫着温馨的情调。

就题目而言，有的译成 The Revision of an Old Dream、Renew Good Old Days、Taking a Trip down Memory Lane 等，显然用词有明显问题，如 revision 是"修订"，并无"重温"之意，而 renew 的本义是 re-establish on a new, usually improved, basis or make new or like new，即更多的是指使更新、复兴、重申等，而与此相关的词应是 retrospection、reminisce、revisiting、reliving 等，如 Revisiting My Dream。

[1] 中，似可按原文词序译成 Italy is an European country that I love most，但实则可简化、变通为 ... one of my favorite European countries，其中的 country 不是单数，而许多人没有注意到。

[2] 中，一般译成 The capital of it, Roman, is a city build on seven hills with 500 churches, big and small, almost all of which I have been to and among which the largest one is St. Peter's. / Located on seven hills, Roman has 500 churches, most of which I've been to, and the largest one is St. Peter's Church. / In possession of five hundred churches in different sizes, Roman is a city stretching between seven mountains. I have been to almost all those churches, among which the St Peter's Cathedral was the biggest. 等，大致不错；当然，对于这几句的词序，译文可作不同的调整，如 Built on seven mountains, Roman is a city with... churches, big and small, ... I visited them all, almost. The largest is St. Peter. 但考虑到前面讲的是国家，此处特意提出其首都，更宜用 Rome 作主语，如 Rome, in particular, is a city ... ，而"最大的是圣彼得"用 with... 作为状语出现；故不妨译为：Rome, in particular, is a city

built on seven mountains with 500 churches of various sizes (with St. Peter's being the biggest). I have visited almost all of them.

[3]中,"梵蒂冈就是在圣彼得教堂附近"可以按原文语序译成The Vatican is in the vicinity of St. Peter church,亦可将"在圣彼得教堂附近"作为"梵蒂冈"的定语后置,如The Vatican, adjacent to St. Peter's, is...,以使句子更为紧凑;"国中之国"是一种通俗的说法,似可用country within a country、state within a state等,但分析起来,state、country的本义为the territory occupied by one of the constituent administrative districts of a nation,而梵蒂冈并非典型意义上的"国家",比如它没有军队,故更宜用kingdom inside the kingdom。"我进去看了,只记得门警是瑞士兵士,穿着黄色制服,别的没有印象了",可按原文词、语序译成I went there to have a look. All I remember now is that the guards at the entrance were Swiss soldiers in yellow uniforms. 但也可将其变通,如I once visited this "kingdom inside the kingdom", but nothing else impressed me except... 等。故此段不妨译为:"The Vatican, adjacent to St. Peter's, is the palace of the Pope. I once visited this "kingdom inside the kingdom", but nothing else impressed me except the Swiss soldiers in yellow uniforms acting as the guards."。

[4]中,"除了……之外",可用apart from...、in addition to...等,而"拴马的铁环"似乎是an iron ring,但实际考察,便会发现,是an iron horsehead to hitch horses to;"十分别致"若单译一句,会显冗赘,如What remains of Florence in my memory is, apart from the sculptures and murals in the art galleries, the lamps on the

walls of the mansions, with an iron ring under each of them, for tying horses at parties and banquets. It was just unique. 对此，若稍加语序变通，会使句子更加通顺、简约、流畅。

总之，冰心散文的笔法轻盈、灵活，译文也要随之有所变化。

参考译文

Revisiting My Dream

(Excerpts)

By Bing Xin

[1] Italy is one of my favorite European countries.

[2] Rome, in particular, is a city built on seven mountains with 500 churches of various sizes (with St. Peter's being the biggest). I have visited almost all of them.

[3] The Vatican, adjacent to St. Peter's, is the palace of the Pope. I once visited this "kingdom inside the kingdom", but nothing else impressed me except the Swiss soldiers in yellow uniforms acting as the guards.

[4] In addition to the statues and frescoes in the gallery, Florence left me with the impression of lamp holders on the walls of the buildings, each with an iron horsehead to hitch horses to under each lamp, which was very nice and chic for a party or banquet.

24

> 原 文

老刀

（节选）

郝景芳

[1] 从垃圾站下班之后，老刀回家洗了个澡，换了衣服。

[2] 白色衬衫和褐色裤子，这是他唯一一套体面衣服，衬衫袖口磨了边，他把袖子卷到胳膊肘。

[3] 老刀四十八岁，没结婚，已经过了注意外表的年龄，又没人照顾起居，这一套衣服留着穿了很多年，每次穿一天，回家就脱了叠上。他在垃圾站上班，没必要穿得体面，偶尔参加谁家小孩的婚礼，才拿出来穿在身上。

[4] 这一次他不想脏兮兮地见陌生人。他在垃圾站连续工作了五小时，很担心身上会有味道。

> 译 析

本篇选自郝景芳的中篇作品《北京折叠》，小说既植根现实，又富于想象，笔法灵活、生动。题目是后加的。

[1]中，"垃圾站"可用waste processing station、garbage station

等;"下班",after the end of his shift、after work;"回家洗了个澡,换了衣服"不必译成 ...had gone home, first to shower and then to change、... went back home to take a shower and then to change clothes、... took a bath at home and changed his clothes、... took a shower and then dressed himself in another clothes 等,而 went home, showered and changed 即可。整句不妨译为:After work, from the garbage station Old Dao went home, showered and changed.

[2]中,"体面衣服",应理解为所谓的 decent suit;而语序既可顺译,亦可调整,如 He put on the only decent clothes he owned—the white shirt and brown pants, rolling the sleeves up to his elbows for the sleeves of the shirt were frayed、The only decent set of clothes he had was a white shirt and a pair of brown trousers. He rolled up the scuffed sleeves to his elbows、White shirt together with brown trousers is the only decent suit he has. Owing to the wear and tear of the cuff, he tucked his sleeves to the elbow 等,但平铺直叙,不妨译为:His white shirt and brown trousers were his only "decent suit". He rolled the sleeves up to his elbow, for the sleeve cuffs were frayed.

[3]中,"老刀四十八岁,没结婚,已经过了注意外表的年龄"似可译成 Lao Dao was forty-eight, single, and long past the age when he still took care of his appearance、Old Dao, an unmarried 48 somethings, is beyond the age to pay attention to appearance、Mr. Dao was 48 years old and single, so he was no longer cared about his appearance and he lived alone 等;其中"没结婚"与

single并不完全划等号，且词序也可调整，如At the age of forty-eight, unmarried, Old Dao has passed the age of caring about his appearance，使其更符合英文表达习惯。"没必要穿得体面"，字面意思是it doesn't require him to wear decent clothes，但此处用动词dress会更加简洁。"没人照顾起居"，一般可译成With no one taking care of his daily life、As he had no one to pester him about the domestic details、For there is no one to take care of his daily life等，但实际可简化为Unattended by anyone, ...；"偶尔参加谁家小孩的婚礼"若译成save a wedding now and then for a friend's son or daughter、except some weddings now and then of a friend's children、It was only when occasionally attending the wedding of some friends' kid he took the set of clothes out and wore 等，不免冗赘而欠妥，如"谁家的"不一定是a friend's...等。整体而言，语序可作调整，故此段不妨译为：At the age of forty-eight, unmarried, Old Dao has passed the age of caring about his appearance. Also, working in a garbage station doesn't call for him to dress decently either. Unattended by anyone, he has kept his "suit" scrupulously for many years, wearing it only rarely, on occasions such as weddings of someone's kids. Every time, after taking off his "formal clothes", he folds them carefully.

[4] 中，对于这种句子，不可按原词序进行翻译，因为那样不仅难以通顺，且意思会走样，如 This time he didn't want to see strangers dirty. He worked at the garbage station for five hours in a row, so he was worried about the smell.、Today, however, he minded

meeting strangers with discourteous image. After the five-hour work at the garbage disposal station, he was anxious about being smelly. / But this time, he didn't want to meet strangers dirty, and he was afraid to smell disgustingly for having been working at the garbage station for 5 hours 等，而应在理解全句的基础上，将词序打乱，重新组合，故此句不妨译为：Today, having worked for five hours in a garbage station, he was worried about his body smell and he didn't want to be seen dirty in front of strangers. 从而，以求在语义上的吻合，而不是字面和词序上的。

参考译文

Old Dao

(Excerpts)

By Hao Jingfang

[1] After work, from the garbage station Old Dao went home, showered and changed.

[2] His white shirt and brown trousers were his only "decent suit". He rolled the sleeves up to his elbow, for the sleeve cuffs were frayed.

[3] At the age of forty-eight, unmarried, Old Dao has passed the

age of caring about his appearance. Also, working in a garbage station doesn't call for him to dress decently either. Unattended by anyone, he has kept his "suit" scrupulously for many years, wearing it only rarely, on occasions such as weddings of someone's kids. Every time, after taking off his "formal clothes", he folds them carefully.

[4] Today, having worked for five hours in a garbage station, he was worried about his body smell and he didn't want to be seen dirty in front of strangers.

25

原文

电商的挑战

[1] 电商营销近年来取得的成绩,对传统百货行业的市场占有率是极大的挑战。越来越多的人去网购,在需求短期之内没有大幅变化的情况下也就意味着相应的百货商场客源流失。业内人士表示,近年来百货业销售下滑较大的品类也正是方便网络购买的品类,比如家电、IT产品和纺织品,甚至是奢侈品。

[2] 同时,一些传统百货商场还面临沦为电商"试衣间"的尴尬。不少人去实体店确定了衣服等物品的款式、尺寸之后到网上支付购买,由此诞生了"抄号族"、"偷拍党"。随着网购市场的日益庞大,服装、化妆品和家居用品等都已经纳入涉猎范围,消费者线下选货线上购买。

[3] 电商侵占市场之外,行业之内的激烈竞争也不容小觑。传统百货商场之间同质化较严重,造成同业之间竞争激烈,近年来全国多个城市都在大力建设购物中心等大型商场,使本来就竞争激烈的百货商场经营更加困难。走在城市的商业街区,几乎所有的百货商场在销售内容、店面设计和产品布局等方面大同小异。一博士生说,从北京走到福州,看到各个城市的商场几乎是一样的。

译 析

该文改写自2012年12月19日《中国商报》的同名新闻报道，属商务报刊类文本。其语言简洁明了、客观中立、新颖活泼；具有一定数量的行业术语和专用名词，但又不乏"中国风味"。

在[1]中，对于"越来越多的人去网购，在需求短期之内没有大幅变化的情况下也就意味着相应的百货商场客源流失"，很容易译成More and more people turn to online shopping, which signifies the loss of customers from the department store correspondingly in the situation when there is no substantial change of demand in short term, 似乎相关的信息都不缺乏，而且结构上也作出自觉的调整，但欠缺了一点：结构的调整为的是疏通相关的信息，甚至要与增删技巧结合起来，同时须意识到商务英语平实表达的特点。再如，With more people shifting to online shopping, brick-and-mortar stores are inevitably losing consumers to their online counterparts if demand remains stable within a short period. 然而，相关的信息（多人去网购、短期内无变化等）似可作进一步的整合，以更突出主要信息（意味着相应的百货商场客源流失）等。

在[2]中，对于"……消费者线下选货线上购买"，很容易译成 ...select goods in the general stores but buy them online / ... offline selection but online purchase 等。其实如果我们从该句所在的整个

段落着眼，认真审视一下，便不难看出，这个意思在前面已经"和盘托出"了，这里再译就纯属画蛇添足了。这就是两种文字表述的差异。在一种文字中是完美无瑕的，翻译到另一种文字时就显得多余累赘，因此就要"舍"，即舍弃不译；须知，"不译"也是一种翻译，正如同中国画里的"留白"，以虚映实，亦似音乐中的"此时无声胜有声"；多了，不是添彩，而是败笔。

对于"抄号族""偷拍党"等流行术语，barcode-copying clan、sneaky photographing tribe、fit-lifters、copy the article number、snapshot the article、number-copying clan、surreptitious-photographing clan 等，这些译法基本上都能表达原意，但有的失去了原文的生动趣味，而 creating 一词的选用在此处亦极不妥当；有的虽保留了原文的生动，但两词叠加使用，英文颇显冗赘，其实不妨用 fit-lifters 加以涵盖，感觉更为地道、贴切。同时，"支付购买"无需 pay and buy，仅 buy 或 purchase 即可；特别是后者，不一定是指大型的、批量购买等，如：He gave his son some money for the purchase of his school books（他给他儿子一些钱买课本）；It is a recent purchase of mine（那是我前几天买来的）等。

在[3]中，这里的"同业之间竞争"不是一般意义上 competition，而应理解为不健康、恶性的，故为 vicious / malignant competition within the trade；"看到各个城市的商场几乎是一样的"，似可正译成：... have found all the department stores are same in every city，但反译更能加深印象：... you are likely to enter a similar kind of department store 等。

The Challenge Presented by E-Commerce

[1] The recent achievements of E-commerce present a tremendous challenge to the share of our traditional department stores. Given that the market demand remains relatively stable in a short period of time, when more and more people go shopping online, it means a loss of customers to traditional department stores. Some insiders have revealed that the types of goods that have recently suffered a sharp decline in sales at department stores happen to be those that can be easily purchased on the Web, such as home appliances, IT products, textiles and even luxuries.

[2] In the meantime, some traditional department stores have embarrassingly been reduced to the "fitting rooms" for E-commerce customers—many of them go to department stores to find out about the size and style of clothes among other things they need and then purchase them online, thus becoming "fit-lifters", so to speak. With the rapid growth of online market, clothing, make-up products, housewares and so on, are all caught in this trend.

[3] Apart from the pressure from the E-commerce, the severe competition within the department store business should also not be

underestimated as a cause for their potential decline. Homogeneity among department stores has caused vicious competition within the trade and, in recent years, a huge number of newly-built large shopping malls in many cities around the country have made the situation worse. Walking on those shopping streets, you can hardly tell the differences between department stores in terms of their layout, store design and goods. From Beijing to Fuzhou, as a PhD candidate put it, everywhere you go, you are likely to enter a similar kind of department store.

26

> 原 文

区块链

林巍

[1] 区块链起源于比特币，在其形成过程中，随着信息交流的扩大，一个区块与一个区块相继接续，形成的结果就叫区块链。

[2] 区块链具有如下特征：去中心化，区块链技术不依赖额外的第三方管理机构或硬件设施，没有中心管制；开放性，区块链技术基础是开源的，除了交易各方的私有信息被加密外，区块链的数据对所有人开放；独立性，基于协商一致的规范和协议，所有节点能够在系统内自动安全地验证、交换数据，不需要任何人为的干预；匿名性，除非有法律规范要求，单从技术上来讲，各区块节点的身份信息不需要公开或验证，信息传递可以匿名进行。

[3] 总体而言，区块链的数据操作会更具安全性，但其应用尚在初创开发阶段。

> 译 析

近来，在经济、金融界走红的一个词是"区块链"，据说将会对我们今后生活的方方面面产生深远影响。

对于[1],有的译得比较"零碎",如The blockchain originates from Bitcoin. With the expansion of information exchange in its formation process, the successive connection of each block has formed the blockchain. / Blockchain originated from Bitcoin. During its forming process, information communication broadening, a block is connected with a block one after another, resulting in the blockchain. 等,固然意思也不错,但应意识到,中文重"意合",英文重"形合",所以在中译英时可尽量将其整合。如,"陈坤是个弃儿,是不幸的,亲生母亲据说是个打工妹,作为非婚生出生即被遗弃"(黄蓓佳《万家亲友团》),似可译成Being an abandoned child, Chen Kun was quite unfortunate. His biological mother was said to be an unmarried worker, and he was therefore abandoned upon birth. 但中文味道太浓,若将其加以"形合"考虑,重新组织,便会大为改观:Chen Kun had a rocky start to his life, being abandoned by his worker mother after having him out of wedlock. 再如,"后来车一直停在那里,司机坐在车里等。再后来,车子开走了"(林那北《今天有鱼》)。若译成:The car has always been parking there, and the driver has been with his car ever since. Later, the car was driven away. 试比较:The car then sat there with the driver waiting and eventually left. 一气呵成,简练而通顺。所以,该段亦应以一句完成,如有的译文:Blockchain, the original Bitcoin system, came into being as a result of one block's successive connect to another with the expansion of information exchange. / Originated from bitcoins, the blockchain is formed when one block is linked to another in succession with increasing exchanges of information. 等，尽管其中加下画线部分有用词不当问题（如 connect 应为 connection; Originate 为 Originating），但总体比较连贯，而更好一些的，如 Originating in Bitcoin, Blockchain formed with the expansion of information communication and the connection between two blocks in succession. 至于"随着信息交流的扩大，一个区块与一个区块相继接续，形成的结果就叫区块链"，为突出其"结果"，亦可将词序调整，如 the first Blockchain was formed as a result of successively connecting blocks with...；"形成过程"不一定译成 formation / forming process，而可将前后通融，如 during the process of Bitcoin development in the... 等，故整段不妨译为：Originating from Bitcoin, the first Blockchain was formed as a result of successively connecting blocks with one another during the process of Bitcoin development in the expansion of information exchange.

　　[2] 中，"特征"可用 feature、characteristic、nature、trait、earmark 等，参赛译文用得最多的是前两个，该二词的细微差别在于：feature——a prominent aspect of something, 即显著特点，如 An interesting feature of the city is the old market（这座城市的一个有趣特征就是古老的市场）; Teamwork is a key feature of the training programme（团队合作是这项训练计划的重要特点）; The software has no particular distinguishing features（这个软件没有明显的特点）等，而 characteristic — the qualities of a person or thing that uniquely belong to them and make them recognizable,

强调性质典型性,如Genes determine the characteristics of every living thing(基因决定每个生物的特征);Mutuality rather than independence is the chief characteristic of human life, whatever we'd like to believe(无论我们愿意相信与否,人类生活的主要特征是相互性,而不是独立性);This characteristic finds an echo in business conduct(这一特征也反映在商业行为中)等。

"去中心化",有的译成technology is not restricted with the central control,显然太繁杂,实则为decentralization,而"没有中心管制"是接续前面的否定句"不依赖额外的……",故其否定词不用not而用nor,其意为in order to introduce the second alternative or the last of a number of alternatives in a negative statement,尽管前面没有neither,如None of us has any idea how long we're going to be here, nor do I(我们没有人知道要在这儿待多久;我也不知道);If he has no future, then nor do we(如果他没前途,我们也都没有了)等。

"开放性",大都译成openness、is open to all,固然不错,但"开源的"为on open platforms,为避免重复,可用publicity,即具有"公众性";同时,"区块链技术基础是开源的,除了交易各方的私有信息被加密外,区块链的数据对所有人开放",有的译成the block chain data is open to all people except that the private information of all parties in the transaction is encrypted,实际词序可调整得更加通顺些,如data, with the exception of ...which is encrypted, can be technically accessed ...等。

"独立性",一般都译成independence / independent,但与

此相关的还有autonomy，二者的细微差别，前者是complete freedom from control or influence of another or others，而后者为usually a degree of freedom that is less than complete independence；此处，区块链虽"不需要任何人为的干预"，但毕竟还在一个系统之内，故不妨采用后者。

"除非有法律规范要求，单从技术上来讲，各区块节点的身份信息不需要公开或验证，信息传递可以匿名进行"，参赛译文有 in terms of technology, the identity information of each block node does not need to be disclosed or verified and information transfer can be performed anonymously unless there are legal requirements / technically, identities in nodes of each block need not to be public or validated. Information can be delivered anonymously unless required by law and regulation / technically speaking, the identity information of each block node does not need to be made known to public or verified and can be delivered anonymously unless required by laws and regulations / technically speaking, the identity information of each block node does not need to be made known to public or verified and can be delivered anonymously unless required by laws and regulations. 应当说，都是基本可以接受的；但词序和标点符号亦可有所调整。故此，整段不妨译为：Blockchain has the following features: Decentralization——its technology does not rely on additional third-party management agencies or hardware facilities, nor does it have a control center; Publicity——operating on open platforms, its data, with the exception of the private transactional information of the parties concerned which is encrypted, can be technically accessed by anyone; Autonomy—based on consensual specifications and protocols, all nodes and data can be automatically and safely verified and exchanged without any intervention from anyone; Anonymity—technically speaking, unless there are legal requirements, information concerning the identity of each block transmission node is not to be disclosed or verified; therefore, information can be transferred anonymously.

[3] 中，"更具安全性"一般译成 is more secure、possesses more safety、will be safer 等；"其应用尚在初创开发阶段"，可译为 still in the early / initial / incipient stage of development 等，但前后两句应有所衔接，如使用 while...。故此句不妨译为 In general, while the data operation of Blockchain can be more secure, its application is still in the initial stage of development.

此文具有科普性质，有其专业术语和特殊表述，翻译时不可望文生义，而应尽可能查阅相关资料。

参考译文

Blockchain

By Lin Wei

[1] Originating from Bitcoin, the first Blockchain was formed

as a result of successively connecting blocks with one another during the process of Bitcoin development in the expansion of information exchange.

[2] Blockchain has the following features: Decentralization—its technology does not rely on additional third-party management agencies or hardware facilities, nor does it have a control center; Publicity—operating on open platforms, its data, with the exception of the private transactional information of the parties concerned which is encrypted, can be technically accessed by anyone; Autonomy—based on consensual specifications and protocols, all nodes and data can be automatically and safely verified and exchanged without any intervention from anyone; Anonymity—technically speaking, unless there are legal requirements, information concerning the identity of each block transmission node is not to be disclosed or verified; therefore, information can be transferred anonymously.

[3] In general, while the data operation of Blockchain can be more secure, its application is still in the initial stage of development.

27

> 原 文

学生比例

[1] 对于学校来说,在国际学生和英国学生之间形成合适的人数比例关系,已经成为了一个棘手的问题。

[2] 学校依赖富有的外国家长支付平均高达27600英镑的寄宿学费,这笔日渐上涨的费用已经超出了不少英国中产阶级的承受能力。

[3] 但是那些有钱家庭的外国学生,仍然源源不断地涌入,在相当程度上,支撑了英国经济的增长,特别是在当前英国脱欧的困境下,更是如此。

> 译 析

就标题"学生比例"而言,有人译成Student Ratio,让人以为是"师生比例",因ratio本义为the relative magnitudes of two quantities (usually expressed as a quotient);有的用了The Proportion of Students,似欠明确,因该文指的是"国际学生和英国学生之间的比例关系",故可译为Proportion of International and Domestic Students。

[1] 中，"棘手的问题"，可以是a thorny / vexed issue、hot potato、tough nut、daunting / knotty problem、challenge等；在语序上，既可放在后面 ... has become a vexed issue for the schools，也可提前It has become a thorny issue for any school...，以表强调。

"合适的人数比例关系"，有的用appropriate scale，但scale是指the size or extent of something especially when compared with something else即主要指的是事物的规模、范围、程度等，而这里指的是人；有的译成a balance between the amount of international students and British students，应知amount is usually used to talk about things that are uncountable nouns，即通常与不可数名词连用，如a large amount of time / money / information等，而此处的人数是可数的，故应用number，如a number of people / books / dogs等。

同时，该句可用名词作主语，如the right mixture of international and British pupils；或用动宾结构，如to properly proportion the number of international and British students等。

故此，该句不妨译为：It has become a thorny issue for any school to properly proportion the number of international and British students.

[2] 中，"寄宿学费"有的用了revenues，但该词本义是the money that a government receives from taxes or that an organization, etc. receives from its business，即主要指政府的财政收入、税收或企业的收益等；"超出……承受能力"一般都译成beyond financial capacity，但分析起来，其中的这种"能力"是一种

ability to be afforded，因而是affordability，如This is a departure from the actual affordability of consumers, the consequences of violating the rules（这就是背离了消费者的实际承受能力，违反规则的后果）；the state's struggle over affordability represents, in extreme form, a national trend（该州人不堪高房价重负以其极端形式体现了全国的趋势）等，而"超出……能力"可以用beyond / exceed ability of...；"平均高达27600英镑的寄宿学费"可直接译成the £27,600 a year average boarding fees，亦可放在括号里表述，如the rising average boarding fees (as high as £27,600 per year)。根据英文形合的特点，固然可以将两句译成一句，如Creating the right mixture of international and British pupils has become a vexed issue for the schools, who rely on wealthy foreigners to pay the £27,600 a year average boarding fees which are rising beyond the reach of UK middle classes. 但为清晰起见，不妨译为两句。故此，该句不妨译为：Schools nowadays rely on the rising average boarding fees (as high as £27,600 per year) paid by the wealthy foreign parents, which exceed the affordability of British middle-class families.

对于[3]，"源源不断地涌入"可以是the continuous influx of foreign students、are still pouring in、...is rising constantly等，似乎都是可以接受的，要看前后语句的搭配；"困境"，大都用了dilemma、predicament、plight、trouble、crisis等，分析起来，dilemma指进退两难的情形，需在相等或相抵触的情况下作出抉择；predicament指一种不知该怎么办的疑难处境；plight指糟

糕或不幸的处境；trouble指令人烦恼、痛苦、危险、匮乏的状态；crisis指危机、危难时刻；就此语境而言，前三个比较恰当，最后一个似乎有些"过"了。综合而言，此句不妨译为：But foreign students from wealthy families are still pouring in, supporting, to a considerable extent, Britain's economic growth, especially in the current predicament of Brexit.

总之，看似相同的词语在译文中亦有细微差别，需悉心辨析。

参考译文

Proportion of International and Domestic Students

[1] It has become a thorny issue for any school to properly proportion the number of international and British students.

[2] Schools nowadays rely on the rising average boarding fees (as high as £27,600 per year) paid by the wealthy foreign parents, which exceed the affordability of British middle-class families.

[3] But foreign students from wealthy families are still pouring in, supporting, to a considerable extent, Britain's economic growth, especially in the current predicament of Brexit.

28

原 文

不可厌倦①

(节选)

梁启超

[1] 厌倦是人生第一件罪恶,也是人生第一件苦痛。厌倦是一种想脱离活动的心理现象。换一句话说,就是不愿意劳作。

[2] 你想,一个人不是上帝特制出来充当消化面包的机器,可以一天不劳作吗?

[3] 只要稍为动一动不愿意劳作的念头,便是万恶渊薮。

[4] 换个方面看,无论何等人,总要靠劳作来维持自己生命,任凭你怎样地不愿意,劳作到底免不掉。

译 析

梁启超不仅是中国近代史上杰出的思想家、政治家,而且是一位大教育家。他的九个子女个个成才,"一门三院士,父子九专家",其秘诀是言传身教。选文是他对学生的演讲,也可看作

---

① 编者注:原名为《教育家的自家田地》,现标题为作者所加。

是对后辈的教诲。

[1]中，关于"厌倦"的译词，参赛者用的是boredom、tiredness、weariness、indolence、ennui等，应当说都不算错，但经辨析：1. ennui为法文，固然有"a feeling of being tired, bored and dissatisfied"之意，但不够常用；2. indolence为inactivity resulting from a dislike of work，更多的是"懒惰"；3. weariness是temporary loss of strength and energy resulting from hard physical or mental work，即暂时性的倦怠；4. tiredness类似于weariness；5. 而boredom（bored的名词形式）为tired、impatient、have no interest in doing anything，是一种常态化的厌倦，故更为确切。

"罪恶"的译法，有的用了crime，需知该词的主要意思是an act which is against the law，即违法行为，然此处并非该意；而evil是morally objectionable behavior，更多道德色彩，同时可泛指一切恶事（见[3]）；guilt本义为an unhappy feeling after having done something wrong，主要是"内疚"，显然不符。当然，用的最多的是sin，该词最初源于宗教，意为an action or type of behavior which is believed to break the laws of God，如original sin（原罪），但又不限于宗教，因the laws of God与natural law（自然法）相通，多指一种本性上的"恶"，如：1. 他们没有任何道德观念，生活中充满罪恶。（Without any moral consideration, they are now living in sin.）2. He saves us from the power of sin.（他使我们摆脱了罪恶势力。）

但该句的译文很容易冗赘，如：Boredom is the first sin of life, and also the first suffering of life. / Tiredness is the guilt of the first thing all one's life and the first pain of one's life. /

Boredom is the most sinful and also the most painful thing in..., 等等。实则可以简化,避免重复,突出主旨。"心理现象",大都译成了psychological phenomena,如Boredom is a psychological phenomenon that someone wants to separate himself or herself from activities. 这未免过于表面化了,实则,这里讲的是一种生活态度,故不妨用mentality,意为a particular attitude and way of thinking,即主要是一种"心态"。此段中第二个"厌倦"显然有递进之意,即"实质上是……(不愿或厌恶做任何事)",而"不愿意劳作"其实就是懒惰!同时,英语口语里说"烦了",还可用sick of,如I am so sick of all the noise and traffic here.(对这里的噪音和交通混乱,我真烦透了。)

故此,[1]不妨译为:Boredom, in my view, is the most painful thing, and a sin to suffer. In essence, it is the mentality of being sick of doing anything at all. In other words, it's lazy!

[2]中,"你想",一般译成了just think、just imagine、think about that等,比较典型的,如Think about that, as humans are not a machine created particularly by God to digest bread but can human not work for a day long? / Just think, a man was not supposed only to be a bread eater when God created him. Could he have a single day without working? / You see, men are not created by God to be bread-consuming machines. How could we live a day without working? 有的将此处三个分句整合为一句:"You may save yourself from hard work only if you were a God-made bread digester which, unfortunately you are not",也是非常可取的,尽管在形式上距原

文较远。其实,这里的"你想",是启发读者意识到(这样一个事实),而"消化面包的机器"是指食而不作。故[2]不妨译为:One has to realize that man was not created by God to be a machine merely to digest food. How can one fail to work?

[3]中,"只要稍为动一动……念头",一般采用了"...don't have a slight error in thought / Don't think a little bit about... / So long as you give rise to the thought... / If you somewhat occur to an idea that (you are averse to working...) / as long as you toy with idea of (unwilling to work) / As if you have an idea of not (work)"等译法,似乎都是一种思路,而"The moment the tendency of being sick of working began to erode your mind, you already fell into abyss of extreme evil"则别开生面!其实,英语里还有一种通俗表达法:not even to think of it /not to even think about that, 如You should not try to smuggle any drugs in that country, where the most severe penalty is in place; don't even think of it!(那个国家对毒品走私有最严厉的制裁;不要试图做那种事——想都不要想!)故[3]可译为:It's best not to even think about that, since boredom is the source of all evils.

[4]中,将"换个方面看"译成From another prospective / On the other hand / Put in another way等,似乎都可接受。"维持自己生命",即"生存""生活"之意,但又不宜简单地译成maintain (sustain) life / to exist through working等。有的译成Anybody needs to work to keep them alive,其中的"keep... alive"是使役句式(causative verb),即"使其活下去",显然有误;此处应为自

动词（intransitive verbs），如make a living，或to survive，其本义continue to live、endure or last，类似的还有endure、hold up、hold out等。总的讲，此句的实际意思是，任何人都别想不劳而获，可表达为：you shouldn't expect to get something without any labor / there is no free lunch in the world / you'd better to know "no pain no gain" / there is no reaping without sowing，等等。故此，[4]不妨译为：Put in another way, whoever wishes to survive has to labor to support oneself, no matter if one is willing or not.

此段演讲，接续的还有一句话（因篇幅所限删去了），"免是免不掉，愿是不愿意，天天皱着眉哭着脸去做那不愿做的苦工，岂不是活活地把自己关在第十八层地狱？"，此处也不妨翻译如下：Fully aware of the necessity to work, should one still frown reluctantly at one's job every day? Is that any different from sinking oneself into the bottom of hell? 仅供参考。

参考译文

Never Be Bored

（Excerpts）

By Liang Qichao

[1] Boredom, in my view, is the most painful thing, and a sin to

suffer. In essence, it is the mentality of being sick of doing anything at all. In other words, it's lazy!

[2] One has to realize that man was not created by God to be a machine merely to digest food. How can one fail to work?

[3] It's best not to even think about that, since boredom is the source of all evils.

[4] Put in another way, whoever wishes to survive has to labor to support oneself, no matter if one is willing or not.

29

原 文

人生即劳作[①]

（节选）

梁启超

[1] 只要当大总统的人，信得过我可以当大总统才去当，实实在在把总统当作一件正经事来做；拉黄包车的人，信得过我可以拉黄包车才去拉，实实在在把拉车当作一件正经事来做，便是人生合理的生活。

[2] 这叫做职业的神圣。

[3] 凡职业没有不是神圣的，所以凡职业没有不是可敬的。

[4] 惟其如此，所以我们对于各种职业，没有什么分别拣择。

[5] 总之，人生在世，是要天天劳作的。劳作便是功德，不劳作便是罪恶。

[6] 至于我该做哪一种劳作呢？全看我的才能何如、境地何如。因自己的才能、境地，做一种劳作做到圆满，便是天地间第一等人。

---

① 编者注：原名为《敬业与乐业》，现标题为作者所加。

译 析

梁启超是中国近代史上的一位杰出的思想家、政治家和教育家，他的一些论述至今不失其价值。本文"人生即劳作"摘选自《梁启超全集》。

就题目而言，容易译成 life is work / job。应知，翻译"劳动""劳作"时，有几个不同的词可以选择：work通常指抽象的工作，如 Depressions throw thousands out of work（经济萧条使成千上万的人失业了）；job是一件具体工作，如 They are paid by the job（他们领取计件工资）；类似的，task则更加具体，意思是 a piece of work imposed（即由别人分配下来的工作），如"他分配给了我一项任务"（He assigned me a task），有时中文的"工作"也可用该词，如"这可不是想象那样容易的工作"（It is not so easy a task as might be supposed）。梁启超这里指的是"辛勤劳动"，故应用labor，该词具有 hard work, strive and make an effort to reach a goal 之意，如 They labored to complete the job（他们努力完成这项工作），"劳动光荣"（Labor Is Honorable / Glorious; Glory to Labor）等，故此处标题可译为 Life Is Labor。

[1] 中的表述颇带有民国语言的特色，需花气力理解原文，否则很容易误译，如将"只要当大总统的人，信得过我可以当大总统才去当，实实在在把总统当作一件正经事来做"译成 To become a president and do the job well only if a president trust in your ability.、As a president, I needed to be trusted and must regard

the position as a serious work and down-to-earth 等；将"拉黄包车的人，信得过我可以拉黄包车才去拉，实实在在把拉车当作一件正经事来做，便是人生合理的生活"译成 The person who pulls a rickshaw must truly believe he can pull a rickshaw, and then seriously performs it as one. That is a sensible life to live in、Believing that they have the competence in doing it, people run the jinrikisha and also consider it a real work. It is the reasonable way of life、One is chosen to pull the rickshaw because the passengers believe him and he takes it seriously too. This is the appropriate attitude towards life 等。其实，对于此段话要作全面理解，即梁启超对于"合理人生"及"工作态度"的领悟，而所谓"总统""黄包车夫"等是一种举例，而非指其具体能力。故此，不妨将词序作较大调整，译出其实质内涵：A rational life is, in my view, a situation where all people, from presidents to carters, spare no effort in doing their duties to the best of their abilities, in accordance with their qualities and wishes, which are deemed to be serious businesses.

[2] 中，"这叫做职业的神圣"，一般会译成 It is called the sanctity of the profession，这里需加甄别：profession，其原义是 a form of employment that is respected in society as honorable and is possible only for an educated person and after training in some special branch of knowledge。如 He is a lawyer by profession（他的职业是律师）、"她打算以教书为事业"（She intends to make teaching her profession）、In the last century there was a great social difference between business and the professions（上世纪，商业界与专业界

在社会上有很大的差异）等；occupation更中性，如What's your father's occupation?（你爸爸是做什么的？）"她是跳舞的"（She is a dancer by occupation）等，故此处不妨选择后者：This is the "sacredness of occupation".

[3] 中，"凡职业没有不是神圣的，所以凡职业没有不是可敬的"，固然可以译成All the occupations are sacred so that all the vacations are respectable、All occupations are sacred, all occupations are therefore respectable、All occupations are sacred, so all occupations are worthy of respect等，但为避免重复，特别是考虑到此处的"职业"与前面的所指有细微差别，故不妨选择trade，该词为an occupation, especially one needing some skills，即指经过一定训练的人所从事的职业，或更为泛指，如walks of all trades（各行各业）、"工会"（trade union）等。同时，作者其实强调的是不可鄙夷任何职业，而应尊重任何劳作，故不妨将此意译出：Every trade in the world is thus sacred, and no one should be disrespected.

[4] 中，对于"惟其如此，所以我们对于各种职业，没有什么分别拣择"，大都按字面意思译成That's why we don't make a distinction and select among the careers、Thus, we do not need to choose in all types of professions、Only then, we can treat all occupations equally等，有的较为深入一层：That is why we should not select and look down upon some occupations、As such, we regard all kinds of occupations without discrimination等。此处的discrimination用得比较好，该词具有unfair treatment of a person

or group on the basis of his or her occupation 的含义。同时，此处还不妨强调作者的"劳作为荣"之意：In this way, people can pursue various careers without discrimination. What matters most is their engagement with their daily work.

[5]中的"总之，人生在世，是要天天劳作的。劳作便是功德，不劳作便是罪恶"，一般容易译成 In a word, life is to work every day. Work is a virtue and not work is a sin、Anyway, we are born to work. Work is of great morality, on the contrary, daydreaming is some kind of unbearable evil things、In short, life, is filled with work every day. Working is virtue, otherwise it would be a sin 等，其实，此处的"罪恶"并非是一般意义上的 sin、evil、crime、offence、misdemeanor、felony 等，而指的是一种人生的堕落，故不妨用 degeneration，其义为 the process of declining from a higher to a lower level of effective power or vitality or essential quality; the process of becoming worse or less acceptable in quality or condition；同时，将词序作必要调整：Labor, whichever type you choose depending on your competence and circumstance, breeds virtue, whereas idleness can only lead to degeneration.

[6]中的"我"是一种泛指，不宜简单地译成 I，而可为 we、you 等；"做到圆满"意为尽全部努力、能力去做；此处的"劳作"又可理解为"每做一事"，即一项具体工作（job）；而"天地间第一等人"是一种夸张表述，译文可有多重变通。较为典型的相关译文：As for which jobs should I choose, it depends on my abilities and situation. Making my <u>labor</u> perfect with <u>taking advantage</u>

of my abilities and situation, then I am the one of most enviable persons in the world、Then, what kind of work should I do? It depends on my talents and conditions. The first-rate people in the world are those who practice their occupations to perfection out of their own talents and conditions、As for me, what should I do? It depends on my talent and mental ground. If a man can do his best, taking advantage of his talent and mental ground, he will be the best man in the world等，其中加下画线之处，有明显的改进空间。综合考虑，此段不妨译为：Therefore, whatever job you may choose depending on your abilities and circumstances, devoting all your heart and soul to a job and making it perfect will make you "a top-class person" in this world.

总之，由于选文具有民国文风，其表述多与现今不同，就更需深入、细致的理解，融会贯通，从而努力在译入语中加以再现。

参考译文

Life Is Labor

（Excerpts）

By Liang Qichao

[1] A rational life is, in my view, a situation where all people, from presidents to carters, spare no effort in doing their duties to the

best of their abilities, in accordance with their qualities and wishes, which are deemed to be serious businesses.

[2] This is the "sacredness of occupation".

[3] Every trade in the world is thus sacred, and no one should be disrespected.

[4] In this way, people can pursue various careers without discrimination. What matters most is their engagement with their daily work.

[5] Labor, whichever type you choose depending on your competence and circumstance, breeds virtue, whereas idleness can only lead to degeneration.

[6] Therefore, whatever job you may choose depending on your abilities and circumstances, devoting all your heart and soul to a job and making it perfect will make you "a top-class person" in this world.

30

原　文

国之少年[①]

（节选）

梁启超

[1] 使举国之少年而亦为老大也，则吾中国为过去之国，其澌亡可翘足而待也。

[2] 故今日之责任，不在他人，而全在我少年。

[3] 少年智则国智，少年富则国富；少年强则国强，少年独立则国独立；少年自由则国自由，少年进步则国进步；少年胜于欧洲则国胜于欧洲，少年雄于地球则国雄于地球。

[4] 红日初升，其道大光。……纵有千古，横有八荒。前途似海，来日方长。

译　析

作为中国近代史上的著名启蒙思想家、政治家和教育家，梁启超生活在清末民初。面对国家的腐败、黑暗、落后和虚弱，他

---

① 编者注：原文为《少年中国说》，现标题为作者所加。

积极参加了"戊戌变法"运动；失败之后，流亡日本，创办了《清议报》，《少年中国说》是1900年发表在该报上的一篇著名文章，影响颇大，被公认为梁启超著作中思想意义最积极、情感色彩最激越的篇章。

就题目而言，有的译成The Country's Young People、Children of the Nation、The State's Youth等，但The Youth of Our Nation似更贴切。

[1]中，许多参赛者没有将"使"译出来，该词此处为"假如、如果"，即if，如《论语·泰伯》有"如有周公之才之美，使骄且吝，其余不足观也已"（即使才华比得上周公的人，如果骄傲、吝啬，别的方面也不值得看了），可译为：If a man is as gifted as the Duke of Zhou, and yet arrogant and stingy, then his other qualities are not worth mentioning. "举国"是"全国"。"老大"，书面语"年老"，有俗语：少壮不努力，老大徒伤悲。"少年"，有人译成了teenage，但该词是"在人口学上界定的青少年"，一般为15—25岁或14—28岁之间，故不如用the young people、youth。

"澌亡"，其中"澌"为"尽"，"澌亡"即"灭绝消亡"，有人译成extinct，但该词本义为：no longer in existence; lost or especially having died out leaving no living representatives; specially, a species of animal or plant that is extinct no longer has any living members, either in the world or in a particular place。如：Unlike in the rest of Canada, the moose has no natural predators on the island, where the native wolf went extinct.（与加拿大其他地方相比，由

于本地狼种灭绝，驼鹿在此毫无天敌。）故该词用在此处有些"过"了。相比而言，perish更为适宜，其意为pass from physical life and lose all bodily attributes and functions necessary to sustain life. 该词最有名的用法出现在林肯的《葛底斯堡演说》中：that government of the people, by the people, for the people shall not perish from the earth（这个民有、民治、民享的政府将与世长存）。故此，[1]句不妨译为：If our nation's youth also become somewhat senile, our nation as a whole will be set back to its previous stage, and will then perish before long.

[2]句，典型的译文如"So those who shoulder social responsibilities are the juveniles rather than anyone else." "It is the juveniles instead of the others, bear the responsibility of today's China." "So it is not others' responsibilities but juniors' to save China." "So the duty of today falls upon none other than the youth."等。其中，许多人用了juveniles，究其本义：A juvenile is a child or young person who is not yet old enough to be regarded as an adult. 且该词是个法律术语，如juvenile delinquency（青少年犯罪）、juvenile court（少年法庭）等，一般文章中不可用来代替young people、youth。如："更有甚者，他们腐蚀青少年。"这句不可译成"What's more, they corrupted the juveniles."，而应为... the young people。故[2]句不妨译为：Hence the duty of transforming our nation today lies in no one else but our youth.

[3]中的"智"，译得最多的是wise，其次为intelligent、clever、bright、brilliant、smart等。但分析起来，a wise person is

able to use their experience and knowledge in order to make sensible decisions and judgments，即 wise 一般多用于有一定年龄、经历、资历的人，如：1. He was widely respected as a wise and statesman like governor.（他作为一位睿智、具备政治家才干的州长而广受尊崇。）2. You're a wise old man: tell me what to do.（您是位睿智的长者，告诉我该怎么办吧。）3. 等你长大懂事后，你会理解我的话。（When you are older and wiser, you will see my point. 注意：此处要用 wiser，而不是 clever。）。

而 intelligent，多指 good at learning, understanding and thinking in a logical way about things; showing this ability，即有才智、悟性强，更多强调理解力好，如：1. The young man did not understand English, but he was intelligent enough to understand my question from the gestures I made.（这个年轻人不懂英文，但他很聪明，根据我的手势便能明白我的问题。）2. a highly intelligent child（非常聪明的孩子）3. to ask an intelligent question（问一个机智的问题）。clever 意为 skillful (or showing skill) in adapting means to ends. 多指心灵手巧，学习和理解比一般人快，如：1. Her younger sister is cleverer than her.（她妹妹比她聪明。）2. 他聪明一世，糊涂一时。（He has been clever all his life but stupid this once.）3. 人们有时聪明反被聪明误。（Clever people may be victims of their own cleverness. 注意：此处的 clever 不可用 wiser，而 cleverness 亦不可用 wisdom。）。bright 常用于口语，强调的是 showing an ability to think, learn, or respond quickly，多指年轻人、小孩反应快，如：1. The boy is bright beyond his years.（这孩子真聪明，不像这么大

的。）2. 我班上有几个非常聪明的学生。（I have some very bright students in my class.）类似的是 brilliant，指某些能力特别突出，如：他才华横溢。（He has a brilliant brain.）。

至于 smart，固然也与知识、智慧有关，但更多是指 showing intelligence and mental alertness，即看起来很灵巧、机警、靓丽；有时也用于贬义，指耍小聪明，如：1. Smart children talk earlier than the average.（聪明的幼童比一般孩子说话早。）2. Do what I say and don't get smart.（照我说的去做，别耍小聪明。）。

同时，"富"的译法，参赛译文中用得最多的是 rich 和 wealthy。二者都指"拥有财物或金钱"，rich 用得更广泛，强调"个人财产和金钱的拥有"，如：He is a rich man.（他是个有钱人。）也指某些物质方面的丰富，如：1. 中国自然资源丰富。（China is rich in natural resources.）2. rich voice（饱满洪亮的声音）3. an experience rich with meaning（富有意义的经验）。前面加上定冠词 the 则指人，如：有时候，富人的烦恼比穷人多。（The rich sometimes have more trouble than the poor.） 而 wealthy 则同时暗指在社会上有殷实的地位，如：He is one of our most wealthy residents in the city.（他家是城里家境相当不错的一户。）而 wealthy 和 rich 会同时用，如：He is not merely wealthy—he is rich. 可译为：他其实不只是富裕，他很有钱！

对于"自由"，用得最多的是 free、freedom、liberty 等，应当说，freedom 用得更为广泛，指某种行为完全不受限制、阻碍、影响，如：1. freedom of speech（言论自由）2. freedom of press（出版自由）3. She is now nineteen, and has the freedom to do as she pleases.（她已19岁了，有自由做自己喜欢做的事。）。liberty多用于正式语体中，具有选择性，如：1. Employees have the liberty to use all the museum facilities.（雇员有使用博物馆设施的自由。）2. 他现在自由了。（He is now at liberty.）。

其实，还可用unrestricted，其义释为"If an activity is unrestricted, you are free to do it in the way that you want, without being limited by any rules."，是一种含义更深的freedom，如：1. The authorities have failed so far to enact a law allowing unrestricted emigration.（到目前为止，当局未能通过允许自由移民的法律。）2. 课外活动，完全自由。（Extracurricular activities are totally unrestricted.）有的用了看似相同的unstrained，其实不妥，因该词强调的是一种自然、轻松状态，如：His playing is facile and unstrained.（他的表演轻巧，无拘无束。）

在句式表达上，一般译文都比较严格地遵循了原文，如If the youth is wise, and our country will be wise. If the youth is rich, and our country will be rich. If the youth is strong, and our country will be strong. If the youth is independent, and our country will be independent. If the youth has freedom, and our country will have freedom. If the youth makes the progress, and our country will make progress. If the youth is superior to Europe, and our country will be superior to Europe. If the youth dominate the world, and our country will dominate the world. 应当说，中文的这种排比句很有气势，颇具感染力，但照搬到英文里效果未必相同，而且还可能读来冗赘重叠。类似的，在第七届"《英语世界》杯"翻译大赛的汉译

英原文中，有句"知识可以占有，智慧只能发挥；知识向外求得，智慧于内感悟；知识越获越丰富，智慧越凝越升华"，一般译文都采取了类似的句式，如"Knowledge may be possessed, while wisdom must be fulfilled spontaneously. Knowledge may come from acquisition, while wisdom must be derived from introspection. Knowledge can be accumulated, while wisdom must be refined."等，当然不能算错，但根据英文形合的特点，不妨将其整合为一句：Knowledge can only be possessed and accumulated externally, while wisdom is brought into play and sublimed internally. 从而求得"整体相等"，同时精简其中重复部分。同样，鲁迅的名言"沉默啊！沉默！不在沉默中爆发，就在沉默中灭亡"，其中有四个"沉默"，在中文里有层层递进的呐喊效果，但若原封不动搬到英文，则显累赘，于是杨宪益、戴乃迭将其译为"Silence! Silence! Unless we burst out, we shall perish in this silence."，既保留原文的强烈感情，又平实、顺畅。故此，[3]句不妨加以相应变通：When the youth become intelligent, the whole nation is; as the youth get wealthy, so does the whole nation. In the same way, when our young people grow to be strong, independent, progressive and unrestricted, so will the whole nation, which will surpass Europe and even stand out in the world with its dynamic youngsters.

[4]中，对于"红日初升，其道大光"，一般都译成了The red sun is just rising、The sun has just risen、The red sun rises brightly等，颇显突兀。其实应该结合其广义和狭义的语境来理解：梁启超将当时封建统治下的中国视为衰落无望的"老大帝国"，而热

切希望出现一个富、强、独立、自由、进步的"少年中国",只有那样,中国才会有前途,因此,译文应加以衔接和变通,如可采用If that happens, ...would be like... 的句式。对于"纵有""横有",有译文用了Longitudinally, ...; Horizontally, ..., 固然清晰,但也多少有些机械,不妨将其融合在整句之中:If that happens, our nation would be like a rising sun or a broad road full of sunlight. ... Sustained by thousands of years of history and a wondrous vast land, China's future is as immense as oceans with ample time ahead.

梁启超写此文时只有27岁,可谓当时的"90后",并把它视为自己"开文章之新体,激民气之暗潮"的代表作。要将其原汁原味地译成英文,则需在词语与句式上颇费斟酌。

参考译文

The Youth of Our Nation

(Excerpts)

By Liang Qichao

[1] If our nation's youth also become somewhat senile, our nation as a whole will be set back to its previous stage, and will then perish before long.

[2] Hence the duty of transforming our nation today lies in no

one else but our youth.

[3] When the youth become intelligent, the whole nation is; as the youth get wealthy, so does the whole nation. In the same way, when our young people grow to be strong, independent, progressive and unrestricted, so will the whole nation, which will surpass Europe and even stand out in the world with its dynamic youngsters.

[4] If that happens, our nation would be like a rising sun or a broad road full of sunlight. ... Sustained by thousands of years of history and a wondrous vast land, China's future is as immense as oceans with ample time ahead.

31

> 原　文

潇洒的欧洲青年[①]

蒋勋

[1] 欧洲有种青年出走的文化。我在翡冷翠认识十四岁的苏格兰小孩，带个毡呢帽，打扫厕所一个学期存的钱，就到欧洲来旅行。

[2] 花完了，一点也不害怕，就去街上吹苏格兰风笛，再继续下一段的旅行。我那时候感触很深，不同的文化，年轻人可以这么不一样。他们将来长大以后，担当的事情也绝对不一样。

[3] 我们宋朝诗人柳永说，"今宵酒醒何处？"

[4] 中国文化里面本来有这个东西。可是这个文化老了，失去了走出去的勇敢。年轻人的生命力没有了，生命力消失了。

> 译　析

选文摘自台湾著名作家、学者蒋勋的《品味四讲》，夹叙夹议，给人启示。

---

① 编者注：原文为《人生需要出走》，现标题为作者所加。

就题目而言，一般译成Degage European Striplings、Rakish European Youth、The Carefree Teenager in Europe、The Carefree Teenager in Europe、European Youth: Living for the Moment、Unrestrained European Youth等，各有侧重，似可接受；但从下文与中国青年逐渐失去生命力、颇负生活压力的现象对比，此处不妨译为：Burdenless European Youth。

[1] 中，对于"欧洲有种青年出走的文化"，比较典型的翻译，如In Europe, it has become a culture for teenager to go far away from home. / In Europe, there is a going-abroad culture of the youth. / Europe has a culture of youth leaving. / In Europe, it has become a culture for teenager to go far away from home. / In Europe, there is a sort of culture featuring youths going out.等，但还有一词，runaway，其特点是a child who has suddenly left home without telling anyone，显示年轻人桀骜不驯闯世界的性格；而对于"打扫厕所一个学期存的钱，就到欧洲来旅行"，意思大都可以译出，但应注意语序的安排，如cleaning the toilet to save money for a semester, traveling to Europe、to Europe after making money by cleaning toilets for a semester、He traveled here all alone, by the money he earned from cleaning the toilets for a whole semester、He saved money for a semester by cleaning toilet, and then traveled to the Europe等。综合而言，该段不妨译为：There is a runaway culture among youth in Europe. I met a Scottish kid in Florence, 14 years of age, wearing a felt fedora. He was bold enough to leave home, venturing around Europe with a little money in his pocket earned

from his casual job of cleaning the toilet during a semester.

[2]中,"感触很深",似乎可以译成 I felt it deeply、I felt very strongly about that...、It touched me deeply、It gave me deep feelings then、it gave me a lot of thoughts、It impressed me deeply then that 等,但鉴于此处体现的是作者冷静的观察和思考,可变通一下,用过去分词短语 Deeply impressed by... 会更加简练。对于"……就去街上吹苏格兰风笛",实则是去街上卖艺,一般译成 for he would play Scottish bagpipes in the street to earn money for his...、he could play the Scottish bagpipe on the street to make it again so as to...、played the bagpipes on the street to earn himself for... 等,其实 busk 的本义是 to perform music in a public place and ask for money from people passing by,故此句为 started to busk his Scottish bagpipes on the street... 即可。(下一段的)"旅行",来稿用得最多的是 travel,还有用 safari 的。一般而言,trip 是 a tour to a place and back again, especially a short one for pleasure or a particular purpose,因而 A trip is often shorter than a journey,但在日常中,trip 用得比 journey 更加广泛,如 a round-the-world trip(环球旅行),故可不必过于死板;safari 则多指 a trip to see or hunt wild animals, especially in east or southern Africa,即多带"野味",如"杭州野生动物世界"为 Hangzhou Safari Park。同时,可用 contemplate,该词本义为 look at something thoughtfully, observe deep in thought;"不同的文化,年轻人可以这么不一样",显出中文表达的简练,实际意思为"在不同文化中成长的年轻人会有这么大的不同"。因而,"这么不一样"可用 huge difference,而

"不同文化中成长的年轻人",与其用从句 young people who grow up in different culture、After they grow up, they will be different culturally、young people should vary remarkably under different cultural backgrounds 等,不如用动名词结构 youths growing up in different cultures;"他们将来长大以后",表面意思是 when they grow up in the future,但前面已经 growing up,此处不宜再用,且"担当的事情……不一样"指的是承担更多的社会责任(shoulder more responsibilities),而这种差距会继续放大(the discrepancy will be magnified),同时要做些词汇和语气上的衔接。故此,该段不妨译为:When his money ran out, he showed no sign of panic but started to busk his Scottish bagpipes on the street, and that kept him going for his next trip. Deeply impressed by his relaxed manner, I could not help but contemplate the huge difference between youths growing up in different cultures. Surely, the discrepancy will be magnified in their later lives once they shoulder more responsibilities.

  [3] 中,所引的词摘自柳永的《雨霖铃》,那原是一首送别的凄婉之作,其中"今宵酒醒何处?杨柳岸、晓风残月",原意是"谁知我今夜酒醒时身在何处?怕是只有杨柳岸边,面对凄厉的晨风和黎明的残月了",而作者在此化用了这一句,赋予其潇洒自在之意,故如果仍然只刻板地译为 Tonight, where shall I find myself, waking from a hangover, 就显然不够确切;比较好的,如 "Where shall I be found at day's early break from wine awake?" "Where am I when awaking from a drunken sleep tonight?" 等,当然最好要做某些增译,如 ...I care not 等。该句可译为:A poet in

the Song dynasty named Liu Yong (984–1053) once wrote, "Where will I wake up after I've passed out drunk? I care not".

[4] 是[2]的自然接续和结果，其中"这个东西"指的显然是作者所赞许的年轻人应有的洒脱之气（natural and unrestrained air），而这种基因（gene）原本植根于中国文化，为强调"原本"（originally），可将其提前，作为副词译出；而这里的"老了"，不是一般意义上的old或getting old / older，而是失去了其往日的光彩（have faded out）；同时，"失去了走出去的勇敢（bravery/guts）"，其主语应为"我们（中国）年轻人"。同时，对于两个"生命力"，译文亦应避免重复。故此处也不妨加以变通：Originally, we had natural and unrestrained genes embedded in our culture, but they've faded out, together with our young people's guts for venturing. With all that gone, they have also lost their vitality.

此文虽短，但涉及中西现代青年文化的课题，翻译时需考虑相关的文化背景，斟酌词义，并深入浅出。

参考译文

Burdenless European Youth

By Jiang Xun

[1] There is a runaway culture among youth in Europe. I met a

Scottish kid in Florence, 14 years of age, wearing a felt fedora. He was bold enough to leave home, venturing around Europe with a little money in his pocket earned from his casual job of cleaning the toilet during a semester.

[2] When his money ran out, he showed no sign of panic but started to busk his Scottish bagpipes on the street, and that kept him going for his next trip. Deeply impressed by his relaxed manner, I could not help but contemplate the huge difference between youths growing up in different cultures. Surely, the discrepancy will be magnified in their later lives once they shoulder more responsibilities.

[3] A poet in the Song dynasty named Liu Yong (984-1053) once wrote, "Where will I wake up after I've passed out drunk? I care not".

[4] Originally, we had natural and unrestrained genes embedded in our culture, but they've faded out, together with our young people's guts for venturing. With all that gone, they have also lost their vitality.

32

> 原　文

女排精神

林巍

[1] 中国女排在此次奥运会上夺冠后，"女排精神"再次成为走红的热词。

[2] 人们一般认为所谓女排精神，就是拼搏、坚持、永不放弃等，似乎有了这种精神，便可在任何赛事中立于不败之地。

[3] 但是，精神固然可以影响，却永远代替不了物质。

[4] 正如女排教练郎平所说："不要一赢球就谈女排精神，也要看我们努力的过程。

[5] "女排精神一直在，但单靠精神不能赢球，还必须技术过硬。"

> 译　析

选文是2016年的时政文体，首先应准确把握原文，然后力求以平实、简练的语言译出。

[1]中，很多参赛者将"（女排）精神"译作了spirit，如the spirit of women's volleyball team has become a hot topic again，看

似不错，但分析起来，这里更多指的是一种体育竞赛中的士气，不妨用morale，其本义为 the amount of confidence and enthusiasm, etc. that a person or a group has at a particular time；而"热词"重在词语方面，多于topic。故该句不妨译为：Following the victory of the Chinese women volleyball team at the recent Olympic Games, the "morale of the Chinese women volleyball team" has once again become a catchphrase.

[2] 中，比较典型的，如："Women's volleyball team spirit" is believed to be the spirit of struggling, persistence, and never giving up, with which people seem to be able to stand in an invincible position in any competition. 这种译法似乎也可接受。但"人们一般认为"不一定永远是believed，而"拼搏、坚持、永不放弃等"亦可加以整合；同时，又不一定恪守原文的标点，即可根据英文的表达方式，将其更加明确：In general, the phrase symbolizes a fighting spirit of persistence which never gives up. To many, it seems that once a team or an individual is imbued with this spirit, any battle can be won in competitions eventually.

[3] 中，这里的"影响"若处理成动词matter，是可以接受的，若译成influence则应有宾语。"物质"问题较多，参赛者一般译成materials、matters、substance等，如 Such spirit indeed matters, but never replaces certain materials，可问certain materials到底是什么东西？显然conditions、real things更恰当，故不妨译为：However, make no mistake, morale, or spirit, can surely influence the outcome but never substitutes for the real thing.

[4] 中,"不要一……就……,也要看……",意思是:不要每当什么的时候,就过分强调什么,而忽视什么。典型的译文,如"People tend to talk of the Women's Volleyball Spirit immediately after the team wins. However, they are also supposed to see the efforts we've made",似乎强调得还不够。过分强调、叨唠,可以用 harp on...,如:I wish you wouldn't harp on about it all the time.(我希望你不要老是喋喋不休地谈论那件事了。)而"也要看"的实质是"请不要忽视""以往重视不够",故该句不妨译为:As their coach Lang Ping said, "People should not harp too much on the 'morale of Chinese women volleyball team' and value too little the hardship of our training every time we win a game."

[5] 中,参赛者一般都能顺理成章地译成"The spirit is always right here. To win the match, we are supposed to combine the spirit with strong skills." "The spirit of our team remains the same, but to win takes more than that. A highly skillful team is a must as well."等,但这里的"技术过硬",固然可以用 superb、strong skills、very skillful 等,但更多是指具有超过对手的技术实力,故不妨译为:"As the morale is always there as before, one should never forget that a game is not won solely by morale but by skills that surpass those of your opponents."

总之,既要吃透原文意思,又不要被原文的句式、标点等束缚,从而使译文得到更加妥善的处理。

The Spirit of Chinese Women Volleyball

By Lin Wei

[1] Following the victory of the Chinese women volleyball team at the recent Olympic Games, the "morale of the Chinese women volleyball team" has once again become a catchphrase.

[2] In general, the phrase symbolizes a fighting spirit of persistence which never gives up. To many, it seems that once a team or an individual is imbued with this spirit, any battle can be won in competitions eventually.

[3] However, make no mistake, morale, or spirit, can surely influence the outcome but never substitutes for the real thing.

[4] As their coach Lang Ping said, "People should not harp too much on the 'morale of Chinese women volleyball team' and value too little the hardship of our training every time we win a game."

[5] "As the morale is always there as before, one should never forget that a game is not won solely by morale but by skills that surpass those of your opponents."

33

> 原 文

杭州师范大学第二届全球青年学者论坛

[1] 杭州师范大学是浙江省重点高校，这所位于杭城西溪湿地之畔的百年学府，培养出了一批杰出校友和优秀人才。学校拥有国家和省级高层次人才80余人，ESI综合排名和论文自然指数（NI）连续多年进入中国百强，国家级研究平台、国际合作科技平台取得了全面进步和显著成效。

[2] 2019年，中国科学院尚永丰院士任我校校长，学校进一步重视人才引进，大力推进人才新举措，吸引集聚海内外优秀学者。

[3] 鉴于当前新冠疫情的特殊时期，2020年，学校将采用线上"云论坛"模式举办第二届全球青年学者论坛，以"展示学校宏伟蓝图、阐述人才引进政策"为主旨，诚挚地邀请海内外优秀青年才俊参加，深入了解杭师大，促进沟通交流，以期合作共赢。

> 译 析

就题目"杭州师范大学第二届全球青年学者论坛"而言，有的译成 The Second Global Forum for Young Scholar of Hangzhou Normal University / The Second Global Youth Scholars Forum of Hangzhou Normal University 等；其实，作为标题，可力求简约，如 The Second Global Youth Scholars Forum of HZNU。

[1] 中，"杭州师范大学是浙江省重点高校，这所位于杭城西溪湿地之畔的百年学府，培养出了一批杰出校友和优秀人才"，若按原文语序，很容易译成 Hangzhou Normal University, among Zhejiang's agenda for key universities, is located near Xixi Wetland in Hangzhou with a centennial history. It has cultivated a number of distinguished alumnus and talents. 其中除了 alumnus 应为复数 alumni 外，整个句式也过于中文化，不如作些结构调整，如以 Located on the banks of... 开头，而将其中的几个要素"重点高校""位于""百年学府""培养出了"，相应变通，融入句子结构。同时，Hangzhou Normal University 首次出现时在括号中加入缩写（HZNU），以便于下面简化表述。

对于"学校拥有国家和省级高层次人才80余人，ESI综合排名和论文自然指数（NI）连续多年进入中国百强，国家级研究平台、国际合作科技平台取得了全面进步和显著成效"，较为典型的参赛译文，如：HZNU is home to 80 talents who are widely acknowledged in Zhejiang and nationwide. It has been listed on China's top 100 in terms of ESI and NI for years running, making considerable progress concerning National Research Platform and International Science and Technology Cooperation Platform. / It has more than 80 high-level talents who are widely acknowledged provincially and nationally, and has been among China's top 100 by ESI ranking and Paper NI for years in a row, making an overall progress and producing a marked effect in terms of national research and international cooperation. / Having more than 80 national and provincial high-level talents now, HZNU has been among China's top 100 by ranking of Essential Science Indicators (ESI) and Nature Index (NI) for many continuous years, with an all-round and remarkable progress in both its national research platform and international cooperation technology platform. 应当说，大致意思都不错，但还可注重时间上的关联和结构上的紧凑，如用些介词、动名词so far、ranking等。

因而，该段不妨译为：Located on the banks of Xixi Wetland of Hangzhou City, as a key university of the province, Hangzhou Normal University (HZNU) has produced a host of outstanding alumni and talents. So far this century-old university has more than 80 high-level talents at the national and provincial levels, ranking in the top 100 universities of China in terms of Essential Science Indicators (ESI) and Nature Index (NI) academic papers for many consecutive years. Meanwhile, the national research platforms and international cooperation technology platforms have made all-round progress and achieved remarkable results.

[2] 中，对于"……任我校校长"，一般译成was appointed as the president of HZNU、became the president of HZNU in 2019、

became our president，其中不宜用our，而且还应有"自从（任我校校长）以来"的意思，尽管原文字面上没有这样写。故此，整句可译为：Ever since Professor Shang Yongfeng, academician of the Chinese Academy of Sciences, started serving as the president of our university in 2019, it has promoted new measures to attract outstanding scholars both at home and abroad.

[3]中，"鉴于"有的译得不太清楚，如For nowadays we have been in a special period of COVID-19 pandemic, we will...，可用In view of、in consideration of等；"采用线上'云论坛'模式"，不一定按字面意思译成to adopt the "online forum" mode，而online即可；"展示学校宏伟蓝图、阐述人才引进政策"，一般译成showing our school's grand blueprint and interpreting our policies for importing talents、showing HZNU's magnificent blueprint and elaborating the talent introduction policy、to roll out the great blueprint of HZNU by elaborating the talent introduction policy等，其中，此处的"学校"显然不是school，"阐述"若用interpret似不够分量，不如elaborate；"共赢"即是"双赢"（win-win）。

因此，整段不妨译为：In view of the current special period of the covid-19 pandemic, the Second Global Youth Scholars Forum will be held online this year, with the theme of "Demonstrating the grand blueprint of the university and elaborating the policy of introducing talent". We sincerely invite outstanding young talents at home and abroad to participate in the event, so as to better understand the university, promote communication and exchange views in achieving win-win cooperation.

　　本文多处涉及词语调整问题，这在汉英翻译中需十分敏感，原因在于两种语言之间在结构和表述方式上的巨大差别。例如，"去年11月，在中国澳门举行的中国－葡语国家论坛上，葡国代表团提出了这一问题"，就其内容而言，是由大到小（时间—宏观地点—微观地点—提出问题者—所提问题），但译成英文时，则要由小至大（所提问题—提出问题者—微观地点—宏观地点—时间）：The issue was raised by the Portuguese delegation at China-Portuguese speaking Forum held in Macao, China, last November；又如，"如果想在有生之年做一点什么事，学一点什么学问，充实自己，帮助别人，使生命成为有意义，不虚此生，那么就不可浪费光阴。这道理人人都懂，可是很少人真能积极不懈地善于利用他的时间"，若按照原文结构，便难以翻译出通顺英文，于是就需将词序，特别是下画线部分，作较大调整：Time must not be wasted if you want to do your bit in your remaining years or acquire some useful knowledge to improve yourself and help others, so that your life may turn out to be significant and fruitful. All that is foolproof, yet few people really strive to make the best use of their time. 应当说，这是汉英（同样是英汉）翻译中的一种基本语言现象，故需要具体语境中相应的翻译技巧。

The Second Global Youth Scholars Forum of HZNU

[1] Located on the banks of Xixi Wetland of Hangzhou City, as a key university of the province, Hangzhou Normal University (HZNU) has produced a host of outstanding alumni and talents. So far this century-old university has more than 80 high-level talents at the national and provincial levels, ranking in the top 100 universities of China in terms of Essential Science Indicators (ESI) and Nature Index (NI) academic papers for many consecutive years. Meanwhile, the national research platforms and international cooperation technology platforms have made all-round progress and achieved remarkable results.

[2] Ever since Professor Shang Yongfeng, academician of the Chinese Academy of Sciences, started serving as the president of our university in 2019, it has promoted new measures to attract outstanding scholars both at home and abroad.

[3] In view of the current special period of the covid-19 pandemic, the Second Global Youth Scholars Forum will be held online this year, with the theme of "Demonstrating the grand blueprint of the university and elaborating the policy of introducing talent".

We sincerely invite outstanding young talents at home and abroad to participate in the event, so as to better understand the university, promote communication and exchange views in achieving win-win cooperation.

34

> 原 文

珠海校区与珠海政府

（上）

[1] 2011年4月国务院侨办、教育部、广东省政府签署共建暨南大学协议；2015年6月学校入选广东省高水平大学重点建设高校。

[2] 为了拓展办学空间，1998年8月28日，暨南大学与珠海市政府签订办学协议，合作组建暨南大学珠海教学点，并于当年开始招生，开创了珠海市全日制普通高等教育之先河。

[3] 2000年4月29日，暨南大学与珠海市人民政府签订共建暨南大学珠海学院协议；6月，暨南大学珠海教学点正式更名为暨南大学珠海学院。

> 译 析

就题目而言，有的没有翻译，有多人的将"珠海政府"译成Zhuhai government，而更准确的为Zhuhai Municipal Government；至于"（上）"一般为（I）或（A）。

在[1]中，"2011年4月国务院侨办、教育部、广东省政府签署共建暨南大学协议"，有的用了被动语态an agreement was signed among...，其实更宜用主动语态；而这里的"入选"并非通常意义上的自下而上的推选，而是自上而下的"选定"，故 designate 比 select 更确切，"他们两个被企业选来复查流水线的定期变化"（The two people are designated by the company to review certain changes of the assembly line）等。而"广东省高水平大学重点建设高校"，许多译文的词序和单复数有问题，如 key universities of Guangdong province high level University、was ranked in the key high schools for development of advanced universities in Guangdong Province 等，实则不妨为 one of the key universities at advanced level to be propped up in Guangdong Province 等。

在[2]中，"为了拓展办学空间"，许多人译成 To expand the schooling space、In order to expand the scope of school 等，其实这里的"办学空间"不只是 space 或 scope，而更多的是 the field of education；而"与谁……签订了……哪方面的协议"，许多译文用错了介词，...to sign an agreement to... 等，实则为 ...signed an agreement with... on ...，类似的，如 The supermarket chain has signed an agreement with a Japanese trading company on exploring new market（该连锁超市与一家日本商行签订了开拓新市场的协议）等；当然，也可将宾语前置，如 They signed a secret deal with their main competitor（他们和主要竞争者签订了一项秘密交易协议），但就此句而言，若以该句式：... signed an agreement <u>of the joint development of its Zhuhai Teaching School</u> with the Zhuhai Municipal Government ...，就显得臃肿，且不易与后面内容连接，

故不妨译为...had signed an agreement with the Zhuhai Municipal Government on the joint development of its Zhuhai Teaching School, which was Zhuhai's ...，以求通顺。"珠海教学点"不是new campus（下段内容才是），亦非teaching point，而是Zhuhai Teaching School。

在[3]中，对于"暨南大学珠海教学点正式更名为暨南大学珠海学院"，许多译成了in June, the campus was officially renamed as the Zhuhai College of Jinan University，其中的campus显然有问题，特别是着眼下面的"珠海校区"，若又译成the college was renamed as Zhuhai campus of Jinan University就混淆了不同概念名词，且句式显得很臃乱，故此处不妨使用括号处理：(the name was formally changed from the previous Zhuhai Teaching School of Jinan University in June of that year)。

汉译英中的一些用语不可想当然，应多查些有关的参考材料，比较已有的不同译法。

参考译文

Zhuhai Campus and Zhuhai Municipal Government

(I)

[1] In April 2011, the Overseas Chinese Affairs Office of the

State Council, the Ministry of Education and Guangdong Provincial Government signed an agreement on their joint development of Jinan University, which was designated in June 2015 as one of the key universities at advanced level to be propped up in Guangdong Province.

[2] To expand the field of education, on 28th August 1998 Jinan University had signed an agreement with the Zhuhai Municipal Government on the joint development of its Zhuhai Teaching School, which was Zhuhai's first full-time tertiary education institute, and started to enroll new students in the same year.

[3] On 29th April 2000, Jinan University signed another agreement with the Zhuhai Municipal Government on their joint development of the Zhuhai College of Jinan University (the name was formally changed from the previous Zhuhai Teaching School of Jinan University in June of that year).

35

> 原　文

珠海校区与珠海政府

（下）

[1] 2009年4月1日，学校实施校区化改革，暨南大学珠海学院更名为暨南大学珠海校区；2016年1月28日，暨南大学与珠海市政府签订共建广东省高水平大学战略合作协议。

[2] 目前，暨南大学珠海校区办学水平和社会影响不断提升，珠海校区已经成为暨南大学一张闪亮的名片。

[3] 展望未来，作为暨南大学"一体两翼"发展战略的重要组成部分，珠海校区将紧紧围绕立德树人这一根本任务与服务国家、广东省和珠海市创新驱动战略需求，着力打造品牌与资源一体化、体制与机制创新化、学科结构差异化的异地大校区发展模式，为建设具有一流办学水平的国际化、特色化和创新型的现代化校区而努力奋斗。

> 译　析

在[1]中，"学校实施校区化改革，暨南大学珠海学院更名为暨南大学珠海校区"，许多漏译了"改革"，或译成a reform was implemented to change its name to Zhuhai Campus of Jinan University，似乎 reform 的全部内容就为了 change its name，实际并非如此；若译为 as a result, ... 即是改革的结果之一，倒是可以的，而确切的则是 as part of the University's own reform, its Zhuhai College was renamed...。"高水平大学"，许多译成 a leading university in...、a high-level College、a high level university 等，但更确切的应为 an advanced Higher Education Institution。对于"改革"有的译成 revolution、transform、change、renovate 等，但更准确的应该是 reform；类似的，如"根本出路在于改革开放"（The fundamental way out lies in reform and opening-up）；"在伟大的改革开放于1979年开始之前，中国完全是另一个世界"（China was really another world before the great reform and opening-up which began in 1979）等。"更名"许多人用了 changed name、changed its name to... 等，其实 renamed 即可。将"共建广东省高水平大学"译成 to build a university with high level for Guangdong、concerted development of a first-level higher education institution of Guangdong、joint development of an advanced higher education institution in Guangdong 等，显然都有些欠缺、不准确之处。同时，鉴于之前所签订的协议，故这里需补充某些信息，如 following previous agreements, 接下来的，不妨译为 Jinan University signed a new agreement with the Zhuhai Municipal Government on the strategy of joint development of an advanced Higher Education Institution in Guangdong Province.

在[2]中，"社会影响"可以是 social impact、social influence 但 social effect / affect 等则显然不妥。"闪亮的名片"，许多人根

据表面意思译得很"实",如 become a shinning business card、a shining icon、representative and twinkling name cards 等;而"暨南大学珠海校区办学水平和社会影响不断提升"应该作为状语处理,即理解为前面省略了"随着(暨南大学……)",故对此不妨译为 ..., with the advance of its education and social influence, the Zhuhai Campus has been transformed into a "shining star" of Jinan University.

在[3]中,"展望未来",有译成 looking ahead、in the future、looking to the future、look forward to the future 等,但根据有关词典解释,look ahead (to sth.)的解释为"to think about what is going to happen in the future 展望未来;为将来设想",故此处译为 looking ahead to the future 似更恰当。"一体两翼"是一种比喻,翻译时当然仍可采用比喻,如"one body, two wings" "one body with two wings",但要注意恰当,如"one main body with two subsidiaries",就有点不伦不类了。

对于"立德树人",有的译成 To high moral values and to cultivate persons、essential mission of moral values establishment and people cultivation、morality establishment and student cultivation、training morality and cultivating people 等,都过于 Chinglish,以至有点儿道德绑架的感觉;还有音译成 Li de shu ren,且没有任何解释,让英文读者不知所云;有的还漏译了。实则,应在指明这是校训(motto)的基础上,将其内容译为 that is to combine the motto of nurturing virtuous talents with the requirements to serve the country 以求明确。

对于"着力打造品牌与资源一体化、体制与机制创新化、学科结构差异化的异地大校区发展模式,为建设具有一流办学水平的……",有的译成 in order to put efforts on building the development model of allopatric big campus, including the integration of brand and resource, the innovation of system and mechanism, and the differentiation of disciplinary structure, so that to establish... 句子结构大致不错,但 allopatric 一词显然是刻意"挖"出来的生僻词,其原义为 of biological speciation or species taking place or existing in areas that are geographically separated from one another(生物学种或物种形成在各区发生的),显然有些牵强附会。其实,核心内容为 by integrating its brand making with resource exploration, reforming its systems and redefining its academic disciplines, so as to form a grand campus model consisting of several branches in different locations,同时,需将其前后的语序结构加以调整。

总之,汉译英有其特殊性,不能以中文思路套用,而要不断在词语、句子结构、表达和思维方式上追求译入语的地道性。

参考译文

Zhuhai Campus and Zhuhai Municipal Government
(II)

[1] On 1st April 2009, as part of the University's own reform, its

Zhuhai College was renamed Zhuhai Campus of Jinan University. On 28th January 2016, following previous agreements, Jinan University signed a new agreement with the Zhuhai Municipal Government on the strategy of joint development of an advanced Higher Education Institution in Guangdong Province.

[2] Currently, with the advance of its education and social influence, the Zhuhai Campus has been transformed into a "shining star" of Jinan University.

[3] Looking ahead to the future, as part of the development strategy of "One Body with Two Wings", the Zhuhai Campus will make arduous efforts to develop an international, world-class and innovation-orientated modern campus with its own unique characteristics, that is to combine the motto of nurturing virtuous talents with the requirements to serve the country, the province and the municipal's strategic initiative by integrating its brand making with resource exploration, reforming its systems and redefining its academic disciplines, so as to form a grand campus model consisting of several branches in different locations.